LOCATING PLEASURE IN INDIAN HISTORY

LOCATING PLEASURE IN INDIAN HISTORY

Prescribed and Proscribed Desires in Visual and Literary Cultures

Edited by

Seema Bawa

B L O O M S B U R Y

NEW DELHI • LONDON • OXFORD • NEW YORK • SYDNEY

BLOOMSBURY INDIA
Bloomsbury Publishing India Pvt. Ltd
Second Floor, LSC Building No. 4, DDA Complex, Pocket C – 6 & 7,
Vasant Kunj, New Delhi, 110070

BLOOMSBURY, BLOOMSBURY ACADEMIC INDIA and the Diana logo
are trademarks of Bloomsbury Publishing Plc

First published in India 2021
This edition published 2021

Bloomsbury Academic
An imprint of Bloomsbury Publishing Plc

ISBN: HB: 978-93-90513-72-7; eBook: 978-93-90513-88-8
2 4 6 8 10 9 7 5 3 1

Typeset in Manipal Technologies Limited
Printed and bound in India by Replika Press Pvt. Ltd.

In memory of my mother Sunandi Bawa,
who taught us the importance of revelling in the small pleasures of life,
and filled not only her own life but also that of everyone around her with
beauty, happiness and moments of sheer joy,
and
my guru, Prof T.S. Maxwell,
connoisseur of 'noble' pickles and well-brewed chai.

CONTENTS

LISTS OF TABLES

LIST OF FIGURES

ACKNOWLEDGEMENTS: LOOKING FOR *HŪR* IN HISTORY

Ilm meñ bhī surūr hai lekin,
Ye vo jannat hai jis meñ hūr nahīñ*
*Learning has its intoxications too,**
It is a veritable heaven but for the absence of houris (epitome of beauty)

This project on the discourse of pleasure in history is an effort to find houris in history. It took shape while introspecting the reasons that initiated many of us into studying history, art and culture. Presumably, we began our history projects because we derive great pleasure from researching and dwelling on the lives of peoples past and, in the process, learning about the peoples present. At times the serious, often arcane world of academia of heavyweight solemn referencing, footnotes, recognition and publication pressures may have dimmed some of this pleasure. This is an effort to reclaim the joys of unusual writing histories based on un/usual archives, unearthing individual and shared experiences of moments of pleasure, beauty and intimacy within the household, court, bazaar and religious spaces.

I am deeply grateful to my colleagues and students at the Department of History, University of Delhi, for the lively and insightful conversations and discussions around the history of pleasure and leisure, many of whom have contributed to this volume. I thank Jaya S. Tyagi and Parul P. Dhar, who have brought their knowledge of ancient literary and visual archives to delve into the deployment and manifestation of pleasure in the households and the court. Preeti Sharma brings in a unique archive and perspective of queens and other women of the harem seeking gendered and voyeuristic pleasures in paintings, for which I am grateful. Kota Neelima readily agreed to bring out the routine and transcendental pleasures of devotion offered to the Gods in a very Indic sensibility that adds a special dimension to the theme.

To Shalin Jain, I am grateful for bringing out the pleasant and unpleasant memories recorded in the autobiography of a 17th century Jain merchant, an individual who stands out as original in an otherwise

* Rishadat Kabir shahab, personal communication via Whatsapp on 21 March 2020.

communitarian world. I would like to thank Raziuddin Aquil, who suggested the poetry of Nazir Akbarabadi. This immediately evoked memories of Agra Bazaar, a play directed by Habib Tanvir for Naya Theatre and based on Akbarabadi's connection with the people, sharing and reflecting on their little pleasures. Saifuddin Ahmad continues exploring the biting satire represented in Mir Jafar Zatali's poetry. A tradition that has very ancient roots as seen in the Chaturbhani plays is explored by Ashish Abrol and Janica Paul, and to both I am grateful not only for working on this theme but also for their research and editorial support. Santosh Kumar Rai has worked on colonial fashion and also discussed the contentious issue of the pain that changes in fashion brought to the producer of these textiles, a much-needed counter perspective to the pleasure project.

To Ashish I would like to extend my sincere gratitude for helping me at every turn, especially in matters technical. Kaveri, my daughter, and her dance have added to the performative element in the book, dinning it into my head and consciousness through constant repetition. In fact, this book owes much to art, music, dance, theatre and even film that has shaped our sensibilities, giving much pleasure to the viewers and audiences. Many of these aspects have not been covered in this book on pleasure—which hopefully is a work in progress—and would be explored later.

Marion Frenger patiently went through my own writing and pointed out any inconsistencies in thought. Yusra Farooqui dug up some literary references in Urdu literature, always willingly and with promptitude. To R. Chandra Sekhar and the editorial team at Bloomsbury, especially Shreya Chakraborti, I am thankful for the promptitude and professionalism with which they approached the project.

There is a caveat to the book—the language of the discourse of pleasure is deeply gendered, since beauty is considered to be the domain of the feminine. All the researchers are deeply conscious of it but it would have become very reader-unfriendly to point it out in every single instance. It is our hope that the specialist would find something of value in this book, and as would the general reader. In the fervent hope that we never become dour gurus like Durvasas or Gautama, this book seeks to bring out the beauty and pleasures of and in history.

October 2020
Delhi

Seema Bawa

INTRODUCTION: PLEASURES—PROSCRIBED AND PRESCRIBED

The experience of pleasure in the partaking of archival artefacts, literature, arts and cultural practices stands as an opaque barrier or gap within the fragmented discourse of recovering and reconstructing the histories of emotions. In appreciating the sheer beauty of the sources that reveal the diverse emotions and experiences embedded in their past, this collection of research studies has let the sources speak for themselves as far as possible and speak with all their biases, attitudes and angularities without the researcher necessarily inscribing on the sources.

The chapters try to incorporate the reflexivity inherent in the work of artists, poets, dramatists and even *śāstrins*, bringing out moments of pleasure in the lives of women and men of past times revealed through anecdotes, narratives, artefacts and objects of aesthetic gratification. While ancient and medieval thinkers, Western or Indian, have explored a rich variety of pleasures (e.g., *voluptas, gaudium, laetitiā* and *dēlectātiō*) and have discovered the idea of pleasure imbued the most sublime, transformative religious experience; pleasure today is assumed to be something banally light, easy and self-indulgent—just pleasantness or fun (Shusterman 1998, 51–52). Zizek locates this banality in the post-modernist 'superego injunction to enjoy that permeates our discourse' where the pursuit for pleasure has become more of a duty than a pleasure (Zizek 2006, 299, 304).

Some academic explorations on the theme of pleasure within the South Asian history include those on pleasure in the context of courtly culture by Daud Ali (2004), Devangana Desai (1985), Orissan temple sculpture by Thomas Donaldson (1987), *Kāma* in theatre, pleasure as an urban phenomenon (Kaul 2010) and so on. Many of these explorations of 'pleasure', however, relate mainly to tracing eroticism in Indian culture. The present project looks at the discourse of pleasure as relating to different types of experiences of pleasure, of which the erotic may form a small part. The contributors try not only to view pleasure—proscribed or prescribed—as an elite privilege but also to recover the experience of pleasure in the context of varied communities, individuals, classes and genders as projected through literary as well as visual mediums. The endeavour also seeks to transcend the boundaries of periodisation to see how some tropes concerning sensual pleasures or renunciation of pleasure inform attitudes and behaviour across time.

Another realm within which materiality, including enjoyment through sensual pleasures, is studied is the philosophical tradition of Lokāyata which marked a materialist scepticism with regards to religious prescriptions or discourses of renunciation and may have served as a parallel tradition of questioning or pleasure.

Perhaps the association of the enjoyment of classical arts with training has led to the notion that elite fine arts may be largely irrelevant to the broader public and that aesthetics is therefore arcane and largely extraneous. However, as has been demonstrated in many of the chapters in this book, literary and visual arts and aesthetics are not only for the elite; rather, the pleasures that their consumption embodies has cognitive value for both the elite and the popular classes. This is not to suggest that pleasure activities are homogenous and class and gender neutral; uncovering these nuances from within the history of emotions can itself be a fruitful exercise.

The chapters, therefore, can be seen as attempts to read histories not just of materiality but also of experiences and the ephemeral histories of emotions attached to these. Pleasure is inherently experiential, and if the aesthetic is tied to it, then the aesthetic is tied to our experience (Nehamas and Shusterman 1998, 49–51).

The engagement with the deeply experiential nature of pleasure in this collection of essays is perhaps the reason why they do not seek to engage with the philosophically and metaphysically deeper and more profound concept of '*ānanda*' (which is a forthcoming project) but of pleasure obtained through beauty, laughter, satire and enjoyment of the senses, including the intellect. The studies explore varieties of aesthetic experiences and their absences or antithesis, tracing pleasure and non-pleasure-centred manifestations. Thus, pleasure in its very nature is dichotomous; it comes alive and is keenly felt because it exists alongside its converse—the experience of pain, discontent, disharmony and, most of all, guilt. One of the reasons that the study of pleasure is not a part of mainstream academic discourse is because pleasure and 'the pleasant' are often conflated, disregarding the fact that the validity and richness of aesthetic experience does not rely solely on its pleasantness, or even on the wide range of deeper pleasures. Mainstream discourse disregards art's vital phenomenological vividness through which not only art's pleasures are partaken but also its other value involving the possibility of serious transformation of the of the person who experiences it.

In Indian aesthetic tradition, this transformation is explored in the rich discourse of *rasa–bhāva* theory and the role of the educated, informed and involved viewer/listener/reader who is the *rasika*. Abhinavagupta, the foremost commentator on Bharatamuni's *rasa–bhāva* theory of aesthetics, sought to link this to philosophy in general and monism in particular. Abhinavagupta locates pleasure in aesthetics—'*natye hi rasah na loke*' (Gupta 2017, vii)—in its *sanatana* or perennial nature. Aesthetic works for him become perennial by their *tadvisheshbudhhi* (synchronic relevance) and *swalakshanaye* (inherent factor, *dhvani* or wavelength). *Rasas* for him can be conveyed only through *dhvani* or the soul of the aesthetic work. What is also termed *gopanasarasāundarya* is explained by him through the simile of a beautiful and noble lady's breasts, somewhat bare and somewhat obscured. The *rasika* gets his pleasure from partaking of that which is both revealed and concealed.

This volume is an attempt to recover some of the 'pleasures' relating to the body self, soul and shared sociality as experienced in literature, arts and practices in both the mundane as well as devout realms of the past of South Asia. This experience or recovery is termed as 'discourse of pleasure' and is distinct from an alternate understanding of the discourse of pleasure as explicated in the Western post-modern tradition of Foucault or Zizek, which relates largely to the analytics of power embedded in how the discourse of pleasure operates. Instead, it seeks to locate not only the discourse of 'prescribed' and 'proscribed' pleasure in Indic textual traditions but also explore how the immanent conceptualisations and Indic life forms may have related to pleasure.

At the outset, it must be said that the fervent hope while compiling this edited selection on the discourse of pleasure in history was that it communicates to the readers how much the editor and the scholars enjoyed researching and writing the chapters in this volume. All the contributions engaged with the different ways in which the peoples in South Asia produced and consumed pleasurable acts and moments, as they are archived in visual and literary artefacts, in a way that is academically rigorous but still fun to read and view. However, the distinction in critical theory between pleasure and bliss, whether in 'readerly or 'writerly' texts, is not the subject of this collection.

PLEASURE IN THE ORDER OF LIFE

In Sanskrit there is no exact term for pleasure alone—*sukha*, *viśoka* and *kāma* are terms that may be used to describe degrees of pleasure from happiness to desire. *Kāma* (Monier-Williams 2002, 271) refers to wish, longing, desire and pleasure, especially sensual pleasure, love and enjoyment. *Prīti* and *Rati* (*Kāmasūtra* 2003, 31–34)[1] are the components of *Kāma* and are indeed iconographically represented as the wives of Kāmadeva (Monier-Williams 2002, 867).[2] *Sukha* relates more to happiness that is linked with ease, comfort and pleasantness.

The two terms *ramana*[3] and *bhoga*[4] are also used to describe pleasurable and desirable activities to be enjoyed in a very material sense.

Pleasure informed, *via positiva* or *via negativa*, the Brahmanical, Buddhist or Jain traditions, as *kāma*, which, along with *artha*, *dharma* and *mokṣa*, is one of the *purusārthas*. It is also discussed under an older categorisation of *trivarga*—where *dharma*, *artha* and *kāma* are the three categories. However, in academic discourse, until recently, it is *dharma* that has taken precedence in with *artha*. More significantly, *kāma* takes a back seat here. In the *trivarga* categorisation, *kāma*, if not dominant, is present as an essential state of being in the Brahmanical *dharmaśāstric* texts.

Before explicating the place of *kāma* in the *trivarga* schemes in the *śāstric* textual tradition, perhaps a reminder that these are meant for the male, preferably of the *dvija jātis*, would be appropriate. Kautilya's *Arthaśāstra*, one of the earliest texts to use *trivarga* in its technical meaning, uses it to refer to *dharma*, *artha* and *kāma* in the context of a king preparing to march into battle. Kautilya presents the three-fold classification of these three possible scenarios (KAŚ 9.7, 60–64)

> "*artho dharmaḥ kāma ity arthatrivargaḥ...*"—*artha*, *dharma*, and *kāma:* that is the *trivarga* of *artha*.
>
> "*anartho 'dharmaḥ śoka ity anarthatrivargaḥ..*"—*anartha*, *adharma*, and sorrow: that is the *trivarga* of *anartha*.
>
> "*artho 'nartha iti, dharmo 'dharma iti, kāmaḥ śoka iti samḥ śayatrivargaḥ...*—"Is it *artha* or *anartha*? Is it *dharma* or *adharma*? Is it *kāma* or sorrow? That is the *trivarga* of doubt. (Ollivelle 2019, 381)

In the expression *arthatrivargah*, the term *artha* appears to signify, in general, an advantage or something beneficial and good, while within the *trivarga* itself, in conjunction with *dharma* and *kāma*, the term refers more clearly to material, political and even military benefits. Thus, according to Olivelle, these three goals are 'similar' in that they all are 'beneficial' and conducive to a persons happiness (*prīti*). He thus argues that the three concepts—*dharma, artha, kāma*—comprehended by *trivarga* represent three major domains of human activities and pursuits that are beneficial to persons who perform them rather than constituting goals or aims of human life (Ollivelle 2019, 381).

In the *dharmaśāstric* tradition, within the hierarchy of values, enjoyment of pleasures, *kāma*, is in normative discourse, considered to be the lowest. *Mahābhārata* (*Mahābhārata* 5.124.,34–8) states that 'a wise man tries to secure all three but if all three cannot be attained, he secures *dharma* or *artha* or only *dharma* if he has a choice of only one'. The *Śāntiparvan* (*Mahābhārata* 12.167.,8–9) of the *Mahābhārata* says that *dharma* is the best, *artha* is the middling and *kāma* is the lowest, and man should so act that *dharma* would be the principal goal of his life. The *Rāmāyaṇa* (2.21.,57–8; 2.53.,13; 4.38.,20–2) too regards *dharma* as the highest of the *trivarga*. Echoing this philosophy, Manu (Manusmriti 2.224) states and the commentator Medhātithi concurs that what is best (*śreyas*) is the triad. However, if *artha* or *kāma* are in conflict with *dharma*, one should give up the former two.

Even the non-*dharmaśāstriya* traditions such as *Kāmasūtra* and *Arthaśastra*, in spite of their inherent valorisation of *kama* and *artha*, echo the normative position.

> He should pursue *kāma* without transgressing *dharma* or *artha*; he should not deprive himself of enjoyments (*niḥ sukha*). Or rather, he should pursue the *trivarga* equally, each intimately linked to the others. For, among *dharma*, *artha*, and *kāma*, when one is pursued excessively, it harms itself as well as the other two. (*Arthaśastra* 1 .7 .3–5 in Olivelle 2019, 384)[5]

With regards to men, the *vargas* are recommended for males at different stages of their lives, where *kāma* is obviously associated with youthfulness, i.e., 'sowing the wild oats when possible' attitude. Further, having partaken in the pleasures of the world, one should pursue *dharma* in old age. Vātsyāyana introduces a new concept: each of the three elements of the *trivarga* should be followed during the three successive stages of a male person's life, the *āśramas*:

> One hundred years, indeed, is a man's lifespan. Dividing that time, he should cultivate the *trivarga*, each intimately linked to the others and none causing harm to the others—during his childhood, *arthas* consisting of knowledge acquisition and the like; during his youth, *kāma*; and during old age, *dharma* and *mokṣa*.... (*Kāmasūtra, 1 .2 . 1–5;* cf. Olivelle 2019, 384)[6]

Feast of the Senses: Bodily and Intellectual Pleasures

The contradiction, conflict and contestation for space—physical, moral and metaphysical between the erotic and the ascetic ideals in art—between the *bhogin*[7] and the *yogi* has a very long history. These existed much before art historians stumbled upon them and debated the apparently problematic relationship between eroticism and asceticism.

As seen above, this relationship is usually seen as binary built on the notion of *moha* and *māyā* versus true *jñāna* or knowledge; thus primal desire weaves a labyrinthine net, which is difficult to escape and from which only appropriate knowledge and true consciousness offer liberation. The only way out of this trap of desire is renunciation and sacrifice of the self in the search for the ultimate truth. The Alambusa Jātaka illustrates this through a bas relief sculpture of Ṛṣi Ṛṣiṣṛnga falling 'prey' to the beauty of the *apsarā* Alambusa, losing his merit and regaining it only after renouncing and denouncing the desire represented by the *apsarā* (Bawa 2013, 263–265, Figs. 7.19, 7.20).

Pleasures related to the senses, the *indriya*[8] or the sense organs, are stigmatised, especially appetites, both alimentary and carnal. In Indian tradition, the primary sense organs are five, which are connected to the organs of action and then to intellect and consciousness. This has been explained in *Samnyāsa Upaniṣads* as follows:

> The fourteen organs such as the eye, each of which is responsible for a single operation, have the following functions; eyes—the perception of form; ears—the perception of sound; tongue—savoring of taste; nose—the perception of smell; voice—the articulation of speech; hands—grasping; feet—washing; anus—evacuation; sexual organ—the perception of pleasure; skin—the perception of touch. Dependent on these the intellect grasps objects. One understands with the intellect, reasons with the mind, and becomes self-conscious with the ego-principle. (*Naradaparivrajaka Upanisad*, 190; cf. Olivelle 1992, 208)[9]

Roger Scruton has argued that thought is internally connected to intellectual but not sensuous pleasure (cf. Savedoff 1985, 313). He distinguishes the intellectual pleasure obtained in art from the sensuous pleasure in food or sex, as intellectual pleasure is seen to be dependent on thought in a way that sensuous pleasure is not. Scruton, however, realising that all pleasure can be affected by thought, seeks to create a hierarchy. For him, sensuous pleasure has only an external, accidental connection to thought, whereas intellectual pleasure has an intrinsic connection with it. Thought is necessary to the experience of intellectual, but not sensuous, pleasure, for intellectual pleasure, unlike sensuous pleasure, has an object and 'any change in the thought involved in intellectual pleasure will automatically lead to a re-description of the pleasure' (cf. Savedoff 1985, 313).

Barbara Savedoff (313–315) contends that both intellectual and sensuous pleasures are dependent on thought and on the fundamental cognition and recognition of the object of pleasure. She observes that when we derive pleasure from a painting, for example, the object of our pleasure is the painting itself. Here, the thought involved in the recognition of the painting as a painting is a precondition for experiencing intellectual pleasure. Our pleasure in a work of art requires not only that we recognise it as art rather than nature but also that we pre-recognise its genre or, in other words, realise the prior notions inherited or cultivated of how the art-object is to be appreciated and enjoyed. Similarly, the pleasure derived from food is as dependent on the pre-recognition of what the food is and perhaps also its taste. Thus, *nāma*, or the essential identity as defined in the Indian tradition, is of seminal importance not only to understanding the nature of a being and of an object but also its enjoyment or its renunciation.

Aquil makes a case for reading about pleasures of the body, of beauty, of the intellect in Urdu literature that at its height is imaginatively romantic, sensual and even pornographic, which prudish and perhaps homophobic modern historians are not equipped to handle. He places Nazir Akbarabadi's works at an intersection between literature, history and society, especially on matters of pleasure, including momentary celebrations of life with a unique *joie de vivre*. Aquil situates Nazir in the history of Delhi at a time of cultural efflorescence actively promoted by later Mughal emperors, especially Muhammad Shah Rangilā—the colourful—even as their political power and authority were being continuously attacked by the invaders from the region to the north west.

The most elemental experience is that of sensuous pleasure—of touch, smell, feel, sound and taste—from whose stimuli the intellectual evolves. '*Kāma* is the activity of the organs of hearing, touch, sight, taste, and smell which are overseen by the mind connected with the self, conductively each with respect to its appropriate object' (*Kāmasūtra*, 2003, xlvii).[10] This, according to Laura Desmond, manifests itself as elemental 'pleasure-in-itself' and throughout the genre of *Kāmaśāstra*, one does not come across the idea that pleasure is an external expression of someone's unique individuality, the gratification of subjective needs and wants (Desmond 2011, 15–39).

Food, or gastronomical pleasures, are reviled as gluttony and greed and anticipated as a feast of taste and the other senses. Ghee, in ancient Indian *samnyāsa*, ascetic tradition, stands for the pleasures of the tongue, of the richness of life, of desires of the flesh to be rejected and denounced. The *Brhat-Samnyāsa Upaniṣad* gives a rather explicit description of the temptation of food, seeking to create a revulsion for these and other pleasures by comparing them with all that is disgusting and/or impure:

> Ghee is like dog's urine, and honey is equal to liquor. Oil is pig's urine, and broth is equal to garlic. Bean cake and the like are cow's meat, and milk is equal to urine. With every effort, therefore, an ascetic

> should avoid ghee and the like. Let him never eat food mixed with ghee, broth, and the like....
>
> He shall avoid ghee as he would blood, a full meal from a single house as he would meat, putting on perfume as he would smearing himself with filth, salt as he would a person of the lowest caste, a garment as he would an unclean bowl, inunction as he would sexual intercourse with a woman, hot water as he would urine, covetousness as he would cow's meat, a region where he is well known as he would a Candala district. (*Brhat-Samnyāsa Upaniṣad*, 267; in Olivelle 1992, 253)

Shalin Jain has looked at this in relation to the Jain ethos, which focuses on the 'thrift' quality that encouraged men to save their money rather than spend it on luxuries and also to avoid laziness and gluttony in order to be better Jains. In this worldview, a man spending money on items such as alcohol was considered wasteful and, in effect, such a man was seen as a failure because he did not spend his time and money in a reasonable and useful manner.

This attitude has parallels in Christian monasticism, where the relationship between sensual pleasures obtained from food and sex are explicated upon by the 4th century theologian Saint Augustine of Hippo. In his *Confessions* as a reformed hedonist, he expounds on three lusts: the lust of the flesh, the lust of the eyes and the pride of life (sensual desires, intellectual curiosity and love of praise) (Gospel of St. John 2:16) (Meilaender 2001). He conflates indulgence in food and sexual pleasures, interrogating whether and to what degree these are necessary for health and procreation—sustenance of the body and the species—and at what point they become justifications for said indulgences (Meilaender 2001, 7, 11).[11]

In the Indic tradition, taste is both celebrated and reviled. The mango, the king of fruits, also figures as the fruit that leads to one's downfall or epitomises heightened gastronomic pleasures, thus attracting both negative and positive attitudes in Indic literature. In Mahakāpi Jātaka, the catalyst is a mango, whose discovery by the king and his desire to possess the source of the mango fruit is so powerful that he ventures into the forest and hunts down a pack of monkeys who live in the mango grove (Verma, IGNCA Weblink) (Marshall 1918, 70).

In the first part of the *Viṣṇudharmottara Purāṇa,* there is a description of how Manu sends *apsarās*, 'wearing ornaments ... roaming amorously and at pleasure' to distract Nara and Narāyana from their penances. Narayāna, the conqueror of Kāmadeva, i.e., one who has conquered his senses, recognises their ruse and shames these *apsarās* by creating from his thigh the *apsarā* Urvaśī using the 'juice of a mango tree, which excites amour'. Urvaśī is more beautiful than any goddess, *gandharvī*, wife of an *asura* or *nāga* damsel or any woman created 'in the world, the very embodiment of feminine beauty and grace' (*Viṣṇudharmottara Purāṇa*, I.129, 1–19).[12] Her description is full of allusions to the entrancing powers of both *samsara* and the joys of heavens. Kālidāsa, while describing the youthful beauty of Pārvatī, compares it to spring season, with 'a tilaka mark marked out with the collyrium that was clinging bees, adorned with the soft red of the young sun her lip that was a mango leaf' (*Kumārasaṃbhava*, 3.30).

While gastronomy, food and recipes are part of many courtly and medical manuals in Sanskrit, Persian and other regional languages, if there is a text that epitomises gourmet delights and desires, it is the illustrated *Ni'matnāmā* (c. 1505 CE),[13] which should have been part of our foray into the world of pleasures but unfortunately will have to wait for another tome. While emperors, kings and nobles would get paeans and eulogies written in the praise of their person and achievements, Sultan Ghiyas-al-din Khijli of Malwa started compiling an illustrated book (which was completed after his abdication by his son Nasir-al-din) that glorified Ghiyas-al-din's greatest love—that of food, recipes and the underlying ingredients.[14]

The illustrations in the book evoke the human and natural landscape and the courtly culture of the Sultan of Malwa that foreground the cooking with clouds, flowering trees, grass and flowering plants in the background and bejewelled female figures in the foreground. The food in the illustrations is a lavish spread with a variety of fruits, meats and vegetable preparations of different scales, shapes, shades and shimmers. The descriptions of recipes range from the lavish to the delicate such as '... a, roast whole camel ... cups of palm sugar ... samosas, green shoots covered in gold and silver or dyed with saffron....' A watermelon on offer includes thin pieces of gold, which the imbiber can preserve as currency. The stems of tubers, cooked greens and the green leaves of jasmine shoots are also wrapped in gold leaf. The food is delivered 'on a tray of seven colours' and 'a tray laden with gold...' (Shaffer 2016, 43). The epicurean Sultan is also portrayed as enjoying aphrodisiacs, rare drinks, freshly prepared food and perfumes in a range of richly textured architectural and textile-adorned spaces. Finbarr Barry Flood is of the opinion that such imagery invokes the idea of *kāma* or sensory pleasure that was central to the performance of Indic kingship, while also owing something to Timurid and Turkmen painting traditions (Flood 2019, 31–32).

Mango as the king of fruits, described by Amir Khusrau as *Naghza Tarin Mewa Hindustan*, is also eulogised in later Urdu literature. Mulla Nizamuddin[15] loved mangoes, and his affection for different kinds of mangoes is reflected in his writings. 'The mangoes should be spotless, no matter if it's the one "ripened on the tree" (*az kism tapka*) or the one which is ripened after falling on the ground'. The gourmet connoisseur's partaking in the pleasures of the different types of the fruit and the distinguishing ways used to ripen are also described (Mahali 1973, 197–98).

Mangoes and Mirza Ghalib have common anecdotal history, with many a story told of his love for the fruit. One day, Bahadur Shah was strolling in *baagh-i hayat bakhsh* or *mehtab bagh* along with his companions. Mirza was also present there. The mango trees were full of mangoes of different colours. These mangoes were reserved for the emperor and the begums of the harem. As Mirza was constantly looking at the mangoes, the *badshah* enquired, 'Mirza, what are you looking with such eagerness!' Mirza replied with folded hands, repeating an old saying perhaps of a *peer* or *murshid* or some other venerable person: '*Bar sar-e har daana ba-navishta ayaan- ka-een fulaan ibn-e fulaan ibn-e fulaan*', which translates to 'on every piece one can see written quite clearly, that this is for so-and-so, son of so-and-so, son of so-and-so. 'I am looking whether my name or my father or grandfather's name is written on any of the mangoes?' (Hali 1897, 70)

Such was his love for mangoes that the residents of the city and even outside used to send him mangoes as a gift. Once, Nawab Mustafa Khan, Maulana Fazl-e Haq, Mirza and many others were present in a gathering and they all were presenting their views on what qualities a mango must have. After hearing every one's views on the mango, Maulana Fazl-e Haq turned to Mirza and asked him for his point of view. Then Mirza said that in his opinion, a mango should have two qualities: it should be sweet and in lots of quantity (Hali 1897, 70–71)!

Aquil has noted that the first letter that employed flattery to acquire mangoes was addressed to a well-wisher in Bengal by Ghalib, who claims that Calcutta's *ahle kalkatta*[16] have a consensus on this: yes, exactly, mango from Hugli, just as flower from the garden (*aare anba az hugli wa gul az gulshan*)!

Pleasures: Somatic and Ritual

Food is one of the supreme offerings made to the gods in the form of ritual sacrifice to put in the *yajña* fire or in *pūjā* rituals. Kota Neelima has emphasised on the pleasure that the devotee partakes in performing rituals, which are pleasing to the deity. The Manifest God receives worship in the form of *pūjā* through sacred rituals following prescribed rules. There may be different kinds of rituals, but a simple *pūjā* consists of offerings of a very basic nature, such as flowers, water, turmeric power, *kumkum* and the like. The more complex *pūjā* requires several sequences of *upacāra* or services accompanied by ritual *mantras* or recitations. Food is one ritualistic way through which the devotee connects with the divine. The offering of *prasāda*, be it the rich viands of *chappan bhoga*, which are the favourite repast of Brij Bihari at Vrindavana, or the *prasādam* at Tirupati or *kada prasāda* at the gurudwara, the devotees seek to please the gods and gurus through pleasing foods and in turn humans partake in the divine pleasure while eating the same redistributed *prasādam*. Perhaps the most popular story is how the tribal woman Śabari tasted the *ber*/fruit before offering it to her divine Lord Rama, to ensure that he was given only the best or the tastiest of them.

Another shared sensuous pleasure is in music and dance that has sublime and sacred moments; it is the activity of the gods and it is also an offering to the divine for their pleasure. The pleasure of song is offered to the gods but is directed at the devotee, as devotion finds the highest expression in lyrics of love and dedication, as seen in the diverse expanse of *bhakti* poetry in India. The highest form of devotion is singing. Thyagaraja personifies and de-personifies god through his timeless *kirtanas* in a magnificent movement between the two realms of thought, creating and erasing dualities.

Śiva dances to express the ultimate pleasure (*Ānanda Tāndava*) and ultimate destruction (*Rudra Tāndava*) at the ultimate cosmic level, while Indra, much like the kings on earth, enjoys the dances by *apsarās* to the accompaniment of music by the *gandharvas* in his court. The performative arts are consumed for pleasure at all levels of existence. Sharma has shown how the *Zenani Dyodi* (women's quarters) of the Jaipur court was culturally organised on the lines of the royal court, and life in it resonated with revelry through periodic gatherings—there were *mehfils* of dance, music and plays. Its inmates were not mere objects of pleasure but they themselves derived pleasure from such performances. My research on Mathura art during the early centuries of the Common Era has revealed the manner in which pleasurable moments derived from dance and music were visualised and displayed, for viewing pleasure, thus implicating the viewer in the visual itself.

The smell of pleasant perfumes and incenses heightens the sense of well-being and experience of pleasure. It is no wonder that *sugandha*, or perfumed objects, are one of the essential offerings to the gods. The god of love and desire, Kāmadeva, dwells in perfumed gardens where gods and goddesses, men and women disport in amorous abandon. This was a pleasure device associated with Kāmadeva, who has five arrows made of different flowers in his quiver that he shoots at those who he wants to bind in the snare of love and infatuation. Scented flowers are one of the recognised ways of experiencing *kāma* (desire) in the Indian *śāstric* literature describing the rules of pleasurable living. Other such devices include precious stones and fine clothing, cosmetics, sandalwood paste, garments smoked in incense, garlands, spiced betel leaf to perfume the mouth, rich food, liquor and the celebration of festivals.[17]

Women have been wearing scented jasmine woven into their plaited hair right from the time of Vasantasenā in *Mṛcchakaṭikā* to the current fashion. In the very recent past, *mālins*, female gardeners would be employed to tuck garlands, *veni* or *gajrā* into the hair of married women in the evenings, before the men returned home from work.

From Pliny[18] to Hegel,[19] European thinkers have focused on the luxuries of the East, especially India, in terms of material objects and in historical imagination as representing opulence, indulgences and decadent pleasures. Perfumes, incense and *ittar/attar* were some of the highly prized luxuries that titillated the senses and were used for medicinal purposes as well to please the olfactory senses. These were particular luxury because like hearing music or watching a performance, the experience was ephemeral. The olfactory object of pleasure could not be used again, as Pliny observes.[20]

The somatic experience of touch, or *sparṣa*, perhaps the most immediate, bodily and sensuous of experiences, is reviled, feared but conspicuous in Indian classical and folk tradition. There is the touch of *vātsalya*, the elemental connection between mother and child, embodied in the Yaśodā–Kṛṣṇa bond, perhaps the most celebrated one at the pan-Indian level, permeating popular as well as classical art forms. It is also at the centre of *śṛṅgāra*, of erotic and amorous love seen through the device of couples, *mithunas* in art as discussed by Bawa, here and elsewhere and also in the rich and diverse textual tradition of *kāvyas*, music and dance. Even trees yearn for the touch of a beautiful young woman (Bawa 2013, 309–335) within the tropes of desire and fertility. The rich and long-lived literary, visual and oral traditions of Bāramāsa[21] and Rāgamāla[22] all speak of these suppressed and expressed desires of lovers longing for the embraces of the beloved, just as Nazir Akbarabadi longs for his beloved Moti's touch in Raziuddin Aquil's account.

To cultivate an amorous and erotic relationship with the beloved, be it human or divine, has been at the heart of much of literary compositions in the poetic forms of *kāvyas*, *dohas*, *ashtapadis*, ballads and folk songs. The devotee's longing for the divine is articulated through bridal *bhakti* or bridal mysticism that speaks of forming a romantic or marital bond with the god/pīr/guru as the bridegroom and the *bhakta* or *bhaktin* as the bride, with the notions of complete loyalty, service, surrender and irrevocableness built into the relationship. This is constructed within the paradigm of longing and sublimation for the beloved, with the entire gamut of experiences and emotions of love, sorrow, separation and ultimate union.

Kota Neelima excavates the devotional depth in Indian traditions not as a historical artefact but as a continuum founded on the notion that essentially, the intensity of devotion marks a subtle rebellion—the pleasure of togetherness through remembering the divine even when not at worship or in religious places. This relationship is not mediated, controlled or charted by authority. Neelima interrogates devotion and pleasure and the relationship between the externalisation of symbolic religion and spirituality with internal devotional space. Devotion without desire is problematic, as the *telos* of seeking salvation is also a desire. However, as pleasure usually has a moral implication, the inherent danger of slipping down the *karmic* scale—as exemplified in the distinction between the good and the pleasant—remains (*Kaṭha Upaṇiṣad* I.2.i).

Visual pleasures are a result of the emphasis on specular beauty, or *saundarya*, in Indian aesthetic tradition, where the entire aesthetic experience of Indian arts is based on experiencing *rasa* at the performance of the arts. A woman looking at her specular self in a mirror reflects such pleasures of beauty. A work of art in itself suggests a cultural authority and a form of dignity, even of wisdom, which is superior to any vulgar material interest, according to Berger (Berger 1973, 218). It is not ephemeral in the way that an art performance would be, but it is like other arts in so far as it is purported to be *sādṛśya* (similitude) and *sahṛdayam* (fostering empathy between the viewer–viewed) and covers the whole gamut of human life experience, be it mundane or sacred, be it in didactic guises or otherwise. In a society that was very comfortable—if not obsessed—with the idea of *kāma*, its representation in art is to be expected. My own chapter focuses on the artistic, physical and ideational spaces in the visual discourse of Mathura art during the early centuries of the Common Era; spaces that privilege and celebrate pleasures of the senses and the intellect.

The world of beauty, desire and leisure in sculptural art though the agency of women and couples is explored within the urban locales of the imagined spaces of palaces, gardens and balconies. Scenes of intimacy, dance and music, feasting and drinking that valorise pleasure and its agents are displayed on pillars and doorways, entrances of *stūpas, vihāras* and other sacred buildings and also on small terracotta plaques at Mathura, Kausambi, Chandraketugarh and many other sites. This trope is seen within the world of *nāgaraka* and *nāgarika* of *Kāmasūtra* and *Mṛcchakaṭikā*, through the ideal urban characters who cultivate their self and seek aesthetic and somatic pleasures in activities such as painting, singing, consorting with beautiful courtesans or *gaṇikās*, participating in intellectually stimulating sessions with like-minded men and public women, *goṣṭhī* and the like. The chapter not only views the display of pleasure but also discusses those who were responsible for producing the objects of pleasure such as jewellery, perfumes and unguents and also for mounting dance and theatrical performances for the *nāgaraka*.

Bodily Pleasures

Since the body is at the centre of the discourse on pleasure, technologies to enhance or control pleasure are often directed at the body, albeit sometimes via the mind. *Rasa bhāva* is one technique that prescribes, sanctions, controls and regulates pleasures by providing a framework for the presentation and enjoyment of a visual or performative experience. Other technologies could be medical techniques, such as Ayurveda and yoga, and other systems of body management or embellishment through external means such as clothes, jewellery and cosmetics or through cultivating it through body movements such as dance, gait, attitude and posture, all of which contribute to the visual pleasure cultures. Not just the body but also the intellect in the form of 64 skills and arts, *chaunsath kalā nipuṇa*, is to be cultivated for a heightened socio-sexual experience, be it for the *nāgaraka*, or the courtesan, the object of desire.

This is true as much of South Asia as it is of other societies, for instance classical cultures and art where the increasing medical involvement in the cultivation of the self appears to have been expressed through a particular and intense form of attention to the body. During the Roman Empire, there was an emphasis on self-care that also imagines others caring for themselves. Michel Foucault in *History of Sexuality* (volume 2) in *The Use of Pleasure* observes that pleasure was largely regulated by regulating the body (Garrison 2014, 108–111).

Desmond in her article on the *kāmaśāstric* tradition, *The Pleasure is Mine: The Changing Subject of Erotic Science* illustrates yet another aspect of the social context through the performance of a large but bounded repertoire of acts that identifies a subject as an agent of pleasure by recasting the subject into a specific kind of sense object—a performative icon. When discussing the *chaunsath kalā*, in which the cosmopolitan is skilled, the work of messengers, courtship, the pursuit of adulterous affairs or the conduct of courtesans, the text describes agents of pleasure that are embedded in the visible and public world of social interaction (Desmond 2011, 17).

Desmond describes that while the *Kāmasūtra's* discussion of sex acts, the defloration of a maiden and the use of secret recipes for bringing others under one's control relates to the private sphere of the bedroom, the remainder of the text delineates acts relating to the public or social sphere of the garden, market and the like. The enhanced bodily and sensory capabilities developed by the *kāmaśāstric nipuṇa* are deployed in response to a complex social environment in which pleasure exists as an 'omnipresent, latent potentiality' (Desmond 2011, 17).

Desmond adds that 'pleasure doesn't just happen, nor does it happen to just anyone' (Desmond 2011, 18).[23] By enacting the prescriptions and procedures described in *Kāmaśāstra*, processes and technologies of self-cultivation and body modification, the likelihood of certain kinds of affective experiences—such as pleasure—increases, largely predicated on the effects one has on the world around oneself.

Aquil has shown the pleasures articulated through the persons of the poet and his lover in Nazir's work and has once again emphasised on the fineness of the woman's body (waist has *lachak*, suppleness, and *nazakat*, elegance), the wonderful features enhanced by captivating gaze, and pearl-like (*moti*) teeth. He has also highlighted the emotions generated by her laughter and the overwhelming quality of her voice, which may cause pearl-like or *moti*-like tears. Both the features of the body and emotions are doubly enhanced by her embellishments and make up—using *paan* (betel) and *missi* (herbal concoction with a sexual connotation, applied by women on their teeth during wedding ceremonies) as well as finely designed dress and accoutrement.

Women Voluptuaries: Renunciation versus Pleasure

Women are central to the discourse of pleasure, as enhancers and agents and as tempters and obstacles to self-restraint and renunciation in popular and classical culture. I quote two lyrics from very popular films of the 1960s that epitomise the conflict between pleasure and renunciation, the material world and its rejection, as has been projected through the person of the moralising *yogi*/sadhu/ascetic and the temptatious woman,[24] embodied by the courtesan, who is not bound by the social order and its behavioural moral codes.[25] These give voice to a cultural consciousness embedded in Indian ethos, from the ancient times to the medieval, in patriarchal stereotypes of Tulsidas and Banarasidas in *Ardhakathanaka* and many others in the popular understanding of *kāma* within the trope of desire being essentially necessary or being a negative force to be contended with, and the counter discourse valorising love, beauty, desire, fulfilment and *bhoga*.

Jao re jogī ... yeh hai premiyon kī nagari, yahān prem hi hai pooja...
Prem ki Pīda Sachā Sukh, Prem binā yeh Jīvan dukh hai
jīvan se kaisa chutakārā, hai nadiyā ke sāth kinārā...
gyān ki kaisi sīma gyāni, gāgar mein sāgar ka pāni.

(Shailendra, *Amrapali* 1966)

> Trans: Depart O! Mendicant for this is the abode of lovers where love is the only worship
> The pining for love is true happiness, the absence of love makes living sorrowful
> What kind of escape from the world where the strand accompanies the river (end is inherent in living)
> What are the limits of knowledge O knowledgeable one, It is like reducing the sea in a pitcher?
>
> *Sansār se bhāge firate ho, bhagawān ko tum kyā pāoge*
> *Is lok ko bhī apnā nā sake, us lok mein bhī pachhatāoge*
> *ye pāp hai kyā ye punya hai kyā, reeton par dharm ki moharen hain*
> *har yug mein badalate dharmon ko, kaise ādarsh banāoge*
> *ye bhog bhī ek tapasyā hai, tum tyāg ke māre kyā jāno*
> *apamān rachetā kā hogā, rachanā ko agar thukarāoge...*
>
> Trans: You who seek to escape samsara, how would you attain God
> Couldn't partake of this world, would repent in the other world
> What is vice (transgression) what is virtue (merit) but traditions sanctified by religion)
> Religions that keep changing with times, how would these be Ideals
> It would be an Insult to the Creator if the creation is rejected)
> (Sahir Ludhianvi, *Chitralekha* 1964)

Āmrapālī embodies both alimentary and sexual desires (mainly male desires for the most beautiful and accomplished woman of her age, and also as a standard for all that is beautiful in the world). The name is derived from *āmra* or mango and *pallava* or young leaves. She is mentioned in *Jātaka kathās*, *Digha Nikaya, Khudda* and also in the visual tradition, and a separate *gāthā* is ascribed to her in the *Therigāthā*, Psalms of the Senior Nuns, where she rejects the notion of the primacy of youth, beauty and body perfections. Āmrapālī's verses (*Therigatha*. PTS, 252–272) repeat the idea of the impermanence of a beautiful female body as if to instruct the viewer about the transience of life. Āmrapālī repeatedly mentions her youthful beauty and its transformation into an ugly old frame with withered breasts, thinning hair, foul odour and wrinkled skin. Vimalā, another former *ganik*ā, says the following:

> Intoxicated by my (good) complexion, my figure, my beauty and fame haughty because of my youth, I despised other women. Having decorated this body, very variegated, deceiving fools, I stood at the brothel gate, like a hunter having spread out a snare. Showing my

> ornamentation. Many a secret place (referring to private body parts) was revealed. I did various sorts of conjuring, laughing at many people. Today (that same) I, having wandered for alms with shaven head, clad in the outer robe, am seated at the foot of a tree, having obtained the stage of non reasoning. (*Therigatha*. PTS, 72–76)

Revulsion with superficial features such as physicality and materiality is to be located in a discourse based on the beauty (or its dissipation) of the body of the woman and carnal pleasures in the religious ideology in textual and oral tradition and fine art (Bawa 2013, 28–29).

This is a continuation of a long-standing contestation between the renunciant and the householder, in this case the Buddhist *bhikkhu* and the householder or the *gahapati/gihi* or even the king as reflected in the *Vinay Piṭaka*, where enjoying luxuries is considered the domain of the latter. Thus, the following questions are raised when the former indulges in pleasurable activities: 'How can these recluses, sons of the Sakyans, dress with their inner robe hanging down … or sit down lolling about … or laugh a great laughter … just like householders who enjoy the pleasures of the sense, *kāmabhogino*' (Chakravarty 1987, 38–39). Temptation to the *bhikkhu* to give up the hard life of begging and abstinence is offered by the sight of 'a *gahapati* or *gahapati puttas* indulging in the five sense pleasures…. A great house, a couch with a scarlet cushions at both ends, a lamp burning and our wives to wait upon him with all their charms' (Chakravarty 1987, 83–84).[26]

The rejection of desire for worldly pleasures is one of the main platforms on which ascetic values are endorsed, granting a superior status to those who control, restrain or reject the sensual and sensory pleasures, in which there is an inherent denunciation of the religious primacy of the householder (Olivelle 1992, 43). The Pali canon reiterates the following:

> The household life is a dusty path full of hindrances, while the ascetic life is like the open sky. It is not easy for a man who lives at home to practice the holy life (*brahmachariya*) in all its fullness, in all its purity, in all its bright perfection.[27]

Thus, those who are attached to the worldly activities of the *gṛhastha*, living in villages, ascribing lineage, performing sacrifices, doing good works and begetting children (especially sons), are subject to rebirth[28] or moral and behavioural unrestraint such as anger. *Moksha* or *nirvana* is available to those who transcend these, and therefore is not available to women who embody the world of sin, temptation, desire, pleasure and physicality (Bawa 2013, 23–28). This is illustrated in the word picture drawn in the *Yājñavalkya Upaniṣad*, where a woman's charms are described vividly only to exhort the renouncer to be vary of the allure.

> What, pray, is the beauty of a woman, who is a puppet of flesh furnished with tendons, bones, and joints, within a cage of limbs moved by machine? [Yogav I.2I.I]
>
> Examine her eyes after separating the skin, the flesh, the blood, the tears, and the fluid, and see if there is any charm. Why are you bewitched in vain? [Yogav I.2I.2]
>
> The same breast of a girl, on which we see the brilliant splendor of a pearl necklace comparable to swift waters of the Ganges rippling down the slopes of mount Meru, is in time eaten with relish by dogs in remote cemeteries as if it were a little morsel of food. [Yogav I.2I.5-6]
>
> With stylish hair and painted eyes, hard to touch but pleasing to the eye, women are like the flame of sin and burn a man like straw. [Yogav I.2I.II]
>
> Burning even from afar, sweet and yet bitter, [316] women indeed are the fuel of hellfire, both lovely and cruel. [Yogav I.2I.I2]
>
> Foolish women are the nets spread out by the fowler called Kama, binding the limbs of men as if they were birds. [Yogav I.2I.I8]
>
> A woman is the bait on the fishhook tied to the line of evil tendencies, for men who are like fish in the pond of birth, wading in the mud of the mind. [Yogav I.2I.20]
>
> I have done forever with women, who are the chains of suffering and strongboxes for all the gems of sins. [Yogav I.2I.23]
>
> A man with a woman desires pleasures. In a man without a woman, where is the room for pleasure? When one abandons women one abandons the world. When one abandons the world one becomes happy. [Yogav I.2I.35] (Yājñavalkya Upaniṣad, 315–316 in Olivelle, 1992, 279)

Shalin Jain's chapter shows the distrustful attitudes towards pleasure and leisure amongst the Jainas, as it is believed that these perpetuated laziness. Indeed, masculinity was defined by the denial of pleasure as an attribute of a 'true man'; thus, it is not an attribute associated solely with ascetics.

Despite the hegemonic contempt of pleasure and pleasurable activities as temptations and obstructions to the attainment of masculine control over the mind and the body, they were celebrated even in their condemnation. Who can be greater sinner than he who rejects happiness, which is the fruit of religious and worldly goods? How can a person who sacrifices the pleasures of the life (*tyakta-dṛṣṭasukha*) to attain happiness in the next life (*janmāntara-sukhaprāptye*) be called a wise one?[29]

The attitudes towards sex for pleasure in Urdu poetry have been highlighted by Aquil, who observes that iconoclastic Urdu literature offers some of the finest articulation and celebration of a variety of ways in which sexual pleasure was possible, whether hidden or in public, and despite attempts to suppress what is termed as 'perversion'. The intricacies of bodily and other features and their celebrations are valorised in the poet's work. It was part of the established tradition in popular Urdu literature to speak about matters of love and sex at a variety of registers, explicit, in double-entendre or in a more sophisticated language.

Domesticated and Gendered Pleasures

Despite the apparent suspicion, fear and rejection of the feminine by the normative male discourse, there is a tradition that provides a window through which women themselves partook of happiness and pleasure. Jaya S. Tyagi has opened up this window for us to look into the lives of the household women as represented in the early Indian textual tradition. The texts chosen for her chapter, the *Purāṇas* (particularly the *Matsyamahāpurāṇa*), visualise pleasure as that which can be attained through power (with its associations with kingship, fame and victory—*rajas*, *yaśa* and *jaya*), status, domestic bliss, carnal satisfaction, health, wealth and overall well-being. All these, however, can be attained only through the performance of rituals, and pleasure is not achieved easily or naturally.

Within the context of ancient Indian textual traditions, domestic spaces are often projected as spaces providing pleasure that is not only conjugal but is also obtained from other relationships—filial ties, paternal, maternal and kinship bonds. There is also pleasure arising from a sense of attachment, of belongingness, and also from the comfort and cocooning within particular spaces—particularly the maternal womb and, by extension, the household and its environs.

Conjugal pleasure was not projected merely as physical or bodily pleasure but something otherworldly, leading to a deep sense of fulfilment and paving the way for familial pleasures. Thus, even the *devas* are projected to be 'enjoying' with their 'lotus-eyed consorts'. This conjugal intimacy is envisaged in a male-centric manner, with the male being both a source of pain and pleasure, especially for those women who threaten and transgress domestic norms. On the other hand, women are providers of pleasure, focused on pleasing the men.

If the opulent, voluptuous and accomplished *ganikā* in her *veśyāvāsa* or courtesan quarters is one trope, the wife, often silent and invisible, the reproductive wife, provides a counter discourse, whose pleasures while hidden from the public eye were differently projected within the household as a 'pleasurable' space. A space that brings *sukha* not only to the householder and its members, says Tyagi, but also to the different social categories dependent on the householder's largesse. This was essential to the notion of social stability that was envisaged in Brahmanical traditions as it would allow for the control of reproductive and productive activities in an organised manner even while allowing the household to emerge as a source of patronage for the Brahman as well as the *śramana* categories, providing sustenance (and 'pleasure') to these categories too with a mutual enjoyment of wealth and resources.

I have argued in another publication that the woman in the visual culture of the post-Mauryan period is represented not just as an object of enjoyment but rather as a participant and even controller of pleasure. In visual culture, pleasure of viewing is often gendered, where the female bodies are constructed as nubile, young and 'playful', primarily to induce and enhance the experience of consuming these as pleasurable spectacle. The head-to-toe description of the perfection of the female body is an established trope in Nazir's poetry, as shown by Aquil, as it is in classical Indian aesthetics on bodily features and practices.

Shalin Jain observes that notions of pleasure require to be differentiated from the usual material concerns of life. Wealth does not necessarily bring pleasure but is required for utilitarian purposes within the Jain worldview. Thus, the interaction between routine life, satisfaction and happiness could have been the prudent cause of pleasure than the need for consumption and utility.

The Jain worldview was conscious of the fact that its followers, who engaged in deliberate and direct pursuits of happiness through the vile of wealth, might end up pursuing immoral activities and experiences, thus missing out on the satisfaction of leading an ideal life.

The situs of pleasure is not fixed; it is in the body and the mind, in the material and the experiential, in rituals, society, nature and culture. It is a fluid category that is based on the individual's experience and the societal and communitarian understanding of what constitutes desire, fulfilment and its display that indicates power, prestige and authority.[30]

The courtly revelry and opulence of Rāvaṇa's abode is explored by Parul Pandya Dhar through visual narratives at Aihole and other temples in western Deccan. She points out that the visualisation of Rāvaṇa's Laṅkā as a paradise of sensual pleasures in ancient Indian sculpture and painting rarely, if ever, parallels its literary abandon, perhaps out of concerns about *aucitya* (appropriateness) that restricts portrayals of erotic excesses. Some artists of the early medieval western Deccan, however, did explore the visual possibilities of portraying bodily pleasures through the *Sundarakāṇḍa* episodes carved on the inner ambulatory of the 7th-century Durga temple at Aihole. They depict the palatial settings of Lanka, aestheticising multiple sensory desires emanating from the particular predilections of the powerful king of Lanka, Rāvaṇa. In a broader frame, her essay attempts to address the nature of prescriptions and proscriptions in the literary and visual portrayals of pleasurable and erotic pursuits in early medieval India and in their differential calibrations when depicting gods, kings and demons.

In India, pleasure may be located within both physical and moral spaces. Bazaars, brothels, gardens, terraces and even the household are sites where pleasure can be experienced. Gardens and open spaces were sites of festivities and enjoyment,[31] as has been shown by me in my essay on the spectacle of conjugal or amorous activities in art of Mathura during the post-Mauryan period. Festivals were special occasions when the elite and the ordinary men and women enjoyed themselves in varied ways, some of which may seem a little strange to us and others that we are more familiar with. (This discourse of leisure has been discussed in a forthcoming publication.)

Festivals presented a public space where the sensual could be exhibited and indulged in. The ancient *Vasantōtsava* and the current Holi in the month of *Phālguna* are well-known examples of this. *Madanotsva, kāmotsava* and other festivities reveal the world of *kāma*, of desire and amour. V.S. Agarwala talks about the *Indra maha* as a festival that marks not just the rite of passage and seasons but as also indicative of the rituals and festivities involved in celebrating this festival. These were moments where popular devotion was combined with celebration, with public gathering at specified time of the year, and often involved dance, music, feasting, offering of flowers, incense or *gandha*, lights and the like.[32] One such festival was known as *Udyāna-maha* or the festival of gardens to be enjoyed in the spring season, where gentle *krīḍā* or play along with leisure activities were organised such as garden excursions, food and drink, flower sports such as the gathering and throwing of flowers at each other, water sports, dance and music and entertainment with friends, relatives and acquaintances.[33]

Aquil speaks of the festivities in Nazir's poems not just around Eid but also around Hindu festivals such as the auspicious Diwali and hooliganistic Holi. These poems also reveal the poet's narrativisation of Hindu beliefs and traditions associated with mythological figures on a scale meant to highlight the excellence of their character and widespread devotion around them as a matter of celebration. Besides matters of bazars, festivities and fun, Nazir's devotional poetry dedicated to the extraordinary powers of religious gurus is equally powerful with love and longing.

The interface between the individual and the community is revealed in Shalin Jain's chapter, which excavates the contours of pleasures and displeasures expressed in the 17th century Hindi text *Ardhakathānak*[34] written by a Jaina merchant Banarsidas. Through this account, he reconstructs a multi-tiered reality in the everyday lives of the individuals around their social, political and economic engagements. The social relations[35] gets expressed in terms of emotions, marriage, friendship, polygamy, concubinage, divorce, remarriage, adoption and other bonds, which have historically provided, created and maintained the kinship groups. Banarsidas's life and time is not just a site for personal legitimate and illegitimate relationships but it also unfolds as a unique site of pleasure in his engagement with sanctioned knowledge and anarchic religious systems. *Ardhakathānak* gives us a rare glimpse of emotions arising from friendships, beyond the usual *sakhā-sakhi* nexus of the hero-heroine and companion-servitor, into those friendships that were based on mutual interest and mutual business enterprises, common pilgrimages and frequent visits.

Jain's chapter discusses the constrains of spaces for individual pleasure and multiple sites of unpleasantness in the early modern society, arguing that pleasure was merely an individual desire far from the realisation beyond normative discourse and still an aspirational goal.

Elite and Popular Pleasure

The production and consumption of pleasure through beauty, laughter and desire are mediated by both class as well as gender. The dominant genders and classes/castes control the discourse of pleasure.

Preeti Sharma's research is based on the Jaipur *suratkhāna* records of the royal women of the erstwhile Jaipur state and demonstrates the Rajput queens' engagement in patronising the art of painting and primarily represents them as women who are purveyors of pleasure and refined cultural vigour. The paintings commissioned included, besides portraits of their male relations, romantic *śṛṅgāra* pictures that idealised women as lovers. In a way, the assumed 'presence' of women, physically 'absent' in the 'public' arena of Rajput courts, from the closed and 'private' quarters of the *zenanā* casts fresh light on the role of women in history.

Her reading of the genealogy of the discourse relating to feminine social spaces locates a hierarchy within women's public and the private realms represented by women's assertive agency in the private sphere through engagements with the arts, aesthetics and literature. Sharma asserts that paintings patronised by the women convey moments of tenderness that integrate visual renderings of the patrons' male relatives with illustrated textual types of romantic *śṛṅgāra* paintings, thereby subverting the patriarchal norm. Rather than being self-portraits, the latter depict idealistic stylised women as lovers. On the other hand, the *zenanā* women commissioned male portraits, a choice that simultaneously questions and strengthens heteronormative ideals and suggests that male images may have been 'objects' of the female gaze. The paintings bring to light the alternate networks of power and pleasure courtly women create from behind the *purdāh* and *zenanā*.

In the light of this public–private dichotomy, usually taken as an indicator of women's subordination, Sharma highlights the women's contributions to the artistic genre and seeks to de-centre the ontological indeterminacy underlying the understanding of the phenomenon of women's pleasure.

The consumption or experience of pleasure is privileged in the sources as well as in their interpretations, neglecting the pain that often accompanies and is inherent in the production of objects and services material, sexual and intellectual. This unequal relationship between the producers and consumers of pleasure, that someone's pleasure must come at the expense of another's pain, has been mentioned in several chapters in this volume. However, Santosh Rai has highlighted this through the lens of the weavers whose fortunes were dependent on the changing fashions in society and the colonial political economy.

Santosh Rai observes that in context of colonial modernity, the pleasure invoked by fashion and creativity of production are not two autonomous domains. Material cultures and the materiality of multiple actors in the fashion industry bind them together. Objects of fashion are highly charged cultural instruments, animated by cross-cultural and transnational flows that actively influence the social world and cultural history. This chapter considers three perspectives on the handloom industry: (a) the changing clothing habits and fashion, (b) the contextualisation of new trends and the documentation of the handloom industry's continued resilience and (c) the weaver's own perception of day-to-day problems of livelihood and survival vis-à-vis the realm of pleasure of production and earnings.

The decline of the handloom industry is connected to the idea of fashion and its evolution; objects of fashion are intimately connected with corporeal, cultural, social and gender-based experiences as well as the economies of fashioning and re-fashioning of these across places and times. The reuse of Indian objects in different European contexts, such as shawls as curtains, or carved tables from Bulandshahr in an Edwardian drawing room, transforms its original purpose, turning it from utilitarian to aesthetic or decorative. These objects speak of this internationalisation of fashion, demand and meaning. Cloth and clothing act as symbols of native pleasures that not only triggered political reactions but were also a symbol of the economic destruction wrought by foreign cloth, dislocating the symbolic meanings attached with cloth and clothing that transmitted messages regarding holiness, purity and pollution.

COUNTER DISCOURSE: SATIRE

As Jain, Tyagi, Rai, Aquil, Sharma and other authors have pointed out, there is no uniform discourse on pleasure. The existing discourse is punctuated and fragmented by counter narratives. Pleasure, its production and consumption and its display are indicators of power and privilege, be it social, political and/or religious power, as much as it is about experience, emotion and aesthetics. Who is allowed to consume, enjoy and witness pleasure is prescribed, sanctioned, controlled and regulated. Who has the power and privilege to laugh at whom, who can have sex with whom, who can step out of the house and be seen and how are these equations to be regulated and controlled so not to disrupt the social order?

Humour and satire are powerful tools to overturn or at least comment on these regulations. The tension is often manifested through laughter and derision of the elite by the lower orders through satire and exposure of their hypocrisy, through the agency of the *viduṣaka*, *viṭā*, poet or artist who highlights the ambivalence of society towards social norms. In the aesthetic tradition, even the *rasas* are recommended for the consumption of elite men and women, and common people are treated differently. It is claimed that men, especially the ones who are educated and belong to higher *varṇas*, can appreciate serious *rasas*, while women and common people can enjoy the lighter *rasas* associated with humour and spectacle.

> Young people are pleased to see (the presentation of) love, the learned a reference to some (religious and philosophical) doctrine, the seekers after money to the topics of wealth, and the passionless the topics of liberation. Heroic persons are always pleased in the Odious and the Terrible Sentiments, personal combats and battles, and the old people in Purānic legends, and tales of virtue. And common women, children and uncultured persons are always delighted with the Comic Sentiment and remarkable costumes and make-up. (*Nāṭyaśāstra*, XXV, 59–61)

This is explored at length in the *parihāsa* and *bhāṇa* dramas in ancient India that often have the courtesan and the dissolute but intellectually perceptive *vīṭā* as protagonists who not only add comic and erotic overtones to the composition but also criticise the hypocritical and bloated pleasures of elite society through satire and lampoons.

Ashish Abrol and Janica Paul's note on the *Caturabhāṇi* showcases a type of classical drama called the *bhāṇa*, which is relatively under-researched but presents an important picture of prescribed and prohibited pleasures that were part of the performative tradition in early India. Here, the protagonists are the *viduṣaka* and the *vīṭā*, or a man about town in form of a jester, and the *gaṇikā* or courtesan par excellence, whose interactions move the narrative forward and also present a counterculture of popular idioms. On the one hand, indulgence in desires is encouraged and even celebrated, while on the other hand, the hypocrisies of the learned elite are exposed to evoke laughter through a satirical impression of contemporary social and behavioural norms.

To quote Ghalib:

> *kahāñ mai-ḳhāne kā darvāza 'ġhālib' aur kahāñ vaa.iz*
> *par itnā jānte haiñ kal vo jaatā.thā ki hum nikle*
> (O Ghalib, The entrance of the tavern and the Moralising preacher are so far apart, yet I only know that he was entering just as I was leaving Ghalib)[36]

Saifuddin Ahmad attempts to investigate the counter discourse of pleasure in the works of Mir Muhammad Ja'far Zatalli (d. 1713 CE) through the use of invective, satire and ribald humour to mount acerbic criticisms of society and its morals. His verses reveal a brave and determined yet intensely socially committed personality of the decaying times of the 18th century, who infused his verses with proverbs, maxims and astute words expressed manifestly. Ja'far's satires are aimed at pointing out the shortcomings of society through the ridicule of accepted standards of thought, exposing the failings of the North Indian society and chastising the hypocrisy of the time. Ja'far shows a mirror to the degeneration of the nobility, rampant corruption, duplicity and immorality of the elites. The distress, pain and affliction in his satire is reflective of the mutilated and dejected soul of the age. He deliberately uses expressions laced with piercing severity meant to shock and injure.

Ja'far's savage and obscene satire was often directed against the women of the high class, who, in his poetry, have been portrayed as sexually promiscuous, whores and cheats with other derisive appellations.

Ja'far's satire is embedded in humour and he also mocks and laughs at his own self-afflicted hardship and also makes others laugh at him in works such as *Joban Nama* and *Hasb-i haal-i khud guftah* among others that describe the hardship Ja'far had to endure because he antagonised his masters/patrons.

The discourse on pleasure is neither hegemonic nor homogenous.[37] The degree of fulfilment is contained within social and cultural contexts and predicaments that communities and individuals situate themselves in. As seen in the chapters of this collection, the pursuit of pleasure and desire is deeply embedded in the attitudes and behavioural codes of the time, constantly being contested and controlled through value judgement, moral and ethical codes of behaviour, ritual and theology. And men and women seem equally determined to defy or modify the moral codes to find moments of happiness and pleasure, to fulfil their desires and make life a little more liveable.

NOTES

1. *Kāmasūtra*: 2.1. The synonyms for sexual pleasure (*rati*) are sexual feeling (*rasa*), sexual pleasure or ecstasy (*rati*), love or ecstasy (*prīti*), emotion, temperament or climax (*bhāva*), passion (*raga*), sexual energy (*vega*) and satisfaction (*samapti*). The synonyms for the sexual act (*surata*) are sex or making love (*samprayoga*), mating or coupling (*rata*), the secret act (*rahas*), going to bed together (*shayana*) and seduction (*mohana*).
2. *Rati*: pleasure, enjoyment, delight in, to find pleasure (of sexual love, amorous enjoyment). *Rati* is also the wife of Kamādeva.
3. Also *ram, ramayin, ramanato*, delight, make happy, enjoy carnally, to couple as in *Harivamsam. Mrigyan ramayati*.
4. *Bhoga*: enjoyment, eating, feeding on; jainas 'enjoying once': sexual enjoyment; experiencing, feeling, perception (of pleasure or pain, profit, utility, advantage, pleasure, delight; any object of enjoyment, such as food or a festival.
5. *dharmārthāvirodhena kāmaṃ seveta, na niḥsukhaḥ syāt . samaṃ vā trivargam anyon- yānubaddham . eko hy atyāsevito dharmārthakāmānām ātmānam itarau ca pīḍayati (KAŚ 1 .7 .3–5)* in Olivelle (2019, 384).
6. *śatāryur vai puruṣo vibhajya kālam anyonyānubaddhaṃ parasparasyānupaghātakaṃ trivargaṃ seveta . bālye vidyāgrahaṇādīn arthān . kāmaṃ ca yauvane . sthāvire dharmaṃ mokṣaṃ ca . anityatvād āyuṣo yathopapādaṃ vā seveta (1 .2 .1–5).*
7. MSWE, *bhogin* (m): a voluptuary, having or offering enjoyments, devoted to enjoyment, wealth or opulence.
8. *Indriya*: the number five as symbolical of the five senses. In addition to the five organs of perception, *buddhīndriyāṇi* or *jñānendriyāṇi*, *id est* eye, ear, nose, tongue and skin, the Hindus enumerate five organs of action,

or *karmendriyāṇi, id est* larynx, hand, foot, anus and generative organs. Between these 10 organs and the soul or ātman stands *manas* or mind, considered as an eleventh organ; in the *vedānta, manas, buddhi, ahaṃkāra* and *citta* form the four inner or internal organs, *antar-indriyāṇi*. According to this, the organs are 14 in number, each being presided over by its own ruler or *niyantṛ*; thus, the eye by the sun, the ear by the quarters of the world, the nose by the two Aśvins, the tongue by Prachetas, the skin by the wind, the voice by fire, the hand by Indra, the foot by Viṣṇu, the anus by Mitra, the generative organs by Prajāpati, the *manas* by the moon, *buddhi* by Brahman, *ahaṃkāra* by Śiva and *citta* by Viṣṇu as Acyuta. In the *Nyāya* philosophy, each organ is connected with its own peculiar element, such as the nose with the earth, the tongue with water, the eye with light or fire, the skin with air and the ear with ether.

9. *Naradaparivrajaka Upanisad*, 190.
10. *Kāmasūtra*, xlvii. Also 1 .2.6–14. Pleasure in its primary form, however, is a direct experience of an object of the senses, which bears fruit and is permeated by the sensual pleasure of erotic arousal that results from the particular sensation of touch.
11. *Kāmasūtra*, 7, 11. What is enough for health is not enough for pleasure, and it is often hard to tell whether it is the necessary care of my body asking for sustenance or whether 'it is a deceitful voluptuousness of greed trying to seduce me' [Conf. 10.3]. 'If one should ask why it was necessary that a helper be made for man, the answer that seems most probable is that it was for the procreation of children....' As we should not grasp for the pleasure of eating apart from the good purpose to which it is divinely ordered, so also, we should not seek the pleasure of the sexual act apart from the good to which it is divinely ordered.
12. Also see *Vishnudahrmottara Purāṇa*, ed. and tr. Stella Kramrisch: 26 fn; also, Part III, Chapter 27, verses 7–26.
13. The *Ni'matnāmā*. London: Indian Office Library.
14. The *Ni'matnāmā* is dedicated to the King of Cockroaches.
15. He was an Islamic Scholar (late 17th and 18th centuries) who belonged to the Firangi Mahal (*madarsa* in Lucknow). He introduced *dars-i nizami*.
16. Ahle Kalkatta implies 'relating to Calcutta' in Urdu.
17. The *Pattinapalai* (1,40) comments that *sandal* and *aghil* came into the Chola markets from the mountains towards the West. The *Silappadikaram*, 'The Lay of the Anklet', described the actress who bathed her tresses in perfumed oil and dried them over the smoke of aloe-wood. Cf. Guy (2011, 168).
18. From the 1st century BC, Rome was the major importer of products from the Far East. In the 1st century CE, Pliny the Elder complained that Rome was already spending 100,000,000 of *sesterces* each year in the Far East. Cf. Tomber (2002, 25).
19. 'India', wrote Hegel, 'as a Land of Desire forms an essential element in General History'. From the most ancient times downwards, all nations have directed their wishes and longings to gaining access to the treasures of this land of marvels, that the costliest which the earth presents, the treasures of nature

–pearls, diamonds, perfumes, rose essences, lions, elephants, textiles, spices –as also the treasures of wisdom. the way in which these treasures passed to the west has at all times been a matter of world historical importance bound up with the fate of nations' (quoted in Panikkar 1969, 21).

20. Pliny says perfume was the ultimate luxury item because it could not be reused (13.20) (Parker 2002, 40–95).
21. Description of 12 months, seasonal changes and the changes in landscape and lovers' psyche.
22. Garland of ragas, that visualises the lyrical melodic ragas in the form of women in various moods and states of being, such as pining for their lovers.
23. Alfred Gell calls 'the technology of enchantment and the enchantment of technology'. He argues that aesthetic power should be understood as the outcome of a technological system in which experts (and through them their patrons) have the means to produce artefacts that are recognised as 'beautifully made, or made beautiful'. Such objects elicit certain responses in those who come into contact with them, compelling them to behave in specific ways.
24. Ascetics shall not speak with śudras, women, outcastes and menstruating women. Ascetics shall not perform divine worship, or which festivals [NpU 176] (Olivelle 1992, 262–263).
25. One is cognizant of the fact that most of the voices that speak for women, elite and marginalised, have been textualised by men, and do not record the 'authentic' experiences of women.
26. *Anguttara Nikaya*, I, 127; cf. (Chakravarty 1987, 83–84).
27. *Digha Nikaya*, I.63; *Majjhima Nikaya*, I.179; III.35, I34. *Sutta Nipata*, 406. On the superiority of the renouncer over the householder, see also *Majjhima Nikaya*, II.197–205; *Sutta Nipata*, I8–34, 393 (see Olivelle 1992, 43).
28. Poison, weapons, seeds, injuring, fierceness, sexual intercourse, observances, such as those of a householder, which were abandoned through renunciation, all social divisions such as lineage, father's and mother's families, and wealth—these are forbidden. He who resorts to them will sink downward. *Brhat-Samnyasa Upaniṣad*, 271.
29. *Brhatkathāśloka samgraha by Buddhasvāmin;* cf. (Shah 2009, 54).
30. Berger (1973, 50) has made similar observation about the arts.

    The visual arts have always existed within a certain preserve; originally this preserve was magical or sacred. But it was also physical: it was the place, the cave, the building, in which, or for which, the work was made. The experience of art, which at first was the experience of ritual, was set apart from the rest of life—precisely in order to be able to exercise power over it. Later the preserve of art became a social one. It entered the culture of the ruling class, whilst physically it was set apart and isolated in their palaces and houses. During all this history the authority of art was inseparable from the particular authority of the preserve.
31. For gardens as ideational and material spaces for deployment of pleasure, see Ali (2003, 223–235).

32. Agarwala has used the term *maha* for festivals and gives the description of many such popular festivities in honour of different mainstream and local gods and goddesses (*Agrawala Vasudeva Sharan* 2015, 744).
33. The names of sports enjoyed on such occasions are found in grammatical literature and in the 'Javamangala Commentary' of the *Kāmasūtra*, e.g., gathering of *asoka* flowers (Asokapushpa-prachayika), plucking of *sala* flowers (Sala-bhanjika), plucking of *uddalaka* flowers (Uddalakapushpa) (*Agrawala Vasudeva Sharan* 2015, 812–813).
34. The *Ardhakathānak* of Banarasidas (a Jain trader from Jaunpur) is an autobiographical poem in the Braj Bhasha, with a touch of Khari Boli, a dialect of Hindi dating from 1641 AD. *Ardhakathanak* is unique because it is, arguably, the 'first autobiography in the Indian tradition' written by an individual, a commoner. See Banarsidas (1641) and Banarsidas (1981).
35. For early Indian attitudes, see Olivelle (1992, 35, 39, 42–46). It is said that the three longings are for sons, wealth and heavenly worlds, the three latent mental impressions selfishness, egotism and the like (Olivelle 1992, I71, fn. 6).
36. Mirza Asadullah Khan Ghalib (1925, 95). Translation courtesy Yusra Farooqui.
37. What Berger says about art applies to the discourse of pleasure also: 'Yet when an image is presented as a work of art, the way people look at it is affected by a whole series of learnt assumptions about art. Assumptions concerning: Beauty, Truth, Genius, Civilization, Form, Status, Taste, etc.' (Berger 1973, 10).

REFERENCES

Agrawala Vasudeva Sharan (A Selection). Edited by Kapila Vatsayana. New Delhi: Sahitya Akademy. 2015.

Anguttara Nikaya, vol. III. Translated by Kausalayana Anand. Kolkata: Mahabodhi Sabha. n.d.

Ali, Daud. *Courtly Culture and Political Life in Early Medieval India*. Cambridge: Cambridge University Press. 2004.

Ali, Daud. 'Gardens in Early Court Life'. In *Studies in History* 19, no. 2 (2003): 221–252.

Ardhakathanak by Banarsidas. Translated, introduced and annotated by Mukund Lath. Jaipur: Rajasthan Prakrit Bharati Sansthan. 1641.

Bawa, Seema. *Gods, Men and Women: Gender and Sexuality in Early Indian Art*. Delhi: DK Printworld Pvt. Ltd. 2013.

Berger, John. *Ways of Seeing*. London: British Broadcasting Corporation and Penguin Books. 1973.

Chakravarty, Uma. *Social Dimensions of Early Buddhism*. New Delhi: Oxford University Press. 1987.

Desai, Devangana. *Erotic Art of India: A Socio-Cultural Study*. Delhi: Tata McGraw Hill. 1985.

Desmond, Laura. 'The Pleasure is Mine: The Changing Subject of Erotic Science'. *Journal of Indian Philosophy* (2011): 15–39.

Donaldson, Thomas. *Kamadeva's Pleasure Garden*. Delhi: BR Publishing Corporation. 1987.

Flood, Finbarr Barry. 'Before the Mughals: Material Culture of Sultanate North India'. *Muqarnas Online* 36, no. 1 (2019). Brill. Available at https://brill.com/view/journals/muqj/36/1/muqj.36.issue-1.xml?language=en.

Foucault, Michel. *The History of Sexuality, Vol. 2: The Use of Pleasure*. New York: Knopf Doubleday Publishing Group. 2012.

Garrison, Daniel H. *A Cultural History of the Human Body: In Antiquity*. New York: Bloomsbury. 2014.

Guy, John. 'A Ruler and His Courtesans Celebrate Vasantotsava: Courtly and Divine Love in a Nayaka Kalamkari'. In *Sultans of the South: Arts of India's Deccan Courts, 1323–1687*, edited by Haidar, Navina Najaf and Marika Sardar, 162–175. New York: The Metropolitan Museum of Art. 2011.

Gupta, Neerja. *Abhinavgupta's Comments on Aesthetics in Abhinavbharti and Locana*. Newcastle Upon Tyne: Cambridge Scholars Publishing. 2017.

Hali, Altaf Hussain. *Yadgar-i Ghalib*. Kanpur: Nami Press. 1897.

Kāmasūtra. Vatsayana and Mallanaga. Edited and translated by Wendy Doniger and Sudhir Kakar. Oxford: Oxford University Press. 2003.

Kaul, Shonaleeka. *Imagining the Urban: Sanskrit and the City in Early India*. Ranikhet: Permanent Black. 2010.

Kumārasaṃbhava of Kālidāsa. Edited by M.R. Kale. Delhi: Motilal Banarsidass Publishers Private Limited. 2011.

Mahali, Muhhamad Raza Ansari Firangi. *Bani Dars-e-Nizami*. Lucknow: Nami Press. 1973.

Marshall, John. A Guide to Sanchi. Calcutta: Superintendent, Government Printing. 1918.

Meilaender, Gilbert. 'Sweet Necessities: Food, Sex, and Saint Augustine'. *The Journal of Religious Ethics* (2001): 3–18.

Michaels, Axel and Christoph Wulf. *Exploring the Senses: South Asian and European Perspectives on Rituals and Performativity*. New Delhi: Routledge India. 2014.

Mirza Asadullah Khan Ghalib. *Diwan-i-Ghalib*. Allahabad: Ram Narayan Lal Publishers and Booksellers. 1925.

Monier-Williams, Monier. *Sanskrit–English Dictionary*. Delhi: Mushiram Manoharlal Pvt Ltd. 2002.

Nàtyasàstra of Bharata Muni. Edited and translated by Manmohan Ghosh. Calcutta: Ganthalya Pvt. Ltd. 1967.

Nehamas, Alexander and Richard Shusterman. 'Pleasure and Aesthetic Experience'. *The Journal of Aesthetics and Art Criticism* (1998): 49–51.

Olivelle, Patrick. *The Samnyasa Upanisads: Hindu Scriptures on Asceticism and Renunciation*. Oxford: Oxford University Press. 1992.

———. 'From Trivarga to Purusartha: A Chapter in Indian Moral Philosophy'. *The Journal of the American Oriental Society* 13.2 (2019): 381–396.

Panikkar, K.M. *Asia and Western Dominance*. New York: Collier Books. 1969.

Parker, Grant. 'Ex Oriente Luxuria: Indian Commodities and Roman Experience'. *Journal of the Economic and Social History of the Orient* (2002): 40–95.

Savedoff, Barbara E. 'Intellectual and Sensuous Pleasure'. *The Journal of Aesthetics and Art Criticism* 43, no. 3 (1985): 313–315.

Scruton, Roger. *The Aesthetics of Architecture*. New Jersey: Princeton University Press. 2013.

Shaffer, Holly. 'The Kitchen Sutra'. *Art India: The Art News Magazine of India*. 2016. Available at https://www.academia.edu/28750436/The_Kitchen_Sutra (accessed on 6-02-2021).

The Ni'matnāmā by Shah, Abd al-Muzaffar Nasir. London: Indian Office Library. n.d.

Shah, Shalini. *Love, Eroticism and Female Sexuality in Classical Sanskrit Literature: 7th–13th Centuries*. New Delhi: Manohar Publishers. 2009.

Shusterman, Richard. 'Interpretation, Pleasure and Value in Aesthetic Experience.' *The Journal of Aesthetics and Art Criticism* 56, no. 1 (1998): 51–53.

Theragatha. Translated by K.R. Norman. London: Pali Text Society. 1969.

Therigatha. Edited by Rhys Davids. London: Oxford University Press. 1909.

The Visnudharmottara Part III: A Treatise On Indian Painting and Image-Making. Second revised and enlarged edition, edited and translated by Stella Kramrisch. Calcutta, Calcutta University Press. 1928.

Tomber, Roberta. 'Indian Fine Wares from the Red Sea Coast Of Egypt.' *Man and Environment*. 2002.

Verma, C.B. *Illustrated Jatakas: Other Stories of the Buddha* IGNCA. 2002. Available at http://ignca.gov.in/coilnet/jatak005.htm (accessed on 31.10.2020).

Vishnudahrmottara Purāṇa, 2 Vols. Edited and translated by Priyabala Shah. Baroda: Oriental Institute. 1958–1961.

Warmington, E.H. *The Commerce Between the Roman Empire and India*. Cambridge: Cambridge University Press. 2014.

Zizek, Slavoj. *The Parallax View*. Massachusetts: MIT Press. 2006.

1

SEEKING PLEASURE: REPRESENTATIONS OF PLEASURE AND DOMESTICITY IN TEXTUAL TRADITIONS

Jaya S. Tyagi

In ancient Indian textual traditions, domestic spaces are often projected as spaces providing not only conjugal pleasure but also that obtained from other relationships—filial ties, paternal, maternal and kinship bonds. This pleasure arises from a sense of attachment, a belongingness, and also from the comfort and cocooning within particular spaces, particularly the mother's womb and, by extension, the household and its environs. In early textual traditions, the domestic domain is represented as providing relationships that lead to long-lasting bonds that alleviate pain and satiate all the senses, associated as they are with pleasure (*sukha*) and conviviality along with combined leisure activities, such as eating, praying, playing, socialising, all leading to connubial, commensal, filial and social fulfilment.

Projecting the household as a 'pleasurable' space which brought *sukha* not only to the householder and its members but also to the members of different social categories that depended on the householder's largesse was essential to the social stability that was envisaged in Brahmanical traditions as it would allow for the control of reproduction and production activities in an organised manner even while allowing the household to emerge as a source of patronage for the Brahmana as well as the *śramana* categories, providing sustenance (and 'pleasure') to these categories too. The *Mānava Dharmaśāstra* (henceforth, MS) states that the four life stages—student, householder, forest hermit and ascetic—have their origins in the householder, meaning that they all gain sustenance from him. The MS also informs that amongst all of them, according to Vedic scripture, the householder is the most important for he supports the other three. 'As all rivers and rivulets ultimately end up in the ocean, so people of all the orders ultimately end up in the householder'.[1]

Pleasure can be associated with a feeling of well-being, contentment and sensory satisfaction, i.e., of sight, sound, touch, taste and smell.

It can also be derived from raising cognitive abilities and creating cultural sensibilities about what is pleasurable on the basis of socialisation and projection of what can be construed as cultural stimuli. This paper will discuss how pleasure was related to the household in early textual traditions. Moreover, it will explore alternative imagery too—for the conceptualisation of pleasure results from its 'othering' from pain, and wherever pleasure is discussed, there is bound to be an awareness of the alternative, pain, even if it is only to avoid it.

Is pleasure gendered? Ideally, it should not be; humans should have similar experiences of pleasure. However, invigoration of the mind should as much qualify as a pleasurable experience as titillation of the senses. Our *perceptions* on what is pleasurable creates the backdrop for our feelings and perceptions, which are encultured and can be indoctrinated. Thus, one observes that representations of pleasure in textual traditions are gendered, as they tend to underline different aspects of pleasure for women and men. Since the texts are male-centric, they focus on male notions of pleasure and also project those notions on women. In the absence of women's voices, we get to know mainly the author's notions on how women may relate to pleasure.

The invigoration of the sensory stimuli, associated with pleasing sensations when combined with the relentless pursuit of such pleasure is, however, associated with hedonistic pursuits in some conceptualisations. This allows for philosophical debates about the purpose of life and the manner in which human life is to be charted. In an interesting twist, we can see the stark reversals of the representation of pleasure vis-à-vis pain in Buddhist traditions wherein anything that is connected to pleasure is believed to ultimately cause pain, or *dukkha*. The domestic space is thus identified not just with transient pleasure but also with pain and distress, and the *sangha* is projected as an alternative to the domestic space, an escape from domestic drudgery, especially for women. In this alternative discourse put forth by Buddhist traditions, human existence and life itself are seen as causes of pain and distress. Here, all that leads to the earlier notions of 'pleasure' is circumspect and seen as leading to desire, or *māyā*, and pain rather than pleasure. The four noble truths work are based on this premise—there is sorrow in this world, this sorrow has a cause, desire is the cause of sorrow and if one removes desire, one can remove sorrow. Thus, notions of pleasure are challenged and revoked, pleasure coming from tantalising and invigorating of the senses is replaced as there is an understanding that this sensory pleasure is accompanied with pain and it is rather spiritual 'bliss', *ānanda*, which comes from controlling these senses and preventing them from becoming too excited or involved is encouraged. Thus the Buddha, *sangha* and *dhamma*, the three institutions with whom the believer seeks asylum and solace, are there to shield the believer from pleasure and pain as one is inextricably linked to the other.

Brahmanical ideology was able to project certain notions about the paths that would lead to pleasure and fulfilment in the elaborate premise of the *puruṣārtha*, literally the purpose of man, which was to be attained through the pursuit of *dharma*, *artha* and *kāma* and would ultimately lead to the escape from the cycle of birth, or *mokṣa*.[2] Following *dharma* was envisaged as essential as it encompasses the moral and ethical code that humans are advised to follow and that helps in maintaining cosmic and social order. A person's *dharma* varied according to their identity; thus, a king was expected to uphold *rājadharma*, a husband, *patidharma* and a wife, *patnīdharma*. *Kāma*, desire, could be for material objects, food or sensual pleasure. It was not the same as but was only one of the aspects influencing the attainment of *sukha*. The role of the householder was projected as being critical in maintaining the balance between the four stages of the life as well as the four *puruṣārthas*. The relationship between the three *puruṣārthas* is summed up by MS 2.24, which states: 'Some say that *dharma* and *artha* are good, others say that *kāma* and *artha* are good, and still others say that *dharma* alone or *kāma* alone is good, but the correct position is that the three should coexist without hurting each other'.

In ancient Indian thought, differences are seen in the attempts made to separate the ethical, material and sensual as seen in the *trivarga* ideology—*dharma*, *artha*, *kāma*—but these converge and are all directed towards attaining the ultimate goal, *mokṣa*. If balanced, all these will lead to the attainment of *sukha*. The conceptualisation naturally relates to the purpose of a *man's* life, and women are by default excluded and do not seem to have the same purpose as men. *Sukha* is therefore clearly gendered.

The texts chosen for this paper, the *Purāṇas* (particularly the *Matsyamahāpurāṇa*, henceforth MMP), perceive pleasure as that which can be attained through power (with its associations with kingship, fame and victory—*rajas*, *yaśa* and *jaya*), status, domestic bliss, carnal satisfaction, health, wealth and overall well-being. All these, however, can be attained only through the performance of rituals, and it is clear that in these texts pleasure is not to be achieved easily or naturally; it is elusive and one needs to constantly work towards it. And that is where rituals and *vratas* become significant as paths that will lead to pleasure.

In Puranic writings it is clear that one has to strive for attaining pleasure—it has to be worked proactively towards, opportunities have to be seized, resources have to be garnered and all the cosmic energies have to be directed and channelised towards the attainment of pleasure. This is where *vratas* and myths related to deities performing such *vratas* become crucial—in these texts, rituals are elaborated upon and myths invoked to give them divine validity as the pursuit of pleasure was portrayed as an active pursuit of the deities themselves, thus giving social legitimacy to humans to unabashedly seek pleasure in their various pursuits.

The proliferation of *vratas* in the *Purāṇas*, especially with regard to women, has to be seen in this light. *Vratas* were projected as a means for achieving specific and cognisable human goals and aspirations. The *Agnipurāṇa* mentions some of these aspirations—*dharma* (*punya*); *artha*, progeny, wealth, beauty or good fortune, virtues, fame, learning, long life, wealth, purity; *kāma*, enjoyment of pleasures and *mokṣa* as well as heaven.[3] The single-minded manner in which Puranic ideology promotes the seeking of individual aspirations, however, couches the fact that one person's pleasure is very often at the expense of others. Myriad resources may be used in this kind of relentless and mindless pursuit of sensory pleasure by the rich and elite, whose notions of pleasure these texts are clearly pandering to.

ELITE ENTITLEMENT TO PLEASURE

In critical passages attributed to Sāvitirī in the MMP, while arguing with Yama, the God of Death, for her husband's life, Sāvitirī describes how the rich *deserve* their good fortunes. In doing so she seems to not only vividly convey what construes as 'pleasurable' for the rich and wealthy in the Puranic world order but also legitimise a lifestyle of opulence and splendour for the rich and powerful.

> They have a golden complexion, riches, stature and wealth, superior seats, golden vases, good food and drink, music, servants, good smell, grain, jewels, fine garments, handsome form, generosity, high attributes, beautiful wives—these are all attained by virtuous persons. The virtuous are blessed with palatial mansions that are decorated with the perforated work with gold because of their virtues. These virtues are asceticism, sacrifices, charities, control of passions, forgiveness, celibacy, travelling to sacred places, reading of the Vedas, service of the good, worship of God, devotion and service of the Guru, veneration of the Brāhmanas, humility—these are all the signs of virtue.[4]

Puranic imagery interlinks pleasure with wealth and resources. It is the rich and wealthy men who seem to seek and gain pleasure; however, it seems to be a vicious circle, as only through lavish donations of what can be construed as wealth (gold, silver, semi-precious stones, vessels and such) can they get access to such pleasures (which are mentioned in the above passage). Further, it is understood that all this wealth comes with high standards of propriety, although there is a hint of entitlement among the elite and the underlying assumption that wealth begets wealth. It will be safe to say that the Puranic texts are catering mainly to a class of patrons, both men and women, who are being encouraged to conduct rituals and lead lives in accordance with the Puranic standards of propriety while pandering to Brahmanical expectations of donations in order to make sure that the lavish gains (which will then lead to worldly pleasure) will accrue.

CONJUGAL PLEASURE

The references to vratas in the *Purāṇas* are juxtaposed with vivid images of conjugality and intimacy, indicating that the aim of worldly life is gaining pleasure *within* the institution of marriage rather than outside it, setting standards of moral propriety for both women *and* men. Conjugal pleasure is not projected as merely physical or carnal but something otherworldly, leading to a deep sense of fulfilment and paving the way for familial pleasures. Thus, even the *devas* are shown to be 'enjoying' with their 'lotus-eyed consorts' in their pleasure enclaves—Viṣṇu and Lakṣmī are inseparable.[5] In the Puranic references to the pleasures of conjugal intimacy, the oblique reference is to women as providers of pleasure. Here, pleasure is envisaged in a male-centric manner wherein it is the man's pleasure that is the focus of attention. Women provide pleasure through companionship and sexual intimacy, performing the requisite religious observances and being actively involved in activities such as management of food resources (their procurement, cooking and dispensation through appropriate rites), all of which are aimed at satiating the male protagonist. However, even while the texts are clearly projecting male-centric notions of pleasure, in a clever twist which is typical of Brahmanical ideology, they constantly reiterate how a husband is integral to a woman's existence.

The MMP clearly highlights the role of the husband as the provider of pleasure. Here, the emphasis is not just on the woman's physical pleasure but her very existence.

> It is difficult for a woman to get a good husband. Without virtue, even a tolerable husband is not obtained, because the natural course for women is to enjoy the company of their husbands for all their lives. The husband of a woman, inspite of his being poor, unfortunate,

> illiterate and void of all fortune, is like a God to her. Dharma without effort, unlimited pleasures and wealth to maintain one's life are all found in husbands.[6]

Despite the projection of conjugality as a source of pleasure, that pleasure and pain come together is implied in a revealing story from the MMP, in which conjugal pleasure cannot be taken for granted and husbands are projected as providers of pleasure but also of pain, particularly when women do not follow the instructions of the husband and seek to challenge the domestic peace. The onus for this conjugal disharmony is squarely placed on the woman's shoulders—she is the one who is irrational, easily enraged and will eventually have to conform if she wants to regain her precarious position in the domestic household, where there is every danger of her being replaced or forgotten, even if she is a goddess.

A certain legend associated with Śiva, Pārvatī and the birth of Skanda narrated in the MMP is revealing as it initiates the reader into the pleasure and pain associated with domestic life as Śiva and Pārvatī have a domestic spat, almost like any other married couple. The legend begins with Pārvatī revelling in her domestic situation as a young bride. Her pleasure comes from her myriad experiences—the comfort of her living arrangements, her beauteous surroundings (on the Kailāsa mountain) which titillate her enthusiasm for nature and the pleasurable times spent with Śiva. As a goddess, the need to keep her away from the process of natural childbirth (which is polluting) is also evident in the myth; so while she takes immense pleasure in her children, she is not subjected to the pain (or pollution) of pregnancy, confinement or gestation. This is because in mythological traditions Goddesses are associated with extra-uterine births and do not undergo the tribulations and pollution of natural birth—which is what distinguishes them from common women.

The discussion about her reproductivity veers off towards alternative ways to have progeny and even implies the need to channelise one's procreativity towards other ends rather than striving for normal childbirth. That Pārvatī virtually adopts the chief amongst the attendants, Vīraka or Vīrabhadra, as a son gives testimony to the inclusiveness of the text. The way she makes him sit in her lap and fusses over him, watches him while he plays are touching images of the affection between a mother and child, so much so that Sūta, the narrator of the legend, is compelled to comment that it is astonishing how Pārvatī, the mother of the universe, is so carried away by maternal love. 'Then what mortal would not be entangled in the bonds of filial love for his son?' he wonders. Thus a domestic tableau is created wherein Pārvatī is projected as having varied pleasurable encounters in her life with Śiva. However, she has problems too, and her insecurities extend to her looks as well as possible competition from other women, as we shall see in the legend.

The story begins with Śiva's marriage with Pārvatī:

> After the marriage rites which are accompanied with singing and dancing of the Gandharvas and Kinnaras, Śiva stays in the night in Himācala's palace and the next day, with his father-in-law's permission, takes his consort on Nandi bull, riding swiftly like the wind. Śiva and Pārvatī spend time in the charming groves and solitary forests of the mountains.

There are numerous references to the interactions between Śiva and Pārvatī—how he leads her inside his palace, her awe at the sight of it, their playing dice for amusement and her gazing through the peepholes of her abode, surrounded by numerous attendants, at the cosmos in its various dimensions. This evokes an imagery of the pleasurable lives of the royal and the elite, associated with grand abodes, aesthetic pleasures and entertaining visual stimulation.

The references to the alternative ways in which Pārvatī's children are born is intriguing. Soon after her wedding, Pārvatī wants to have a son and makes several dolls to play with to channelise her maternal instincts. The legend relating to the birth of Vināyaka is distinct in the MMP. On one occasion, with the dirt of her body, she makes a human form with an elephant head and throws it into the Ganga, where it becomes enlarged. Brahmā names the boy Vināyaka and appoints him as the head of all attendants. It is Pārvatī's desire for progeny that makes her plant Aśoka saplings and care for them. When the *devas* ask why she is engaged in planting trees, she gives a stunning answer (which is an environmentalist's delight):

> One who makes a well where there is scarcity of water lives in heaven for as many years as there are drops of water in the well. One large reservoir is worth ten wells. *One son is equal to ten reservoirs and one tree is worth ten sons.* These are my ethics (*maryādā*) and I'm prepared to protect the universe towards this end.[7]

The larger vision of preservation of the universe that is associated with the Goddess is significant—for her, making reservoirs and wells and planting trees is part of her ethical existence and much above birthing sons. Finally, the story comes to the point where Śiva and Pārvatī are about to be separated because Śiva mocks Pārvatī. The fact that Pārvatī is livid at his words seems to reflect on the fragility of the pleasure derived from conjugal relationships. Of course, all this is according to the grand plan of the *devas* who seek the birth of Skanda.

Śiva goes to sleep with the dark-skinned Pārvatī and he jokingly tells her that while his body is lustrous and resplendent, she looks black. He compares her embrace to that of a serpent coiled around a sandalwood tree. Incensed, Pārvatī spews the following words:

> One despises others because of one's own faults. Such a person is sure to meet with misfortunes. Constant despise is the reward I get for attaining you after rigid austerities; I am neither mysterious nor wicked. O one of streaming hair! You are well known to be vicious because of contact with evil things .... You call me black; but you are well known as very black, *Mahākāla*. I am going to the mountains to practice austerities and will give up my life. What is the use of my life under the subjugation of a cunning husband?

Śiva lovingly and meekly tries to appease her, saying that he mocked her in jest. Adamant, Pārvatī prepares to leave Kailāsa. He then gets angry and calls her a true daughter of her father—unapproachable, hard (as a stone) and crooked. Pārvatī, furiously grinding her teeth, retorts that he should not despise other worthy people by trying to find fault in them.

> You are full of faults because of your company. Your crookedness is derived from you contact with serpents. You are devoid of affection, like ashes. Your heart is more spotted than the moon with her spots. You live in the cremation ground and are fearless. You are inferior even to this bull in understanding. You are shameless and naked; you cannot distinguish things as you are wearing skulls and mercy has left you totally.

The fact that she makes such angry statements reveals the extent of her pain. She is so insecure that she has to make arrangements to ensure that Śiva does not go to some other woman behind her back. As she leaves, all the attendants including Vīrabhadra run up to her in tears, begging her not to forsake them. Pārvatī fondles him but insists that she has to go and assigns him the task of guarding the gate so that no other woman takes her place in the night. Vīrabhadra agrees to be watchful.[8] This is not sufficient though, as when Pārvatī sees the Mountain Goddess Kusumamodinī (a friend of her mother's), she confides in her and asks her to remain as the Mountain Goddess and keep an eye in case any woman comes to Śiva.

Pārvatī (Umā) then enters her father's pleasure gardens to carry out severe penance—she dons barks of trees and, in summer, envelops herself in fire, remains submerged in water in monsoon, living on jungle fruits or observing a fast. She sleeps on the floor and continues her penance, and her body becomes lean and thin. This imagery seems to link a woman's pleasure to her husband: as long as she is with him, her life brims with pleasurable experiences, but the moment she is apart from him, her life is one of misery and rigour, even if it is self-inflicted.

In the meantime, the demon Āḍi seeks to avenge Śiva. Taking a serpent's form, he manages to slide past Vīrabhadra. He then takes Pārvatī's form in order to kill Śiva. Śiva realises something is amiss and kills the demon. The Mountain Goddess, on seeing a dead woman, reports this to Pārvatī, who curses Vīrabhadra (who was supposed to guard Śiva against any such alluring women), saying that his mother will turn into a piece of stone—without a heart, inanimate, rough and rugged. Pārvatī is so angry that the curse escapes her mouth in the form of a powerful lion. Seeing the lion, the enraged (and perhaps hapless) Pārvatī is prepared to enter his mouth. Brahmā, reading her mind, attempts to thwart her. Making an appearance, he tells her to ask for a boon. Pārvatī asks for her complexion to become golden (*kāñcanākārā*) so that she may adorn herself in the arms of her lord.

It is ironical that after her indignation, she displays the typical insecurity of a wife and feels the urge to change her complexion. Brahmā not only grants her the wish but also states that henceforth she will also become a part of Śiva's body—*bhartṛrdehārdhdardhāriṇī*. This is the ultimate state of pleasure envisaged for a woman, that she become inseparable from her husband and be part of his very body. Pārvatī's complexion immediately changes to a golden hue from lotus blue. Her dark skin separates from her body and takes form as the Goddess Rātrī.[9]

Pārvatī goes to Śiva, where Vīrabhadra, not recognising her, does not allow her to enter and tells her that once a demon had gone past him and the lord himself had chided him for not keeping careful watch.[10] Pārvatī identifies herself, after which Vīrabhadra offers obeisance to her and she then goes to Śiva. The couple enjoy intimacy and, after a thousand years have passed, the *devas* send Agni to find out what has happened. Agni, disguised as a parrot, spies on them. Annoyed at the interruption, Śiva ejaculates. Agni catches the virile semen in his palms. The semen passes through the *devas* stomach and ends up in the pool of the Krittikas. When Pārvatī drinks the water from that pool, she gets impregnated and from the right side of her stomach, Kārtikeya (another name for Skanda) is born.[11]

This extra-uterine birth shows how even the feminine ability to give birth is sought to be appropriated. It seems the deity cannot be born out of normal birth conditions since it is polluting. Thus, even while the female body is associated essentially with reproduction, reproduction itself is projected as polluting, rendering most women contaminated!

This is why goddesses have to be disassociated with normal uterine births. Thus, an elaborate frame is created to show the extra-uterine birth of Skanda.

Once the Goddess is detached from the natural process of birth, she can be imbued with emotions, and all other qualities associated with common women (according to the Puranic authors) are incorporated in her persona—she gets angry at her husband's mocking but is also anxious that no woman should replace her in her absence, so she puts both Vīrabhadra and her aunt on the lookout. The anxiety surrounding women's insecurity regarding their men is a real and a recurring thing. But where these texts deviate is that the men in them are encouraged to practice monogamy and it is Śiva himself who chides Vīrabhadra for not keeping proper vigil and allowing a demon impersonating a woman to get through to him.

The fact that Pārvatī encounters so many experiences and changes herself sharply contrasts with Śiva, as there is no reference to what happens to him when Pārvatī leaves. Is it business as usual, and is he not impacted at all? Is it only Pārvatī who feels domestic pleasure and pain, and is Śiva above all this? Pārvatī's humanisation, her experiencing anger, jealousy, rage and insecurity (to the extent that she is willing to change her appearance), is offset by Śiva's apparent calm and equanimity. It is not that Śiva is always calm, but in the domestic context, the projection of him as a jocular, calm and only mildly angry being, unable to placate Pārvatī, seems to imply that for the male the domestic domain is one of relaxation and pleasure and not something to lose calm over. Śiva will only display his famous anger over more important issues. And ultimately, despite all his nonchalance, things do go his way as Pārvatī goes through severe tribulations to change her skin colour. For women, whether divine or human, domestic pleasure is not to be taken for granted; it is fraught with anxieties and will lead to pain if they do not conform and comply.

JAYANTĪ PROVIDES PLEASURE TO ŚUKRA

We have already discussed how one person's pleasure is usually at the cost of another. In this way, women are expected to cater to and provide pleasure to men. Here, the woman's pleasure is not taken into consideration; when the men in her life are pleased, she is expected to be pleased too. The need for women to provide hospitality to and please the sages who visit them is therefore a recurring motif in textual traditions. The legend of Jayantī[12] shows how women, especially daughters, are used as pawns for achieving political and ideological ends by ambitious fathers (and husbands). Indra sends Jayantī, his daughter, to 'please' Śukra with her service and conduct, to do as he (Śukra) wishes and serve him with all diligence and to worship him and strive towards achieving his (Indra's) end as she has been told to dedicate herself to him by Indra:

> Go to him and work for my cause. After going there you will have to rid yourself of laziness, and have to conduct yourself in a way that the sage is pleased. You should adore him so that he is fully satisfied. Go and dedicate yourself to him from today, make efforts for my welfare.[13]

This is noteworthy as Śukra and Indra are sworn enemies and to send his own daughter to the enemy's camp is realpolitik. The observances that she has to practice are directed towards moulding herself entirely to suit Śukra's needs and pleasure. She not only pleases him but also persuades him to marry her and retreat from the world in order to be intimate with her. Bṛhaspati takes advantage of Śukra's absence to deceive the *daityas* by posing as Śukra.

> Jayantī goes to the sage who was suspended with his head downwards and inhaling the smoke of the chaff, even while a *yakṣa* had thrown him down the side of the *kuṇḍa*. Absorbed in austerities, lean and covered with ashes, she begins to serve him according to her father's directions. She washes his legs and wins his pleasure with sweet and flattering speech, adapting herself to suit his pleasure. She practices penances with him for many years. Śiva, pleased with Śukra's austerities, grants him many boons and riches that make him the master of mankind and also invulnerable. Śukra, pleased to the tip of his hair with the boons, sings a hymn of praise for *nīlalohitam*, the blue-red God.[14]

After singing elaborate praises of the deity, and being blessed by him, the seer turns to Jayantī and asks her who she is and why she is performing these austerities for him. Jayantī asks him to use his divine powers to discern her will and the sage, through his powers, realises that she wants to live with him. So he takes her home and marries her. To enjoy himself in her company undisturbed, he makes himself invisible such that the *daityas* also cannot find him. Bṛhaspati comes to know of this and, further incited by the *devas*, impersonates Śukra and rallies the *daityas* around him. The *daityas*, overjoyed to think that it is Śukra training them, begin to take lessons from him. Ten years later, when Śukra emerges from his invisibility, he tells Jayantī that he is going to see his disciples, which Jayantī supports. Śukra, finding the disciples deceived by Bṛhaspati, urges them to come to him but the bewildered Dānavas do not know what to do as they cannot recognise the real Śukra. The Dānavas choose to stay with Bṛhaspati since he has been their mentor for the last ten years. In a fit of anger, Śukra curses them that they would be routed by the *devas*. Prahlāda asks for forgiveness on behalf of the *daityas* and Śukra relents, curbing his anger, and tells them that what has been declared cannot be averted but they would not have to go to *Rasātala*, the abyss. A great battle between *devas* and *asuras* ensues, lasting for over a century. In the battle the *devas* are defeated and the *asuras* emerge victorious. The *devas* decide to conduct a sacrifice and invite Śaṇḍa and Mārka and make friends with them because of which the Dānavas become weak and are defeated. In Puranic traditions, Śaṇḍa and Mārka are represented as the priests of the *asuras* and also as the sons of Śukracārya. Thus, when they are called for the sacrifice, it weakens the *asuras* considerably. They eventually have to enter Rasātala.

The text shows how women feature in the grand plans of males—as pawns and providers of pleasure.[15] Jayantī goes to Śukra according to her father's will, wins him over and even marries him. The end result, the victory of the *devas*, justifies the means and shows women to not only comply with but actively participate in and fully cooperate in the political strategies of first their fathers and then, switching loyalties effortlessly (and predictably), to their husbands.

GODDESSES AS PROVIDERS OF PLEASURE

The *Purāṇas* describe an evolved notion of pleasure to be gained through the control of power manifested as feminine energy—śakti. The idea may have been born from the goddesses' progenitive capacity and reproductivity but has moved into abstract and metaphysical force/s far beyond reproductivity. These came to encompass notions of power, domination, fame leading to pleasure and glory as tangible manifestations of this energy. Thus, notions around the 'Divine Feminine' revolved around the 'male' need to gain pleasure, control power and generate wealth, all of which were interrelated. This must be seen in the specific context of the aspirations of the state and the elite vis-à-vis a consolidation of power, acquisition of territory and the active pursuit of pleasure. In that sense, the conceptualisations of the Goddesses seem to reinforce the idea of the feminine as desirable, elusive, transient and potentially destructive, and hence the need to control and venerate it.

In the male-centred pursuit of pleasure, feminine attributes are given to the conceptualisation of pleasure itself, which is also then seen as something that needs to be pursued. Thus, whether it be the Saptmātṛkas, Lakṣmī or Guḍa Dhenu, they are associated with power, wealth and prosperity, all means of obtaining pleasure. However, pleasure seen in the form of *sukha* is in direct contrast to *dukkha*, sorrow. One of the ways in which sorrow can arise is through śoka, from death and destruction. The Goddesses are invoked, not only for pleasure but for *viśoka* (the opposite of śoka), to keep away death and destruction and the resultant sorrow.

Discussions on kingship help us derive notions relating to the interconnections between power and attainment of pleasure. The worship of the Saptmātṛkas, the seven mothers, is indicative of the aspirational nature of kingship and the need for the king to have all his wishes fulfilled (and anxieties allayed) relating to power, disease, knowledge and pleasure. The *Devī Purāṇa* mentions the protection offered to a king who possesses the seven banners of the Goddess.

> The king who has the banner with the lion of Umā shall know no fear of his enemies. For one who has the banner with the monkey king, his enemies will be destroyed and his best desires will be fulfilled. The purpose of the swan banner is to bestow knowledge, pleasure and progeny on the king. All disease will be destroyed for the king who has the Garuḍa banner. The king who has the banner with the *triśula* of the destroyer of the demon Mahiṣa accomplishes all deeds. The banner with the lotus confers dharma, kāma, artha and mokṣa. The banner with the symbol of the skeleton will be eternally free from animals.[16]

Katherine Harper attributes the emergence of the Saptamātṛkās into mainstream Hindu religion to the notions of kingship of the Gupta sovereigns. They were the 'religio-political symbols that ensured the success of the kings' imperial programme to establish *rājadharma* (righteous rule) in territories controlled for centuries by foreign invaders'. She defines śakti as a universal and all-embracing dynamic that manifests itself in human experience as a female divinity, claiming that both the goals of *bhukti* (domination) and *mukti* (liberation) are conferred by the Goddesses, whereas Śiva and Viṣṇu confer only *mukti*. It would seem as if the pleasure derived from the worship of Goddesses is manifold.[17]

While the desires and aspirations of the king were a real concern for the Puranic authors, along with that, the need for wealth and prosperity and its inherent link to pleasure made the authors covet Śrīdevī Lakṣmī, and many *vratas* and rituals are devoted to her in the MMP. The care with which the text deals with the iconography describing how the image of Śrīdevī Lakṣmī should be made reveals the anxiety related to her veneration.[18] The image of Lakṣmī is very different from the ferocious Yogeśvarī. The emphasis is on her youth and ornamentation, her desirability. The reference to her youth and beauty underlines the gendered way in which the feminine is represented. Thus, as Lakṣmī, she is to be coveted and represented in a desirable manner, indicating high standards of beauty. This is in contrast to the male deity of wealth, Kuvera, who has a 'huge abdomen, huge form', *mahodaram mahākāyam*.[19]

> The image of Śrīdevī Lakṣmī should be made with a very youthful appearance, having thick cheeks, red lips, knitted brows, with thick and raised breasts, adorned with jewels and earrings, with a round face, wearing head ornaments and lotus, having a conch, and beautiful separated tresses of hair, adorned with garlands, armlets, having arms like the trunk of an elephant, holding a lotus in the left hand, the fruit of an wood apple tree in the right, adorned with a lotus, a svastika, a conch, earrings and Alākā, breasts covered with a bodice and adorned with a necklace, with a girdle of bells shining like gold, dressed in finery.
>
> Close to the image should be made the images of two female attendants, holding *camaras* (fly whisks) in their hands.
>
> The Goddess should be seated on a lotus bed surrounded by buzzing black bees and bathed by a couple of elephants with vases, prayed to by the Gandharvas, Guhyakas. Similarly should be made the image of Yakṣinī prayed to by the Gods and placed close to Lakṣmī Devī. Urns should be placed near her image.... A pleasure grove with a pool of water reached by pleasant steps nearby. The God Cupid should be well dressed and his posture should be slightly bent.[20]

The detailed iconography related to Lakṣmī shows how crucial she is towards the fulfilment of pleasurable desires relating to material wealth for the authors of the MMP. Several *vratas* are dedicated to her, one of them specifically for the attainment of *viśoka*, the *Viśokadvādaśīvrata*.[21] The term *viśoka* needs further scrutiny, as at first glance it would mean an absence of sorrow, and it so possibly indicates the attainment of pleasure. However, sorrow, particularly śoka, is also related to death and destruction, so the term indicates the need to keep away death to attain pleasure and contentment. The fact that the *vrata* highlights conjugal bliss and also the need for prosperity in order to attain this state of *viśoka* shows that conceptualisations of domestic pleasure were related to keeping death, destruction and sorrow at bay.

The reference to the image of Lakṣmī made of sand gravel for the *vrata* seems to show customs related to making votive figurines. Although

Viṣṇu is mentioned, it is clear that the focus of the *vrata* is the Goddess. The *vrata* is 'revealed' by the Lord in the form of Matsya, who states that though kept secret from *suras* and *asuras*, the *vrata* has been specially revealed to Manu on account of his intense devotion.

> The *Viśokadvādaśīvrata* falls in the month of Āśvina—on Ekādaśī day, an altar is to be made on the ground after making a circle on it. An image of Lakṣmī made of river sand/gravel should be placed in a winnowing basket and worshipped according to the rites mentioned. Lakṣmī should be worshipped after reciting the following mantras—*Devyaī namah, Śāntvaī namah, Lakṣmyai namah, Śrīyai namah, Puṣṭyaī namah, Tuṣṭyaī namah, Vṛṣṭyai namah, Hṛṣṭyai namah.* The devotee should also say, 'O Viśoka Goddess, destroy all grief, grant some boon, give wealth and fulfil all desires'. After this he should wrap up the winnowing baskets in a piece of cloth and worship Lakṣmī with fruits and various kinds of clothes and with a golden lotus. The devotee should drink the water purified by the *kuśa* grass and carry on music and singing throughout the night and on the lapse of three quarters of the night thus passed in vigil and prayer, the devotee should sleep in the last quarter and then, waking up, go and worship them along with three couples of Brahmanas and Brāhmaṇīs according to his means; if not three, then at least one couple should be worshipped. The night should pass with keeping watch and listening to music and songs. The devotee, after bathing in the morning, should worship the Brahmana couples. They should be fed according to his means, free from niggardliness. And then, after taking his meals, he should pass that day in listening to the *Purāṇas*. The devotee should observe the same rituals every month till the period is over after which he should give away a bedstead along with the *guḍa dhenu* (sugar cow), pillows, bedding, sheets and cloth. Then he should say, 'O Lord! As Lakṣmī does not forsake you, similarly, beauty, health and pleasure may always be mine. As Lakṣmī does not go without Viṣṇu, let there always be happiness with me. Let my devotion always remain centred in Viṣṇu.' With the above words, the devotee should give away the bedstead and the *guḍa dhenu*, the image of Lakṣmī and the winnowing basket, to the Brahmana.
>
> This Viśokadvādaśī is most sacred and dispeller of all sins and is auspicious. He who fasts on this Dvādaśī goes to Viṣṇu's highest seat. He attains prosperity, longevity and health in this world, and after death he goes to the city of Viṣṇu, remembering him always at that critical moment. The virtuous devotee never gets grief or pain for a period of nine *arbuda* and eighteen thousand years. A married woman observing this Viśokadvādaśī fast with music and dance also obtains the same benefits.

Performing rituals to avoid grief and pain implies that pleasure can be gained from ritual activities. In the Puranic world view, the association of the feminine with wealth and prosperity and food and the inherent link of food with pleasure coupled with the anxiety related to the procurement of food underline the need for rituals. The symbolism connecting the cow with food and prosperity is evident in the *Guḍadhenudānavidhivarṇam*.[22]

> The image of *guḍa dhenu* should be made with four *maunds* of raw sugar and the calf with one *maund* of raw sugar, which is considered to be superior; the image of the cow made of two *maunds* and the calf of half a *maund* of raw sugar is considered to be the next best. The image of the cow made of one *maund* and the calf of ten *seers* of raw sugar is considered to be the least preferable. After thus making the images of the cow and the calf, the devotee should worship them with incense, lights and such with the following prayer:
>
> 'The Goddess, who is inherent in all beings in the form of Lakṣmī and who also resides among the Devas, let that Goddess in the symbol of a cow confer peace upon me. The Goddess who is known as Rudrāṇī, the favourite of the Lord Śiva in whose form she resides, may that very same Goddess, in the symbol of the cow, dispel all my sins. The Goddess, who reclines on the breast of Viṣṇu as Lakṣmī, who is present in the form of Svāhā in the fire, and is called the power and the energy of the sun and the moon and Indra, the same Goddess, in the symbol of the cow, may grant me wealth. She who is the Lakṣmī of Brahmā, Kuvera, Lokapālas may grant me boons in the symbol of the cow. She who is Svadhā of the highest Pitṛis, is Svāhā of the Devās, may she remove all my sins and bring me peace in the symbol of the cow.'

DOMESTIC TRIBULATIONS AND SORROW

While the Brahmanical texts were concerned with formulating conditions relating to the pleasures to be gained from marriage, wealth and religious piety and linking it to sociocultural propriety, alternative models of existence were projected in Buddhist texts—the *sangha* is one such, the *srenis* or guilds another. The MS, Buddhist and Jaina texts and literary works seem to be trying to capture the patronage (and minds) of wealthy and elite households by referring to them, determining the norms of inheritance and property and thus redefining notions of pleasure while delineating norms related to household linkages, kinship and domesticity. There is also careful discussion on attitudes related to wealth and resources and their link to pleasure and pain, which, along with vested proprietary interests, is regarded as the reason for dissatisfaction and sorrow.

A counterpoint to Brahmanical projections of pleasure is discernible in Buddhist and Jaina texts, which view social order, desire and aspirations from a different perspective. The unbridled seeking of pleasure, material resources and accumulation of wealth is scoffed at and replaced with soteriological aspirations. These texts represent the Brahmana critically, as an object of derision, greedily seeking material wealth and pleasure, or one who gets convinced to join the order after debate and deliberation. Rituals centred around the fire are replaced with rituals centred around the individual body and mind and donations to the sangha, either by dedicating one's own life and services (as *bhikkhus* and *bhikkhunīs*) or material wealth (or both).

These texts reveal an alternative image of the household—as a space for sorrow and drudgery—and discuss how women may feel that there is a need to escape it. They also surrender to the agency of women by including them as *bhikkhunīs* and give space to the lay *upāsakas* and *upāsikas*. By emphasising the monastic order and eschewing production and reproduction activities, they seem to be making a direct and frontal attack on the institution of the household, projecting it as a source of pleasure and pain.[23]

Thus, an alternative image of domesticity and conjugality emerges in the Buddhist texts. One of the sources revealing the tensions and conflict that exist in households is the *Therīgāthā*.[24] The *therīs* references to tribulations shows that women turned to monasticism in extreme circumstances, such as when they faced personal loss in the domestic space.[25] Social relationships, which are sought for pleasurable purposes but cause immense pain, are also categorically explored in the *Therīgāthā*. Kathryn Blackstone refers to how kinship ties, conflicts, filial and maternal emotions, grieving and longing are all explored in the hymns of the *bhikkhunīs*.[26] Conflicts and contestations in the household are constantly referenced and simmer on the surface of the poems, as in the case of Isidāsi, who is pawned off from one family to another by her male kinsmen (father and husband). She has to earn her position in the marital household by being subservient and respectful.

In some of the activities, the texts do reveal expectations from women as wives. This is in stark contrast with the Brahmanical notion that the husband gives pleasure to the wife. In these texts, the wife pays obeisance to his parents, gives up her seat respectfully to his relatives, serves food, wakes up before him, approaches him respectfully, waits on him, 'helps him get ready like a servant', cooks and does the washing. Despite all this, her husband rejects her, making her return to her father. She then marries twice more but is rejected by these men too, after which she joins the *sangha*.[27] In this representation, domesticity is not associated with pleasure but with drudgery and sorrow. The *sangha*, in contrast, offers an outlet from the extremes of pleasure and pain which are seen in normal lay life. It is en route to total renunciation, wherein soteriological escape from the cycle of birth and death is the only path for the ultimate bliss, *ānanda*, which is over and above the sensory entrapment of pleasurable pursuits that ultimately lead to pain.

It is a fact that entry into the *sangha* was fraught with tensions and conflict, more so for women than men. Commentaries such as Dhammapāla's *Paramatthadīpanī* (6th CCE) highlight the role that the *bhikkhunī sangha* played in the propagation of Buddhist ideals. Dhammapāla refers to how once the *bhikkhunī sangha* was established in villages, towns and country districts, women, daughters-in-law and daughters of clans had to seek the permission of their husbands, parents and kin to renounce the world. Instances of conflict with the family while joining the *sangha* are also more pronounced in case of the *therīs*, while monks like Ātuma find it difficult to go forth because of the 'wife who has been brought home'. However, these are a rarity.[28]

Sumedhā has long discussions with her parents and fiancé about the futility of material wealth and sensual pleasures even as they try to lure her with the prospect of becoming a queen. She throws herself on the ground and finally cuts off her hair, which convinces her fiancé to argue her case with her parents and finally 'allow' her to join the *sangha*. In contrast, Cāpā's poem shows her vehemence in resisting her husband's decision to renounce worldly life by promising to obey him, highlighting the beauty of her body and also threatening to kill their son. But finally, she succumbs to the ideology herself.[29]

Kathryn Blackstone also shows how there is a larger proportion of *therīs* who are free from family responsibilities before joining the sangha. Their families are either old, dead or have renounced them or are ex-courtesans or ascetics.[30] This goes to show that women were expected to carry out their domestic responsibilities before having the luxury of joining a monastic order.

One of the most vivid images from these texts is one of the household being a space for tribulations. Muttā refers to the drudgery of domesticity by describing being liberated from the three crooked things: the mortar, pestle and her crooked husband. Other episodes of intense domestic sorrow are recounted in the *therīs*' hymns. Kisāgotamī faces the loss of her two sons, husband, parents and brother, Candā and Vāsiṭṭhī also refer to their distress—Candā is a childless widow who has to beg from door to door while Vāsiṭṭhī, crazed by her son's death, wanders naked for three years living in rubbish heaps, cemeteries and highways.[31] This understanding of the household as fostering sorrow and loss and the need to remove oneself spatially from it gives us a deep insight into the thought process of the compilers of these texts. Of course, earlier references to the need to forsake households exist. The Brahmanical conceptualisation of the fourfold *aśrama* system also got ingrained around this time in fact, three of the four—*brahmacarya*, *vanaprastha* and *sannyāsa*—were meant to be lived away from the household. But the household is mostly projected as a sacred and ritual space—luxurious, seductive and safe rather than one where one faces conflict and sorrow.

However, amongst the gamut of emotions ranging from pleasurable to painful, one stands out—the bonds of friendship and the remarkable sense of bonding amongst the *bhikkhunīs* that come through in the texts, which would certainly have been one of the least specified but pleasurable outcomes of joining the *sangha*. And this was specifically so for the *bhikkhunīs*. Thus, as Blackstone reveals, 13 of the 73 poems (17.8%) refer to friends or teachers in the *sangha*, whereas only 20 of the 264 (8%) of the monks' poems refer to mentors in the *sangha*. Uttamā refers to a *bhikkhunī* 'fit to be trusted', Paṭācāra and Vijayā mention being taught by a *bhikkhunī*, Paṭācāra taught thirty *bhikkhunīs*, Candā and Uttarā and Subhā Kammāradhītā refer to Uppalavaṇā as their teacher. Sundarī and Sumedhā also encounter friendly and benevolent *bhikkhunīs*. Sumedhā's friendship even transcends previous births. This seems to show that the *therīs* seek solace and social relationships in the *sangha*, which seems to replace the household.

The above discussion shows the complexity of the notion of pleasure in early texts. One needs a thorough and nuanced understanding of the different ways in which pleasure is referred to. In the context of the Puranic texts, it is seen as an elite privilege, attained by maintaining Puranic standards of propriety and through rituals and *vratas*, allowing occasions for patronage of the Brahmanas. Knowledge, following the path of *dharma*, power, wealth, sexual pleasure and domestic bliss obtained from familial bonding, conjugal relationships and friendships are some of the ways in which pleasure can be attained.

However, these texts also point towards the fragile nature of such pleasure from material wealth and relationships and the need to nurture and maintain them with constant infusions of *vratas* and *dāna*. Gods and Goddesses themselves are in pursuit of pleasure and subject to human emotions and angst. Moreover, these visions of pleasure are plagued by the anxiety related to death. One aspires always towards the attainment of *sukha* and also particularly, *viśoka*. It is this anxiety related to death, destruction, greed and unhappiness that the Buddhists texts warn against, juxtaposing pain with pleasure and greed. The ultimate goal in these conceptualisations is a soteriological one, escape from cycle of repeated births—the ultimate *sukha* seems to be related to *mokṣa*, *nirvana* or *kaivalya*.

NOTES

1. Patrick Olivelle, *Manu's Code of Law: A Critical Edition and Translation of the Mānava Dharmaśāstra* (New Delhi: Oxford University Press, 2005), 153.
2. For further details on how the concept developed within the Brahmanical traditions, see Stephen Hay, ed., *Sources of Indian Tradition, Modern India and Pakistan* (Columbia: Columbia University Press, 1988) and Patrick Olivelle, *The Āśrama System: The History and Hermeneutics of a Religious Institution* (Oxford: Oxford University Press, 1993).
3. *Agnipurāṇa* 175.44, 57.
4. MMP CCX.
5. MMP CXLVII, 37.
6. *durlabhah stpatihstrīṇāmviguṇo~pi patihkil/ naprāpyate vināpuṇyaihpat-ināryārkadācana/yato nihsādhanodharmarmahparimāṇojbhiktā ratih/ dha-nam jīvitaparyaptampa taunāryahpratiṣṭitam/ nirdhano durbhago mūrkhah sarvalakṣaṇavarjitah/ devatam parmam nāryāh patiruktah sadaiva hi.'* MMP CLIV, 155–174.
7. MMP CLIV, 495–513.
8. MMP CLV, 1–25.
9. Rātrī is addressed by Brahmā as being blessed with her contact of Pārvatī, and the lion would now be her conveyance. She is asked to proceed to Vindhyācala, where she will do the work of the devas. Henceforth she will be known as Ekāvamśā. The *yakṣa* Pāñcāla is given to her as an attendant, well versed in various kinds of māyā and with 100,000 *yakṣa* attendants following him.
10. MMP CLVII, 1–22.
11. MMP CLVIII, 1–41.
12. MPS XLVII.
13. *gaccha sansādhayasvainam śramāpanayanaih śubhaih/ taistairmanonukūlaiśrca hyupcārairatandritā//kāvyamārādhyasvainam yathā tuṣyeta sa dvijah/ gaccha svam tasya dattā~si prayatanamkurūmatkṛte//*
14. MMP XLVII.
15. See Gerda Lerner, *The Creation of Patriarchy* (New York: Oxford University Press, 1986).
16. *Devī Purāṇa* 23.12–16. Udayagiri, according to Gupta inscriptions, was the basecamp from where Candragupta launched his campaign against the Śakas and was able to consolidate his power there, cited in Katherine Anne Harper, 'The Warring Śaktis: A Paradigm for Gupta Conquests,' in *The Roots of Tantra*, ed. Katherine Anne Harper and Robert L. Brown Harper (Albany: State University of New York, 2002), 117.
17. Ibid., 117.
18. MMP CCLXI, 40–47.
19. Ibid., 21.
20. Ibid., 40–47.
21. MMP LXXXI.
22. MMP LXXXII.
23. A close reading of the texts shows that the *sangha* organisation could exist only because of household production and thus the emergence of the

sangha was integral to the existence of a household economy, as I have shown in an earlier work, viz., Jaya S. Tyagi, 2007, 'Organized Household Production and the emergence of the sangha' in *Studies in History*, July-December 2007, Volume XXIII, Number 2, pp. 271–288.

24. Kumkum Roy refers to this transition from being in a home to being homeless (from *āgāra* to *anāgariya*). She also shows how renunciation and marriage are constructed in a dramatic conflict. Kathryn Blackstone and Kumkum Roy have shown how vivid descriptions of the social world of the women prior to their joining the sangha is drawn up in these poems.
25. Kumkum Roy, *The Power of Gender and the Gender of Power: Explorations in Early Indian History* (New Delhi: Oxford University Press, 2010), 25.
26. Kathryn R. Blackstone, *Women in the Footsteps of Buddha, Struggle for Liberation in the Therigatha* (Richmond: Curzon Press, 1998), 55.
27. Ibid., 42.
28. Ibid., 46.
29. Ibid., 43–47.
30. Ibid., 47.
31. Ibid., 43.

REFERENCES

Blackstone, Kathryn R. *Women in the Footsteps of Buddha, Struggle for Liberation in the Therigatha*. Richmond: Curzon Press. 1998.

Harper, Katherine Anne. 'The Warring Śaktis: A Paradigm for Gupta Conquests.' In *The Roots of Tantra*, edited by Katherine Anne Harper and Robert L. Brown Harper, 115–132. Albany: State University of New York. 2002.

Hay, Stephen, ed. *Sources of Indian Tradition, Modern India and Pakistan*, 2nd ed. Columbia: Columbia University Press. 1988.

Lerner, Gerda. *The Creation of Patriarchy*. New York: Oxford University Press. 1986.

Leslie, Julia. 'Śrī and Jyeṣṭa: Ambivalent Role Models for Women.' In *Roles and Rituals for Hindu Women*, edited by Julia Leslie, 107–127. New Delhi: Motilal Banarsidass Publishers Ltd. 1992.

Matsyamahapuranam. *Matsyamahāpurāṇam*. Delhi: Nag Publishers. 1983.

Olivelle, Patrick. *The Āśrama System: The History and Hermeneutics of a Religious Institution*. Oxford: Oxford University Press. 1993.

———. *Manu's Code of Law: A Critical Edition and Translation of the Mānava Dharmaśāstra*. New Delhi: Oxford University Press. 2005.

———. *The Āśrama System: The History and Hermeneutics of a Religious Institution*. Austin: Oxford University Press. 1993.

Roy, Kumkum. *The Power of Gender and the Gender of Power: Explorations in Early Indian History*. New Delhi: Oxford University Press. 2010.

Tyagi, Jaya S. 2007, 'Organized Household Production and the Emergence of the Sangha', in *Studies in History* XXIII, no. 2 (July-December 2007): 271–288.

2

IDYLLIC, INTIMATE, BEAUTIFUL PLEASURES IN VISUAL CULTURE AT MATHURĀ*

Seema Bawa

Scenes of intimacy, dance, music, feasting and drinking that valorise pleasure and its agents are displayed on pillars, doorways and entrances of *stūpas, vihāras* and other sacred buildings and also on small terracotta plaques at Mathurā, Kausambi, Chandraketugarh and many other sites. My chapter focuses on the artistic, physical and ideational spaces in the visual discourse of Mathurā art during the early centuries of the Common Era; spaces that privilege and celebrate pleasures of the senses and the intellect. The world of beauty, desire and leisure in sculptural art though the agency of women and couples is explored within the imagined urban spaces of palaces, gardens and balconies.

Indulgence in desires is represented in the world of *nāgaraka* and *nāgarikā* of *Kāmasūtra* and *Mṛcchakaṭikā*, the ideal urban characters who cultivate their self and seek aesthetic and somatic pleasures in activities such as painting, singing, consorting with beautiful courtesans (*gaṇikās*), participating in intellectually stimulating sessions with like-minded men and public women (*goṣṭhī*) and the like. The chapter not only looks at the display of pleasure but also discusses those who were responsible for producing objects such as jewellery, perfumes, unguents and props for mounting dance and theatrical performances for the *nāgaraka*.

The discourse of pleasure can be read at many levels: the pleasure of looking, listening, eating, reading, art, music, dance and poetry. Physical (experienced with the sense organs) and social pleasure (in being a *nāgaraka*, being recognised, being a wife/mother, and the like). Pleasure and satiation go together. In the literary tradition, the agents of pleasure are usually urban young men and women of leisure called

* An early and brief version of this chapter was presented at CERES, Bochum. I am grateful to Marion Frenger and Ashish Abrol, who read the chapter and whose comments and suggestions have enriched it.

nāgaraka. These occupy spaces for the consumption and production (urban the public and the private—the inner quarters or the *antahpura*) of pleasure that may be recovered from the art of Mathurā, especially from the post-Mauryan period, which is the focus of my chapter.

Laura Desmond in her article *The Pleasure is Mine: The Changing Subject of Erotic Science* illustrates another aspect of the social context as she describes that it is through the performance of a large, but bounded, repertoire of acts that one becomes, and can be recognised as, an agent of pleasure. Whether discussing the 64 arts in which the cosmopolitan person is skilled, the work of messengers, courtship, the pursuit of adulterous affairs or the conduct of courtesans, the *Kāmasūtra* describes agents of pleasure that are embedded in the visible and public world of social interaction (Desmond 2011, 17). In the visual discourse, the agents of pleasure are couples and young women, including *apsaras* and *yośitās* and their attendants, amplifying the life of luxury and comfort, with accessories such as flowers, cosmetics, clothes and the like. While in the visual discourse-like in the *Kāmasūtra*, sexual activities which may have been a prelude to the actual lovemaking, including scenes of grooming, dressing up and the use of unguents take place in the interior spaces such as bedchamber, the textual tradition prescribes that the *nāgaraka* also appear in the public sphere—the streets, assembly and outer chambers of the home at festivals or parks (Desmond 2011, 17). The enhanced bodily and sensory capabilities developed by the *kāmaśastric* actor find execution *qua* a complex societal matrix imbued with pleasure as a latent presence. Urban spaces that are socially complex converge during festivals (*utsava*), in soirees (*goṣṭhī, samāja*), at music, dance and theatre performances (*sangītaka, preksā*) or on picnics (*goṣṭhīyāna*) (Kaul 2010, 212).[1] These are depicted in the visual culture at Mathurā and elsewhere in detail and with care.

It is only fitting that it is in Mathurā, the land of Krișṇa, that the discourse of pleasure, leisure and beauty not only intersect, but also coalesce (more on the discourse of leisure in a forthcoming paper). There is a sensualisation of the visual space in the city unparalleled in the history of early Indian art. Even in the more prominent later temples (such as at Khajuraho) that are imbued with *maithuna*, copulation and *mithuna* or couples, the sensualised scenes are fewer in proportion to the total available production than those that are actually projected and are more conventionalised, that do not refer to the social and material setting as we see at Mathurā.

Mathurā, for the purpose of this paper, implies the ancient city of Madhurā, part of the Surasena *janapada*, but more importantly a centre of art whose influence spread to other sites in North India that are characterised by features of the Mathurā art style (as is understood as such by art historians). There is an interesting reference to a naked *yakṣīnì* in the *Manorathapurani* of Buddhaghoṣa. Commenting on the *Anguttara Nikāya* (2.646), where the Buddha speaks of the five disadvantages of Modhura (modern Mathurā), including its fierce *yakṣas*, Buddhaghoṣa recounts a story describing a visit of the Buddha to Mathurā. The story says that just as he entered the outer precincts of the town, a naked *yakṣīni* stationed herself before him with her hands outstretched and her tongue sticking out.[2] The Buddha, apparently disgusted, turned back from the town and set up residence in a monastery outside the city.[3] The Buddha may have disliked such acts of public indecency, as seen in the arts of the period, but it seems that the patrons of art had a distinct taste for feminine beauty and charms, lovers' world of intimacy and sensual pleasures. It is the city of Vasavadattā, the famed and much desired *gaṇikā*, the very representation of *kāma*, who is converted to *dharma* by the monk-teacher Upagupta (Strong 1992).

The world of desires, beauty and enjoyment, of pleasures of the body and the intellect, whose overlord is Kāmadeva (Figure 2.1) may be termed *kāmaloka*.[4] In early Indian tradition, the three components of pleasure have been defined as *prīti, rati* and *ramana-bhoga* that have been discussed in the introduction.

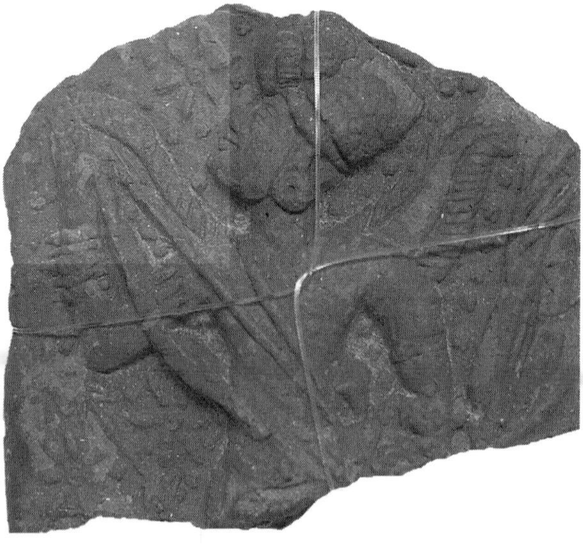

Figure 2.1: Kāmadeva with a Bow and Quiver of Arrows, 2nd Century CE, Terracotta, Mathurā Museum

Kāmaloka (world of pleasure) is a term used by Vogel (1971, 17) for describing amorous scenes on *toraṇa* and railing pillars found from

Mathurā. But I think the term may be effectively applied to a larger body of both architectural and small terracotta objects. In these narrative, apotropaic and descriptive artworks, the everyday world of seeking out and enjoying the big and small pleasures of life is represented in a visual form.

PILLAR OF PLEASURE

One such significant work is what I would like to call 'The pillar of pleasure' (Mathurā Museum Accession No. 0001.11). This may have been the doorway to a monastic or religious establishment; it is evocative of the context as well as the content of activities associated with such places. This relatively large and partly broken pillar seems to have been originally square-shaped and was at some later date sliced down the middle. What is left is a tall, thin rectangular slab (Quintanilla 2007, 56). As it stands today, the pillar measures about 5 ft in height. The carvings on the three sides of the pillar are divided into eight panels, each set apart from the other by a *vedikā* (Figure 2.2). The lowermost registers have dwarf *yakṣas,* like *bhāra putrakas*, holding up on their shoulders the weight of the architectures and all that it represents.

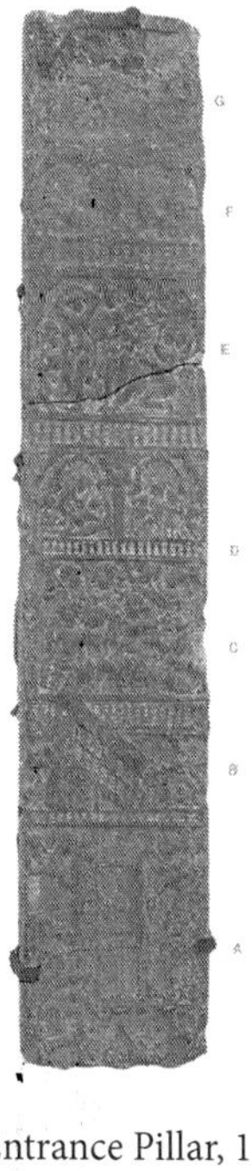

Figure 2.2: Pillar of Pleasure, Entrance Pillar, 1st Century CE, Red Sandstone, Mathurā Museum Accession No. 0001.11

The most significant face, for the purpose of representing and locating pleasure, is the front one. The whole pillar describes a scene that is partly horizontally set and partly vertically arranged but due to the exigency of fitting it all onto a pillared structure is seen in these seven rising registers, each used to depict the location, the protagonists and the narrative.

The lowest one, panel A, indicates the setting of the scenes, with two tall city gates, behind which two palm trees are seen that represent an *udayāna* or a park/garden/orchard. Within this a multi-storied structure is situated that brings out the spatial setting of the urban residential architecture, with the entrance flanked by a tall city fortification wall.

On both sides of the gates are two spear and shield-carrying *dvāra pālas*, guarding the entrance. These figures wear a Scythian dress—a tunic with a belt and a conical helmet/hat. These are repeated more clearly on the narrower side of the pillar. Adjacent on the narrow right side has been carved one half of a two-story tower, the other half being effaced but originally situated on the front panel, so the structure wraps around the corner of the pillar (Quintanilla 2007, 56).

The next panel, B, on the front side, has a diagonally set *sopāna* or a stairway leading up to the right side, covered with a barrel-vaulted roof that ends at the top in a small enclosure or chamber with a window (Figure 2.3). Two male figures, one pot-bellied and bejewelled and the other with a sword, are seen around and on the staircase (indicating their varied social statuses). More stock figures of *bhāra putrakas* are seen at the ends of the panel, almost spilling over to the sides.

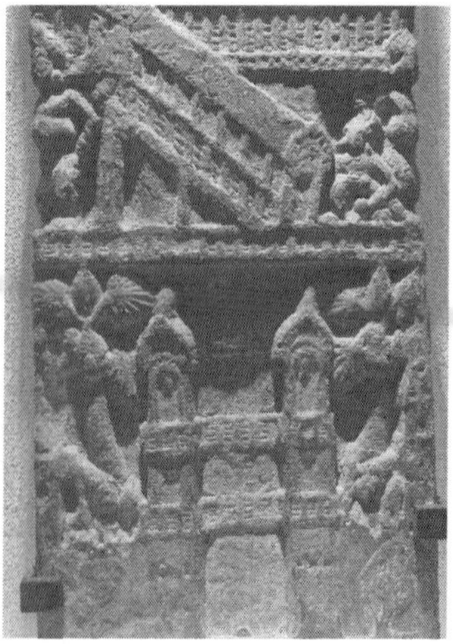

Figure 2.3: Detail Showing the Entrance Gateway and Stairway, Pillar of Pleasure, Entrance Pillar, 1st Century CE, Red Sandstone, Mathurā Museum

The staircase leads up into the next panel, C, that depicts a crowded composition, filled with male and female figures engaged in various activities. The principal figures seem to be a couple in lower left corner, seated in an intimate posture and looking towards each other, with the woman's hand resting on her companion's thigh. There are two attendant figures behind them, one of them holding a *chowrie* aloft, suggesting the elite status of the seated couple. On the right in front of the couple are dancers and musicians (two drummers and a woman playing the harp), engaged in their activities with energetic movements. The female dancer is shown with her feet planted on the ground, her legs bent and her left arm bent and upraised. She wears heavy roll anklets, a girdle that is slung low on her hips and a sash tied loosely around her waist.

The next panel, D, is relatively shallow: it depicts male–female interactions, set under two *gavākṣa* arches, divided by a pillar (Figure 2.4 [lower half]). The figures on the right are abraded but a male in the centre flanked by two seated females can be made out, with the male holding them in a loose embrace. On the left are three figures, the principal couple and another female figure on their right. The amorous couple is in a reclining position, with the man bending over and embracing the woman, engaging in coitus, *maithuna* or in *ālingana mithuna*.

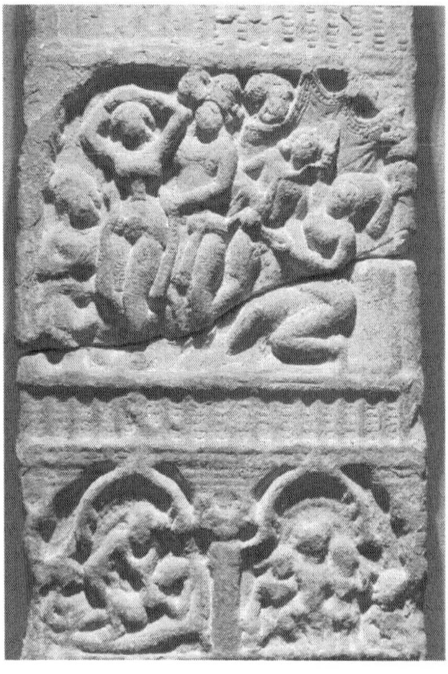

Figure 2.4: Detail Showing the Scenes of Intimacy and Pleasure Activities, Pillar of Pleasure, Entrance Pillar, 1st Century CE, Red Sandstone, Mathurā Museum

In the fifth panel, E, there is again a dancing scene (Figure 2.4 [upper half]). A dwarf, maybe a *yakṣa*, looks up at a provocatively delineated female figure,[5] with arms held above her head in a dancing posture, or indolently stretching; the turbaned male figure on her left is undoing her waist band. Another couple is seen on the right, with the male leaning over the kneeling woman, who is wearing a tasselled conical cap and seems to be in the act of removing the male's turban. There is a curtain-like device on the right top corner from which a spectator figure is looking down on the couple. The curtain device is reminiscent of the Vasantasenā scene from the Doris Wiener collection (Bawa 2013, 282).

The narrative must have continued in the uppermost two panels, F and G, but unfortunately these are much abraded. It can be said that there were many figures in the upper panel, including three male figures, one of whom holds a sword. The presence of an elephant can also be made out. Sonia Rhie Quintanilla says, 'The bellicose male figure in association with an elephant recalls the story of King Māndhātā and his conquest of *kāmaloka*', as told in the Divyadāna and Māndhātā Jātaka.[6]

Other male and female figures, perhaps indicating the presence of servitors, *cetas* and *cetikās*, are carved on the two narrow sides of the pillar. These may be attendant figures who enhance the narrative and descriptive element of the main composition on the front panels. The sides also depict women carrying pots and a male figure with a broad sword raising his right hand and pointing, as if to draw attention to the scenes above and on the side. A woman holding a square object resembling a birdcage is also seen. A birdcage is one of the objects associate with desire and is also mentioned as part of the birds seen in Vasantasenā's aviary mentioned below.

The physical setting of the interior of a house may refer to the *vesāvāsa*, the courtesan quarters that later, in the early modern period, were also known as *kothās*, literally meaning the roof where amorous activities were carried out, often outside sanctioned, familial set-ups. Inhabited by women, *yossita*, who can be had without any effort, who can be had merely by making advances: a woman who stands at the door; a woman who looks out from her rooftop porch onto the main street; *prasādarājamārga avalokini* (Kamaustra, 5.52). The courtesans were also known as *prakāśanāri*, those exposed to light and associated with the *bāhya* or the outside world, according to Arthaśastra and Nāṭyaśāstra respectively. The upper registers lead to an open-pillared chamber, a pavilion called a *kūṭāgāra*,[7] or *harmya*, which is often the location for lovers' trysts and which is discussed later in this paper, in context of Sudraka's play *Mṛcchakaṭikā*. The entire scene is thus so compiled as to reveal the many layers of pleasurable anticipation and activities, from passing the lofty entrance with doorkeepers and servants, to climbing the stairway, to reaching scenes of music, dance and romantic dalliance, among others.

Similar but abbreviated scenes showcasing the spirit of enjoyment of leisure activities such as music and dance in mixed company are often seen on terracotta plaques. The exact purpose of this is not known, but it may have been for simple viewing pleasure. These have not been found from Mathurā per se but from other sites in North India; for example, a round plaque from Bhita shows a couple in a pleasure garden framed by a broad margin with oblique incised lines.[8] A little to the left of centre, there is a house within a railing which has a gable roof, while in the background there are trees and in front there is a pond filled with lotuses. On the right is a depiction of a bullock cart and, in the centre, a jungle and a deer. In the uppermost part is a couple inside an enclosure, but the details are not clear. There are other plaques also with couples in arboreal settings of gardens or *udayānas* enjoying picnics with music and dance such as the two specimens from Kausambi (Figure 2.5).

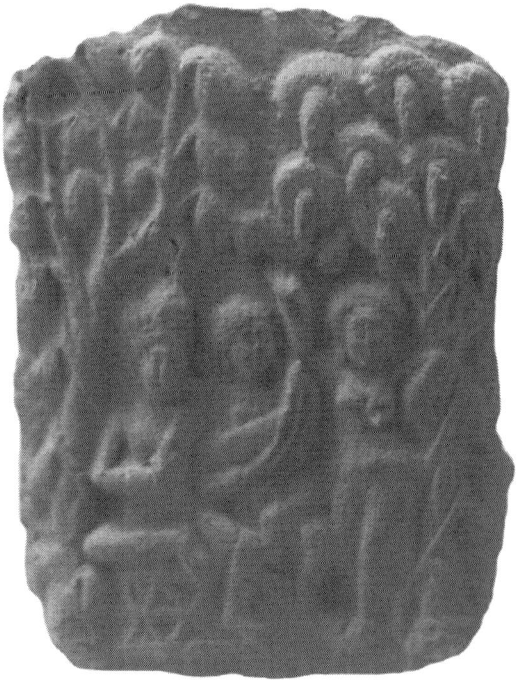

Figure 2.5: Couple in an Orchard Setting Enjoying Music and Dance, 1st Century BCE, Terracotta, Kausambi, Now in National Museum, Acc. No. 60.436

PILLARS OF INTIMACY

A rather popular composition that seems to enjoy a wide appeal, as there are many versions of the same basic arrangement, is that of couples or *mithunas*,[9] with attendants indulging in acts that may be considered intimate, within the interiors of a palace, a big house and religious buildings. I call these pillars of intimacy. These are not confined to *dvāraśākhās* or doorjambs from the Mathurā atelier but go on to influence the creation of *mithuna śākhās* seen at the entrances of Buddhist caves such as Nasik Cave No. 3 and later temples dated to the Gupta era. One such category is that of so called *Saundarananda* panels, discovered from various sites that are associated with the Mathurā atelier, such as Kankāli Tilā,[10] Jamālpur, Sankissa and Sanghol. Intimacy between couples indicated here and in other *mithunas* panels at Mathurā can be traced back to its visual lineage from earlier art and architecture at Bharhut, Bodhgayā, Kausambi and other contemporary bas-relief sculptures from the late Mauryan period onwards. The context of *mithunas*, gendered and otherwise, has been traced in an earlier work of mine and does not bear repetition and dangers of self-plagiarism (Bawa 2013, 204–232).

The scenes on the pillar cited above are within the trope of amorous interactions between couples seen on several of the railing pillars at Mathurā, where there is one principal couple, with or without the company of some attendant figures. Within the larger tradition of the *mithuna śākhās*, there is often the adoration and adorning of the feminine by the male, by putting on jewellery and offering clothes. P.K. Agarwala refers to this motif as the lovers' apology, arising from temporary quarrel and resulting in reconciliation (Agarwala 1992). The device of the male helping the female adorn herself, or offering her clothes, is a very popular topic in folk songs and classical performing arts; similarly, the asking, offering and receiving of gifts of ornaments and apparel for the embellishment of the physical body is repeatedly used in classical literary texts to exhibit romantic and erotic relationships. As I have stated elsewhere, the connection between the feminine and the physical is well established in early Indian cultural traditions as not only essential to describe the desirable female but also as a symbol of the auspicious and fertile female body. This is voiced in canonical Buddhist and Brahmanical literature, *śāstric* traditions and visual tradition, in which the ornamentation of the female body, by herself and through the help of the male partner, is considered to be a prelude to consummation (with the wife and the courtesan). This does not preclude it being considered *mangala* or auspicious and thus adding value to the ornamental or *alaṃkāra* of the structure while also evoking pleasure in scenes of intimacy and love between a couple at Mathurā. This is in consonance with the greater 'secularisation' and 'sensualisation' of art during the post-Mauryan period at Mathurā (Desai 1985, 17).

One composition that is found on various sites with varied permutations and combinations has been identified as the one detailing the interactions between Sundarī and Nanda based on the Aśvaghoṣa's *kāvya Saundarananda* (Agarwala 1963, 32–33; Bawa 2013, 233–242). Aśvaghoṣa invests considerable effort in painting a verbal picture of the love between the prince Nanda and his wife, with whom Nanda spent innumerable hours in play and passion. He describes how, in the process of love, 'he covered her with ornaments, not that she should be decorated but only to serve her …' In response, she put a mirror into her lover's hand, saying, 'Just hold this up while I paint myself,' and he obeys her request (*Saundarananda* II, 12–13). The most complete depiction of the *mithuna* pillar is found in Chaurasi ka Tila, GMM. 57.4446 (Figure 2.6). This pillar must have been a tall jamb at the entrance of a Buddhist structure.

The pillar has eight figural panels on the two sides and a scroll with a vine of leaves on the third side. Each panel is separated from the other by *vedikā* railings at the bottom and a row of *gavākṣa* window or pavilions at the top, framed by pilasters completing the setting of a palace/shrine interior. The bottom panels on both sides have a large male figure with folded hands, perhaps offering homage to a turban-like object held aloft by a dwarf figure, while on the reverse, the figure is holding a bunch of lotus flowers. On the top of each side, there is a figure of the Buddha with a halo around his head seated on a throne, gazed at by male figures with folded hands, Indra and Brahmā. The intervening six panels on each side contain *mithuna* dyads, usually not looking at each other, offering prayers and devotion with folded hands, or objects such as flowers, garlands and cloth, presumably to the Buddha. The interaction and aura of the *mithunas* depicted on the Chaubārā in their deeply devotional postures is very different from the amorous interactions on other pillars such as the *Saundarananda* panels[11] that refer to a *kavya*, a poem of the same name attributed to Asvasgosa, who is believed to have lived in the time of Kaniska, c. 2nd century CE.

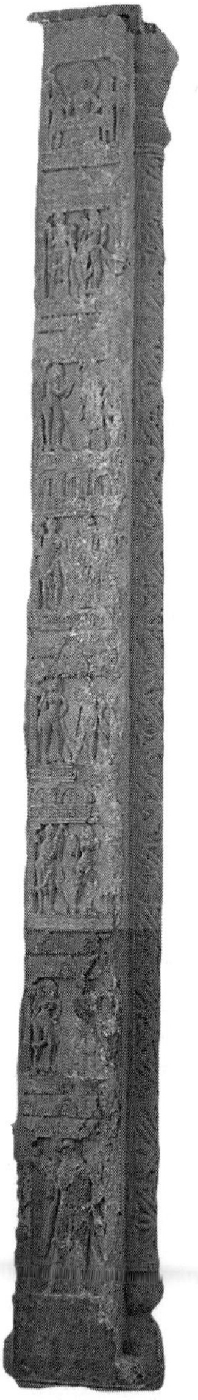

Figure 2.6: Pillar of Intimacy and Devotion, Doorjamb, 2nd Century CE, Red Sandstone, Chaurāsi ka Tilā, Mathurā Museum, Acc. No. 57.4446, ht: 3 m 71 cm

A three-sided second-century jamb from Mathurā, known as the *Saundarananda* panel (SML J. 533, red sandstone, height 143.5 × 29 cm, 1st century AD, Kankāli Tilā, Mathurā) and now housed in the Lucknow

Museum is broken off from the top. Of the three complete panels on each side that are visible, significant depictions are of a couple seen seated on a couch with the man offering a cup to a woman on his right with an attendant woman standing behind, who is carrying a *surāhi*-like pot. The *surāhī*-like vessel is repeated in another panel where the woman is seated on a stool, her legs crossed at the knees, with this vessel placed behind her on a table (Figure 2.7).

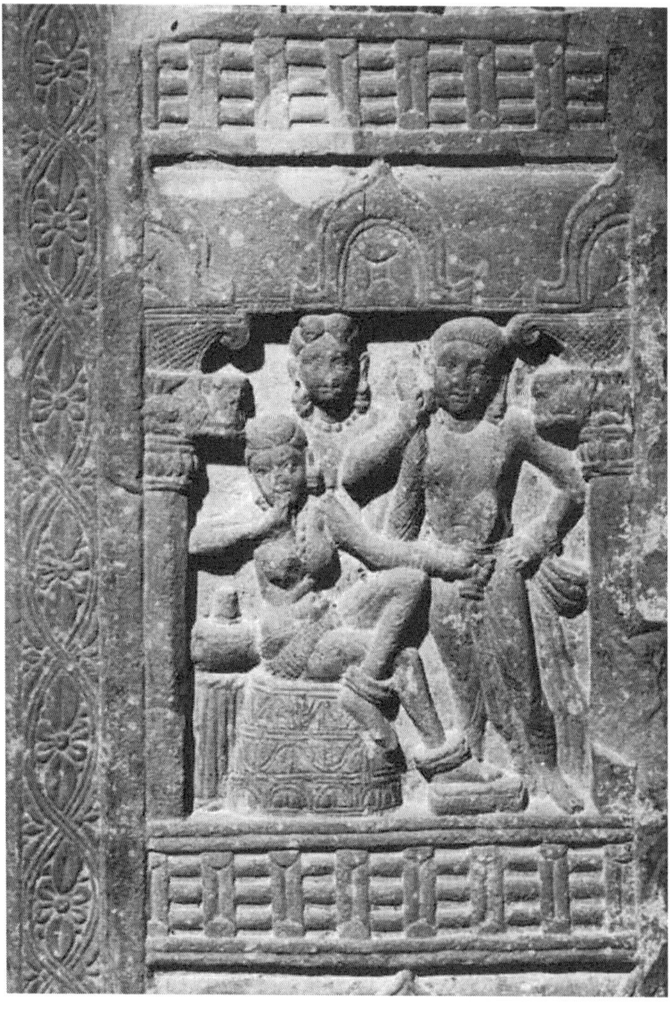

Figure 2.7: *Saundarananda* Panels, 2nd Century CE, Red Sandstone, Kankāli Tilā, Mathurā, Now in the State Museum, Lucknow, Acc. No. J 533.
Courtesy: AIIS.

One hand is raised to her lips and the other holds a mirror. The male is holding a cloth roll or thick garland in his hand. The female attendant figure stands behind. The man offers clothes to the woman seated in a similar posture. The combing/adorning of the hair composition is also seen in another panel with the dwarf attendant figure holding a basket of garlands in the foreground.

In a third example from Isāpur, Mathurā (Figure 2.8), the top panel depicts the seated Buddha, the centre panel shows the woman dancing with her arms raised, of which the male holds one. The lower panel shows a male holding an object near the mouth of the female while he embraces her with the other arm; the woman holds a cup in her hand.

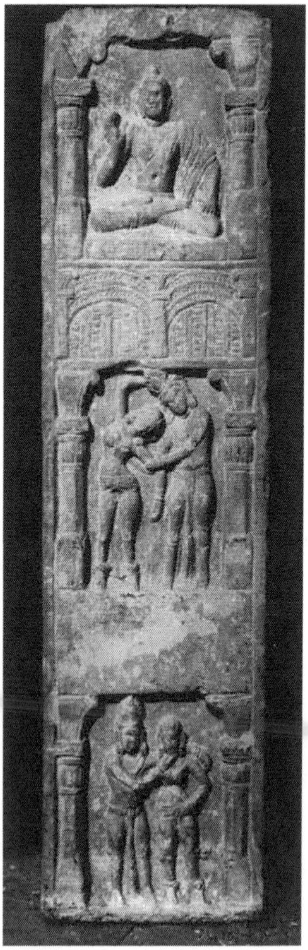

Figure 2.8: Couples Dancing and Enjoying Amorous Pleasures, Railing Pillar, 2nd Century CE, Isapur, Mathurā Museum
Courtesy: AIIS.

Another beautiful pillar (Figure 2.9) found from Gurgaon[12] (Acc. No. 12.168) has two panels showing the usual setting with a long architrave with ogee arches, a *vedikā*, pilaster on the obverse and a *yakṣī* on the reverse. The lower panel on the obverse shows a smiling man holding the edge of what seems to be a roll of striped cloth placed on the tray. The woman to his left is taking off or putting on a garland or necklace around her neck, which she holds with both her hands. She is looking into a mirror held up in front of her face by a dwarfish female figure (or perhaps a eunuch). To her left is a male figure holding a garland tray. The male is clad in a dhoti that covers him from the waist downwards, while the woman seems to be wearing a transparent dhoti that is discerned by the edges near her feet, for her lower half is exposed, as are her breasts, in the fashion of *yakṣī/yośitā* figures of the 1st–2nd century Mathurā. The panel above this has the order of the figures reversed. The female attendant figure on the right holds the tray with the garland *utpala-mālābhāriṅī kanyā* (Agarwala 1963, 32), while the main female figure has her back towards the viewer and her face is in profile as she looks into the mirror held in her right hand and tries to arrange her frontal hair with her left, while another female attendant looks on. The smiling male figure seen standing behind her seems to be adorning her hair by interweaving it with a garland of flowers or unknotting her coiffured hair. With his other hand, he holds the sash around his waist that is looped at the end in a typical Kuṣāṇa period fashion of a dandy.

A similar scene has also been retrieved from Sankissa,[13] with the woman in a frontal standing position, putting on a thick garland, with a man on her left. He seems to be holding a stretched, heavy garment, perhaps an *uttarìya*, in his hands, seemingly waiting for her to accept it from his hands. A diminutive female attendant is also visible.

There is tenderness about the postures of the couple identified as Sundarī and Nanda; it was a popular theme for the visual and literary productions of writers, sculptors as well as donors who funded the production. Perhaps this popularity was linked to the great difficulty faced by Nanda in leaving his beautiful and virtuous wife and his prolonged battle with temptation. This struggle may have struck a chord with the Buddhist brethren who faced similar difficulties in forsaking the material world with its pleasures, as is reflected in the poems of the monks recorded in the *Theragāthā* (Theragāthā 1969, 32, 48) and also in the tales of the many backsliding brothers admonished by the Buddha in the *Jātaka kathās*.[14]

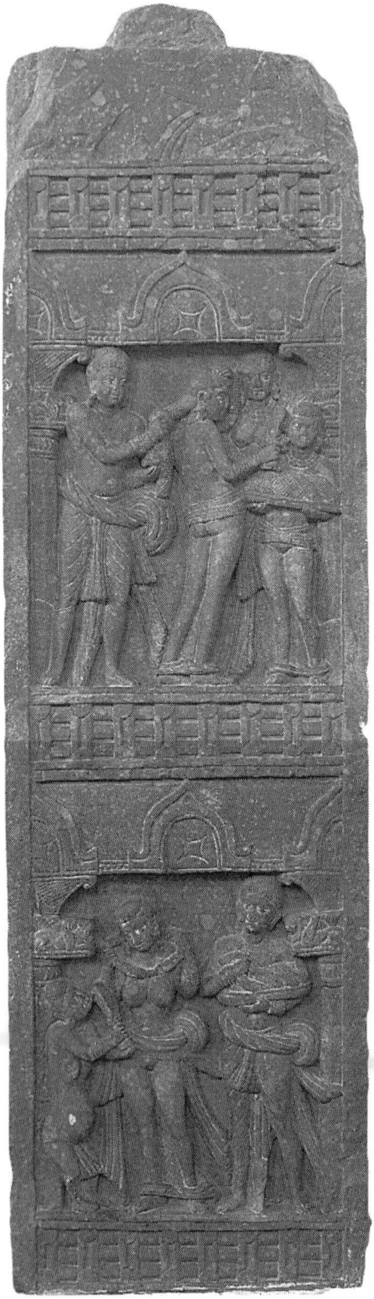

Figure 2.9: *Saundarananda* Panels, 2nd Century CE, Red Sandstone, Gurgaon, Mathurā Museum, Acc. No. 12.158, ht: 1 m 4 cm

FEAST OF THE SENSES

There are vignettes of enjoyment of the senses, revealed through scenes of revelry that are part of larger compositions. The most attractive and expressive in terms of emotions is a small stone plaque, probably a fragment of a larger architectural piece that displays five women eating, drinking and dancing (Figure 2.10), set inside an interior space, indicated by pilasters on both sides. Three women are visible at the back; the one on the left has her hand raised to her mouth as if eating from the bowl held in her lower hand. Of the two on the right, one is embracing the one directly in front of her, who is holding a cup like vessel in her right hand, which she covers with her left. The figure on the lower left has her one arm raised while the other hand rests on her waist in a dancing posture. The figure on the right has her hand on her cheek, perhaps dancing or acting. The allure of this composition is not just in the beautifully bejewelled figures but also in the animated movement and smiling faces of the women enjoying themselves.

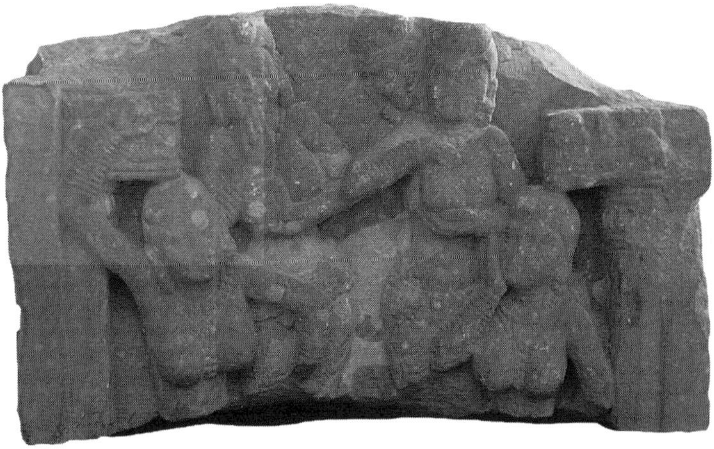

Figure 2.10: Five Female Figures Feasting, Drinking and Sharing Intimate Moments, 2nd Century CE, Kathauti ka Kuan, Mathurā Museum, Acc. No. 14.405

A more conventionalised circular terracotta plate with five fe/male figures dancing in a circle has been found from Mathurā and has at least two versions, one at Mathurā Museum (Figure 2.11) and other at the Museum of Asiatische Kunst, Berlin. All figures have their heads towards the outer edge and legs placed together near the centre and are performing different movements, clapping, arm upraised in dance, hand on the mouth. A rattle recovered from Kausambi (?) also shows men dancing in a circle with their heads towards the centre and legs stretched outwards (Poster 1986, 118). The celebratory dance by women and men on a child's toy (?) or a small plaque made for the amusement of the children or elders does speak of the little pleasures in the act of viewing pleasurable moments, perhaps recalling such festivities of shared music and dance.

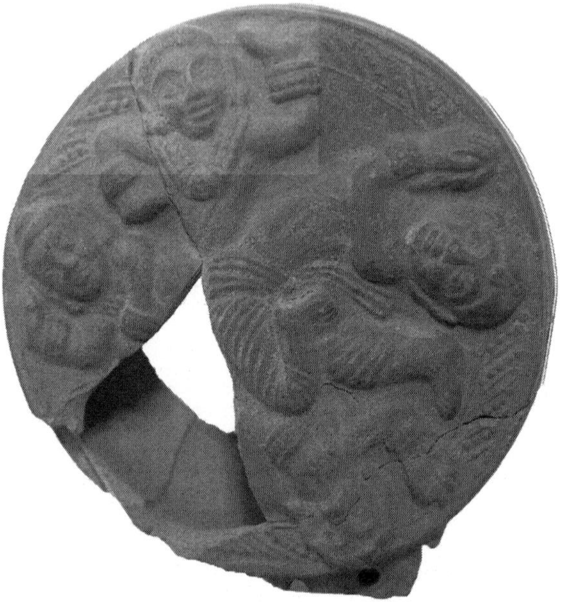

Figure 2.11: Five Figures Dancing in a Circle, Rattle (?), 1st–2nd Century CE, Terracotta, Mathurā Museum

PILLARS/PANELS OF BEAUTY

One of the characteristic features of the *abhisarikā*/wife, who waits for her lover, berates him and then allows for reconciliation that has been referred to above. The *yośitā*, the young woman, is the heroine not only of many of the dramas and *kāvyas* but also of the railing pillars, especially within the Mathurā region from the 1st to the 3rd centuries (Figure 2.12). The nature and typology of this so-called *yakṣī* figure has been discussed in another publication (Bawa 2013, 309–336) but suffice it to say here that the *yośitā*, with her abundant youth, was constructed as an object of male desire. The courtesan, the *yośitā* par excellence, was one archetype that was constructed for pleasure, mostly for catering to the male 'gaze'.

Typologically, in sculptural art at Mathurā, women are shown as large-breasted and small-waisted with wide hips, usually engaged in *lilā* and *krīḍā*, activities that were considered as adding to feminine allure. They sport elaborate coiffure and rich ornaments.

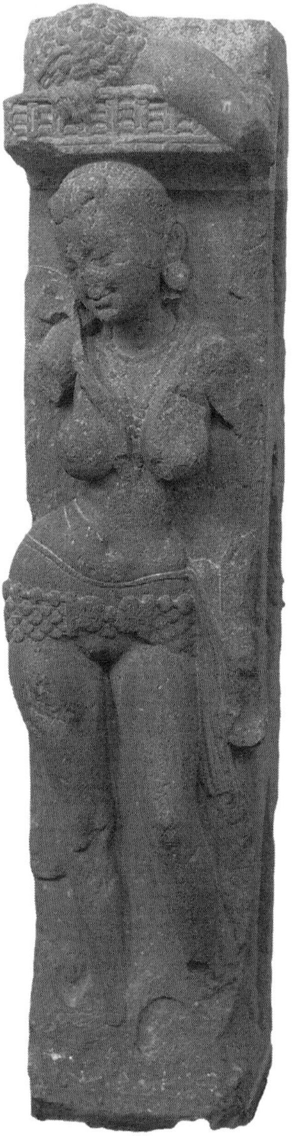

Figure 2.12: *Yakṣī/Yośitā*, Epitome of Feminine Youthful Beauty, Railing Pillar, 2nd Century CE, Mathurā Museum

Śṛṅgāra or decorating the self seems to be a feminine domain. *Śṛṅgāra* is also a *rasa-bhāva* that evokes erotic love and is considered incomplete without women; women are considered essential to evoke a sense of beauty and desire while performing dance and drama (*Nāṭyaśāstra*, VI. 45–48). In sculpture this is demonstrated in the form of beautiful young women adorning the *viharas* and *stupas* of Mathurā. As seen on the pillars of intimacy and in the *yakṣī/yośitā* pillars, women themselves or their male lovers are shown as aiding women who are engaged in augmenting their physical beauty through the application of make-up, combing of hair, bathing and looking at themselves in the mirror.

The raison d'etre for this emphasis is to be found in contemporary attitudes towards youth and beauty as the main attribute of femininity reflected in literary cultural products such as the *Nāṭyaśāstra* and the *Kāmasūtra*. This has been elaborated in Aśvaghoṣa's *Buddhacarita*, where Śuddhodana, Gautama's father, ordered the women of the palace to tempt and distract Gautama from renouncing the world by enthralling his senses with worldly pleasures. The attempts described include women being intoxicated 'with liquor (*madaneniya varijitah*) and touching him with their firm, rounded (*pinaih*), close-set (*samhaitaih*) and charming breasts (*stanaiā*); they repeatedly exposed their body by allowing their blue lower garment to fall (*strasta-nila*). Wet with ointment (*ardhā nulepana*) ... and smelling of spirituous liquor, they displayed their bosoms like golden jars' (*Buddhacarita*, IV, 29–35). While the verse is a paean to Gautam's firm resolve, the description of the attractive bodies, naked and captivating, does match many of the representations of feminine figures found in post-Mauryan art.

While most part of canonical literature is silent on the identity and symbolism of these young women chiseled out of stone,[15] two *Śvetāmbara* Jaina texts, the *Rājaprasniyasūtra* and *Jivajivābhigamasūtra*, dateable to the 1st century BC (Roth 1957, 91–116) give a vivid and detailed description of the ideal desirable feminine beauty, postures and movements of the *śālabhañjikās*. Roth has translated a passage related to this as follows:

> ... on both sides of each of the doors, on the double flankers, rows of 16 branch bending females on each side are arranged well supported. These branch bending females stand sportively, well adorned, with dresses of different colors, covered with different garlands; they have beautiful waists, which can be grasped by the length of a hand's grip, and breasts which are plump, fashioned, swollen, raised and round like a couple of diadems worn on top of the head, who have impassioned side glances and dark hair,

> their hair is covered at the top with tender, spotless, auspicious symbols. Their bodies are leisurely inclined against Aśoka trees and they seize the prominent parts of the branches with the left hand. They, who seem to captivate (the senses of gods and men) with the gestures of their side glances, having turned their eyes aside, and who seem to exhaust themselves on account of embraces with their looks, whose features resemble the maturity of earth, who have entered into eternal existence, who have faces like the moon, who have foreheads like a half moon with an appearance even more pleasing than that of the moon, they who are shining like a meteor, with a splendour even more than the shining flow of the sun and the light particles of the lightening clouds, whose dresses are beautiful, because they are like an abode of ornaments, they are gracious.... (*Ràjaprasniyasūtra* 1957, 114–115; Pali original with Hindi translation, Ratan Muni 1982, 66–67)

This sculptural device represents the desirability and the erotic availability of women in visual imagination for the pleasure of the audience. This notion of physical beauty, charm, playfulness and eroticism as the essential elements of femininity is discussed elsewhere. Suffice it to say here that *bahya* (lit. outside) women, not belonging to the household, are like the youthful sculptures who represent the first stage of feminine youth (*Nāṭyaśāstra*, XXV.43).[16] This does not negate the association of the *yakṣī/yoṣitā/śālabhañjikā* with the *mangala* or auspicious scheme; indeed women have been linked with pleasure in offering devotion, in classical as well as folk visual and performative cultures.

In *kāmaśāstriya* literature, drinking wine, especially in the company of women, is *de rigueur* for the *nāgaraka*, enhancing the erotic and amorous potential of the encounter (Figure 2.13). But epigraphic references to the making and perhaps the consumption of wine have also been found in monastic contexts (Falk 2009), where wine was also used for ritualistic purposes. However, in art, it is often depicted as a pleasurable activity of the better off *yakṣa* such as Kubera and rich people depicted as *mithunas*, elite couples, *gaṇikā* or courtesans or even the pillar *yakṣī/yoṣitā* who are often shown holding a pitcher (presumably) of wine or a goblet. The inebriated pot-bellied *yakṣa*, in all probability Kubera, holding a goblet-like cup, found on the double-sided panel in Palikhera illustrates not only the identity but also wine drinking in its socio-ethnic context. Women and men surrounding him wear Scythian, i.e., north-western dresses, which is in keeping with the popularity of bacchanalian cult and art of the region of Gandhara (Carter 1968).

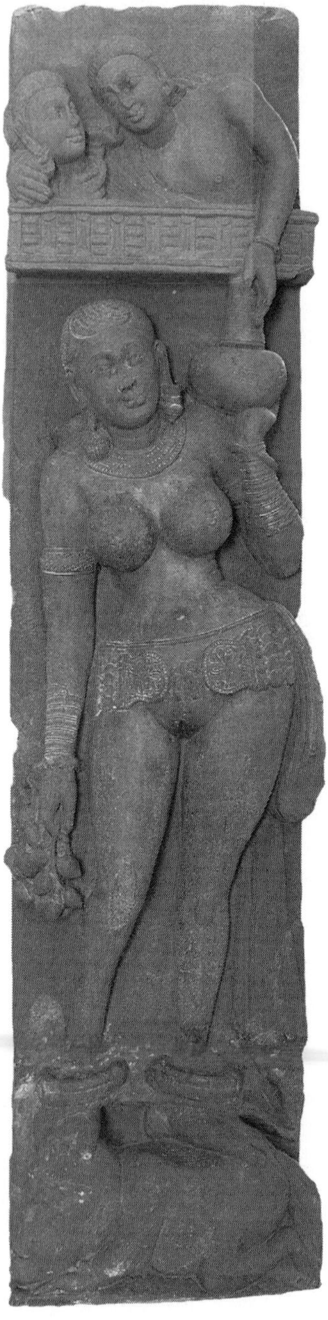

Figure 2.13: *Yakṣī/Yośitā*, with a Flask Probably of Wine, Railing Pillar, 2nd Century CE, Mathurā Museum

One depiction of intoxication is that of *Vasantsenā* that is repeatedly sculpted on double-sided images or pillars; these have been found at monastic sites in and around Mathurā such as Maholi (Agarwala 1939, 71), Kankali Tila, Narauli and the related site of Sanghol. For the sake of brevity, I take up only the Maholi[17] example as these panels are the best-preserved and most complete specimens (Figures 2.14 and 2.15). They are found on a stone panel made of red sandstone and carved on both sides. On one side is a scene of a woman kneeling, apparently drunk or overwrought, being supported on the right by a diminutive man and on the left by a man of natural proportions. On the far right is another woman, less voluptuous than the central figure, and behind rises a pilaster terminating in a bowl at the top.

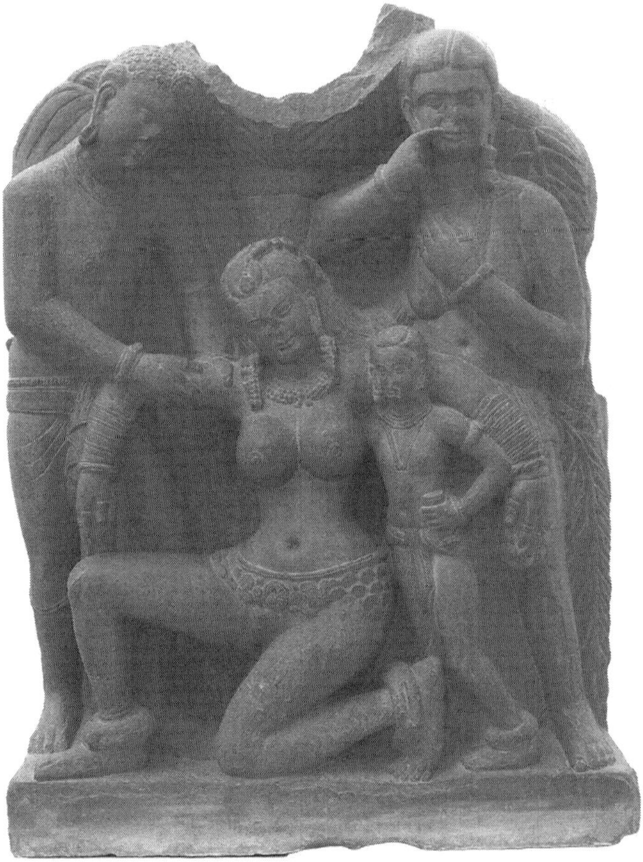

Figure 2.14: Kneeling Courtesan (Vasantasenā) Supported by Companions, Double-sided Panel, 2nd Century CE, Maholi, Mathurā, Now in National Museum

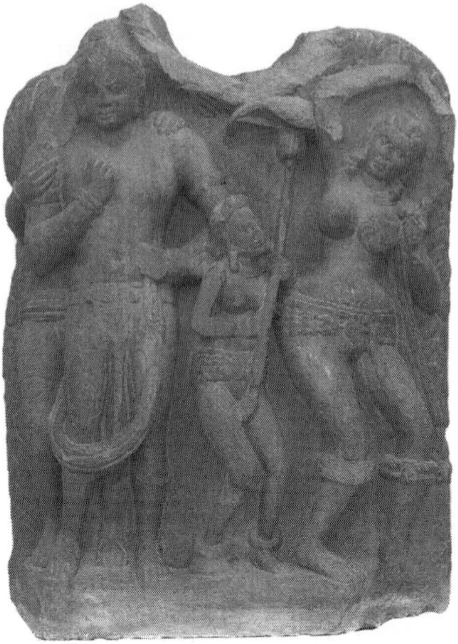

Figure 2.15: Vasantasenā Fleeing from Unwanted Advances, Double-sided Panel, 2nd Century CE, Maholi, Mathurā, Now in National Museum

On the reverse side on the far right, the standing figure of a (same?) woman bent at the knees and the waist is seen, wearing clothing and jewellery that resemble those worn by the standard representation of *yakṣī* figures of the period. This includes voluptuous delineation of the body with rounded, full breasts, a narrow waist and wide hips. She is shown to be naked from the waist up, wearing a *mekhalā* and a profusion of necklaces, earrings and the like. The striking feature is the anklets that are worn under her knees rather than at her ankles, which is curious element in comparison with the other depictions of female figures, including the ones on the obverse. Her right arm is stretched above her head, as if she is arranging her shawl or *uttarīya* above her head. On her immediate right, positioned in the middle of the composition, is a diminutive female figure holding up a parasol or *chatra* above the main female figure. On the left there are two men of which only one is fully visible, since the other is hiding behind. The man in the front appears to be well-dressed like an aristocratic though not a divine person. The whole piece is apparently a stand for a bowl, which can be seen on the top of the pilaster, carved in the middle of the slab.

C. Śivaramamurti first identified the Maholi relief with a scene from the Sanskrit play *Mṛcchakaṭikā* by Śudraka dated variously between the

2nd and 5th centuries. He sets the drunken lady on the obverse in a *veśāvāsa* or courtesan's house, where she is being offered wine by her girl attendant even as she drops down inebriated and is supported by a youth on the other side who, in Śivaramamurti's opinion, represents 'one of the many ... lured by the charm of the *vesāvāsa*' (Śivaramamurti 1961, 36–37). Standing beside the principal female figure is the old prostitute, *kuttanì*, manager of the *gaṇikās*' quarters. There is a general consensus among art historians accepting this identification of the double sided panels as representing moments from the *Daridracāruduttam/Mṛcchakaṭikā*, a narrative that was in circulation at the time, and the main figure being that of Vasantsenā, the famed *gaṇikā* of Ujjayini.

One must understand the main thread of the plot related to this depiction before interpreting it. The reverse refers to the first act of the play, where Vasantsenā is fleeing the unwanted advances of the royal brother-in-law Samsthanaka, whose parasitic but cunning boon companion, the *vīṭā*, warns Vasantsenā that the tinkling of her anklets and the scent of the flowers in her hair are giving her away. She takes off her ornaments and covers her hair and enters the house of Carudutta, the romantic hero of the play, to take shelter. As another character comes out of the house, the cowardly Samasthanaka hides behind the *vīṭā* (*Mṛcchakaṭikā*, 41–47). In the visual version, she has pulled up her anklets up to her knees to prevent them from jingling and covered her perfumed hair. The two men are Samasthanaka and the *vīṭā*, as described in the play. On the obverse, it could be the depiction of the courtesans' quarter with a drunk *gaṇikā* and her retinue of lovers and dependents. It could be another moment from the play where a newly converted Buddhist monk rescues her after being left for dead by a desperate Samsthanka who had strangled her (Bawa 2013, 281).

The depiction of the *gaṇikā* is quite evocative of the male fantasy of the cultured but sexually available women, construed to fulfil every male desire and fantasy (for a price of course). She is the female counterpart of the *nāgaraka*, accomplished in sexual and cultural matters, as will be discussed at length later.

It is also suggestive of a new vein of sensualised narratives as art centres shift to more urban, mercantile-denominated areas such as Mathurā. Here, art catered to the urban populace's desire for visual pleasure. This was not just for the sophisticates but also the craftsmen, merchants, kings and performers mentioned in inscriptions and literature. Men and some women patronised the making of beautiful sculptures on beautiful monuments so that they could indulge in the pleasure of looking and also in devotion and charitable piety. Amongst these were prostitutes, *vesa* or *vēśyā* like Vasu and her junior Lonashobhika who donated a shrine (*devakula*) of the Arahat (Arhat), an *ayayasabha*, a reservoir (*prapa*) and stone slabs (*silapata*) in the Arhat temple (*Arahatayatana*) of the Arahatas (Arhats) (GMM, Acc No. 00.Q7) (Luders' List 1909–10 [LL], 102).

HISTORICISING PLEASURE AND BEAUTY

There is textual evidence of pleasure in the discourse of *kāma*, through *ninda* (criticism) or otherwise in *kāvya* or in canonical texts;[18] however, inscriptional references are rare. References to Kāma (deva) form a constant refrain in the literature of the early period that indicate the discourse of desire and beauty.[19]

While the texts are largely silent about the voluptuous sculptures adorning the *stupas* and *vihāras*, Harry Falk has published an inscription that sheds light on the associations between the young, sensually posed women and sculptures at Mathurā. Only the lower half of a free standing female figure in the typical Mathurā red mottled sandstone remains; it is dateable to the 2nd century CE. Unlike the majority of *stambha* or pillar *yakṣī/yoṣitā* figures, she is shown standing in *sambhanga*, i.e. balanced on her feet, not in movement or activity, with a dwarf near her right foot. There is an inscription on the pedestal that tells us that this was the *pratimā* or sculpture of *kāmukī ibhaye*, established by Sirsu (?) for the pleasure of the deity (lit. not to the dislike of the deity, *priyata bhagava mahatr*; Falk 2014, 13–17). The operative word here is *kāmukī*, a desirous (for sexual or other material objects such as wealth), lustful or libidinous woman (Pāṇini, *Astadhyayi* 4–1, 42).[20] She is an *ibhī*, literary meaning an elephant mare, a woman of the *hastinï* type that *Kāmaśāstriya* literature, as part of its obsession for classifying the human race according to region, desirability, body type and the like, has established as one of the categories (doe, horse and elephant) to classify women. This inscription is significant in shifting these females forms on the pillars at Mathurā from the fecundity explanation 'model' to the discourse of pleasure. It also establishes that the 'cultured' society of the time was comfortable enough with the idea of desire, amour and the archetypes set out in the *Kāmaśāstriya* concept of lustful women, to not only sculpt them onto presumably religious buildings but also offer them for the pleasure of gods. Interventions regarding the identity of figures such as the one on the railing pillars seem significant in this context. Doris Meth Srinivasan has suggested that the Didarganj *yaksi* is not a divine/semi-divine figure but rather a *gaṇikā*, a courtesan par excellence or deluxe (Srinivasan 2005). In another publication, I too have suggested a close connection between eroticism and women (Bawa 2013, 23, 32–40).

An inscription from Jogimara caves dated to 1st century CE informs us as follows: 'The temple servant (*Devadāsi*) Sutanukā by name (the copyist) Devadinā by name the Balanaseya (native from Banares) loved her'. There are debates about the exact social-economic identities of the figures (Banerji-Sastri 1923, 278, 280). Bloch offers the most plausible interpretation of Devadinā to be a sculptor, a *rūpa dakha*. If we accept Bloch's interpretation, then this evidence of a *devadāsi* or a temple 'prostitute' being associated with a sculptor is significant and she may have been his model (Bloch 1903–1904, 128–130).[21] This should be read in conjunction with another inscription from the Sitabenga caves at Jogimara that provides further context: '... poets venerable by nature kindle the heart ... at the spring festival of the full moon, when frolic and music abound, tie around their neck thick garlands of jasmine' (Gupta 1980, 197–198).[22] The Sitabenga cave has a large semi-circular opening about 1.8 m high with a vaulted roof, which, according to S.P. Gupta, was perhaps a gathering place for festive occasions. Mirashi agrees with this premise, adding that it is credible that the *nāgaraka* engaged in pleasurable activities in the company of courtesans—*devadāsis* (Mirashi 1982, 17–32)—in caves and gardens just outside the town (such as the Puśpakarandika *udyāna* mentioned in the *Mṛcchakaṭikā*).

The last piece of contextual evidence comes from a terracotta example of a *dampati-mithuna* from northern India, belonging to the later Gupta period. The male is seated cross-legged, while the female is in half-*bhadrāsana*. Her right arm is extended and rests at the elbow on the knee of the male. Her left hand is placed on the calf of her folded leg. The male's left arm is folded with the elbow resting on the shoulder of his partner and his other hand is placed on the thigh. The depiction of this intimate, warm scene is amplified by the word *ramana*, meaning sensual enjoyment, which is incised in Gupta Brahmi characters at the lower left of the piece.

Mathurā not only provides a visual world of pleasurable activities but also gives context to the production of such activities by craftsmen and artists who catered to the tastes of the sophisticated urban men and women depicted in the literary and visual cultures; which alludes to the demand for flowers and garlands, perfumes and unguents, jewellery, personal grooming and, most of all, entertainment. It is a world not only of the mendicants and the householders but also of *artha*, economic activities that emerge not only from the texts but also inscriptions. This is a world populated by actors, *śailalaka,*[23] and dancers or *naṭakas* (Kumar 2019, 144), goldsmiths or *hairanyaka* or *soavanika, suvarnakāra* (Kumar 2019, 127, 129), perfumers or *gandhikas,*[24] dyers,[25] garland makers or *malakara,* barbers or *nāpita*[26] and jewellers. Significantly, the Sarasvati image inscription from

Kankali Tila was donated by Ranganarttano, a person related to the theatre (Kumar 2019, 120).[27]

There is thus a confluence of the consumers of pleasure, the *nāgaraka* and others, and the producers of pleasures, the craftsmen, entertainers and the like, as seen from the sculptural and inscriptional evidence. The inscriptions also give detail of workers and craftsmen (*sippīs, śilpīs*) who perform the services that underlie 'pleasure' for the *nāgaraka*, the sophisticate. Services that no doubt were handsomely paid for enabling these workers to indulge in socially and religiously accepted donative practices (Salomon 1989).

One can view the Mathurā panels, especially the Maholi–Vasantsena double-sided panel, and also consider other *yakṣī/yośitā* depictions in light of the inscription published by Harry Falk discussed above along with Srinivasan's contention regarding the Didarganj *yakṣī*. This would suggest that the discourse of beauty has an important role in constructing pleasure for the viewer; especially when the object of pleasure is a socio-culturally and erotically available figure of a sophisticated *gaṇikā*. The courtesan along with the *nāgaraka* forms a dyad, in which the female is designed for the pleasure of the *nāgaraka*. The discourse is generally silent on her 'pleasure'.

ALLURING ART AND ARCHITECTURE

Though the art and architecture of the period available till now was created largely in a religious context of shrines and monasteries, or *caityas* and viharas, it still engages with the discourse of pleasure either in endorsing or condemning it. In the textual tradition, the Sanskrit terms *prassana, abhiprassana* and *saāvega* (Schopen 2007, 309) valorise the beautiful as it 'pleases' not just the senses but also the more supra-mundane being. Thus, aesthetics, as manifested in literary, architectural and artistic beauty as emerging from contemporary sources, elicits and attracts patronage and attention not just of men and women but also of gods. Such a scenario perhaps calls for a redefining of the relationship between *kāma, artha* and *dharma*, where *kāma* functions as a catalyst for *artha* and *dharma*.

One level of the *nagara–vihara* dichotomy is where the sheer architectural grandeur of the monastery or vihara stands on its own rather than in relation to any piety and renunciation within. Gregory Schopen has drawn attention to the many examples cited in the canonical early *Mulasarvastivadin Vinaya* text, a Buddhist monastic code, where merchant-patrons are drawn to *adbhuta* as in *bhavya*, the wonderous, abundant beauty of a particular monastery (Schopen 2007, 304, 309). He says, 'Narratively, the merchants can only be responding to the beauty and elaborate character of the monastery, not to what the monks are or do' (308).

The other benchmark of beauty highlighted is the bucolic pastoral beauty, the aesthetic artifice of the 'park', the well-maintained microcosm of the *araṇyaka-nagara* (forest-polis), which are part of the contemporary worldview. Efforts made by monks to maintain parks, beautiful gardens and orchards of monastic establishments are valorised (Schopen 2007, 309), embellishing these with paintings on walls and on cloth. A monastery with 'lofty gateways and ornamented with open galleries on the roof' is explicitly said to 'captivate both the heart and the eye' (309). As a consequence, when 'merchants from the North Country' see this beautiful monastery and discover its monks have left, they promptly re-endow it on an even more lavish scale (307). Architectural beauty is not only a source of aesthetic pleasure but also ensures continuing patronage.

A condemnatory voice is also found in Buddhist sources, where lofty and luxurious buildings are considered as signs of lofty conceit that indicate impermanence, revealing the dialectic between the aesthetic beauty of the lofty architectural structure and the ephemerality of edifices, secular and monastic. 'At that time the Licchavis of Vaisali built houses with six or seven upper chambers. As the Licchavis built their houses, so too did they build *vihāras* .... As a consequence, because of their great height … they fell apart' (Schopen 2007, 306). Other textual sources (as seen in the discussion below, refer to the seven *prakoṣṭhas* in *Mṛcchakaṭikā*) are replete with references to seven-storeyed structures.

Beauty as a device to attract and entice towards the path of *dharma* is alluded to in Aśvaghoṣas *Saundarananda*. References to the beauty of Sundarī and her idealised relationship with Nanda are seen as a device for the ultimate *telos* of disseminating non-attachment to disenchant Nanda and consequently others from women and other worldly desires. Aśvaghoṣa, in his defence of the beauty of his poem, also says how things that give pleasure such as *kāvya* can entice even the recalcitrant:

> This poem, dealing thus with the subject of salvation, has been written in the *Kāvya* style, not to give pleasure, but ... with the intention of capturing the hearers devoted to other things. For, that I have handled other subjects in it besides Salvation … in accordance with the laws of *Kāvya* poetry to make it palatable, as sweet is put into a bitter medicine.... Since I saw mankind given over to the pleasures of the objects of the senses and averse from Salvation. (*Saundarananda* XVIII.63–64)[28]

The Indian visual and literary traditions—both religious and secular—are saturated with thick and sensuous descriptions of such pleasurable spaces.

By the time we come to the 5th century, aesthetic pleasure, *saundarya* is cited as a goal in itself, for example in the poetics underlying the Sanskrit *kāvya* of Kālidāsa that exalts all that is beautiful in the world (Smith 2010). This is further explicated upon by Mammaṭa in *Kāvyaprakāśa*, a later text on poetics that says, 'A creation that is free from the constraints of nature's laws, consisting entirely of pleasure, totally independent'. The emphasis on the *viewerly* pleasure for its own sake can also be seen in Gupta art, which focuses on the beauty, rather than didacticism and narrativity, that marked the art of Mathurā during the post-Mauryan period. The paeans to beauty, of nature and human and divine beings become progressively more lyrical in the subsequent period, both in Kālidāsa's poetry and in Gupta art (for example, in *Kumārasaṃbhava*, Pārvatī's physical allure is described in detail, 1.31–39).[29] This is the world of *kāma*, and *Kumārasaṃbhava* and *Raghuvamśa* are replete with references to Kāmadeva and his work of creating an environment fit for love and dalliance.[30] In fact, the consummation of love marks the culmination of the poems of Kālidāsa: in *Raghuvamśa*, after Rāma and Sitā return to Ayodhya, Śiva and Pārvatī's amorous love play (*ragavanprakshya*) on the marital bed (*Kumārasaṃbhava*, 8.81–91) and the memory of love (*sambhogānte*) between the *yakṣa* and his *yakṣī* in *Meghadūta* (*Uttaramegha* 36).

PHYSICAL AND CULTURAL CONTEXTS OF VISUALLY REPRESENTED PLEASURE

Dramas, poems and even prescriptive texts give us information about the physical and cultural contexts in which humans and other beings partook of pleasure. The plan of the architecture seen on the pillar of pleasure approximates the description given by the awestruck Maitrerya (the *vidūṣaka*) in the fourth act (*chaurtha ank*) of Sudraka's play *Mṛcchakaṭikā* of the *veśavāsa* or the courtesan's mansion, which he describes at length. The gateway, stairs, windows, arches, pavilions, railings and the dramatis personae all find a reflection in the textual description provided by the play, especially in the description of the seven *prakoṣṭhas*.

The first element that strikes Maitreya is the *toraṇa* and its *stambha* (gateway, pillar) as he wondrously describes its decoration and splendour: 'It is raised on top to a great height.... It is adorned with string of a garland of jasmine flowers … it is decked with a lofty arch of ivory. It is decorated with a number of auspicious banners (*saubhāgya patākā*)' (Figure 2.16) (*Mṛcchakaṭikā*, 157). As he steps into the first quadrangle (*imaṃ prathamaṃ prakoṣṭhaṃ*[31] *praviśatvāryaḥ*), he sees rows of balconies resembling beautiful objects like flowers and jewels, with golden stairs (*sopāna*) and crystal windows (*saphitakavatayana*). *Dvārika* or gatekeepers guard the entrance; in this case, they are sleeping at ease, enjoying sleep as is enjoyed by Brahmins (who presumably do not have a care in the world). He passes two more *prakoṣṭhas* to enter the fourth (161), where dance and music by young maidens are the focus. Cymbals, bamboo-pipes and lutes accompany courtesan girls (*dārikā*) learning songs and dances that are full of *śṛṅgāra* (rasa)[32] (*Mṛcchakaṭikā*, 161).

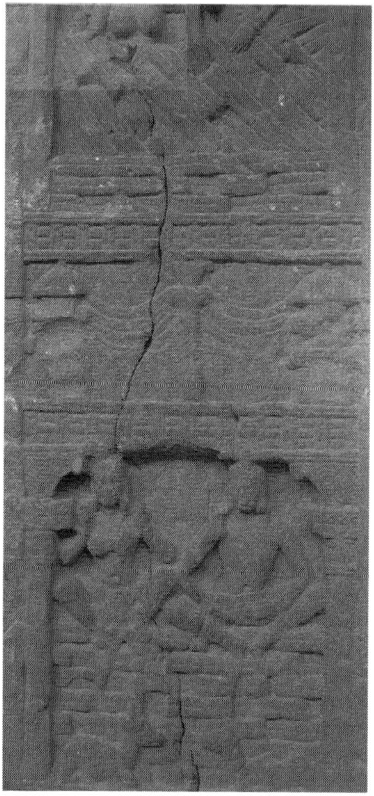

Figure 2.16: Seated Couple with Two Deer in Front, Banners or *Patākās* Hanging on the Panel Above, Railing Pillar, 2nd Century CE, Mathurā Museum

The fifth quarter caters to alimentary appetites where choicest dishes are prepared. The sixth *prakoṣṭha* (165), has architectural arches, *karmatorani*, made and embellished with precious metals and stones. Significantly, the business of the prostitutes' quarter takes place here. The narrator describes the pleasures of the senses—alimentary, visual, emotional and behavioural—that are on offer.

> Betel rolls with camphor (*sakarpura tambulam*) are being offered to the lovers of the courtesans, *kāmukana*; side glances are being cast; laughter is going on; and wine (*madirā*) is incessantly drunk with sounds of merriment. Here are drinking these men-servants, these maid servants, *chetas* and *chetikās* and also these men who have forsaken their children, wives and property, and left (to themselves) by courtesans who have drunk from liquor cups. (Mrcch. 165)

The next two courtyards are reserved for an aviary and a splendorous garden, a fitting setting for Vasantasenā, the chief courtesan. The *vidūṣaka*, partly envious and partly disapproving, registers physical and moral judgments for these splendours.

The scenes on the pillar of pleasure also find visual correlation with terracotta plaques found from all over northern India, dateable to the 1st BCE to the 2nd century CE. These show amorous couples in various postures and activities (Bawa 2013, 218–222). One such scene is of a couple seated on a couch in an arboreal setting, watching a dance being performed by women accompanied by musicians, such as the one seen in panel C of the Mathurā pillar discussed above. These do not have the elaborate setting of the palatial seven-storeyed structure but do visually construct an intimate ambience imbued with enjoyment, set in a garden or *udyāna* (see Figure 2.5).

Probably the largest range of *mithuna* depictions is of couples seated and standing without being associated with a sacred object within a composition, in representations carved on the railing pillars of religious structures. Some of these may be delineated as slightly amorous pairs, meant both for ornamentation and for highlighting physical intimacy as a pleasure. The loci or sites for *kāma* are also the various congregational occasions in form of festivals and gardens discussed in the previous chapter: the *madanotsavas, vasantotsavas, kāmaotsavas, kāma udayanas*. In the early medieval period, the splendours of the court are visually represented in the sculptural bands on the base of temple structures, which has been discussed by Parul Pandya Dhar in Chapter 4 of this book.

IDEATIONAL CONTEXTS

In Indian aesthetic tradition, the arts should be *sadrishay* and *sahridayam*, i.e., have verisimilitude and empathy with the viewer/audience. Thus, the entire gamut of human and divine lived experience, *laukik* and *alaukik*, is to be represented, in didactic guise or otherwise. In a social order that seems very comfortable with the idea of *kāma*, its representation in art is to be expected in sculptures, plays and poetry and in dance and music.

Behind the man–woman pairing, a concept translated into art as *mithuna*, was the belief that *kāma*, or sensual desire,[33] is all-pervasive and as such influences the entire world. While the canonical texts sought to control and channel this powerful force, preferably to overcome *kāma*, it suggested that through the renunciation of desire (Buddha and the Jina), or by following Śiva's path of a householder, who with Pārvatī transcends *kāma* through *dāmapatya* or married bliss, *moksa* or *nirvana* becomes achievable (Bawa 2013, 228).

Ideationally, pleasure is located within the sphere of *kāma*, which constitutes one realm of the *trivarga* that represents three major domains of human activities and pursuits that are beneficial to persons who perform them, i.e., *dharma, artha* and *kāma*. According to Olivelle, these three are 'similar' in that they all are 'beneficial' and conducive to a person's happiness (*prīti*) (Olivelle 2019, 381).

Nonetheless, while striving for all three, says Manu, if *artha* or *kāma* are in conflict with *dharma*, one should give up the former two. In spite of the inherent valorisation of *kāma* and *artha*, even the non-*dharmaśāstriya* traditions, such as those in the *Kāmasūtra* and *Arthaśastra,* regard *dharma* as the highest of all goals (Olivelle 2019, 384). *Kāma* and *artha*, pleasure, knowledge and gain, should be pursued when young, and *dharma* and *moksha* when one grows old (384). Youth is the time for *kāma*, and this is translated in visual terms where youth and beauty are celebrated in the sculptured forms of men and women. A good life can be achieved through a balance of all three. It is through theorisation and incorporation of the *trivarga* scheme that *kāma* is contained within a communitarian and religio-philosophical realm.

Vasantasenā performs the daily ritual of worshipping the gods even as she pursues her profession as a prostitute of the first quality (*Mṛcchakaṭikā*, 67). Similarly her love interest Cārudatta, a virtuous and married Brahmin householder gambles and dallies with prostitutes but regards daily meditation and prayer to the gods as an inviolable duty (25). Other characters are also shown to perform their daily rituals centred on worship such as Viṣṇunāga, a lover of courtesans, who objects when one of them kicks his head in love-play. His head is a symbol of 'high status … where his mother bound the *śikhandaka* (ritual top knot) with careful hands … and on which *brāhmanas* sprinkled water ...' (Pāda, 108, verse 9).

The pursuit of *kāma* is idealised though the urban sophisticate *nāgaraka*, who is the protagonist of literature such as the *Mṛcchakaṭikā*, *Caṭuṛbḥāṇī*, *Malatimādhava* and *Kuttanimatta*. The entire fourth *adhyāya* or chapter of the first book of the *Kāmasūtra* is devoted to *nāgarakavṛtti* (*Kāmasūtra*, 1.4, 5–26), which is the mode of life, behaviour, moral code, style or movement of the *nāgaraka*. The daily routine prescribed for him involves leisure activities that ultimately lead to the fulfilment of intellectual and physical desires, the physical manifesting in sculptural evidence and the intellectual in textual.[34]

Caturbhāṇī, discussed later in this book, valorises the sensual and intellectual, the material and the mundane realms:

> Between the two, the present and the future, the present is superior .... Here men enjoy the pleasures of discussing ... means for pacifying women after a love quarrel.... These bashful and sweet words [of women] ... half uttered due to liquor, how can we hear these in heaven which knows no drinking? *Dhūrtavitasamvāda*

Mathurā is also the centre of multi-religious efflorescence where donations are made by and to Buddhist and Jaina mendicants and establishments. It is a city inhabited by *bhikṣu, sakyabhikṣu, vācaka* (preacher), *ṣisya* (pupil), *antevasin*, *savaka* (lay hearer), *samanasavikā* (female lay hearer), *śramana* (ascetic), *devakulika* and the like (LL 63, 75, 93).

The pillars and panels discussed above at Mathurā demonstrate a close relationship between beauty, sex, gender, power and asceticism. The *gaṇikā* and the *yoṣitā* represent the ultimate lure that warns the ascetic not to wander away from the renunciatory path. These are reflected in the *Theragāthā*, Psalms of the Monks. The text contains two significant verses attributed to *thera* Nāgasumala and *thera* Sundarasamudda. Nāgasumala addresses a prostitute: 'Ornamented, well dressed, wearing a garland, anointed with sandal, in the middle of the road, a dancing girl dances to music ... disgust was established' (*Theragāthā* 1969, 32). Sundarasamudda is even more explicit and says the following:

> Ornamented, well dressed, carrying a garland, adorned with her feet reddened with *lac*, having put on slippers, a courtesan.... Abide in my teachings, enjoy human sensual pleasures; I shall give you wealth.... When we are both old, supported by sticks, we shall both go forth .... *And when I saw the courtesan beseeching me with cupped hands, ornamented, like a snare of death spread out*. (*Theragāthā* 1969, 48)[35]

This makes it clear that a prostitute is like a snare that binds and tempts at the same time. The verses above centre on the omnipresent danger presented by the physical charms of a female prostitute, inviting the male ascetic to eschew the path of enlightenment; the feminine *gaṇikā* figure in a sculptural panel personified temptation in its totality or female-induced enticement against which all followers of the faith, especially men, had to brace themselves. Courtesans tempt the nuns saying, 'What are you almswomen doing with the holy life? Why not now enjoy the pleasures of the senses and join the holy life when you are old' (cf. Horner 1999, 231).

In the religious discourse, whether Buddhist or Brahmanical, there is an ambivalence towards pleasure and beauty, a tension between asceticism and pleasures associated with lived reality. In addition, the contexts of pleasures for males and females are distinct and deeply gendered given that the female body is the object of pleasure rather than controller of her own pleasure; the pleasure described through prescription or proscription is that of the male. The discourse of female pleasure is difficult to extract, given the relative silence in most sources; while when the monastic *Thera* and *Theri-gāthā* describe female domains of pleasure such as adorning the body and the self and revelling in one's youthfulness, the description is in the context of criticism or in terms of the impermanence of such pleasures. The gendered nature of the discourse of pleasure is predicated on who produces, provides patronage for and finally consumes sculptures and texts. The discourse of pleasure and beauty is constructed, patronised and consumed largely by men. Even when depicted through didactic or apotropaic devices, the idealisation of the female body takes place for this purpose.[36]

In the art of Mathurā during the early centuries of the Common Era, beauty and pleasure are deployed as both aesthetic as well as didactic tool. If there is one city that may be associated with 'pleasure' in art, not only that of looking at and enjoying art but also witnessing the themes in the depictions, then that is Mathurā. Here, *kāma, artha* and *dharma*, contiguous and sometimes contesting worldviews, are reconciled; devotion and religious duty are resolved with partaking of desires and beauty in the visual discourse. The discourse of beauty and pleasure can also be recovered from various literary genres: directly and explicitly from *kāma shatras* and obliquely or through criticism from religious texts, *kāvya* and epigraphic sources.

The visual and literary sources dwell on the imagined pleasures of beauty if only for the purpose of attracting attention and obtaining patronage. The need to be aesthetically attractive and pleasurable underlies the architectural design and artistic depictions on pillars, *toraṇas* and architraves created on *stupas* and *vihāras*.

Indirectly, through this art, there appears to be a certain legitimisation of the pursuit of production and consumption of objects and spaces for pleasure. This legitimisation extends consequently from those who were involved in providing pleasure to those who were the purveyors of sexual pleasure or otherwise were allowed to be engaged in the visual, religious and ritual life of the city. These include, among others, the *vēśyās* or prostitutes, actors, performers, dancers, perfumers and the like.

In the narratives of the discourse of pleasure, the setting or milieu seen in the reliefs of couples, young women, is urban or suburban with the social context, whether pertaining to the *nāgaraka* or to the *vēśyā* quarters. is one of plenty, of opulence, complete with all accruements to heighten the experience of sense pleasures. This milieu points to sophisticated pleasure that has been socially and intellectually cultivated by the connoisseurs of fine things. This is important for understanding the operations and *situs* of the discourse of pleasure. The world of *kāma* is not a subterranean world or even a marginalised one. The congregational nature of this world seems to suggest that it is very much on the surface. The world of *kāma* is, therefore, not hidden but celebrated in art and architecture.

Beauty, emotion and pleasure are not merely sublimated in the art of Mathurā or were pushed to the periphery as mere *alamkara* or auspicious symbols but celebrated and central to the underlying *rasion d'etre* for the viewer-oriented art.

NOTES

1. Games and gatherings also seem to be depicted in certain sculptures, for example in reliefs from Bhārut and Rajghat.
2. *Atheka mâcchaditthika yakkhini aceta hutva dve hatthe pasretva jihvam ninnametva dasabalassa purato atthasi* (Kopp 1966, 329).
3. The same story is related also in the Bhatsajya vastu section of the Gilgit Manuscripts, with the difference that this naked goddess of Mathurā is called *devata* instead of *yakkhini* (see Dutt 1984, 14–15).
4. There is no exact term in Sanskrit for pleasure alone; *sukha*, *vishoka* and *kāma* are terms that may be used to describe degrees of happiness and pleasure. *Kāma* is (MWSE, 271) wish, longing, desire and pleasure, especially sensual pleasure, love and enjoyment. *Sukha* relates more to happiness that is linked with being easy, comfortable and pleasant. See the Introduction.
5. 'In later literature these females are sometimes styled as *Alasà Kanyà* whose special feature was the stretching of youthful limbs specially by throwing the arms above the head in a languid manner' (Agarwala 1963, 28).
6. According to Sonia Rhie Quintanilla, it might be a depiction of the Buddhist version of the story of King Māndhāta

   > set up in front of a Buddhist establishment a reminding the practitioners to overcome desires for worldly and erotic pleasure and extolling monastic life as the ideal. At the same time, the carvings on the *kāmaloka* pillar fulfill the Indian propensity for depicting dance scenes and amorous encounters celebrating life and abundance on the exterior of sacred monuments. (Quintanilla 2007, 60)

7. *Kūṭāgāra* is basically an apartment on the top of a house (*kūṭāgāraiśca saṃpūrṇāmi-ndrasyevāmarāvatīm*) (Rām.1.5.15). It is a building with a peaked roof or pinnacles, possibly gabled, or with an upper storey. (upari Aśvaghoṣa places Sundarī on the palace roof when she is alone and abandoned: 'Surrounded by those women *on the palace roof th*at slender beauty, wasted with anxiety, seemed like [cintātanuḥ sā sutanur babhāse] the crescent moon in an autumn cloud encircled by lightning flashes') (6.37); (*kūṭāgāra* dhaja has a flag on the summit; kutagara sālā refers to a pavilion (see description of *Maṇḍalamāḷa* at DA. I, 43) Vin. III, 15, 68, 87; IV, 75; D. I, 150; S. II, 103 = V. 218; IV, 186.
8. *Mithuna*, round plaque form Bhita, Indian Museum Calcutta, AAA/1650–74; Dhavalikar (1977, 29, 35).
9. *Mithuna* literally means paired, forming a pair; pairing, copulation, a pair or a couple, also twins. It can also signify the other part, complement or companion of anything (MWSE, 816).
10. The well known piece is found from Kankali Tila Lucknow Museum J.533; Seema Bawa (2013, 23); *Indian Journal of Archaeology* 4, no. 4 (October 2019–January 2020): 62–1167; Agarwala (1963, 32–33).
11. Many such pillars with couples have been found from different sites at Mathurā, including Kankali Tila, Rangeshwar Well, Isapur, Mogarra Police Station and the like.
12. The Museum labels it as the *veni prasadhan* scene from the *Saundarananda*.
13. Sankisa, Etah Dist., red sandstone, 2nd century AD, height: 35.5 × 18.5 cm. Indian Museum Acc. No. A 24250/Sa. 2A.S.B/ 5173. Architectural piece with tenons at the bottom and top to secure it.
14. Cowell 1990, i.42, 44, 128, 133, 137; ii.13, 23, 79, 81, 89, 81, and others speak of monks who are tempted and/or weak-willed.
15. For further discussion, see Bawa (2013, 309–336).
16. Women are classified according to the stages of youth: through dresses, posture, appearance of the limbs as well as [inner] qualities. It is clear from the description of these four stages that the body and its ornamentation are of primary importance when it comes to imagining the female as a woman, especially as a public, or *bāhya* (lit. outside), woman.
17. It measures 104 cm in height and is 76 cm in width and has been dated to the Kuṣāṇa era, 2nd century AD. It has often been published and is housed in the National Museum (Acc. No. 2800).
18. The *ninda stuti* of Kamadeva called *Kamachatura*, set in Raga Lathangi, composed by Serfoji Maharaj, the Maratha ruler of Thanjavur, around the late 18th century. This is a condemnation of Kamadeva by Śiva and is still performed in the *Bharatnatyam* dance tradition.
19. In *Sundarakāṇḍa*, Hanumān sees the flying Puṣpaka palace where the mechanical birds have their wings sportively (salīlam) extended as if they were accomplices of Kāma (5.6.13); in *Kumārasaṃbhava*, Kāma's bow with its five flower arrows that aim at lovers has its ends beautifully curving (*cāruśṛṅgam*) (2.64), beautiful, fine feathers (*cāru patre*) … bāṇe (3.27); in 4.14, the mango flower and Kāma and his wife Rati are mentioned. There

are mentions of Śiva and Pārvatī and Kāma's ploy is explored in Sarga 3, resulting in Kāma being burned to ashes and Śiva leaving in Sarga 5.

20. Also, *Mrchh* as mistress; in the *Devi Bhagvata Purana* translated by Swami Vijnananda, Chapter 30, verse 53–102, the Devi is called Kamuki in the region of Gandha Madana, the fabled mountain from where Hanuman carried the Sanjivini plant.
21. That a *devadàsì* during the era in question meant a temple prostitute is not clear. The *Arthaúàstra* has the first identifiable reference to a *devadàsì*, where it prescribes that old devadàsìs who have ceased to attend temples for service, mothers of prostitutes, mendicants or ascetic women should be employed to cut wool, fibers, cotton, hemp, panicle and flax. *urnavalkakarpa satulasanaksaumani ca vidhavanyanga kanya pravrajitandandapratikarinibhi rupajivatrkabhirvrdhharajada sibhir vyauparatopasthanadevadàsìbhis ca kartayet* (AS, 2.32.2). There is a mention of a *veshyà* dancing for Śiva in the temple in *Meghadūta* (verse 34–35) but the first connection between prostitution and the temple is found in only early medieval literature.
22. Gupta (1980, 197–198); *adipayanti hådyaý. Svabhāva guru kavayo ae ratayam … dūle vasantìya. Hasavanabhūte. Kadusphataý evaý alaòg.*
23. *Epigraphia Indica Vol X*, 1909–10, LL. 85.
24. *Epigraphia Indica Vol X*, 1909–10, LL. 32. 68,76.
25. *Epigraphia Indica Vol XXXII*, p. 2110.
26. Mathurā inscriptions, MI. 111.
27. Smith (2010, 55); *Indian Journal of Archaeology* 4, no. 4 (October 2019–January 2020): 62–1167.
28. *Saundarananda*. XVIII.63–64, *prayenalokya lokaý viûayaratiparaý mokûàtpratihataý kàvyavyajen tatåvam kathitamih mayàmokûaá paramiti, tadbudcva samikaý yatradavahitamito yahyaýna lalitaý pamúubhyo dhatujebhyo niyatamupakaraý camikàramiti.* XVIII.64.
29. Kale (1981); *Kumārasaṃbhava*, Pārvatī (1.39) 'bore three beautiful folds at her waist'; 'her hands with their beautiful nails' (1.42).
30. *Kumārasaṃbhava*; Kāma's bow has its ends beautifully curving (2.64), his arrow has beautiful, fine, feathers (3.27); in 4.14 the mango flower Kāma used to use is said by his widowed wife Rati to have a 'beautiful red and green stem'; Śiva sees Kāma with 'his lovely bow drawn right back to form a circle' (3.70); just as Kāmadeva is about to release his arrow (3.68).
31. *prakoṣṭha:* a court in a house, a quadrangle or square (surrounded by buildings); इमं प्रथमं प्रकोष्ठं प्रविशत्वार्यः *Mrcch*, 151.
32. *Rasas* recommended for the consumption of men and women are different in the normative aesthetic tradition. It is assumed that men with their higher mental faculties are capable of enjoying the more serious *rasas*. However, women can enjoy the *hāsya-rasa*. The *Nāṭyaśāstra* XXVII.61 says that 'Young people are pleased to see (the presentation of) love, the learned a reference to some (religious and philosophical) doctrine, the seekers after money to the topics of wealth, and the passionless the topics of liberation. Heroic persons are always pleased in the Odious and the Terrible Sentiments, personal combats

and battles, and the old people in Purānic legends, and tales of virtue. And common women, children and uncultured persons, *mūrkha*, are always delighted with the Comic Sentiment and remarkable costumes and make-up'. Women (and children) are classified as a gender with other uncultured people. Bawa (2013).

33. For Màra as Kāma and as such an epitome of Evil, see Bawa (2013, 343–356).
34. Discussions around 'sophisticated' subjects such as poetry and art as hallmarks of social and cultural superiority have continued over millennia, from the salons of Paris to the art soirées of socialites today accompanied as they are by wine and hors d'oeuvres. The idyllic and idealised life of a *nāgaraka* is described in the *Kāmasūtra*. In the morning and afternoon, the *nāgaraka* eats and after eating, passes the time by teaching parrots and mynahs to speak, goes to quail fights and cock fights, engages in various arts and games *kalakrida* … goes to *goshthi* and *sabhas*, salons with amusing and intellectually stimulating companions, the *viṭa* and vidūṣaka, to amuse himself. Picnics, *udayanagamana*, may be described in the same way where they enjoy daytime events and theatrical spectacles. In the evening, there is music and dancing, *sangita* … await, *praktisksha*, the women, *abhisarikas*, who are slipping for a rendezvous. Though visually it is the female counterparts that are more aptly shown performing this routine, in the railing sculptures that is reflected in art *kāmaloka* scenes (with his *abhisarikā*/ love-interest). Then he goes to visit the *vesya's* prostitute's house, where he again engages in *buddhishila* discussions on *kavya* and *kala*, has wine (commentary calls it sura) made of honey, fruits, cloves, intoxicants and aphrodisiacal food (1.4.20). He consorts with the *gaṇikā* if he has the money and is not married. He gets up in the morning, relieves himself … bathes every day, gets himself shaved every fourth day … and thus places himself, as per Desmond, '…to be a subject in the kāmasūtra means being a certain kind of object in the world'. The 64 arts include music skills, techniques for coiffing, decorating and ornamenting the body, skills in painting, dancing and the like and suggest a material, physical culture replete with objects of pleasure: jewels, flowers, precious metals, palaces and pleasure gardens. Desmond (2011, 19).
35. *Alamkata suvàsanà màladhàrì vibhūûità alaþþakatapàdà padukarugha vibhusita vesika; pàdukà oruhitvana purab panjatikata sa mam sanhena muduna mhitapubbam abhasatha; yuvasi tvam pabbajitotittahi mama sasane, bhunja manusake kame, aham va te haram aham; yada jinna bhavissama ubho dandaparayana, ubho po pabbajissama, ubhayattha kataggaho; tan ca disvana yacantim vesikam panjalikatam alamkatam suvasanam maccupasam va odditam* (Theragatha 1966, 459–465).
36. *Kāmasutra*, xlix. According to Yashodara, the base of *kāma* is the woman, and the subsidiary limbs are garlands and such things. *Kāma* is pleasure, and its limbs are jewellery, perfumed oils and garlands; as well as forest groves, roof-top gardens, the playing of lutes and wine; its base is women—unrestrained, beautiful, young, amorous, flirtatious, clever at flattery, drawing to themselves the minds and hearts of men.

REFERENCES

Agarwala, P.K. 'The Motif of Lovers Apology in Early Indian Sculpture'. *Proceedings of Indian History Congress* 53 (1992): 649–659.

Agarwala, V.S. *Catalogue of the Mathura Museum: Architectural Pieces*, Varanasi: Prithvi Prakashan. 1963.

———. *Mathura Museum Handbook*. Allahabad: Superintendent Printing and Stationery. 1939.

Banerji-Sastri, A.P. 'The Jogimara Cave Inscription'. *Journal of Bhandarkar Oriental Research Society* 9, no. 3–4 (1923): 273–293.

Bawa Seema. *Gods, Men and Women: Gender and Sexuality in Early Indian Art*. Delhi: D.K. Printworld. 2013.

Buddhacarita. Edited and translated by E.J. Johnston. New Delhi: Motilal Banarsidass. 1972.

Carter, Martha C. 'Dionysian Aspects of Kushana Art'. *Ars Orientalis* 7: 121–146. 1968.

Chaturbhani. Edited and translated by Moti Chandra and V.S. Agarwala. Bombay: Hindi Granth Ratnagar Karyalaya Pvt. Ltd. 1960.

Cowell, E.B. and R.A. Neill, eds. *Divyàvadàna*. Cambridge: Cambridge University Press. 1886.

Cowell, E.D., ed. *The Jātaka or Stories of Buddha's Former Births, Six Volumes*. Delhi: Motilal Banarsidass. 1990.

Desai, Devnagana. *Erotic Art of India: A Socio-Cultural Study*. New Delhi: Tata McGraw Hill. 1985.

Desmond, Laura. 'The Pleasure is Mine: The Changing Subject of Erotic Science'. *Journal of Indian Philosophy* 39, no. 1 (2011): 15–39.

Devi Bhagvata Purana. Translated by Swami Vijnananda. Allahabad: Allahabad Pannini Office. 1922.

Dhavalikar, M.K. *Masterpieces of Indian Terracotta*. Bombay: D.B. Taraporevala. 1977.

Dutt, Nalinaksha, ed. *Gilgit Manuscripts in IV Volumes*. New Delhi: Sri. Satguru Publications. 1984.

Falk, Harry. 'An Inscribed Statue of a Lustful Woman from Mathura'. *Indo Asiatsche Zeitschrift* 18 (2014): 13–17.

Falk, Harry. 'Making Wine in Gandhara under Buddhist Monastic Supervision'. *Berlin, Bulletin of Asia Institute. Essays in Honour of Richard Salomon's 65th Birthday*, New Series/Volume 23 (2009): 65–77.

Gupta, S.P. *Roots of Indian Art*. New Delhi: B.R. Publications Corp. 1980.

Horner, I.B. *Women Under Primitive Buddhism*. New Delhi: Motilal Banarsidass. 1999.

Janert, K.L. and Heinrich Luders. *Mathura Inscriptions*. Gottingen: Vandenhoeck & Ruprecht. 1961.

Kaul, Shonaleeka. *Imagining the Urban: Sanskrit and the City in Early India*. Ranikhet: Permanent Black. 2010.

Kopp, H., ed. *Manorathapurani*. London: Pali Text Society. 1966.

Kumar, Vijay. 'Catalogue of Antiquities of State Archaeological Museum, Lucknow, U.P. India Part I: Jain (from Kankali Tila, Mathura & other places of Mathura), Bauddha (from Mathura) & Gandhar Antiquities'. *Indian Journal of Archaeology* 4 (2019–2020), no. 4: 62–1167.

Kumārasaṃbhava. Edited and translated by M.R. Kale. New Delhi: Motilal Banarsidass. 1981.

Luders List (LL). Calcutta, *Epigraphia Indica Vol X, Appendix: A List of Brahmi Inscriptions from the Earliest Times to About AD 40*. 1–235. 1909–1910.

Mirashi, V.V. *Indological Research Papers*. Nagpur: Vidharbha Sansodhan Mandal. 1982.

Mṛcchakaṭikā. Translated by M.L. Kale. Delhi: Motilal Banarsidass. 1962.

Nàtyasàstra ascribed to Bharata Muni. Edited and translated by Manmohan Ghosh. Calcutta: Ganthalya Pvt. Ltd. 1967.

Olivelle, Patrick. 'From Trivarga to Puruṣārtha: A Chapter in Indian Moral Philosophy'. *Journal of the American Oriental Society* 139, no. 2 (2019): 381–396.

Prasad, Nandkishore, ed. *The Manorath Purani: Anguttaranikaya, Attakatha*. Nalanda: Navnalanda Mahavihar. 1976.

Poster, Amy. *4000 Years of Indian Earth*. New York: Brooklyn Museum of Art.

Quintanilla, Sonia Rhie. *History of Early Stone Sculpture at Mathura, Ca. 150 BCE–100 CE*. Leiden: Brill. 2007.

Ratan Muni, Shri. *Ràjaprasniyasūtra*. Beawar: Sri Agam Prakashan Samiti. 1982.

Roth, Gustav. 'The Women and Tree Motif'. *Journal of The Asiatic Society, Letters and Science* XXIII, no. 1 (1957): 91–116.

Salomon, Richard. 'Daily life in Ancient Mathurā'. In *Mathurā a Cultural Heritage*, edited by Doris Meth Srinivasan, 39–45. New Delhi: American Institute of Indian Studies. 1989.

Saundarananda of Asvaghosa. Edited by E.H. Johnsons. New Delhi: Motilal Banarsidass. 1975.

Schopen, Gregory. 'Art, Beauty and the Business of Running: A Buddhist Monastery in Early North West India'. In *On the Cusp of An Era: Art in the Pre Kushana World*, edited by Doris Meth Srinivasan, 287–318. Leiden: Brill. 2007.

Śivaramamurti, C. *Indian Sculpture*. Delhi: Allied Publishers. 1961.

Smith, David. 'Beauty and Words Relating to Beauty in the Rāmāyaṇa, the Kāvyas of Aśvaghoṣa, and Kālidāsa's Kumārasaṃbhava'. *The Journal of Hindu Studies* 3 (2010): 36–52.

Srinivasan, Doris Meth. 'The Mauryan Ga1⁄2ikå from Dïdårgañj (På¶aliputra)'. *East and West* (Rome) 55 (= Mau- rizio Taddei Commemoration Volume, eds. Pierfrancesco Callieri & Anna Filigenzi), 345–362. 2005

Strong, John S. 'Lay Life, Ordination, and Arhatship'. In *The Legend and Cult of Upagupta: Sanskrit Buddhism in North India and Southeast Asia*. New Jersey: Princeton University Press 1992. http://www.jstor.com/stable/j.ctv3hh47b.10 (accessed on 27 March 2021).

Theragāthā. Translated by K.R. Norman. London: Pali Text Society. 1969.

Vogel, J.P. *Catalogue of the Archaeological Museum at Mathura*. New Delhi: Indological Bookhouse. 1971.

3

SATIRE AND DESIRE IN CAṬUṚBHĀṆĪ

Ashish Abrol and Janica Paul

The stated dominant discourse of wisdom and otherworldliness of ancient classical culture is punctured by earthy and often very candid poetry and drama. Over time, Orientalist perspectives and chronological distance from early India have painted a picture of a sombre people steeped in arcane philosophical issues regarding the nature of death, *karma* and *dharma* or composing beautiful verses in ornate Sanskrit. However, early Indians seem to have been connoisseurs of laughter and fun, albeit that they framed rules for enjoyment, fixing a hierarchy of literature and performance to be enjoyed by each class or varna and gender. In fact, the Caṭuṛbhāṇī may be seen as incorporating a number of aspects that are a part of popular culture—the gossiping underclass, imposture whether in the lovelorn (lustlorn) elite masking their desire as 'higher' love or in the notion of the *dhongi* baba, the imposter in guise of a wise mendicant, all having been at the butt of folk tales, jokes, proverbs and idioms in popular culture. Thus, diverging from the beaten path and jaded taste of patron rulers, the Caṭuṛbhāṇī makes us enter the intimate life of humans through its humour, otherwise unparalleled in Sanskrit literature.

The Caṭuṛbhāṇī, a very early set of four dramatic texts, sets out some of the counter attitudes towards the sanctimonious hypocrisy of the ritually pure as well as the ruling elite that valorised a rigid code of righteous behaviour. This code focused on the stock idealisation of the self-restraint and reasoning of the male and the compliance of the dutiful wife (Bawa 2013, 23–27), while the deviant others were condemned as frivolous or unworthy. The Caṭuṛbhāṇī and similar narratives of the Gupta and early medieval period reveal a counter discourse that instead highlights hedonism and pleasure-seeking on the one hand and, on the other hand, exposes the hypocrisy of the pretentious elite or the renunciant through satire, witty dialogues and lampooning.

The roots of satire, according to Bḥaṛaṭā's *Ṇāṭyāśḥāṣṭṛā*, can be traced to Bḥaṛaṭā's sons, who after mastering the scripture of dramatic arts began ridiculing the universe with farces and performed a satire on the divine sages (Seigel 1989, 57). *Bḥāṇa* and *pṛāḥāṣaṇa* evolved from these divine farces. *Bḥāṇa* plays are monologues or one-act and social plays distinct from the better-known multi-act, solemn heroic and divinity-based plays. *Bḥāṇa* literature introduces its readers to a fresh form of entertainment in which dozens of characters play a part but only obliquely, because only a single actor occupies the stage for the entire performance (Clasquin 2001, 107, 116) who is 'at once a spokesman for the satirist … and also an object of satire, a satirist self satirized' (Clasquin 2001, 107).

> ēkā mūkḥēṇāīvā bḥāḥyaṇṭē ūkṭḷṃaṇṭāḥ kṛīyaātē apṛāvīṣcḥā apī pāṭṛīāvīṣḥēḥā yāṭṛā īṭībḥāṇā
> (A *bḥāṇa*, is one so called because the multitude of it's characters do not come on stage but are spoken by one mouth.)
> (trans. mine) (NS, XX.10)

Bḥaṛaṭā says,

> The bḥāṇa is to be acted by a single character and it is of two kinds: that (with one's) recounting of one's own feelings and that (with) describing someone else's acts. The Bḥāṇa, which is to include somebody else's words addressed to oneself, should be acted by means of replies in course of conversation with imaginary person (*ākāṣḥabḥāshītā*) along with the (suitable) movements of the limbs. The Bḥāṇa should include characters of Ḍḥūṛṭā and Vīṭā and treat their different conditions, and it always consists of one Act, and should include many incidents which are to be acted by a Ḍḥūṛṭā or a Vīṭā. (NS, XX.107–10) (Varadpande 1987)

The *bḥāṇa*, Bḥaṛaṭā states, must have its character in *baḥūcḥēṣḥṭā* or multiple movements and also include characters of rogues (*ḍḥūṛṭā*) and parasite (*vīṭā*) (XX, 110). The term *baḥūcḥēṣḥṭā* is used in another context by Sūśṛūṭā as an anatomical term to describe a *sandhi* or joint that allows movement in all directions. The *bḥāṇa* is just as fluid and mobile, connecting different worlds and presenting the situation from varying perspectives so as to contextualise renunciation, social pride or esotericism. It does not allow its depiction to be contained within any single paradigm.

The earliest *bḥāṇa* plays are the *Caṭūṛbḥāṇī* (*Cbh*)[1] comprising of four plays dated around the 5th century CE, viz. *Ubhayābhisārikā* (*Ubhayā*) by Vararuci, *Padma-prābhrtaka* (*Padma*) by Śūdraka, *Dhūrta-vita-saṅvāda* (*Dhūrta*) by Iśvaradatta and *Pādatāditaka* (*Pāda*) by Śyāmilaka. These plays not only provide coarse comic relief (Das 2005, 63) through certain urban characters and atmosphere but also comes closer to portraying lived emotions and experiences than the more stylised and ornate courtly literature. In each of these plays, the setting for an irreverent mode is usually laid out from the very invocation. For instance, in *Padma*, the God Rudra—the renunciant, the wailer or the angry one—is invoked as one who either out of anger or benediction (*kripa*) has made women the subjects of desire and beauty. Iśvaradatta, on the other hand, in his *Pāda* dispenses with the customary blessing at the beginning of the play and declares instead his own view about the value of learning and high regard for honest people (Das 2005, 63).

The plays do use the classical and conventional conceit-ridden verses, for instance the arrival of Vasant in *Padma* is defined though the all-pastoral *ālamkārika* of classical drama and *kāvya* and the erotic overtones of fruition and fertility. Though the ornate verse provides for the underlying fertility tropes a more earthy context, despite the earthiness, it ensures a lyrical and even accessible quality. However, there is a tendency that one notices in the later *bḥāṇas*: *Ṣṛīṇgāṛa bḥūṣaṇā*, *Ṣṛīṇgāṛa-ṭīḷakā*, *Ṣṛīṇgāṛa-ṣaṛvaṣvā*, *Ṣṛīṇgāṛa ṃāṇjaṛī* and *Pāṇcabanā-vījayā* emphasise the erotic and have a diminished interest in comedy or satire (De 1926, 63–90) and therefore deploy rigid *ālamkārika* prescriptions that push them towards stylised and stultified conventional imaginary. This has led to later commentators such as Ḍḥaṇaṇjay in *Ḍasāṛūpakā* and Vīśwaṇāṭḥ in *Sāḥīṭyaḍarpan* stating that the *bḥāṇas* should only represent the heroic and the erotic rasas (and not *hāsya*). This prescription is not true for the *Cbh*, in which, while the erotic is used, if only to satirise, the heroic does not appear and *hāsya* dominates. The confusion may be on account of the containment of the *vītā's* character in later dramas, where his humour is aimed less at religious and political targets but, like the *vīḍuśākā*, works to intensify the dominant rasa and the hero's quest (Pamment 2017, 73). As Dasagpta and De note in their history of Sanskrit literature, '[…] The comic and satiric tendency […] so prominent in the *Caṭuṛbḥāṇī*, gradually disappears in the later bhānas, which become in [the] course of time entirely erotic' (Dasgupta and De 1962, 492). The later *bḥāṇas* actually dilute *hāsya* rasa, as do the more established genres of *prakarana* and *nātaka*, which very occasionally include the *vītā* and often place the character in the service of Brahmanical reform. 'The Brahminisation of these literary types, take them away from the fluid mixing of order and chaos, which for viṭạ of early bhānas had the effect of playful socio-political critique' (Pamment 2017, 74). This quality of a Brahman jester speaking back to the powerful apparently re-emerges in jester literature of the Muslim Rule during the later Sultanate period (Pamment 2017, 74) and may have remained in popular performances.

The plot of the plays may differ, but the characters and broad themes centre around the trials and travails of lovers, one of whom is often of the courtesan. The lovers are helped by the *vīṭā* (Ghosh 1975, XXXII). The *bhāṇa Padma* includes Karniputra Ṃūḷaḍevā wanting to please his beloved Ḍevasēṇā. Thus, to help in their love affair, he exhorts Śaśa (as the *vīṭā* is named) to successfully carry out the commission and is ultimately gifted of lotus flower as a souvenir from Ḍevasēṇā on his return. The task is delicate and, according to Śaśa, requires perspicacity care and foresight, for which Śaśa seeks the appropriate messenger in Pāṭaliputra. The *vīṭā* meets a number of persons and shares their secret weaknesses and dalliances, satirising them one by one. A striking example is that of the Pāṇini system grammarian Ḍaṭṭākaḷāsī, son of Ḍaṇḍāsūkā, who is described as being enamoured by courtesans. He pretends to be very cultured while courting the sensitive and cultured Ṛāsaṇavāṭīkā though according to the *vīṭā* he possesses as much sensitivity as a camel would for a *vina*. Further, through Ḍaṭṭākāḷāsī, the *bhāṇa* makes an erudite reference to the then topical dispute between two schools of grammarians—the Kaṭaṇṭṛīkās and the Pāṇini—described by *vīṭā* as a battle of crows and owls, a reference to a Pañcatantra-based symbol of pointless arguments. The bone of contention, the patronage of the rulers, also comes into play. Despite some of the references in the descriptions being topical, the humour transcends time. In his descriptions of Ḍaṭṭākaḷāsī's erotic dalliances, the *vīṭā* wishes that he may require to have enough *triphala*, *gokṣūra* and iron dust that is a regular supply of a purgative, aphrodisiacs and hair dye to mask his age.

Ḍhūṛṭā opens during monsoon and centres on the *vīṭā* being depressed by the weather. He is in a dilemma over enjoying gambling or visiting the *veśyās'* street. As he is short of *panas* for gambling or even for a drink, he gravitates to the *veśyās'* street but cannot afford the courtesans either. He ultimately lands up in the house of the roughish couple Vīśvāḷākā and Sūṇaṇaḍā, where he passes the day in discussing knotty erotic problems put to him by Vīśvāḷākā. *Ubhayā*, on the other hand, discusses the *vīṭā's* commission to propitiate Ṇāṛāyaṇaḍaṭṭā, beloved of Kūbēṛaḍaṭṭā, who is offended because her lover praised a singer in her presence. However, he finds that, urged by the magic of the season, the lovers have already set out in search of each other and have forestalled his effecting a reunion (De 1926, 63–90). Lastly, in *Pāda*, the *vīṭā* sets out to attend an assembly of *vīṭās* and rakes to consider the question of expiation (*prāyaścitta*) put forth to them by Ṭaūṇḍīkōkī Vīśṇūṇāgā, the son of a mahamatra and himself an officer of the king, for the indignity he has suffered by allowing an intoxicated courtesan, Ṃaḍaṇasēṇīkā, to playfully kick a Brahman's sacred head.

The assembly's proposition of the modes of expiation proposed for Vīśṇūṇāgā is indeed amusing and indicates 'a natural gift of polite banter' (De 1926, 63–66). Some think that it is not Vīśṇūṇāgā but the girl herself who should expiate for setting her foot upon such a beast (De 1926), while others suggest that Vīśṇūṇāgā should rub and shampoo her dishonoured feet (De 1926, 67). Another proposes that he should bathe his head in the water with which she washes her feet and drink the same, while the poet Ṛūḍṛāvāṛṃaṇ prescribes that his dishonoured head should be shorn. But in the end, it is agreed, on the proposal of the presiding rake, that Ṃaḍaṇasēṇīkā should knock more sense into her lover by setting her foot on the president's own head in Vīśṇūṇāgā's sight (De 1926, 84–87). The text thus discusses frivolous problems with frivolous solutions to evoke laughter, thereby trivialising overt intellectualism, a sentiment that will evoke a sympathetic response from the audience down the ages. Early western commentators of the *bḥāṇas* saw in them a quintessential Indian humour and considerable literary quality:

> In spite of the unedifying character of their general subject and even in spite of the occasional vulgarities, have real literary quality. They display a natural humour and polite, intensely Indian, irony which need not fear comparison with that of Ben Jonson or a Moliere. The language is veritable ambrosia of Sanskrit speech. (Thomas 1924)

The narrator in the plays is always the *vīṭā*,[2] who is the single actor, jester and entertainer. He is no ordinary fool but a high caste personage, known for his wit and camaraderie. He steps into the role of a 'love counsellor' as he mediates between couples, guides them and answers their several queries. He is the 'voice of the countryside and its people' as he ridicules and dismisses the Brahmans, monks and the intellectuals and as a 'rulers' spy' when he checks cases of misgovernance, corruption and bribery.

The *vīṭā* is otherwise part of the *vīṭā–vīḍuśākā* pair, as the other boon companion of the *ṇāgāṛākā*. Yet there's a significance difference between both characters. The *vīḍuśākā* is hunchbacked and dwarfish, limps (Shulman 1985, 156), has crow's feet on his head and is recognised by his deformities (Zin 2015, 381). The *vīṭā*, on the other hand, evokes laughter and romantic interest through his *ābḥīṅāyā*, expressions, dialogue delivery and satirical courage. The *ābḥīṅāyā* techniques include *ṣāṃāṇyabḥīṇaya*, which is through the body to enact monologues; *ākāśābḥāṣīṭā*, or 'speech in air technique'; *ēkāḥāṛyā*, whereby a sole actor impersonates more than one characters without changing the costume or get-up (*āhārya*); and lastly *ḷāṣyāṇgā* (sung with *ābḥīñāyā*) to enhance the *bhava* sentiment (Mehta 1995, 375).[3]

For Pamment, the *vīṭā* appears to be upholding the social order even while opposing its rigidities. With his 'playful inconsistency, potent critique, wide-ranging interactions and aided by solo shape shifting role', the *vīṭā* sets apart his character from the more constrained *vīḍuṣḥākā*. However, both *vīṭā* and *vīḍuṣḥākā* are high-ranking Brahman identities operating as parasites or serving low-status servant roles, often to Kshatriya householders and kings. Pamment thus argues that this pairing of the Brahman jester and Kshatriya king lends insights into the workings of caste and its complex interrelations of order and chaos in the sacred spaces of early Indian comedy (Pamment 2017, 71).

The *vīṭā* evokes laughter by mocking his patrons, exposing hypocrisies regarding class, gender, corruption and hollow piety (Pamment 2017, 71). To give an example, in Śyāmilaka's *Pāda,* the *vīṭā* describes Vīśṇūḍāsā as a judge and a staunch Vaishnava who pretends to devote most of his time to meditation, to the extent that he neglects his official duties but actually indulges in bribery and dozes in court 'like an ox of the market place' (Śyāmilaka 1996, 116). The *vīṭā* taunts the powerful officer over his ineffectual sexual efforts that result in 'disappointing the honoured (courtesan) Aṇaṇgaṣēṇā. When offered a citrus by the judge to avoid these allegations, the *vīṭā* turns to political satire hinting at his corruption in the courts. 'You cannot deceive me in such a case as you can your retainers, by a bribe' (Śyāmilaka 1996, 206).

In the *bḥāṇa* the single actor playing the part of a parasite has been seen as the satirist, a cultured and often enthusiastic expert in sexual etiquette and amorous arts who earned his livelihood as a counsellor or go-between for a wealthier patron, an aristocrat or a merchant aspiring to aristocratic manners. The parasite walks through the streets of a city frequently for the sake of conducting an erotic business transaction for his patron; he describes the people he meets, exposes the degradations around him, '… pays heavy amounts to doctors for regaining his lost youth, gives money generously to courtesans and though himself had gone weak in limbs takes great interest in sex talk' (Varadpande 1987, 174).

The setting for the genre pre-supposes an urbane as well as eclectic setting of multifarious pleasure where 'recitation of the vedas, jousting, elephant rathas and horse sport, archery, theatre, kavya, ships laden with goods from the four oceans, song, music, gambling' (Śūdraka, 7) form the matrix for pleasure and laughter evoked by the banter of the *vīṭā* is to be contextualised. Similarly, for the sophisticated *nāgāṛakā*, pleasures associated with the sense of taste or the tongue are sophisticated as epitomised in the gastronomical trope of the *chutni* with mixed flavours which is used both for gastronomical pleasures and those associated with partaking the spicy and sharp flavour of the beloved.

The privileging of the urban, erotic and satirical in the *Cbh* poses an important question not only about the audience for whom these were composed but also about power. Who can laugh at whom? Who wields the power of dispensing and enjoying pleasure? The *bḥāṇas* create a relatable world where the *vīṭā*, as a Brahman, can mock almost all. Thus, *Cbh* parodies almost all members of the court society except the king and the queen, not sparing even the king's brother-in-law. It reveals the psyche of the members of this elite class who found entertainment in a subverted image of themselves in performative arts (Verma 2011, 33). The ascetics, religious moralists, fathers, who are figures of authority, are lampooned for their hypocrisy, foolishness or frivolity. The courtesan-prostitute may be condemned for mercenary tendencies but is considered as an object of desire, an agent of pleasure, necessary for the life of leisurely pursuits of the *nāgāṛākā*, especially the *vīṭā*. In *Dhūrta.*, most of Iśvaradatta's courtesans play a part, including Ṛāmaḍāsī, Ṛaṭīṣēṇā and Pṛaḍyūṃṇāḍāṣī after having enjoyed lovemaking. Revealing the courtesans' nobler traits, the *vīṭā* is seen admiring Kūṃūḍvaṭī in Śūdraka's *Padma* as she offers sacrifice to the gods and feeds the crows for the safe return of her lover from a punitive expedition (Chandra 1973, 198). The one with the intelligence and birth to make fun of the rest is the *vīṭā*, the highborn *bon vivant* whose authority on matters of pleasure and humour is accepted and celebrated (Pamment 2017, 71). Śyāmilaka in his *Pāda* says '... austere ascetics do not attain salvation by weeping. Words of merriment do not stand in the way of reaching heaven. Hence with a firmly resolved mind, the wise should have laughter by all means' (Śyāmilaka 1996, 106).

Further, in privileging pleasure, treatment of the art of love in *bḥāṇa* literature is posed as a serious concern and hence is discussed, debated and projected through intellectual gatherings or *goshthis*. In Iśvaradatta's *Dhūrta*, the *vīṭā* showcases his knowledge of love affairs in a set of 19 answers on issues such as distinguishing a courtesan's true and false love through beautiful signs, loving glances and show of courtesy; ways of propitiating an offended women by placing her left foot on his head rather than falling at her feet; reconciling women estranged on hearing other women's name in her presence by lying, praising, joking and changing the topic; remedying frigidity with a four-step formula of simplicity, money, wisdom and appeasement to win the love of a young girl, greedy woman, wise woman and angry woman respectively and various ways of lovemaking.

The two-facedness embodied in religious purity on one hand and engaging in disguised sexual relationships on the other is exposed in numerous incidents. For example, Pavīṭṛakā, a Vaishnava in Śūdraka's *Padma*, makes it a point to avoid being defiled by the touch of a stranger by 'holding his moist clothes close to his body, contracting his limbs, closing his nostrils with his fingers, (to the extent) picking jasmine flowers with a pincer' (Śūdraka, 194) but is revealed by the *vīṭā* to be maintaining disguised love relations with Vaṛūṇīkā (courtesan). Similarly, Saṃgḥīḷākā, an inmate of Dharmaranya monastery, who is caught running out of the courtesan's house, hiding the ringworm marks on his shaved head with a scarf (197), pretends to have come to perform his 'religious duty' to console Saṃgḥāḍāsīkā on the loss of her mother with Buddha's words (196). Similarly, Śaīsīḷākā, the son of a Brahman is reminded of having raped a Buddhist nun. Thus what becomes apparent is that the Buddhist nuns or monks not only indulge their base senses but also act as 'go-betweens' for young lovers, arranging romantic meetings. The dereliction of religious and ascetic virtuous codes is exposed and contested through the *bḥāṇa* tradition and may have resonated with the audience.

On the other hand, the plays often centre around winning the attention and affection of the *veśya*, who brings *Cbh* characters 'indescribable pleasure'. Śyāmilaka in *Pāda* advises his audience and readers that when caught between paying either a *kāyasthā* or a courtesan, 'it is better to give money to a courtesan because that is bound to yield some pleasure at least'.

Therefore, besides satire, the plays dwell on the mundane, earthly pleasures of the senses, especially in the company of the courtesan and the prostitutes, the *veśyā*, valorising these over the distant pleasures of the heavens. They make a persuasive case in observing that paradise lacks the satisfaction of the senses in the spring season when '… the perspiration wipes away the *tilakas*, when the koels begin swarming the garden, when women begin wreathing their zones, when the mango trees begin blossoming and the breeze is full of fragrance, when a woman gives up her pride and approaches the lover seeking reconciliation' (Chandra 1973, 208). While heaven may tempt renunciants with everlasting union with the beyond or in the presence of nymphs, *Cbh* rejects the same saying '… the pleasures that love making gives can never be found in the company of those women' (208) and adds that

> It is said that there are trees and houses of gold in heaven … the pleasures which the women derive from young trees, reared and treasured like their own sons, and yielding flowers for their coiffure,

can such pleasures be ever obtained from hard lifeless golden trees? (209)

Consorting with courtesans does not have universal approval; in fact, the parents of impressionable young men along with the mothers of the *veśyās* often try to deter and sever such relationships, turning villains in the path of romance and pleasurable companionship. In Iśvaradatta's *Dhūrta,* the *viṭā* vilifies the obdurate banker father of Kṛīṣḥṇaḷākā, saying '... these bastard fathers act as though they themselves had never tasted the pleasures of youth ...' (Chandra 1973, 198). The usual solution of all parental problems regarding their sons' misjudged alliance is to get them married, which according to the *viṭā* is 'a matter of sorrow, for you will abandon the broad road of the courtesan in favour of the narrow lane of a wife'. The wife versus courtesan dichotomy and the underlying politics of creating archetypes is thus highlighted.

The courtesan's mother's motives are more mercenary in forcing the courtesan to consort with a rich man against her wishes as in in the case of Ṃāḍavasēṇā in *Ubhayā* or in restricting them from visiting impoverished men such Aṇaṇgaḍaṭṭā of the same text. The mother also robs the male lover of his money, as Ḍḥāṇaṃīṭṛā loses all his wealth to the courtesan Ṛaṭīsēṇā's mother. His stupidity is mocked by the *viṭā* in these words: 'Wicked kings pass on the responsibility of their evil deeds to the shoulders of ministers and crafty courtesans on to the shoulders of their mothers' (Chandra 1973, 211).

Recovering context from the stock characters and plots is difficult. However, *bḥāṇa* plays, as pointed out before, have a distinctly urban air about them. Satire in play is an urban technique (Seigel 1989, 79). Such plays open with a conventional description of a real or imagined city in which the play is set (Seigel 1989, 79). The *viṭā* in *Ubhayā* praises the splendours of the King's Road in Kūṣuṃāpūṛā, the City of Flowers: '... life here is an everlasting festival of joy ... the city is an ornament upon the forehead of the goddess Earth, making her look like heaven' (Seigel 1989, 79). *Dhūrta* and *Ubhayā* hail Pāṭaḷīpūṭṛā for its lofty houses, crowded markets, and the citizens for being both charitable and cultured (Chandra 1973, 209). Similarly, Śaśa, the *viṭā* of *Padma* set in Ujjayīṇī, portrays its 'incomparable charm' (190) and talks about the different sounds heard around the city, including the recitation of the Vedas, learned discussions on drama and poetry, songs, musical instruments, gossip of rakes, chirping of birds and tinkling of girdles and bracelets (190). However, the last *bḥāṇa* in the collection, *Pāda*, is set in the imagined city of Sārvabhauma-nagara, the Universal Kings's City, to prevent identification with an actual capital whose scandalous gossip the poet may have had to record in a disguised form (De 1926,

63–90). Urban pleasures and socio-sexual spaces form the picturesque backdrop for the characters and their activities in *bḥāṇa* plays. For example, *Pāda* talks of taverns (*panagara*) lining the paths leading to the *veśyā* houses, which gamblers, after having won some money in gambling, visit with wine bottles in their hands to enjoy their drinks in the company of courtesans (Varadpande 2011, 26).

The existence of plays such as the *Cbh* does not imply that these represent stark reality compared to the normative literature such as the *Dharmashastras*. It does, however, reflect attitudes and behaviours that fracture the normative ideal. The *Cbh* is in Sanskrit, which by implication suggests that the literate, if not the elite alone, formed its audience. Śūdraka, the author of *Pāda*, is also credited with the ten-act play *Ṃṛīcḥḥākāṭīkaṃ*, and both may have been written for a common audience.

The characters whose stories are narrated in the play are not kings and divine heroes as in the better known classical Sanskrit plays of Bḥāsā and Kālidāsa. Rather, in *Cbh*, they are merchants, ministers, *gaṇikā* and *nāgarakās*. The origins of *bḥāṇas* and *pṛāḥāṣaṇas* may be traced to 'popular farcical comedies which were never written down ...' and '... are probably court imitations in the kavya style and in Sanskrit of popular models in popular dialects' (Jha 2009, 210). It has been argued that Sanskrit drama was not performative in the character-based way on the premise that it does not follow the Western model of dramatic progression or classification. However, it has been demonstrated that the *bḥāṇa Kaṛpūṛācāṛīṭā* of Vatsarāja was performed at the festival of Nilakantha yatra at the behest of 'learned spectators' and the *pṛāḥāṣaṇa* called Ḥāsyācūḍāṃaṇī also of Vatsarāja was ordered to be performed at a similar occasion (Dalal 1972, 23, 112). Performances at temples, festivities and public gatherings would have had a wide audience from the city inhabitants. In fact, *Kāmasūtra* talks of *pṛēkṣāṇākā* or public show including drama, where the actors, or *kulilavas*, came from various places to perform and were producers of pleasure, as mentioned in Chapter 2. One-act plays, the *bḥāṇas* were performed by actors well-trained in *abḥinayē sūsīkṣīṭō* (Jha 2009, 223).

The *Cbh* and its performative and narrative aspects not only bring out the presence of urban agents of pleasure through its dramatis personae but also give us a glimpse into the world where wit, humour and erotic presentations were valorised. The *vīṭā* perhaps mediates between the popular and the courtly, criticising the 'nobler' lot through jest about the corruption in bureaucracy, varna disorder, ascetic hypocrisy and other topics. The importance of gossip on the raja-marga, of Viṣḥṇūḍāṣā or about administrative lapses as a means of communicating popular attitudes is captured in the *bḥāṇas*. By insult of the high and mighty, such as the *niṛāpēkṣḥā*, or poet, who sells poetry to the Brahmans well-versed in the Vedas for a glass of wine (*Cbh*, 85), a Brahman who rapes a Buddhist nun or a Buddhist monk who, in the name of duty, visits courtesan's quarters in hiding, the *Cbh* invokes the power of the grapevine to carry information and to not only subvert the archetypes of important personages but also strengthen the hierarchy of power by spelling out who can mock whom. The plot, the characters and the satire of *Cbh* is part of a living tradition that celebrates little pleasures and vast beauties of an imagined urban world.

NOTES

1. 'F.W. Thomas called attention to these plays in his paper *Four Sanskrit Plays* in the centenary supplement of the *Journal of Royal Asiatic Society*,' points out Sushil Kumar De (1926). This paper has relied on the Sanskrit test and its Hindi translation by Moti Chandra and V.S. Agrawal (1959) for the analysis.
2. He is depicted in *Deśopadeśa* by Kshemendra in stanza 'Śūro dosākarah strīnām vakraścitte khalo budhah' interpreted by C. Shivaraju as '"sūra" (*sūrya* or hero) and "dosākara" (candra or defiler) of women, "vakra" (*mangala* or crooked) in mind, wicked and "buddha" (intelligent), "guru" (heavy) in sin, "śukra" (semen) in spending and "sanaiścara" (*śani* or moving slowly on the path)' metaphorically presenting the *vīṭā* as the seven 'grahas' (Shivaraju 2003, 114).
3. Mehta describes the *vīṭā* on the basis of a Kusana Mathura frieze (1st century AD) now in the National Museum and Ajanta frescoes (Vakataka, 5th century AD) as

   > blue body paint, with artistic designs of *tilaka* on the forehead; arms and chest are smeared in designs with saffron and sandalwood. Fashionably draped dhoti in pale green colours, with a mauve coloured jacket with full sleeves. Foppishly tied multicoloured turban. A pale magenta coloured upper garment modishly draped on shoulders and arms (along with)…. Stylishly ornamented … golden ornaments covering the neck, waist, forearms, fingers, ears and waist …(and) a garland with perfumed flowers.

REFERENCES

Bawa, Seema. *Gods, Men and Women: Gender & Sexuality in Early Indian Art.* Delhi: D.K. Printworld. 2013.

Chandra, Moti. 1973. *The World of* Courtesans. New Delhi: Vikas Publishing House.

Chandra, Moti. *Chaturbhani: Sringara Hata*. Edited and translated by Moti Chandra and V.S. Agrawal. Bombay: Hindi Grantha Ratnakara. 1959.

Clasquin, Michel. 'Real Buddhas Don't Laugh: Attitudes towards Humour and Laughter in Ancient India and China'. *Social Identities* 107, no. 7 (2001): 97–116.

Dalal, C.D., ed. *A Collection of Six Dramas of Vatsraja. Baroda*: Oriental Institute. 1972.

Das, Sisir Kumar. *History of Indian Literature*. New Delhi: Sahitya Akademi. 2005.

Dasgupta, S.N. and S.K. De. A history of Sanskrit Literature Volume 1. Calcutta, University of Calcutta. 1962.

De, Sushil Kumar. 1926. 'A Note on the Sanskrit Monologue Play (Bhana) with Special Reference to the Caturbhani'. *Journal of the Royal Asiatic Society* 58 (1926): 63–90.

Ghosh, Manmohan. *Glimpses of Sexuaḷ Life in Nanda-Maurya India: Translation of the Caturbhāni*. Calcutta: Manisha Granthalaya. 1975.

Jha, Vishwa Mohan. 'Medieval Sanskrit Drama as a Literate Medium for Non Literate Communication'. In *Mind Over Matter: Essays in Mentalities in Medieval India*, edited by D.N. Jha and Eugenia Vanina, 207–227. Delhi: Tulika Books. 2009.

Mehta, Tarla. *Sanskrit Play Production in Ancient India*. New Delhi: Motilal Banarsidas. 1995.

Nàtyasàstra. Ascribed to Bharata Muni. Edited and translated by Manmohan Ghosh. Caḷcutta: Ganthalya Pvt. Ltd. 1956.

Pamment, Claire. *Comic Performance in Pakistan: The Bhānd*. York: Palgrave Macmillan. 2017.

Shivaraju, C. *Humour in Sanskrit Literature*. Mumbai: Himalaya Publishing House. 2003.

Shulman, David Dean. *The King and the Clown in South Indian Myth and Poetry*. New Jersey: Princeton University Press. 1985.

Siegel, Lee. *Laughing Matters: Comic Tradition in India*. New Delhi: Motilal Banarsidas. 1989.

Sreenivasrao. 'Ten Forms of Sanskrit Drama'. Available at https://sreenivasaraos.com/tag/ten-forms-of-sanskrit-drama/ (accessed 14 October 2020).

Śyāmilaka. *The Pādatāditaka*. Translated by G. H. Schokker. Paris: Mouton. 1996.

Thomas, F.W. 'Four Sanskrit Plays'. *Journal of the Royal Asiatic Society* (Century Supplement) 13 (1924): 123–136.

Varadpande, Manohar Laxman. *History of Indian Theatre: Classical theatre*. New Delhi: Abhinav Publications. 1987

———. *Love in Ancient India*. New Delhi: Wisdom Tree Publishers. 2011.

Verma, Archana. *Performance and Culture: Narrative, Image and Enactment in India*. Newcastle upon Tyne: Cambridge Scholars. 2011.

Zin, Monika. 'The Jester and the Musician'. In *Studies in Indian Culture and Literature,* edited by A.A. Esposito, H. Oberlin, B.A.V. Rai and K.J. Steiner, 379–396. Wiesbaden: Harrrassowitz Verlag. 2015.

4

COURTING PLEASURE IN RĀVAṆA'S LAṄKĀ: THE AESTHETICS OF POWER AND DESIRE IN EARLY MEDIEVAL DECCAN

Parul Pandya Dhar

The fifth book of the *Rāmāyaṇa*, the *Sundarakāṇḍa* (*tr.* the book beautiful) is set in the sumptuous opulence of Laṅkā.[1] This is the kingdom of the epic's anti-hero, Rāvaṇa, full of pleasure groves, glistening mansions, rich treasures, intoxicated lovers, luxuriant interiors and sensory enchantments that composers and writers from the time of the great poet Maharṣi Vālmīki have recounted in rapturous detail. Such descriptions of the awe-inspiring beauty of the land and the rich revelry of its inhabitants soon acquired a canonical status in ancient Indian literature and offered a template for poets describing heavenly and courtly pleasures.[2] But the visual translation of Rāvaṇa's Laṅkā as a paradise of pleasure and of its powerful king Rāvaṇa's colourful and complex characterisation in early medieval Indian sculpture rarely, if ever, parallels such literary abandon. Some artists of the early medieval western Deccan, however, did explore the visual possibilities of portraying the unparalleled pleasures of Laṅkā, translating in stone some of the sensual pursuits emanating from the proclivities of the powerful king of Laṅkā. Of special note is the portrayal of the *Sundarakāṇḍa* episodes carved on the inner ambulatory of the 7th-century Durga temple at Aihoḷe in northern Karnataka (Meister and Dhaky 1986, 49–52), which have thus far not received nuanced analysis, especially in the context of the history of pleasure in early medieval India.[3]

My essay interprets this exceptional delineation in stone of Rāvaṇa's city of pleasure by locating it within the larger history of courtly cultures and the presence of erotic imagery[4] in early medieval Indian art. It approaches the visual imagery in its relationships with texts of different genres to analyse its layered iconography and the semiotics of its location within the Durga temple. In the latter part, I extend this theme to explore if, and to what extent, the creative experiment at Aihoḷe was carried forward in later visual translations of the narrative on two other temples from the extended early medieval western Deccan region. Situating this discussion in a broader frame, I address the nature of prescriptions and proscriptions in early medieval India in the literary and visual portrayals of pleasure and eroticism and in their differential calibrations when depicting gods, kings and demons.

LAṄKĀ AND RĀVAṆA IN THE SUNDARAKĀṆḌA'S TEXTUAL IMAGERY

If Laṅkā is the imagined emotional and physical landscape for locating the narrative in *Sundarakāṇḍa*, the three main characters on its stage are undoubtedly Rāvaṇa, the king of Laṅkā; Hanumān, the monkey-emissary of the epic's hero Rāma; and Sītā, the abducted wife of Rāma. Rāma's physical absence is evoked through the recurrent motif of 'recall', especially in the minds of his closest confidantes, Sītā and Hanumān. Sītā, as the forlorn yet strong-willed wife of Rāma, in deep despair at being held captive in a foreign land, is the undisputed principal female character of this book. She is an embodiment of pathos, evoking the sentiment of compassion, *karuṇā rasa*, and a kaleidoscope of transient emotions, *vyābhicārī bhāvas* such as repentance, anger, fear, restlessness, dejection, hope, faith and more.[5] But it is Rāvaṇa and Hanumān, two immensely powerful and near-infallible beings with magical powers—one a *rākṣasa,* demon; and the other a *vānara,* monkey—who are at the centre of action. The book commences with Hanumān's giant leap into Rāvaṇa's Laṅkā in search of Sītā and concludes soon after his successful return. Through this unique configuration of the characters and setting, the poet has distanced the book's narrative frame from the world of humans and human-kings, from the norms of divine-human kingship and their codes of ethical behaviour and social etiquette. This allows for the expression of unrestrained sensual pleasures in Laṅkā and gives the poet a unique opportunity within the larger epic to explore the depths of *saṃbhoga śṛṅgāra* (the sentiment of love in union) in ways that were not possible with the more subtle expressions of *śṛṅgāra* between Rāma and Sītā in other *kāṇḍas* of the epic. Pleasure and sensory gratification in their different hues form a recurrent theme in the *Sundarakāṇḍa*. The king and his city—Rāvaṇa and Laṅkā—both harbour a range of polarities. The splendorous city, often compared with Indra's Amarāvatī, and its extraordinarily accomplished, desirable and powerful ruler have an equally dark side. Rāvaṇa's immense intelligence and talent coexist with arrogance, indulgence and an uncontrollable lust; Laṅkā's desirable women of unsurpassed beauty and handsome men of unmatched grace are contrasted with disfigured, grotesque and fearsome beings who also inhabit Laṅkā; knowledge, talent and the cultivation of fine arts meet their contrast in savage and ruthless behaviour and paradisiacal pleasure groves harbour cruel demons of the dark.[6]

Laṅkā's heavenly locale, its towering mansions, blossoming trees, glittering lights, bejewelled residences, singing birds, blissful chatter, riveting music and dance, alluring fragrances and luxurious living spaces manifest as *uddīpana vibhāvas* (emotional excitants) that evoke every imaginable circumstance to arouse desire in men and women. Laṅkā is imagined by Vālmīki as a beautiful and unassailable woman, protected by the formidable Rāvaṇa.[7] In the early parts of the *Sundarakāṇḍa,* Rāvaṇa's handsome form, exuding strength comparable to mythical mountains and his insatiable appetite for women are reciprocated by the eager willingness of his besotted women.[8] The poet revels in the excesses of sensory pleasures and erotic love and conveys these through the gaze of Hanumān, who witnesses all this as he scours every inch of the city and Rāvaṇa's palace in search of Sītā. In the process, Hanumān's celibacy and sexual innocence are brought face-to-face with carnal pleasures and sexual excesses.

The *Rāmāyaṇa*, as is well-known, has been read, recited, performed, sculpted and painted over centuries and across distant regions. Before exploring visual translations of the *Sundarakāṇḍa's* description of sensual pleasures in the city of Laṅkā and in the inner sanctum of Rāvaṇa's palace in the early medieval Deccan, it is important to foreground some keys issues crucial to their interpretation. The first issue relates to the transmediality of this epic and the ways in which narrative strategies and representational concerns for telling this story would have adapted to different mediums of communication. What may be effective in poetry, for instance, may not be suited to the visual medium. Second, the early medieval period in India was characterised by socio-cultural and political conditions that would have had a direct bearing on the sculptural narratives under consideration. It is important to address the nature of political patronage and social reception of erotic pleasures in courtly and temple settings to better contextualise visual articulations of pleasure in Rāvaṇa's Laṅkā. Finally, the temporal and regional distance between the two (Vālmīki's poem and early medieval sculptures) suggests the possibility of additional sources of inspiration for the sculptures. How closely does the poetic rendition of Vālmīki's *Sundarakāṇḍa* match the visual narratives carved on early medieval temples in the western Deccan? How far is it possible to locate intermediate presences that may have shaped a related yet altered rendering?

POETRY, THEATRE AND SCULPTURE: AESTHETIC NORMS AND NARRATIVE ATTRIBUTES

In early medieval India, artistic expressions in different mediums, verbal–textual and visual–theatrical, are known to have been closely interlinked.[9] Poetry (*kāvya*), theatre (*nāṭya*) and sculpture (*śilpa*) complemented each other, often exploring shared themes but presenting them with distinct artistic techniques, narrative strategies and representative norms specific to each medium. For example, the aesthetic criterion of *aucitya* (propriety/decorum) would be different in poetry, theatre and visual arts. In the case of classical Indian theatre, the display of uncontrolled anger, extreme disgust, death and erotic excesses was prohibited on stage. In the chapter on *sāmānya abhinaya*,[10] the *Nāṭyaśāstra* prescribes that:

> … No woman, whether she is of a high, low or middling status, should be shown scantily dressed (lit. exposed) or wearing only one garment; nor should her lips be painted. Though natural to women of a low status, even they should not be shown doing improper things on the stage.... There should be no sleeping on stage....If the context requires it and one has to sleep, either alone or with someone else, kissing, embracing, any other private acts, biting the lips (of one another), marks of nails (on the woman's breasts), loosening the *nīvī* (front knot), crushing the lips or breasts—such things should not be shown on stage. For, a drama is seen by a father, a son, a daughter-in-law, a mother-in-law (all sitting together); so, these must be avoided.[11]

The *Nāṭyaśāstra* exerted a lasting influence on performance and visual art traditions in ancient and early medieval India; specifically, its knowledge and practice are recorded in a few early Calukya inscriptions (Padigar 2010, 269–270: nos. 186 and 187). The prohibitions mentioned in this text may be attributed to the immediate corporeality of theatrical performance that involved human actors and may have caused concerns about *aucitya* (appropriateness). This consequently would have led to restrictions on displays of violence and erotic excess, which were to be conveyed only through subtle suggestions.

Looking at the numerous sensual portrayals of the female form, the frank sensuality of *mithunas* (loving couples) and other sexually explicit depictions in ancient and early medieval sculpture (Figure 4.1), one may surmise that the norms and prohibitions for ancient Indian theatre were stricter as compared to those imposed on the visual arts. Sculpture and painting are more visceral and tangible as compared to

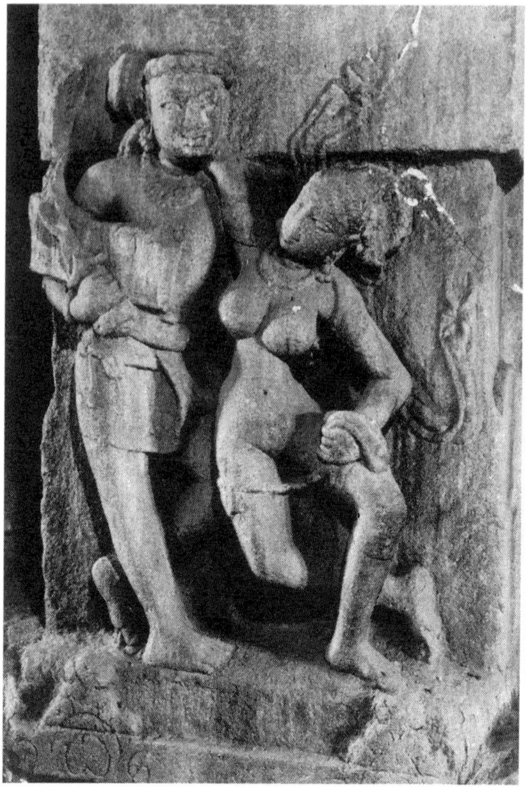

Figure 4.1: *Mithuna*, Huchchappaya Maṭha (Temple No. 7), Aihoḷe, c. Late 7th Century
Courtesy: American Institute of Indian Studies, Gurugram.

literature but less immediately so than dance and theatre. The standards of propriety for the visual arts in the portrayal of erotic and violent attitudes appear to fall between those for literary and performance arts. The *śāstric* texts on the visual arts, however, are not explicitly vocal on the issue of propriety in the display of eroticism in painting and sculpture. These concerns are subsumed within *śāstric* preoccupations with categories of characters, types of women and men, proportions and measures suitable to the different types, deliberations on corresponding typologies and metaphors drawn from nature for their body parts: *aṅgas* (primary limbs), *pratyaṅgas* (secondary limbs) and *upaṅgas* (tertiary limbs),[12] the elements, materials and techniques of visual representation and a continued engagement with key sentiments and emotional states, *rasa* and *bhāva*, especially *śṛṅgāra* (the erotic sentiment).[13] There is the occasional specific reference to permitted and prohibited themes in the specific contexts of residences, palaces and temples. The *Śilparatna*, for example, states that 'scenes of war, even between gods and demons, death, misery, performances of ascetics and depiction of naked figures should not be executed in houses' (Nardi 2006, 26). Similar proscriptions for residences, but interestingly not for palaces and temples, are to be found in the *Viṣṇudharmottara Purāṇa.*[14]

EROTIC PLEASURE IN EARLY MEDIEVAL COURT AND TEMPLE CULTURES

Recent decades have seen a shift in interpretations of early medieval Indian courtly cultures, bringing attention to royal courts as socio-political institutions with specific protocols of conduct, bodily discipline, gesture and performance among its members, in which beauty, refinement and love held a special place.[15] Daud Ali has emphasised that the immediate, inhabited world of a king's court—which included courtiers, advisors, women, poets, scribes, artists and other palace personnel—was a site of production and reception of different forms of cultural knowledge. His work draws attention to the sociology of court art and the necessity to integrate material practices when interpreting relationships between aesthetics and political power in early medieval India. Viewed in this light, the themes and content of court poetry, drama, music, temple arts and architecture (epic literature and art were a part of these artistic expressions) were closely entwined with the aspirations of the court society, which acted as an 'interpretive community' (Ali 2011, 1–25).

Erotic pleasure, courtship and a preoccupation with *śṛṅgāra* in court art were unavoidably tied to ethical concerns among court society about attachment and dependence. The terms (*anurāga, vaśa* and others)[16] used to conceptualise erotic love shared much in common with those used to explain political affiliations and control (for example, a vassal's or courtier's dependence on the king). In both cases, attachment was a necessary virtue to transact the relationship but also a limitation to self-autonomy, as this implied submission (Ali 2011, 251–261). The ideal king or elite, in the moral order of court societies, was not enslaved to erotic excess. As observed in Vātsyāyana's *Kāmasūtra* and in early medieval inscriptions, erotic love and political negotiations were conceptualised through a shared set of similes and metaphors—as a play, contest or battle (Figure 4.2). Specific to our context, the *Tembhurṇi* grants of the early western Calukya king, Vikramāditya I, liken his capture of the unassailable city of Kāñcī from Pallava Parameśvaravarman I to grabbing the girdle of a damsel (Padigar 2010, xlvii and 87–89: no. 51).

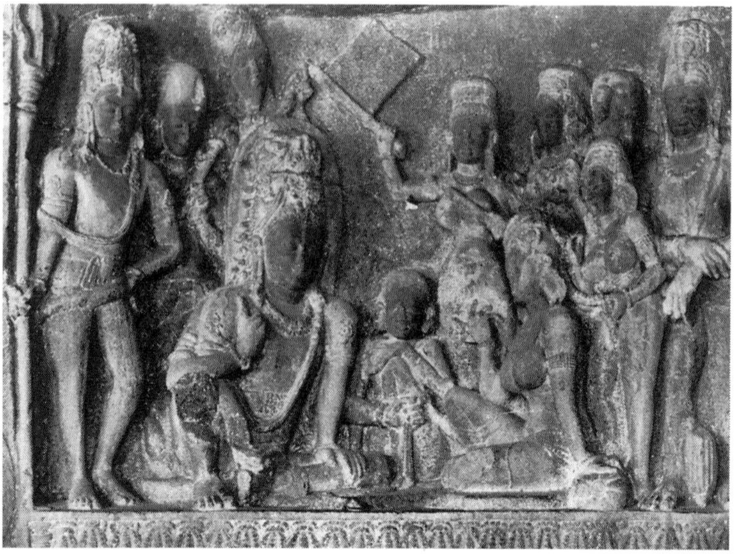

Figure 4.2: Śiva and Umā Playing a Board Game, Ellora, Rāmeśvara Cave (No. 21), c. 7th Century
Courtesy: American Institute of Indian Studies, Gurugram.

Court poetry and drama, including that based on the *mahākāvyas* or epics, delighted in the erotic sentiment. The science of *kāma,* alongside language, grammar, logic, politics and more, was part of an aristocrat's education (Desai 2013a). A close nexus existed between royal courts and temples in early medieval India, and this relationship also revealed itself in the art and architecture of these temples. The portrayal of sex and eroticism on temple walls during the early medieval period, however, was a result of a confluence of many circumstances. Tāntrism and the consequent revalidation in the belief of the magical and ritualistic powers of sex added fuel to the already prevalent exaltation of *śṛṅgāra* in courtly and temple arts. This led to the proliferation of explicit sexual imagery on the temple surfaces during this period. Erotic motifs such as *mithunas* (loving couples) and other symbols associated with fertility and auspiciousness, discussed by Seema Bawa in the context of post-Maurya art,[17] were already part of the temple's sculptural vocabulary and continued being so through the early medieval period (see Figure 4.1). The coming together of the Smārta and Tantra traditions led to greater acceptance of the visual portrayal of erotic themes, and sexually explicit imagery became more pervasive on temples (Desai 2013b). It is important to qualify, however, that erotic imagery on Indian temples was almost always generic and did not depict specific personalities. Specific gods and kings, although pictured with their consorts in pleasing attitudes, were represented with restraint appropriate to their dignity, a prerequisite for the pursuit of higher objectives in the case of kings, as for example, in the portrait of the Hoysaḷa king Viṣṇuvardhana with his consort and courtiers near the entrance to the Cennakeśava temple in Belur (Figure 4.3).[18]

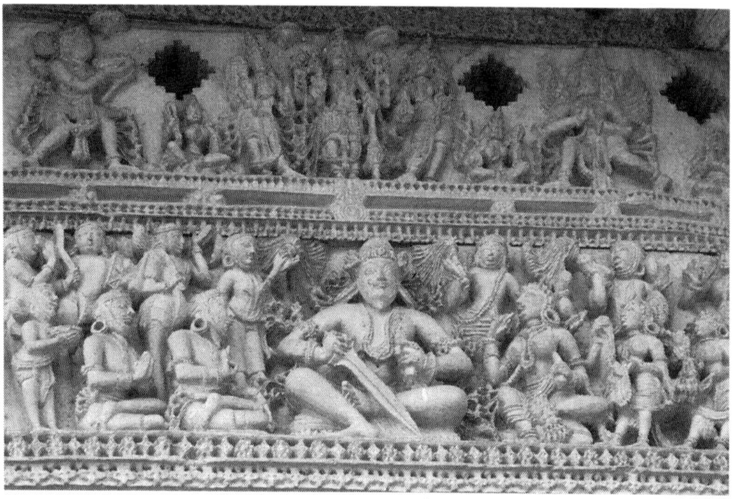

Figure 4.3: Portrait of the Hoysaḷa Patron-King Viṣṇuvardhana, with His Consort and Courtiers, Protected by Viṣṇu Above, Belur, Cennakeśava Temple
Courtesy: Parul Pandya Dhar.

NARRATIVE AS IMAGE: LOCATING TEXT AND CONTEXT

Attempts by art historians working on the narrative art of ancient and early medieval India to arrive at specific text–image relationships have been fraught with difficulties. Given the gaps in our sources for this period, the precise text or performance tradition that may have guided a sculptor's chisel in carving mythological or historical narratives is difficult to indicate with precision. The inherent creativity of artistic expression also implies that innovation and fluidity are an integral part of the process. This is true of repetition in the same medium (for example, multiple theatrical performances of the same narrative) and even more so when a narrative is translated from one medium to another (for example, from text to image).

These issues become important when we attempt to correlate textual versions of the *Sundarakāṇḍa* with those carved in stone. How do we compare the pursuit of pleasure in Rāvaṇa's palace as elaborated by Vālmīki with its visual counterparts carved on temples in Aihoḷe,

Paṭṭadakal and Amritapura in the early medieval Deccan or Karnataka? Which version of Rāma's story was the Deccanī sculptor familiar with? How does one begin to accommodate the separation in time and location between the ur-text of the *Sundarakāṇḍa* ascribed to Maharṣi Vālmīki and the sculpted versions in early medieval Deccan?[19] Was the *Vālmīki Rāmāyaṇa* well-known and followed in early medieval Deccan, or were Deccanī artists, elites and spectators more conversant with some related variant?[20] What of the oral and theatrical versions that are no longer accessible? This complicates any attempt to unequivocally draw direct correlations between Vālmīki's text and the early medieval narratives in stone. I have on occasion drawn parallels with other texts, specifically the *Bhaṭṭikāvya* (*Rāvaṇavadha*); the *Kamba Rāmāyaṇa* (*Irāmavatāram*) and the *Adhyātma Rāmāyaṇa*.[21] However, I should add the disclaimer that it has not been possible for me within the scope of this essay to also consider other available court dramas, such as Bhāsa's *Pratimā-nāṭaka* and *Abhisheka-nāṭaka,* which may be useful for further investigation.

CARVING RĀVAṆA'S PALATIAL PLEASURES IN STONE AT AIHOḶE

The Durga temple at Aihoḷe is dated stylistically to the 7th century CE and was built during the rule of the early western Calukyas, also known as the Bādāmi Calukyas (Meister and Dhaky 1986, 49–52). The dominant language of early western Calukya (c. 550–750 CE) courtly culture was Sanskrit, but early Kannaḍa was also in use (Padigar 2010, xxviii–xxx). Calukya courtly practices and notions of kingship were inspired by Sanskrit prose and poetry, and many fine architects, sculptors, actors, singers and dancers practised their art in the temple and court environs.[22] Bharata's *Nāṭyaśāstra* and works of celebrated Sanskrit poets such as Kālidāsa and Bhāravī are mentioned in their epigraphic corpus; some epic narratives have been sculpted in stone and several are likely to have been performed.[23]

The entrance porch (*mukhacatuṣkī*) of the Durga temple at Aihoḷe bears episodes from the *Rāmāyaṇa* carved as a continuous narrative on the recess (*kaṇṭha*) of its base mouldings (*adhiṣṭhāna*). The northern side of the entrance porch harbours episodes from the *Araṇyakāṇḍa*, whereas themes from the *Sundarakāṇḍa* are the most prominent on its southern side. It is interesting to note that in the Calukya heartland, wherever the *Rāmāyaṇa* has been carved on temple surfaces, episodes relating to Laṅkā are most often found in the southern direction. This suggests a general understanding that Rāvaṇa's Laṅkā was located to the south of the Calukya kingdom. In the available visual rendition of episodes from the *Sundarakāṇḍa* at the Durga temple, Aihoḷe, Sītā is missing; Rāvaṇa and Hanumān dominate the narrative.[24]

The Aihoḷe artists have imaginatively conjured the luxurious interiors of Rāvaṇa's palace and his encounter with Hanumān. Rāvaṇa is the undisputed focus of this long narrative register. His unshakeable strength and towering presence is visualised majestically, comparable to textual metaphors of the Kailāsa and Meru mountains, with his many heads resembling the mountain peaks and his multiple arms resembling tree trunks;[25] the king of Laṅkā occupies the entire height of the panel, which for all others (except Indrajit) is divided in two registers (Figure 4.4). He sits comfortably amidst a bevy of beautiful and eager damsels vying for his affections; his many hands caress them as he admires their beauty with his many eyes. Rāvaṇa's handsome presence contrasts with and complements the grace and delicate beauty of his female companions. The sculptor has effectively recreated an ambience in which the scent of unguents and other delicacies brought in and placed in baskets seems to mingle with the fragrance of the flower that he holds close to his chest—a metaphor for his heightened erotic desire while revelling in the company of his women in the *pānabhūmi* (drinking hall) inside his flying palace (Puṣpaka-vimāna).[26] In the midst of all this beauty and revelry, the more austere qualities of the king of Laṅkā offer a counterpoint: a *yogapaṭṭa* (yogic band) is tied across his legs and a *yajñopavīta* (sacred thread) crosses over his chest, a reminder of his half-Brahman lineage and the severe austerities that he had performed to gain power through a divine boon.

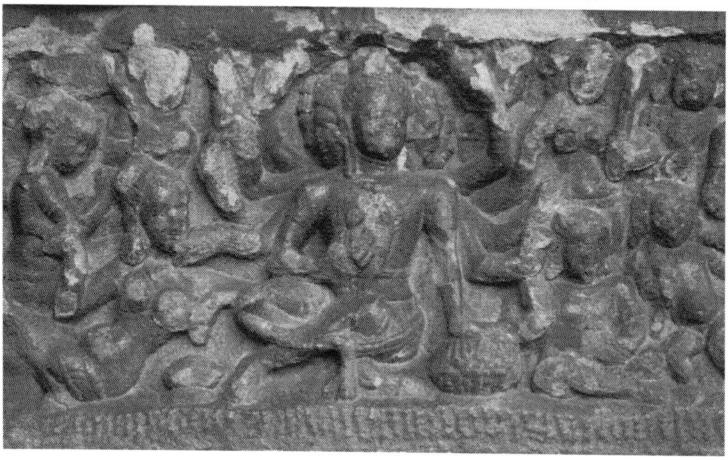

Figure 4.4: Rāvaṇa in the Company of Women in His Palace Interiors, Durga Temple, Aihoḷe, c. 7th Century
Courtesy: Parul Pandya Dhar.

In visualising Rāvaṇa in his palatial chambers, the artist has successfully brought forth the contrary qualities that coexisted in him and the extremes of virtue and decadence that he was capable of. His uncontrolled desire and arrogance, his attachment and dependence on the excesses of sensory indulgence—qualities that spell the nemesis of a king—are elaborated here. It is indeed a rare depiction in early medieval Indian sculpture of a king simultaneously enjoying multiple women and other pleasures in his harem. Rāvaṇa, by reason of his birth as a demon and as the king of *rākṣasas* (demons), was beyond the norms of righteous conduct to be followed in the world of humans. Such an exception owes its visual presence in part to the imagination of the stone sculptor, Mudyasili, to whom I shall soon return.

The *Sundarakāṇḍa* narrative at the Durga temple in Aihoḷe commences as a conflation of two events that proceed simultaneously.[27] Such practices of simultaneous narration and *śleṣa alaṃkāra* (a figure of ornamentation in Sanskrit poetics conveying double meanings) are shared across *kāvya* (poetry) and *śilpa* (sculpture) in the intellectual histories of the period. The first episode relates Hanumān's stealthy entry in the guarded palace interiors and the scenes of revelry that he witnesses. But it also connects with a later passage in the *Sundarakāṇḍa,* when Hanumān positions himself at the garrisoned gateway as a challenge to assess the enemy's power, after his meeting with Sītā and his devastation of Rāvaṇa's pleasure grove (Aśokavana).[28] Hanumān is first seen at the extreme right corner outside of the palace, which is guarded by a row of soldiers on the upper half of the register (Figure 4.5). Here onwards, the narration overlaps, and the two strands of the larger narrative conflate: the residences that Hanumān spied on and the revelry he saw in his search of Sītā crowd the scene. Hanumān's form appears several times in the continuous narrative mode. The second parallel event is the episode occurring after Hanumān allows himself to be captured by Indrajit (son of Rāvaṇa), who does it with the aid of Brahmā's noose (*nāgapāśa*) and brings him before Rāvaṇa (Figure 4.6). This event should have been presented in a court setting and not in Rāvaṇa's pleasure hall. But in this case, the two locations have been accommodated in a single composition. The majestic, multi-armed and multi-headed king is shown seated regally, even as revelry and women surround him in place of his courtiers. A depiction of Rāvaṇa in his court on the base mouldings of the 7th-century Upper Śivālaya at Bādāmi, the capital of the early western Calukyas, offers an interesting comparison (Figure 4.7).

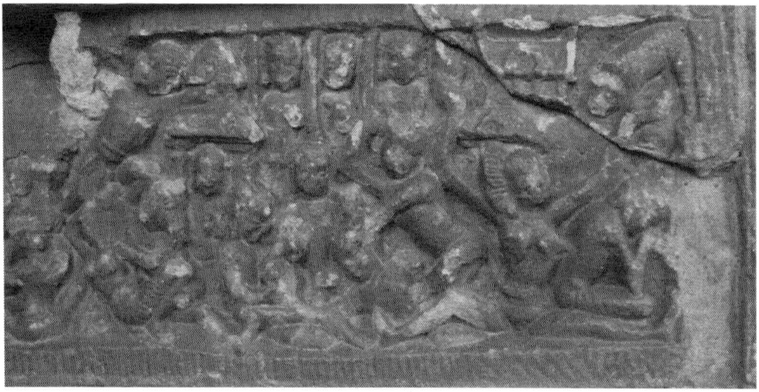

Figure 4.5: Hanumān's Entry in Laṅkā and in Rāvaṇa's Palace Complex, Durga Temple, Aihoḷe
Courtesy: Parul Pandya Dhar.

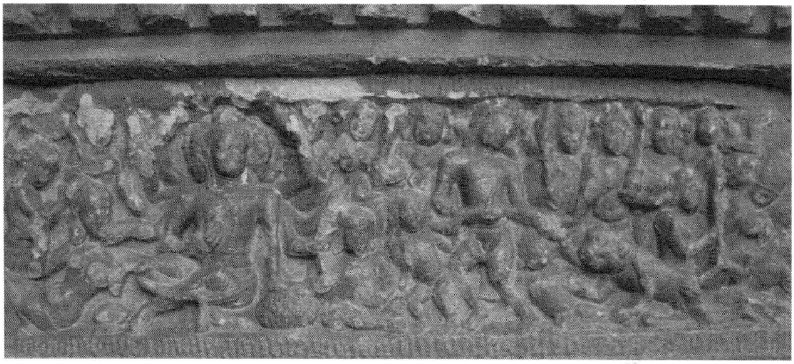

Figure 4.6: Indrajit Brings a Captured Hanumān before Rāvaṇa, Durga Temple, Aihoḷe
Courtesy: Parul Pandya Dhar.

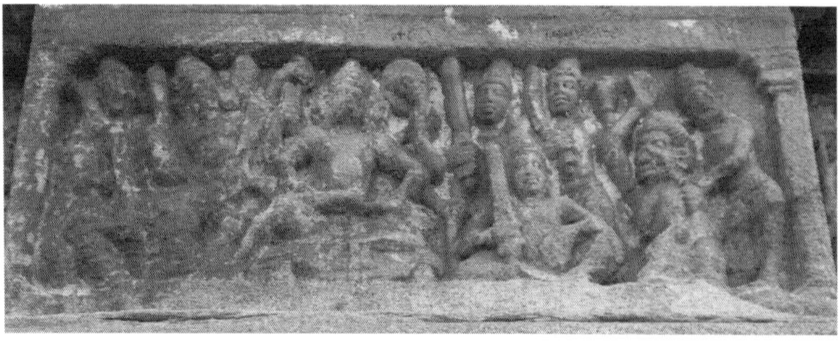

Figure 4.7: Śūrpaṇakhā's Lament in Rāvaṇa's Court, Upper Śivālaya, Bādāmi
Courtesy: Parul Pandya Dhar.

To the right of the king of Laṅkā, elaborate scenes of revelry continue, which are witnessed by Hanumān: a bed chamber with a couple occupying it is in view (Figure 4.8). Further right, scenes of the loving couples of Laṅkā offer visual parallels of erotic poetic renditions of the theme. Much vandalised, the panel still reveals passionate couples in union (*saṃbhoga śṛṅgāra*), drinking, embracing and enjoying other sexual pleasures.[29] Mudyasili, the artist who carved these erotic scenes, has engraved his name beneath this panel (Figure 4.9). Interestingly, the inscription records his name as 'Śrī Mudyasili' and describes him as '*anaṅga* (god of love) to women/wives' (*Śrī Mudyasili peṇḍir-anaṅgan*) (Padigar 2011, 259, no. 165). Mudyasili's name is a twist on the term *Silemudda*, meaning a stone sculptor (Padigar 2011, 259).[30] Evidently, Mudyasili, who postures himself as an attractive man, a 'god of love' to women and hence given to sensual pleasures, appears to have taken special pride in carving an elaborate portrayal of erotic revelry in the Laṅkā of Rāvaṇa, who is known to have been attractive to many women.

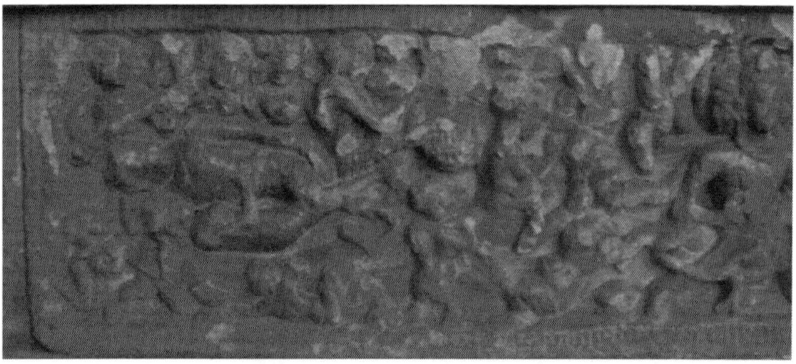

Figure 4.8: Hanumān Witnessing a Couple in a Bed Chamber Inside Rāvaṇa's Palace, Durga Temple, Aihoḷe
Courtesy: Parul Pandya Dhar.

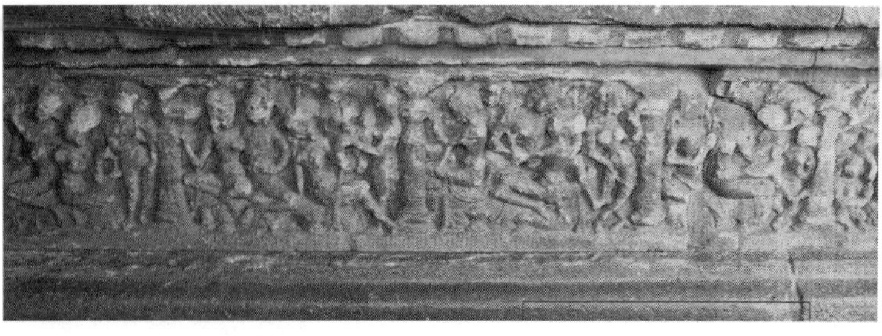

Figure 4.9: Intoxicated Lovers in Laṅkā, with Artist Mudyasili's Signature and Message Engraved Below, Durga Temple, Aihoḷe
Courtesy: Parul Pandya Dhar.

The visual narrative of erotic pleasure in Rāvaṇa's Laṅkā at Aihoḷe needs to be interpreted further in its architectural context. Like the *Rāmāyaṇa* narratives on some Gupta-period stone temples in northern India, the 7th century early western Calukya temples also harbour the epic scenes in narrative registers located on base mouldings of the temples (Dhar 2019, Figure 1). This is also the location for the depiction of *mithunas* and other sexually explicit imagery on temples from this period onwards. Mudyasili certainly knew how to imaginatively exploit this context and sculpt an elaborate excursus into the theme of 'love in Laṅkā'.

The epic portrayals at Aihoḷe find textual reverberations in the *Vālmīki Rāmāyaṇa*, *Bhaṭṭikāvya* and *Kamba Rāmāyaṇa* (*Irāmavatāram*). Some nuances are of special interest, especially in their inter-relationships with the visual imagery. Vālmīki's poem luxuriates in the wealth, grandeur and beauty of Laṅkā with its mansions, towers, archways, gardens, beautiful women and intoxicated lovers. Rāvaṇa's glory and revelry is extolled. Hanumān witnesses Rāvaṇa sleeping on his bed with several women resting at his feet and sees the beautiful Mandodarī sleeping on a bed apart from all others.[31] Bhaṭṭi's Hanumān encounters scenes of revelry in the interior of Laṅkā's mansions, especially in Rāvaṇa's palace, where he finds women of incomparable beauty eager to partake of sensual pleasures. Bhaṭṭi visualises Rāvaṇa's lordship, lustre and lust for women and compares him to Kailāsa and Meru.[32] In the same text, as Rāvaṇa retires (to his bed chamber) with a lover, Hanumān leaves the palace to continue his search for Sītā.[33] Kamban's Hanumān finds Mandodarī resting in luxury, attended upon by *apsarās* in her palace, and Rāvaṇa sleeping in his own magnificent palace.[34] Poetic and artistic freedom render the search for direct correspondence of the visuals with a single text difficult, but the visualisation corresponds well at times with the *Bhaṭṭikāvya* and at other times with the *Vālmīki Rāmāyaṇa*.

FURTHER VISUALISATIONS: PAṬṬADAKAL AND AMRITAPURA

The Virūpākṣa, Mallikārjuna and Pāpanātha temples at Paṭṭadakal, built under the direct patronage of the early western Calukyas, belong to the first half of the 8th century and harbour *Rāmāyaṇa* narratives (Meister and Dhaky 1986, 75–90). The architectural context of the epic scenes now shifts from the recessed bands on the base mouldings (as at Bādāmi and Aihoḷe) to the outer wall surfaces and pillars in the interior of the temple halls, resulting in greater visibility. The inherent contradictions in Rāvaṇa's character have been sensitively portrayed at

Paṭṭadakal, where he is encountered both as a powerful adversary and a passionate demon-devotee.[35]

The pillars in the interior of the Virūpākṣa temple's great hall (*mahāmaṇḍapa*) are carved with epic and *purāṇic* scenes laid out in horizontal registers, presaging, thematically and stylistically, the long and expansive layout of the *Rāmāyaṇa* and *Mahābhārata* carved on the walls of the lower storey of the Kailāsa temple complex at Ellora (Markel 2000, 59–71). The *Sundarakāṇḍa* narrative of Hanumān's entry into the inner chambers of Laṅkā's mansions, his encounter and defeat of the demoness Laṅkā-devī, his gaze into the inner apartments of the elites of Laṅkā, his capture and audience with Rāvaṇa and the burning of Laṅkā are themes carved on one of the pillars of the *mahāmaṇḍapa* of the Virūpākṣa temple at Paṭṭadakal (Figure 4.10). Hanumān is portrayed several times in three registers, encountering demons, jumping over mansions in his search for Sītā and watching the pleasure pursuits in the palace, including a couple in a sexual embrace on their bed. The rendering though is much abbreviated; its location at eye-level within the temple's interior, not far from the sanctum, as well as the space limitations on the pillar may have guided the sculptor's chisel towards a mere suggestion of the erotic rather than any detailed experiment as was noticed at Aihoḷe.

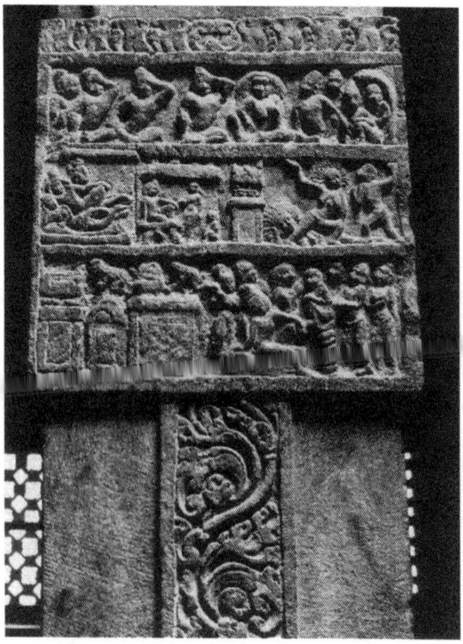

Figure 4.10: Hanumān's Entry and Gaze into the Palace Interiors of Laṅkā and His Audience with Rāvaṇa, Virūpākṣa Temple, Paṭṭadakal, c. 745 CE
Courtesy: American Institute of Indian Studies, Gurugram.

At the late 12th-century Amriteśvara temple in Amritapura built during the rule of the Hoysaḷas of Dorasamudra in Karnataka, the textual inspiration aligns with the philosophical approach of the slightly later *Adhyātma Rāmāyaṇa.*[36] This suggests that the *Rāmāyaṇa* sculptures at the Amriteśvara temple were based on a version of the epic that was moving closer in content to the *Adhyātma Rāmāyaṇa*. In this temple, the details of Hanumān's encounters with sensual pleasures in the palaces and residences of Laṅkā are completely missing; Rāvaṇa is shown performing a fire sacrifice before the final epic battle (Figure 4.11), and Rāma's allies, the *vānaras* (monkeys), are seen entering Rāvaṇa's harem and assaulting his women (Figure 4.12).[37] In all these instances, the visuals relate more closely with the *Adhyātma Rāmāyaṇa* and not with the *Vālmīki Rāmāyaṇa.* There is a decided shift in favour of ever greater deification of Rāma as an *avatāra* (incarnation) of Viṣṇu and in the release to be found in his grace. Rāvaṇa too is aware of his destiny

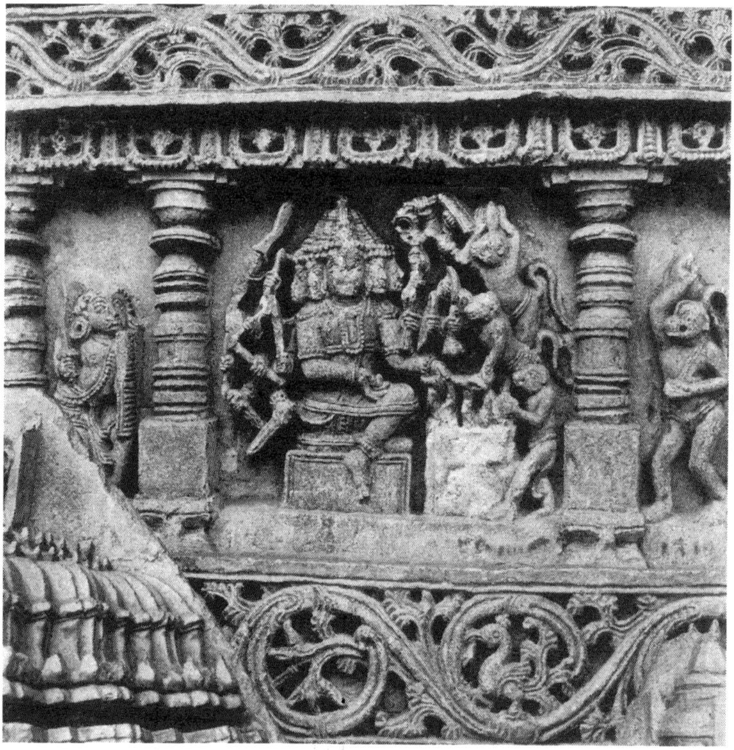

Figure 4.11: Monkeys Disrupting Rāvaṇa's Sacrifice Prior to the Epic Battle, Amriteśvara Temple, Amritapura, c. 1196 CE
Courtesy: American Institute of Indian Studies, Gurugram.

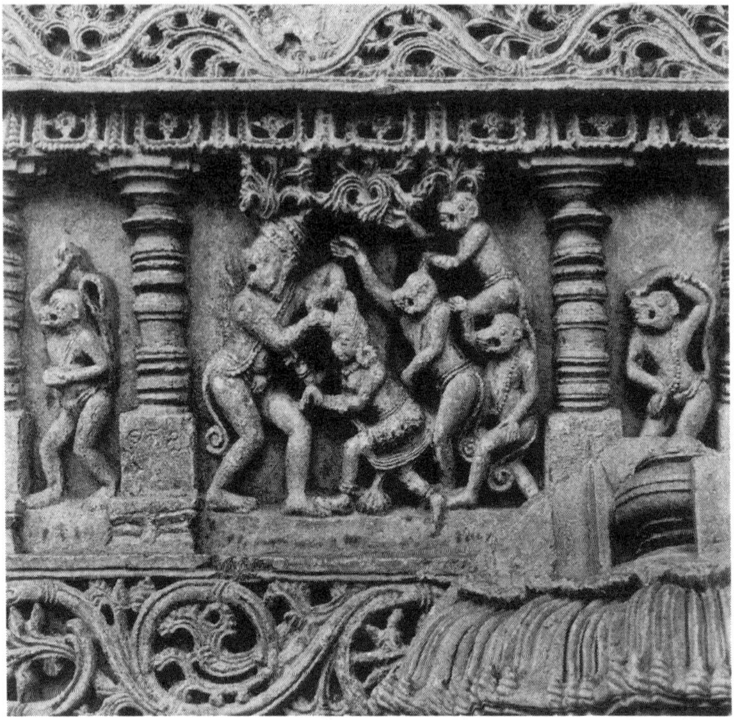

Figure 4.12: Monkeys Molesting the Women in Rāvaṇa's Harem, Amriteśvara Temple, Amritapura
Courtesy: American Institute of Indian Studies, Gurugram.

and desires release at the hands of Rāma. Increasing Vīraśaiva influence in Karnataka during this period also meant that the nobler qualities of Rāvaṇa as an ardent devotee of Śiva gained him increasingly greater regard. This is also revealed through the changing representations of the *Rāvaṇānugraha* ([Śiva's] benediction upon Rāvaṇa) iconography found on the Hoysaḷa-period temples, where the emphasis shifts to Rāvaṇa's nobler qualities: his ardent devotion to Śiva and his profound austerities, talents and abilities (Dhar 2015). It is in this context that the deliberate omission of pleasures in his harem and the absence of the unrestrained sexual exploits of the residents of Laṅkā on the Amriteśvara temple at Amritapura are best interpreted. The portrayal of *vānaras* in Rāvaṇa's harem—their wreaking havoc and behaving in an unruly manner with erotic undertones—has perhaps been introduced to highlight the baser instincts of *vānaras*, for social codes of conduct in the kingdom of monkeys, who dwell in the wilderness of forests, fall outside the codes of conduct applicable to humans.

CONCLUDING OBSERVATIONS

A contextual understanding of erotic pleasure in early medieval India through the prism of the aesthetics of desire and power in Rāvaṇa's Laṅkā offers a useful vantage point to understand how such themes were perceived, reimagined, enacted and reinforced, especially in the context of the court and temples of this period in early medieval western Deccan. The cultivation of social graces and pleasures—of beauty, sexuality, etiquette and aesthetic pursuits—were an integral part of early medieval elite society. These predilections also reflect in the arts of the early medieval temples. Religious developments such as Tāntrism, which advocated a belief in the magical powers of ritualised sex, gave further impetus to the already prevalent exaltation of *śṛṅgāra* in literature and the arts during this period. This promoted the proliferation of explicit sexual imagery on the temple walls, alongside a host of motifs relating to fertility and abundance. At the same time, righteous behaviour and restraint were crucial virtues in the world of humans and kings in transacting social and political inter-relationships.[38] The visuality of erotic desire was influenced by a confluence of all these circumstances. So although overtly erotic imagery of a generic nature is in evidence on early medieval temples, gods and kings, even when in the pleasurable company of a consort, have been portrayed with restraint. The *śāstric* texts on sculpture and painting had by this time codified a host of different typologies for portraying situations, emotions and characters of various types, which reflected in the sculpted imagery on the temple walls.

The *Sundarakāṇḍa* includes the most detailed imagery of erotic pleasures in the entire *Rāmāyaṇa*. Rāvaṇa and his kingdom, Laṅkā, belong to a realm where prohibitions on uncontrolled erotic pleasure were not the same as those that defined virtuous conduct in the world of human kings. This perhaps inspired Vālmīki and some of the later writers to conjure a luxuriant imagery of carnal pleasures in the city of Laṅkā. Such literary elaborations find resonance in some visual narrative sculptures at the Durga temple in Aihoḷe, built during the rule of the early Calukyas of Bādāmi. However, a degree of restraint is still evident in the visual vis-à-vis the textual because of the very physical nature of the visual medium. Mudyasili, the likely artist of this sculpted narrative, ingeniously locates a celebration of erotic pleasures in Laṅkā, with a splendorous and passionate Rāvaṇa as the focus, on the base mouldings of the temple's front hall, far below the eye-level and hidden from direct gaze. This was the architectural context for epic narratives on temples of the period of Gupta dominance, which preceded the early Deccan temples and was continued on the Upper Śivālaya at Bādāmi and the Durga temple at Aihoḷe.[39] From about the 7th-8th century, recessed bands of mouldings in different locations on temple surfaces became one of the preferred locations for placing certain types of debased sexual congress (*bhraṣṭa mithunas*).[40] The sculptor Mudyasili appears to have creatively exploited the interspace between both these visual conventions.

The Aihoḷe experiment is exceptional, and later imaginations—as at the 8th-century Virūpākṣa in Paṭṭadakal—were comparatively summary in their treatment of the theme. By the 12th century, as noticed at the Hoysaḷa-period Amriteśvara temple at Amritapura in Karnataka, detailed depictions of erotic pleasures in Laṅkā were given up in favour of a more idealised and spiritual interpretation, based on a tradition or text that predates the *Adhyātma Rāmāyaṇa* with which the sculptural panels show affinity. Only a minor erotic excess in the guise of the *vānaras* transgressing and assaulting the women in Rāvaṇa's harem serves to remind us of the very different attitudes towards pleasure, its prescriptions and proscriptions, not just in the realm of the *rākṣasas* but also in that of the *vānaras*.

NOTES

1. The *Rāmāyaṇa* is divided into seven parts or *kāṇḍas* that tell the story of Rāma from the events leading up to his birth and culminating in the end of his journey on earth. The story proceeds from the *Bālakāṇḍa*, followed by the *Ayodhyākāṇḍa, Araṇyakāṇḍa, Kiṣkindhākāṇḍa, Sundarakāṇḍa* and *Yuddhakāṇḍa*, ending in the *Uttarakāṇḍa*. The first and last among these were written later than the ones in between. On the issue of the geographical identity of Rāvaṇa's Laṅkā in the epic poem and Sri Lanka (Ceylon), I accept Robert Goldman's view:

   > … it seems improbable that the authors of the original portions of the epic had any very detailed knowledge of Sri Lanka (Ceylon). There is some evidence in the poem that the island was known but is distinguished from Laṅkā. The most that can be said with any certainty is that the poet knew of an island kingdom, whether real of mythical, said to lie some distance off the coast of the Indian mainland. (*The Rāmāyaṇa of Vālmīki, Vol. I*, 3–13, 28)

2. See, for example, the description of besotted women enticing Prince Siddhārtha in the *Buddhacarita*, 4.25–4.53. Also, *The Rāmāyaṇa of Vālmīki, Vol. V*, 9, note 9.
3. For a brief discussion of this aspect, see Dhar (2019).
4. Throughout this essay, I have used the term 'erotic' in the sense of the pleasures of love between man and woman, especially love in union, as it has been understood in the interpretation of *śṛṅgāra rasa* in Indian aesthetic theory.

5. The aesthetic theory of *rasas* (essential sentiments) and *bhavas* (emotional states) applied here is explicated in a range of ancient Indian texts on theatre and poetics, including its early discussion in the *Nāṭyaśāstra*. See, for example, *The Nāṭyaśāstra*, 53–77.
6. For a more detailed exploration of some of the ideas presented in this section, see *The Rāmāyaṇa of Vālmīki, Vol. V*, 3–86. The editors of that volume, however, do not consider Rāvaṇa to be as important a character as Sītā and Hanumān.
7. *The Rāmāyaṇa of Vālmīki, Vol. V*, 116–120, *vv.* 2.19–22, 3.1–2 and 3.18.
8. Ibid., 129–142, *Sargas* 7–9.
9. See, for example, the dialogue between sage Mārkaṇḍeya and Vajra about the inextricable connections between various art forms, in the *Viṣṇudharmottara Purāṇa* (Nardi 2006, 23).
10. *Sāmānya abhinaya* refers to theatrical communication through a harmonious blend of speech and physical and natural gestures suited to express common or general concerns specific to an emotional state.
11. *The Nāṭyaśāstra*, 197–201: Chp. XXIV, *vv.* 238–241 and 291–296.
12. This corresponds with the division of the body parts into six primary, six secondary and six tertiary limbs in the ancient Indian art treatises.
13. For a more detailed understanding of how these are explicated in the text, see Nardi (2006), *passim.*
14. Nardi (2006, 172, note 10):

    > This text [*Viṣṇudharmottara Purāṇa* (III.43.13b–17ab)] explains that scenes such as the preparation of battles, funeral grounds, the tragic, death, pain, people tormented with grief and the villainous, bulls without horns and elephants without trunks are regarded as inauspicious and they are not allowed to be painted in houses. They are only permitted in the royal assembly halls and temples.... The portrait of oneself or self-portrait must never be made in one's own house.

15. See Ali (2011), in which Daud Ali offers a perspectival change by moving away from theories that focus exclusively on kingship and legitimation in early medieval Indian history.
16. Approximately translated as 'affection or attachment', and 'bringing under control', respectively. See also Ali (2011, 252).
17. See, Chapter 2 by Seema Bawa in this volume.
18. In the entire range of early medieval Indian sculpture, there are very few such 'portraits' of actual kings.
19. The earliest portions of the *Rāmāyaṇa* are accepted in academic scholarship to have been written around the 4th–5th century BC, with accretions over time up to the 4th century CE.
20. Given the Sanskritic cultures prevalent in early western Calukya court, direct familiarity with the *Vālmīki Rāmāyaṇa* is not unimaginable. See Padigar, ed. (2010, Inscription Nos. 8 and 22, pp. 12–15 and 37–40).
21. See Bibliography for the editions used. The *Bhaṭṭikāvya* belongs to the region of Valabhī in southern Gujarat and has been dated by scholars to the 6th–7th century CE; Kamban's *Irāmavatāram* is later than the carved

versions at Aihoḷe and Paṭṭadakal, and the *Adhyātma Rāmāyaṇa* is dated by scholars to about the 13th–15th centuries. The latter has affinities with the portrayals at Amriteśvara in Amritapura.

22. The names of several sculptors and actors, composers and teachers, musicians and dancers are mentioned in the Calukya records. For an overview, see Padigar, ed. (2010, xxvii–lxxx).
23. See Dhar (2019). Visual narratives of the *Rāmāyaṇa* are carved on the early Calukyan temples at Bādāmi, Aihoḷe and Paṭṭadakal. Calukya King Maṅgaleśa's Mahākūṭa Pillar inscription compares the king's qualities to various gods, including Rāma, and includes a phrase from the *Raghuvaṃśa*. Ravikīrti's Meguti temple inscription of Pulakeśī II (634/5 CE) compares Ravikīrti's fame on account of his poetic skill to that of Kālidāsa and Bhāravī. See Padigar, ed. (2010, 12–15 and 37–40, Nos. 8 and 22).
24. The Durga temple, Aihoḷe, was carved with more narratives, especially on the outer ambulatory, but these are either incomplete or far too effaced to be identified.
25. *Bhatti's Poem*, 171, *vv.* 8.51 and 8.54.
26. *The Rāmāyaṇa of Vālmīki, Vol. V*, 139, *v.* 9.3.
27. Taboji (2011, 38) and Padigar (2015, 24) do not suggest such a simultaneous depiction of two parallel narratives. Padigar (2015, 24) briefly mentions the following scenes on the southern side: 'Hanuman destroying Ashokavana at Laṅkā; Indrajit leading a shackled Hanuman to Rāvaṇa's court; and loving couples in Laṅkā.'

    My interpretation here is a slightly revised version of the simultaneous narration that I first discussed in Dhar (2019).
28. *The Rāmāyaṇa of Vālmīki, Vol. V*, 227–244, *vv.* 39.8–46.30.
29. Ibid., 119–142.
30. Padigar further notes that Mudyasili's signature is inscribed on the lower moulding near the *Rāmāyaṇa* narratives on the southern side of the front hall and that he is most likely to have been the artist who carved the *Rāmāyaṇa* narratives on the southern side.
31. *The Rāmāyaṇa of Vālmīki, Vol. V*, 118–138.
32. *Bhatti's Poem*, 171, *vv.* 8.51 and 8.54.
33. Ibid., 165–171.
34. *Kamba Rāmāyaṇa*, 216–224.
35. For further details on this theme, see Dhar (2019) and Wechsler (1994).
36. The *Adhyātma Rāmāyaṇa* is connected with the *Brahmāṇḍa Purāṇa* and has been dated by scholars between the 13th and 15th centuries CE. This 'philosophical *Rāmāyaṇa*' is a retelling of the epic by Śiva to Umā. It is seen as an attempt to reconcile Śaṅkara's Advaita Vedānta with a belief in the saving grace of Rāma. See Rocher (1986, 158–159).
37. See also, Evans (1997, 70–74), and Settar (1992, Vol. II, Figures 188–189), for further visual reference.
38. This argument has been developed at length in Daud Ali's important book on courtly cultures (Ali 2011).
39. See Bawa (2018) and Dhar (2019, especially Figure 1).

40. See, for example, Desai (2013b, especially Figures 13.1, 13.2 and 13.9). Tantric sexual imagery of yet another category was located at the place of juncture or *sandhi-kṣetra* on temple exteriors where successive temple halls connected with each other. See Desai (2013c). In the context of sculptures depicting explicit sexual congress on base mouldings of Hoysaḷa temples, see Settar (1992, Vol. II, Figures 261–266).

REFERENCES

Ali, Daud. *Courtly Culture and Political Life in Early Medieval India*. Cambridge: Cambridge University Press. 2011 [2004].

Bawa, Seema. 'Visualising the *Rāmāyaṇa*: Power, Redemption and Emotion in Early Narrative Sculptures (5th to 6th centuries CE)'. *Indian Historical Review* 45, no. 1 (2018): 92–123.

Bhaṭṭi's Poem: The Death of Rāvaṇa by Bhaṭṭi [Bhaṭṭikāvya], trans. Oliver Fallon, edited by Isabelle Onians. New York: Clay Sanskrit Library. 2009.

Desai, Devangana. 'Erotic Literature'. In *Art and Icon: Essays on Early Indian Art*, 195–206. New Delhi: Aryan Books International. 2013a.

———. 'Tantrism and Erotic Temple Sculpture'. In *Art and Icon: Essays on Early Indian Art*, 207–231. New Delhi: Aryan Books International. 2013b.

———. 'Beyond the Erotic at Khajuraho'. In *Art and Icon: Essays on Early Indian Art*, 232–246. New Delhi: Aryan Books International. 2013c.

Dhar, Parul Pandya. 'Challenging Cosmic Order: Ravana's Encounters with Shiva at Belur and Halebidu'. In *Art, Icon and Architecture in South Asia: Essays in Honour of Dr. Devangana Desai*, edited by Anila Verghese and Anna L. Dallapiccola, 169–186. New Delhi: Aryan Books International. 2015.

———. 2019. 'Characterizing Contrariety: Representing Rāvaṇa in the Early Western Deccan'. In *Berliner Indologische Studien/ Berlin Indological Studies*, 24 (2019): 131–164, edited by Gerd J.R. Mevissen. Berlin: Weidler Buchverlag.

Evans, Kirsti. *Epic Narratives in the Hoysaḷa Temples: The Rāmāyaṇa, Mahābhārata Bhāgavata Purāṇa in Haḷebīd, Belūr and Amṛtapura*. Leiden-New York-Koln: Brill. 1997.

Markel, Stephen. 'The *Rāmāyaṇa* Cycle on the Kailāsanātha Temple at Ellora'. *Ars Orientalis* 30 (Supplement 1, 2000): 59–71.

Meister, Michael W. and M.A. Dhaky, eds. *Encyclopaedia of Indian Temple Architecture, Vol. I, Part 2: Upper Drāviḍadeśa, Early Phase, A.D. 550–1075*. (Text and Plates). New Delhi and Philadelphia: American Institute of Indian Studies. 1986.

Nardi, Isabella. *The Theory of Citrasūtra in Indian Painting: A Critical Re-evaluation of Their Uses and Interpretations*. London and New York: Routledge. 2006.

Padigar, Shrinivas V., ed. *Inscriptions of the Calukyas of Bādāmi*. Bangalore: Indian Council for Historical Research. 2010.

Padigar, Shrinivas V. *Aihole* (Heritage Series). Edited by C.G. Betsurmath. Mysore: Department of Archaeology, Museums and Heritage. 2015.

Rocher, Ludo. *A History of Indian Literature, Vol. 2, Fasc. 3: The Purāṇas*. Edited by Jan Gonda. Wiesbaden: Otto Harrassowitz. 1986.

Settar, S. *The Hoysaḷa Temples, Vols. I & II*. Dharwad: Institute of Art History, Karnatak University and Kalā Yātrā Publications. 1992.

Taboji, Chandrashekhar B. 'Narrative Sculpture in Early Karnataka'. PhD diss., Dharwad: Karnataka University Dharwad. 2011.

The Adhyātma Rāmāyaṇa by Maharshi Vedavyasa, with the commentary of Ramavarmah, edited by Pandit Jibananda Vidyasagara. Calcutta: New Vālmīki Press. 1884.

The Buddha-Carita or Acts of the Buddha, Part II, edited with an introduction and notes by E.B. Johnston. Calcutta: Baptist Mission Press. 1936.

The Kamba Rāmāyaṇa. Translated by P.S. Sundaram, ed., N.S. Jagannathan. New Delhi: Penguin Books. 2002.

The Nāṭyaśāstra, English translation with critical notes by Adya Rangacharya. Delhi: Munshiram Manoharlal (fourth edition). 2003 [1996].

The Rāmāyaṇa of Vālmīki: An Epic of Ancient India. Vol. I: Bālakāṇḍa. Translated by Robert P. Goldman and Sally J. Sutherland. New Delhi: Motilal Banarasidass. 2007 [1984].

The Rāmāyaṇa of Vālmīki: An Epic of Ancient India, Vol. V: Sundarakāṇḍa. Translated by Robert P. Goldman and Sally J. Sutherland Goldman, 2007 [1984]. New Delhi: Motilal Banarasidass.

Wechsler, Helen J. 'Royal Legitimation: Rāmāyaṇa Reliefs on the Papanatha Temple at Pattadakal'. *MARG* 45, no. 3 (1994): 27–42.

5

PLEASANT AND UNPLEASANT MOMENTS: THE LIFE AND TIMES OF A JAIN MERCHANT IN EARLY MODERN NORTH INDIA

Shalin Jain

The study of pleasure, its material affiliations and the structures of sociability in South Asia—whether conceptualised as the histories of entertainment, manners and ethics, life cycle or even as the history of 'private' or 'everyday' life—has been strikingly neglected in Indian historiography. Since the 1980s, social relations have been a much-celebrated topic of historical research; however, little attention has been paid to the forms of pleasure as an individual experience and its relative social dynamics. The historians who largely focus on the social aspects of history have neglected the dimensions of human experiences such as growing up, courting, getting married, bearing and rearing children, living in families, becoming old and dying from the perspective of pleasure and displeasure. However, such relationships, when developed in historiographic terms, can foster a sense of complexity and differentiation in the course of social change.

INTRODUCTION

In this backdrop, the critical issue is how one can historically conceptualise and measure pleasure in the South Asian context and how the struggles to actualise pleasure have been revealed in the popular perception. For example, how have the issues of pleasure been engaged with the literary imagination? What methods and practices have been used to construct and implement initiatives aimed at securing individual pleasure? Have understanding and realising pleasure been able to address issues such as gender, friendship and social networks as well as the tensions around them? In what ways have religious and philosophical traditions engaged with the challenges of securing mundane pleasure and how has the enjoyment been conceived within the institution of family? While discussing the social life of pleasure, one needs to understand individual persona, constraints shaping individual lives and both the access and denial to pleasure in private and public spheres within the historical context.

In terms of the individual life, the tasks individuals perform and the larger responsibilities they take in the domain of social existence, there are still significant gaps in the social history of medieval India. In the South Asian scenario, histories of common people have been largely overshadowed by royal histories.[1] Here historiography has celebrated the life of the royalty and the nobility while commoners still await their due in the narratives. The problem cannot simply be conceptualised in terms of a presumption of values, attitudes and beliefs and an assumption about the physical environment of social life. What constituted the appropriate ways to produce and maintain pleasure within families and the community is still a question to be answered. Individual passions have rare chances to get accommodated in the communitarian societies as personal pleasure always remains subject to social approval. Thus, the individual life emerges as the sole site for venting inner feelings of sorrow and a desire for affection, care and comfort. The social relations get expressed in terms of emotions, marriage, friendship, polygamy, concubinage, divorce, remarriage, adoption and other bonds, which have historically provided, created and maintained the kinship groups. These functions have also predetermined the character of larger kinship groups such as clans, lineages and communities defining property rights, legal interventions and thus the role of state.[2] In a way, family life has also governed social life; thus, an exploration of the ways in which common people in early modern South Asia shared various responsibilities and pleasures of family life is required.

This paper moves around the contours of pleasures and displeasures expressed in the 17th -century Hindi text *Ardhakathanak*[3] to reconstruct a multi-tiered reality in the everyday lives of individuals around their social, political and economic engagements. Eugenia Vanina and Farhat Hasan, while discussing the *Ardhakathanak* within specific contexts, refer to a constant tension persisting between the medieval 'individual' and his 'social' ambience. Vanina sees it as a conflict of cultural values with an emphasis on individuality and self-realisation while Hasan sees it in terms of an 'engagement that contemporary norms and values had with individual subjectivity'.[4] One needs to extend these arguments further—that the terms of negotiation between the individual and society at large were also simultaneously creating forms of pleasure and displeasure. One should also pose questions about how the normative social code of conduct expecting an explicit morality was being dealt with by the agency of the individual. 'Interconnectedness' across the various Jain lifestyles is as visible as the tensions cutting across them.

For example, the life of a householder always follows the role model setup by the ascetics. However, it is only the householder who breaches the principles of austerity.

THE ETHOS AND PRACTICES OF PLEASURE

Before leaping into the world of pleasure of Banarsidas, it is pertinent to point out that he exhibits a strong sense of identity of his religious and spatial affiliations as well as family genealogy. But Banarsidas has an inclination towards the spaces beyond familial ties where he delves into the unrestrained joy of erotic love and enjoyment of worldly success and pleasure. Thus, the way Banarsidas situates himself is a reflection of his selfhood in a historical consciousness. His story began with his individual identity as the slave of the Jain Tirthankars Parshava and Suparshava and carrying the name Banarsi. He indicated his birthplace as Benaras, the birthplace of two Jain Tirthankars as well.[5] He takes pride in identifying himself with the geographical boundaries of *madhyadesha*, as he resided and travelled across Agra, Jaunpur and Khairabad. The repeated references to geographical space reveal a great deal about his sense of regional pride. He identified with great satisfaction his textual language as that of *Madhyadesha—Madhyadesha ki boli*. The sense of belonging to a particular linguistic zone is as apparent as his attempt to associate himself with a particular lineage of Shrimal Jains who claimed conversion from the Rajputs of Biholi, a place near Rohtak. These claims are signifiers of a multipolar identity drawing legitimacy from various sources of social existence. Banarsidas again asserts his identity while summing up his text through his sense of belonging to the geosocial world of Jain Shrimal clan of Agra, Banarsi Biholia by name, and an *adhyatmi* by conviction:

> I now live in Agra and I am, let me repeat, a Jain of the Srimal clan, Banarasi Biholia by name and an *adhyatmi* by conviction.[6]

Here is an individual acting under various influences and responding to them through his own agency.

While talking about a complex personality like Banarasidas, one needs to situate the medieval worldview of the Jains vis-à-vis their religious morality. The five Jain vows known as *anuvratas—ahimsa* (non-violence), *satya* (truth), *asteya* (non-stealing), *brahmacharya* (chastity) and *aparigraha* (non-possession)[7]—are meant for householders with certain reliefs in practicing these vows. The Jain worldview also claimed that work was the key to success and that a 'true man' was always willing to work hard. Leisure was distrusted because they believed that it perpetuated laziness. A man who indulged himself in leisure was not considered a 'true man', for a 'true man' denied himself pleasure to practise self-denial. Being concerned with thrift, the Jain ethos encouraged men to save their money rather than spend it on luxuries and also to avoid laziness and gluttony in order to be better Jains. In this worldview, spending money on items such as alcohol was wasteful and in effect made the buyer a failure because he did not spend his time and money in a reasonable and useful manner.[8]

Despite belonging to a merchant community, Banarsidas's desire to make money has been narrated as an abhorrent orientation in an apologetic manner in *Ardhakathanak*. After lamenting his good virtues, big and small, which were not free of shortcomings, Banarsidas relates his vices. He says he has little anger, pride or cunning, yet his greed for money was great.[9] The early modern context of pleasure vis-à-vis the merchant communities gets narrativised not only in the course of Banarsidas' actions but also through his thoughts. He takes an intellectual stand, philosophically explaining the criteria for defining pleasure. While describing the persecution of his father in the hands of Qilich Khan, he takes a fatalist view.[10] For him and in the eyes of common men, the circumstances of joy and sorrow, so close in time, may yet seem so utterly different as to have nothing whatever is common between them. But one has just to look at the matter from a slightly different angle to realise that joy and sorrow are, in truth, near kin. Only a man who has known suffering can taste joy, and a man who has experienced happiness must also have known suffering. Yet the ignorant man can think of nothing but joy when fortune is smiling on him and times are good. In days of hardship, he is completely overwhelmed with pain. To him joy and sorrow are utter opposites. Wise is the man who strives for equanimity, remaining equally unmoved by joy or sorrow. Such a man is like the sun, which has the same red hue whether it rises or sets.[11] More than the experience of pleasure, the criterion of experiencing the pleasure is more significant in social terms.

Notions of pleasure must be differentiated from the usual material concerns of life. Wealth did not necessarily bring pleasure but was required for utilitarian purposes within the Jain worldview. Thus, the interaction between routine life, satisfaction and happiness could have been the more wise cause of pleasure than forms of consumption and utility. The Jain worldview took into account that the followers who engaged in deliberate and direct pursuits of happiness through the evil of wealth might wind up pursuing immoral activities and experiences, thus missing out on the satisfaction of an ideal life. This normative approach is challenged the moment we take the examples from *Ardhakathanak*, as on the one hand luxuries are less easily justified and on the other utilitarian consumptions are prized. The normative Jain worldview was being broken and challenged not only in the intellectual domain. Entertainment and luxuries were ingrained in the individual lifestyle beyond religious constraints. The Mothiya business family of Agra was one of the wealthiest Shrimal families then living in Agra. In 1615–1616, when Banarsidas was going through a financial crisis along with his partner Narottam, Sabal Singh Mothiya invited them to Agra. Banarsi calls himself partner of Sabal Singh.[12] The description of Sabal Singh given by Banarsidas explains the lavish standard of life of the 17th-century traders of Agra:

> He was a spoilt, rich man, revelling in his possessions. Whenever I went to him I saw him surrounded by musicians. Famous singers sang before him with wonderful art while skilled players on string instruments displayed their virtuosity to the accompaniment of sonorous *pakhawaj* drums. He was always sitting in court like a prince distributing bounty and gifts. Poets, bards and minstrels stood before him reciting eulogies in his praise. From morning till evening he was in the midst of a dazzling exhibition of affluence such as I can find no words to describe.[13]

The usual mercantile cunning was part of the tactics of Jain businessmen as well and they ruthlessly exercised it with their competitors and customers to earn profits. Banarsidas had to face lot of problems in settling his business transactions with Sabal Singh. The narrative of Banarsidas about Sabal Singh certainly comes out of the anguish of a failed partnership, but at the same time, it shows the independent luxurious lifestyle of the merchants of Agra. Forms of enjoyment were mundane here, with a secular sense of pleasure far away from the theological constraints. At the same time, this narrative sidelines many an oriental assertion that Indians merchants had to hide their wealth and live a humble life to avoid the wrath of the authorities.[14] No sources exist to indicate the response of Jain ascetics to the hedonistic lifestyle of Sabal Singh Mothiya as expressed by Banarsidas, which is more a narrative in nature than voicing loathing. The polarities of experiences of Sabal Singh and Banarsi indicate that social and economic status mattered a lot in the application of public morality.

THE JOY OF KNOWLEDGE

Just as in the political, social and religious realms, early modern times were periods of intellectual transformation as well. As a commoner of the early modernity, Banarsidas's life and time unfolds a unique site of pleasure in terms of his passion for knowledge. His unending quest and complex engagement with forms of knowledge and knowledge production are a story of his incessant joy, pleasure and relentless pursuit for intellectualism. Banarsidas's curiosity about literary and spiritual matters and at times erotic as well meant that he was widely read. While the thematic range of literature he discussed was predominately Jain, his vocabulary was cosmopolitan, interacting with the larger context. Like many of his contemporaries,[15] he was a multilingual intellectual who translated several Jain treatises from Sanskrit and Prakrit into Brajbhasha (*Samaysaar natak/Gommatsaar*) and composed *Dhyanbattisi*, *Shivmandir*, etc. During his days of penury in Agra, he passed his time singing Qutban's *Mirigavati* and Manjhan's *Madhumalati*, two mystical Sufi poems.[16] His very knowledge of these Hindavi Sufi classics speaks of a literary culture that was not hindered by religious boundaries and indicates his knowledge of the Persian literature. That is why Banarsidas could freely accommodate Persian words such as *mulk, shariyati, dervish, fakir* and *aashiqui* within his narrative. He was aware of various literary trends, which is reflected in his compositions in the *sorath, dhola* and *chaupai* metres. This typical literary genre happened to be the trend of majority of the medieval Jain compositions in the region of Rajasthan and Gujarat and is explicit in his scholarly career. He very generously liberated himself from linguistic boundaries, borrowing from various languages and putting together a liminal form of creative expression that was both attractive and meaningful across the linguistic barrier.

Banarsidas's linguistic elasticity and his conscious choice of writing his autobiography in Brajbhasha, despite his fluency in both Sanskrit and Persian, is a sharp signifier of the emergence of a public domain, which was prepared for such production beyond the sphere of elite literary production. Writing a commentary on the philosophical treatise *Samaysaar*[17] was filtering down a tradition according to his own worldview. His literary knowledge came at hand when he circulated texts through oral performance. On several occasions, Banarsidas and his intellectual circle assembled to recite various popular literary texts. I argue that these moments empower individuals with the status of agency between a text and its audiences across time and beyond the realm of normative discourse.

The newly emerging intellectual domain was another space to fulfil human desires and express creativity. The pleasure of intellectual expression was a quest that could often move beyond existing societal norms. Being rational was almost equivalent to the discovery of the individual self but at the cost of socially acceptable behaviour. Such rationalisation of individual thought certainly led to the secularisation of culture beyond the societal boundaries of religion and caste. Banarsidas was condemned by contemporary sects for drifting away from his parent faith, the Shwetambar sect. However, his attraction towards the Digambar sect could not hold him for long, as he could not accept the formal practices of the Digambars, such as use of the *picchika* (a broom made of a bunch of peacock feathers) and *kamandalu* (water vessel). He also had some reservations in his belief in the Digambar Purāṇas, particularly about their aim of enjoining rituals and formal traditions of conduct.

One sees the individual's rational disenchantment and sense of displeasure both with the prevalent Shwetambar lifestyle and the extremist Digambar sense of non-possession.[18] By this time, Jain theology had become so orthodox in its practices that the urge to reform was common to many a contemporary Jain thinkers and philosophers. Ultimately, Banarsidas wrote a commentary on *Samaysara*, propagating his own views in order to win over more people to his way of thinking. He declared that the *bhattaraks*[19] of the Digambar sect were not worthy of veneration: no man, he argued, who has any possessions, however small (*tilatusamatro*), deserves the name of a monk (guru).

Banarsidas's doctrines gave rise to a separate sect in 1680 VS (AD 1623). He writes about the rational practices of the *adhyatama* movement inspired by one Arathmal Dhor from Khairabad and appropriated the literature of this movement. He studied hard and wrote profusely and very soon renounced all rituals and outward forms of his religious faith.[20] It seems he became a member of a liberal group at Agra, which included his friends Chandrabhan, Udaykaran and Thaan. In a way, pleasure has been organised and taken around knowledge practices throughout the *Ardhakathanak*. However, whether it is implicit or explicit depends on its functionality in the private or public domain. In 1692 VS (AD 1635), Pandit Rupchand, an authority on Jain scriptures, came to Agra and stayed in a temple built by the merchant Tihuna Sahu. All *adhyatmis* requested him to explain the *Gommatsaar*, a profound work on Jain doctrines.[21] The argument about the rise of a literary public becomes handy to explain this, as the quest to know the 'text' was quite explicit across the religious spectrum of early modern history.[22] A 'protestant' puritan culture was emerging against the established orthodoxy and the 'text' was being revisited in the autonomous sphere of individuality. The text was not only stimulating the intellectual prowess of the individual but was also providing the pleasure of creativity in terms of understanding and debate.

The above-mentioned 'literary radicalism' was contradictory to the established religious norms and thus a matter of grave concern for the Jain theology of the time. Banarsidas and his friends had to face a lot of criticism from the Jain community, which he himself acknowledged. He mentions that, along with his friends, he became blasphemous, engaged in indecent acts and his image was tarnished.[23] However in the milieu of early modernity, knowledge and its acquisition was still such a social act that individuals had no natural prerogative or access to it. In Jaunpur, Banarsidas had to face the elders of his community, who censured him and advised him to mend his ways:

> Pursuit of learning is meant for Brahmans and bards and that son of a merchant should tend the shop. If you study too much you shall beg, you must adhere to what the elders' advise.[24]

Here knowledge is withheld as community-based experience and whatever is supposed to be individual pleasure is being asked to be sacrificed as per the standards of the community.

A contemporary text, *Yuktiprabodha*, written by the Shwetambar monk Meghavijay of the 17th century, discussed the rise of the *adhyatama* sect in Ugrasenpura (Agra). Many followers of the Shwetambar faith began to call themselves *adhyatmikas*. They were also known as *Varanasiyas* because their views were 'inspired by the imaginary but attractive ideas propagated by a Jain named Banarsidas who has succeeded in deluding them and leading them astray'. Meghavijay critically examined the ideas and lifestyle of Banarsidas, even more so because Banarsidas posed a theoretical challenge to normative Jainism. The community saw whatever Banarsidas believed in or practised as acts of defiance and indiscipline.[25] Here, the choice of individual pleasure was constrained by the normative public ethos. Meghavijay was conscious of the fact that Jain monks and householders of coming generations might confusedly think that the *adhyatmikas*, like the Digambars, 'are an ancient sect and that their views (though heretical) have a basis in age-old religious canons'.[26] He denounced Banarsidas as he was worried that neo-Digambarites, the Varanasiyas, wished to win over the followers of the Shwetambar sect to their own heretical beliefs. In his perception, men became base and self-seeking due to the evil nature of the contemporary epoch—'they do not practise charity and have no faith in the *tirthankars* or their monk-gurus'.[27]

In such a scenario, public demonstration of religiosity too had to be projected as a site of pleasure. Throughout his young life, Banarsidas tried out various forms of belief and kept rationalising Jainism through his actions. However, while he confessed his 'sins' in his autobiography towards the end of his life, he also moved towards the standardised life of a Jain *shravak*. In his retrospective recasting of his life-experiences only in the late stages of his youth did he become a genuine adherent of the religion to which he was born. The first thing he did every morning was to visit a Jain shrine even without brushing his teeth to pay homage to the Tirthankara. He strove diligently to put the precepts of his faith to practice and follow the 14 prescribed rules of conduct. He performed the decreed penances for the expiration of sins and sat religiously for the enjoined *samayika* meditations designed to instil an attitude of detachment towards the world. He gave up eating green vegetables, for these are forbidden to a Jain, and took a vow never to touch brinjals and other prohibited food for the rest of his life. For eight days in a year, he observed the special ritual of paying homage to the Tirthankaras, singing hymns to their glory and imploring them for grace and mercy. After breaking all the norms of the faith, he gradually projected himself as a truly devout, faithful Jain, spending hours listening to the glory of the religion.[28]

To maintain the norms of the public life of a religious man, individual desires and passions had to be suppressed. However, pleasure as an individual quest had to seek its space even in such constraints. The relation between pleasure and sin in the life of an individual leads to the assessment of that particular vice within the medieval spiritual value-system, emphasising the significance of values in providing the religious needs of particular communities. Even the slightest deviations from the prescribed morality, which could be condemned simply as illegitimate, could be presented in a nuanced way to sustain pleasure.

THE FAMILY AS A SITE OF PLEASURE

When one explores the individual domain of pleasure, it emerges as a complex phenomenon metamorphosing into multiple forms. Banarsidas draws a clear distinction between filial and fraternal emotions on the one hand and erotic emotions on the other. He depicts the love for his parents and his wife in vibrant and perceptive language and doesn't shy away in doing the same for his other relatives. Banarsi says:

> After settling my belongings at a *sarai* and after having my lunch at the banks of Ganga, I now walked down alone into the city to meet my father, Kharagsen. I was seeing him after a long time and was thrilled with joy. I ran to touch his feet and he embraced me with great tenderness.[29]

However, the moment one seeks to define pleasure in the context of family relations, it again becomes a complex issue, as more than being an emotive value it is treated in our referred text only with a fatalist approach. For example, when Banarsidas was married for the first time and brought his bride home, his father's grandmother was breathing her last and his mother was giving birth to his sister. He felt that a thoughtful man would have discerned in this a profound irony, the mockery and the wretchedness of life. Only a fool would remain unruffled.[30]

The times of Banarsidas are interesting in terms of human sexuality and human procreation vis-à-vis notions of pleasure. Banarsidas rarely describes sexual encounters between husband and wife, and even then he does so in a very subtle manner. Thus, from the ways in which occasions of birth have been narrated in the text, it seems as if the primary evolutionary purpose of sexual activity is not pleasure but procreation. So, in terms of familial sexuality, reproduction is the purpose rather than pleasure. Thus, the act of procreation was purely patriarchal. The birth of baby boy was much celebrated, and only the father was given credit for this auspicious feat. For example, Muldas, Banarsidas' grandfather, had two sons.[31] Another instance occurred when Banarsidas was born eight years after the death of his elder brother, and the event occasioned much joy. The whole household rang with propitious songs for the young woman and generous gifts were distributed to the poor. Festivities continued in the family for not less than six months.[32] In another instance in Jaunpur, when Kharagsen and his mother reached to the house of Madan Singh Shrimal, an older brother of Chhachmal, the maternal grandfather of Kharagsen, to take shelter and help, Madan Singh consoled them saying, 'a son even though an only son can be a great source of happiness'.[33] Again, when Kharagsen was blessed with another child, the event proved that both pleasure and displeasure move around the birth of a male child. The high mortality rate in pre-modern societies could simultaneously cause both pleasure and displeasure, and this becomes apparent when Kharagsen celebrates the birth of another child with great pomp and show, but the child passes away within ten days of birth.[34]

However, there are moments when pleasure becomes passionate; rather, it extends to such a level of spiritualism that a fatalist approach towards the mundane world of the family life cycle can easily be undermined. Banarsidas was very conscious about concealing his erotic emotions and seems highly elusive about what he experienced in the space beyond the household. Though he mentions them as part of his narrative of growing up and experiencing worldly pleasures, he makes a clear distinction between the two. He talks of his amorous relation as an 'all-consuming passion', comparing his intense devotion towards his beloved with those of a Sufi *shaikh* and a *faqir* for God. However, this individual infatuation could not be publicly acknowledged for the fear of social stigma associated with such socially disapproved relationship. Banarsidas consequently does not elaborate or mention any details of his 'beloved'. Here again the limitations of individual pleasure against social constraints are quite apparent. For the sake of his love, Banarsi could not refrain from stealing his father's belongings.[35] Whenever he is engaged in secret acts of sexuality, he describes it as pleasure (*rasmaahi*).[36] He stole money to gift his beloved. He called himself the *dasa* (slave) of his beloved, referring to himself as *garib* or poor.[37]As per the Jain norm, a *shravak*, i.e., a Jain householder, cannot relinquish copulation as such but should abstain from sexual and lustful contacts with all other women except his nuptial partner.[38] As discussed earlier, the one who follows the five Jain vows (*anuvrat*) must abstain from carnality and unchastity.[39] One should observe the following five meditations to observe chastity:

1. Refrain from reading or hearing stories about women
2. Abstain from seeing their arousing body parts
3. Avoid recalling past enjoyment or pleasure with women
4. Renounce all exciting and aphrodisiac food
5. Renounce self-beautification.[40]

THE PLEASURES OF FRIENDSHIP

While locating the forms of pleasure in early modern times, the emotional and the personal forms of bonding are subjective and significant enough to be raised here as a much-neglected dimension of South Asian history—friendship. Banarsidas's *Ardhakathanak* is replete with affective themes, especially friendship and its pleasures and sorrows. In the 17th century, friendship comprised intimate personal values deeply public in nature as well. Friendship was a social capital, as it shaped and in turn was shaped by social norms. The elite-prone public sphere inaccessible as an everyday experience for commoners makes friendship a significant virtue as well as bond of socialisation. Friendship also emerges as a site of collaborative networking to create dynamics of pleasure. Both personal and social lives converge as well diverge as a matter of experience, as in the case of Banarsidas—the emotions of friendship constantly faced material constraints. On the one hand, Banarsidas and his circle could express themselves collectively though not socially to have moments of pleasure, but on the other hand, the moment their relations were scrutinised in terms of communal good, they could no longer fit into the frameworks of social norms. Yet the secular domain of friendship emerging as an alternative against communitarian constraints made it a rational world of mutual exchange.

As a parallel example away from the *madhyadesa* of Banarsidas in the 17th century, in the *marudesa* of Ahmedabad another thick friendship of elites unfolded in the persona of Shantidas Jauhari, a great merchant magnet of the time, and his Jain ascetic friend Muktisagar (who later on took the title of Rajsagar Suri). The affective bond between Rajsagar Suri and Shantidas brings out the complex relationship of early modern asceticism and materialism through the particular lived experiences of these individuals. Shantidas was actively engaged in manoeuvres and bargains in the contemporary Jain religious domain of Ahmedabad.

According to Jain tradition, the spiritual mentor of Shantidas was a monk called Muktisagar who was affiliated to the breakaway Sagar faction of the Tapa Gaccha. This faction was a reflection of the dissent with the main Tapa Gaccha and was established in AD 1600 by Dharmasagar. According to hearsay, Shantidas believed that he owed his prosperity to the miraculous mantras given to him by Muktisagar, which helped Shantidas amass a great fortune.[41] Throughout their lifetime, both remained very close friends, and this friendship influenced the sphere of sectarian discourse as well. This was the bond of a teacher, disciple and a friend.

Shantidas used all his material resources to establish his friend and preceptor as well as the Sagar Gaccha in the religious world of the Jains. He constantly tried to pressure the Tapa Gaccha leader, Vijaysen Suri, to bestow the title of 'Upadhyaya' on Nemisagar and Muktisagar, but Vijaysen Suri obliged only in the case of Pandit Nemisagar in AD 1608, leaving out Muktisagar. The issue of bestowing of the title of 'Upadhyaya' on Muktisagar became an issue of contention between the Tapa Gaccha and Shantidas. In AD 1625, Shantidas attempted to organise a public debate in Ahmedabad between Muktisagar and Vijaydev Suri, the Tapa Gaccha leader, to establish which of the two groups was superior.[42] At the last moment, Muktisagar did not appear for the debate and Vijaydev Suri was declared the winner. Muktisagar was expelled from the Tapa Gaccha on that very day.[43]

The Parshvanath Temple of Ahmedabad was built by Shantidas in AD 1621 on the advice of Rajsagar Suri, and in AD 1625, he performed the consecration of the idol of Lord Chintamani Parshvanath. According to *Chintamani Prashasti*, in 1686 VS (AD 1630), in spite of all the protests by the leading Jain pious and affluent laity, Shantidas successfully used his influence to ensure the title of the '*Acharya*' for his pontiff friend Muktisagar from the Tapa Gaccha head Vijaydev Suri, the successor of Vijaysen Suri. In this mission, Shantidas took the help of Shrimalla, a businessman of Cambay, to get Vijaydev Suri's support. Earlier, Shrimalla had helped Vijaydev Suri in his elevation as *Acharya* in AD 1614. The title bestowing ceremony was held at the temple of Mahavira Swami at Ahmedabad, and the family of Shantidas celebrated the occasion with great pomp and show. Shantidas's nephew Vashipal, the son of Vardhaman, spent a large amount in celebration on the accession of Muktisagar as Suri. On this occasion, Muktisagar took a new name—Rajsagar Suri. According to the Jain tradition, to counter the influence of the Tapa Gaccha, Shantidas ultimately instigated Rajsagar Suri to establish a separate Jain *gaccha* or sect in Gujarat known as the Sagar Gaccha.[44]

Shantidas constantly challenged the supremacy of the Tapa Gaccha. According to one *farman* of 1629–1630, Shantidas established three *poshals* of the Sagar Gaccha in Ahmedabad, four in Khambat, one in Surat and one in Radhanpur. But the Sagar faction could not hold out for long against its rival Tapa Gaccha. In AD 1630, several of the leading laity from Cambay left the Sagar Gaccha to accept Vijaydev Suri as their preceptor.[45] Shantidas made another attempt to appoint Satyavijay as Suri of the Tapa Gaccha after the death of Vijaysingh Suri in AD 1653. This attempt could not succeed because Satyavijay backed out and initiated his own reformist lineage of the Samvegi Vjayshakha of the Tapa Gaccha.[46]

Tilaksagar Suri, in *Rajsagar Suri Nirvana Raas* of AD 1666, has mentioned the sorrow of Rajsagar Suri on the death of his dear friend Shantidas. Though the Suri lived up to the age of 84, his lament on the death of Shantidas—'*Sah Shantidas surlok ko prapt huye, hum niradhaar ho chuke hain, us kaaran Shantidas mera sahodar bhai usse milene ke liye main bhi praan tyag ki iksha rakhta hoon*' [Sah Shantidas has left for heaven thus now I am without any support, so for that reason to meet my brother Shantidas I want to leave my life][47]—clearly establishes a personal bond going beyond the materialistic considerations between the piety and the laity.

Such gestures of friendship within the merchant community certainly carried the social and material virtues of pleasure. *Ardhakathanka* also dwells upon the formation of a close nexus of friendship, maintaining intimate links in various ways through mutual business enterprises (?), common pilgrimages and frequent visits to each other. The first instance of friendship in *Ardhakathanak* is of Banarsidas's father Kharagsen with Karamchand Mahur, a Baniya of Shahzadpur.[48] The affection of friendship between them is expressed in terms of Karamchand's material generosity in Kharagsen's days of hardship. Banarsidas's own experience of friendship was with Narottamdas and Thanmal Badaliya, who shared various forms of companionship.[49] Their experiences varied from common pilgrimage trips to shared business interests. However, the platonic value of this companionship becomes quite explicit the moment Banarsidas narrates how Narottam discarded his father's warning for the sake of his friendship with Banarsidas, and Banarsidas poetically renders himself as Narottam's true friend.[50] Even in his literary pursuit Narottam left an undeniable mark on Banarsidas. Banarsidas credits Narottam, on whose behest he composed one of his literary compositions, *Banarsi-Naammala*.[51]

However, such individual compassions were certainly constrained by material factors, as after this instance ultimately both Banarasidas and Narottam had to wind up their partnership. Henceforth in Banarsidas's narrative, Narottam gets represented through his father's business activities only until his demise. Banarsidas recounts that while he was heading towards Agra, the unfortunate news of the loss of Narottamdas was received through a letter of another friend, Benidas. Banarsidas fell unconscious and remained inconsolable for a few days. This was the moment of reckoning for Banarsidas's bond of friendship.[52]

Another instance of Banarsidas's friendship was more in the nature of an intellectual companionship being shaped by the social practices of reading, writing and collecting, when his interaction with Arathmal Dhor or Chandrabhan, Udaykaran and Thaan begins. They followed virtually a secret anarchist way of life against the established norms of Jainism. Banarsidas himself says that they would dance naked in the house and claim to be ascetics.[53]

In the narrative of Banarsidas, his whole life cycle has moments of pleasure getting expressed through familial life, a friendship circle and individual passions. However, these very bonds of pleasure ultimately prove to be the occasions of sorrow as well. While interacting with the materiality of the social world of early modern times, constrains to individual pleasure were apparent. This is in spite of Banarsidas's comment that 'a little gain makes me inordinately happy and little loss plunges me into the depth of despairs'.[54] Pleasure does not seem to be only a matter of spirit, whether it was acquisition of knowledge, a matter of faith, the earning of a livelihood or the familial cycle of birth, marriage and death. Whatever the desires of Banarsidas were, they were so constrained that even while summing up his narrative when he imagines his own sense of pleasure he writes,

> I am over fond of laughter and love to poke fun at everything. I delight in playing the clown and acting the buffoon, indulging in these capers with great relish and gusto. I often utter things that should not be said without any sense of shame, revelling in narrating unutterable stories and escapades with much glee. I love to relate fictitious stories, often quite scandalous, and try to pass them off as

> true, especially when I am in the midst of a large gathering. When I am in the mood for fun, nothing can restrain me from telling fanciful lies or untruths.[55]

To conclude, in 17th-century India, pleasure was still far away from being an individual experience as the individual's life was still controlled by medieval norms of familial and community control. One must appreciate the fact that what was the act of procreation ultimately remained subservient to the social normativity. Except in his writings, one comes across rare examples where Banarsidas is able to express his pleasure in his individual capacity within the public space, while multiple instances can be found for shared occasions of experiencing and expressing pleasure. Thus, while discussing the constrained spaces of individual pleasure and the multiple sites of unpleasantness in early modern society, this paper argues that pleasure was merely an individual desire far from realisation beyond normative discourse and yet to be aspired for. A dualism prevailed between individual's social conduct and personal passion. Private moments of pleasure could be juxtaposed to the phases of public sorrow as far as the everyday life of a early modern Indian individual is concerned. The everyday life of a early modern Indian individual certainly had private moments of pleasure; however, such endeavours and desires had to constantly face the 'sorrows' surrounded by the public life of the times. Thus, pleasure is also a contradictory value in terms of being both individual and communitarian.

NOTES

1. Harbans Mukhia, *The World of Mughals and Works on Mughal Household* (USA: Blackwell, 2004); Ruby Lal, *Domesticity and Power in the Early Mughal World* (New York: Cambridge University Press, 2005).
2. Jack Goody, *The Development of the Family and Marriage in Europe* (Cambridge: Cambridge University Press, 1983).
3. The *Ardhakathanak* of Banarasidas (a Jain trader from Jaunpur) is an autobiographical poem in Braj Bhasha, with more touch of Khari Boli, a dialect of Hindi dating from AD 1641. *Ardhakathanak* is unique because of its being, arguably, the 'first autobiography in the Indian tradition' written by an individual, a commoner. Banarsidas, *Ardhakathanak* (1641), trans. Mukund Lath, *Ardhakathanak: Half a Tale* (Jaipur: Rajasthan Prakrit Bharati Sansthan, 1981).
4. Eugenia Vanina, 'The *Ardhakathanak* by Banarsi Das: A Socio-cultural Study', *Journal of the Royal Asiatic Society of Great Britain & Ireland*, 5, no. 2 (July 1995): 211–224; Farhat Hasan, 'Presenting the Self: Norms and Emotions in *Ardhakathanak*', in *Biography as History: Indian Perspectives*, ed.

Vijaya Ramaswamy and Yogesh Sharma (New Delhi: Orient Blackswan, 2009), 105–122.

5. Banarsidas, *Ardhakathanak*, verses. 1–2, p. 223.
Paani-jugul-put sees dhari, aani apanshau daas I
Aani bhagati chint jaani prabhu. andau paas-supaas II 1 II
Gangmaahi aaee dhasee daeu nadi baruna asi I
Beech basi banarasi nagari bakhani hein II
Kasiyaar des Madhya gaaon taaete kaasi nau I
Shrisupaas-paaski janambhumi maani hein II 2 II
6. Banarsidas, *Ardhakathanak*, 198, verse no. 671, p. 275.
Nagar agre mein basein, Jaindharam Shrimal I
Banarsi Biholia, Adhyatmi Rasaal II
7. Umasvati/Umasvami, *Tattvartha-sutra* (That Which Is), trans. Nathmal Tatia (Delhi: Motilal Banarsidass, 2007), 176.
8. Acharya Samantbhadra, *Ratnakarandakshravakachara*, trans. Vijay. K. Jain, *Ratnakarandakshravakachara: The Jewel-Casket of Householders Conduct* (Dehradun: Vikas Printers, 2016), 110.
9. Banarsidas, *Ardhakathanak*, verse 652, p. 274.
Kahe Banrasike gun jatha I *doshkatha ab barnau tatha* II
Krodh maan maya jalrekh I *Pai lachhimeekoun lobh bisekh* II 652 II
10. Banarsidas, *Ardhakathanak*, verses 110–113, p. 232; *Bipada udai bhai is beech, purhakim nauwab Qilich.* (A number of dire and tragic events occurred in between; Nawab Qilich Khan was then the governor of the city.)
11. Banarsidas, *Ardhakathanak*, pp. 20–21; verses 128–130, pp. 233–234.
Ek drishti bahuantar huiye I *Ek drishti such dukh sum doi* II
Jo dukh dekhe so suckh lahee I *Sukh bhunjae soi dukh sahe* II (128)
Sukh mein mane mein sukhi, dukh mein dukhmae hoi I
Moodh purushki dishtimein, deesae such dukh doi II 129 II
Gyani sampati vipati mein, rahee eksi bahnti I
Jyoon rabi ugat aathwat, tajae na raati kaanti II 130 II
12. Banarsidas, *Ardhkathanak*, verses 406–407, 475, pp. 254, 259.
Tab hatth kari raakhae ghar maahi I *bhai kahae judaai naahi* II
kahoo divas narottamdas I *tarachand mothiyae paas* II 406 II
Baithae tab uthi bole sahu I *tum banarasi patne jaahu* II
Yeh kahi raasi daee tis baar I *tika kaadhi uttarae paar* II 407 II
Sabalsingh mauthiya masand I *nemidas sahu kau nand* II
Likhyon lekh tin apne haath I *dou saajhi aavhu saath* II 475 II
13. Banarsidas, *Ardhkathanak*, verses 558–562 , p. 266.
14. Francois Bernier, *Travels in the Mogul Empire, 1656–1668*, trans (Delhi, Low Price Publications, 2005), p. 225; Jean-Baptiste Tavernier, *Travels In India*, ed. Vincent Ball, vol. I (Delhi: Low Price Publications, 2000), 115.
15. In the 16th and 17th centuries, as pointed out by various scholars, a literary revolution both in classical and vernacular languages was going on. Jain literary culture was no exception. Banarsidas and his contemporaries were constantly engaged in the production of knowledge through copying, translating, creating and transmitting texts and ideas. They also actively

held and participated in *vichaar goshthis* where they discussed, debated as well as sermonised. They were multilingual and knew not only the classical Sanskrit along with Prakrit but also strongly espoused vernaculars. Banarsidas also be friended Arathmal Dhor of Khairabad, who gave him *Samaysaar natak*, which greatly impacted Banarsi's quest for spirituality. Banarsidas refers to Pandit Rupchand, who lectured extensively on *Gommatsaar* (Jain philosophical treatise) at Tihuna Sahu Temple, Agra. Interestingly, such literary productions took place beyond the networks of patronage. This intensification of the literary production needs to be contextualised within the frame of increased circulation of the literati, which led to the dissemination of texts as well as eased the mobility of languages across geographical and social boundaries and would have certainly contributed towards the pleasure of the public engaged in literary pursuits. Banarsidas, *Ardhakathanak*, verses 591–594, p. 269; verses 630–631, p. 272; John E. Cort, 'Making It Vernacular in Agra: The Practice of Translation by Seventeenth-Century Jains', in *Tellings and Texts: Music, Literature and Performance in North India*, ed. Francesca Orsini and Katherine Butler Schofield (Cambridge: Open Book Publishers, 2015), 61–105; Thomas de Bruijn and Allison Busch, 'Introduction', in *Culture and Circulation: Literature in Motion in Early Modern India*, ed. Thomas de Bruijn and Allison Busch (Brill: Leiden-Boston, 2014), 1–20.

16. Banarsidas, *Ardhakathanak*, verse 335, p. 249.
    tab ghar mein baithae rahae, jaahi na haath bazar I
    madhumalti mirgawati, pothi doee udaar II 335 II
17. Banarsidas (1636), *Natak Samaysaar*, Commentary by Buddhilal Shravak (Bombay: Jain Garnthratnakar, 1929).
18. Meghavijay, 'Yuktiprabodha', verse 9, pp. 217–218.
19. Title of respect for a versatile scholar, generally applied for Digambar temple managers who do not observe nudity and other ascetic aspects. The *bhattaraks* manage the abodes of the ascetics and religious properties.
20. Banarsidas, *Ardhakathanak*, text, verses 592–600, p. 269.
21. Banarsidas, *Ardhakathanak*, verses 630–631, p. 272.
    *anayaas is hi samay, nagar aagrae thaan*I
    roopchand pandit gunee, aayon aagam-jaan II 630 II
    tihuna sahu dehura kiya I*tahaan aaee tini dera liya* II
    sab aadhyatmee kiyon bichaar I*granth bachaayon gomatsaar* II 631 II
22. Francesca Orsini and Katherine Butler Schofield, 'Introduction', *Tellings and Texts: Music, Literature and Performance in North India*, eds. Francesca Orsini and Katherine Butler Schofield (Cambridge: Open Book Publishers, 2015), 1–30; John E. Cort, 'Making It Vernacular in Agra: The Practice of Translation by Seventeenth-Century Jains', *Tellings and Texts: Music, Literature and Performance in North India*, eds. Francesca Orsini and Katherine Butler Schofield (Cambridge: Open Book Publishers, 2015), 61–105.
23. Banarsidas, *Ardhakathanak*, text, verses 608–610, p. 270.
    Kahhi log shravak aru jati I *Banarsi khosramati* I
    Tini purush ki chalae na baat I *yeh pandit taatae vikhyaat* II 608 II

Ninda thuti jaisi jis hoi I *taisi taasu kahae sab koi* II
purjan bina kahe nahi rahae I *jaisi dekhae taisi kahae* II 609 II
suni kahae dekhi kahae, kalipit kahae banai I
duraradhi ae jagat jan, inhasau kachu na basai II 610 II

24. Banarsidas, *Ardhakathanak*, verse 200, p. 239.
bahut padhae baabhan aru bhaat I *banikputra to baithae haat* II
bahut padhae to maange bheekh I *maanhu poot badeki seekh* II 200 II

25, Meghavijay, 'Yuktiprabodha', *Ardhakathanak: Half A Tale*, Mukund Lath. Appendix I (Jaipur: Rajasthan Prakrit Bharati Sansthan, 1981), 214–215.

26. Ibid.

27. Ibid., verse 24, p. 222.

28. Banarsidas, *Ardhkathanak*, verses 274–275, pp. 244–245.
Nit uthi praat jaai jinbhaun I Darsanu binu na karae dantaun II
Chaudaha name virti ucchre I samaik padikauna kare II274II
Hari jati raakhi parwaan I jaavjeev baigan-pachkhaan II
Pujabidhi saadhe din aath I Padhai binti pad mukh-paath II275II

29. Banarsidas, *Ardhakathanak*, verses 429–430, pp. 63, 256.
*Jaai saraee utaara liya*I *ganga ke tat bhojan kiya*II
Banarasi nagar mein gayon I *Kharagsen kau darsan bhayon* II 429
Dauri putranai pakre pai I *pita taahi leenau ur laai* II
Poonchai pita baat ekant I *kahiyo banarasi nij birtant* II 430

30. Banarsidas, *Ardhakathanak*, verses 107–108, p. 232.
Nani maran suta janam, putrabadhu aagaun I
Teeno kaaraj ek din, bhay ek hee bhaun II 107 II
Yeh sansar vidambana, dekhi pragat dukh khed I
Chatur chhit tyagi bhaye, moodh na jaanhi bhed II 108 II

31. Banarsidas, *Ardhakathanak*, verses 17–18, p. 225.
Saawan sit panchami ravivaar I *Muldas-ghar sut avtaar* II
Bhayo harakh kharche bahu daam I *Kharagsen dino yahu naam* II 17 II
Sukh sau baras doi chali gaye I *Ghanmal naam aur sut bhae* II
Baras teen jab beete aur I *Ghanmal kaal kiyo tis thor* II 18 II

32. Banarsidas, *Ardhakathanak*, verses 84–86, p. 230.
Ekadasi baar rabi-nand I *nakhant rohini vrishkau chand* I
Rohini tritiya charan anusaar I *kharagsen-ghar sut avtaar* II 84 II
Deenau naam vikramiit I *Gawahee kamini mangal-geet* I
Deejhi daan bhayo ati harsh I *Janmayo putra aatham varsh* II 85 II
Ehi bidhi beetien maas cheh saat I *chale su parshavnathki jaat* I
Kul kutumb sab leeno saath I *bidhisau puje parasnath* II 86 II

33. Banarsidas, *Ardhakathanak*, verse 43, p. 227.
Sarbas looti liyo jyon meer I *so sab baat kahee dhari dheer* II
Kahee madan putrisau roi I *ek putrasau sab kichhu hoi* II 43 II

34. Banarsidas, *Ardhakathanak*, verse 77, p. 230.
Kharagsen ghar sut avtaryon I *kharchayon darab-haras man dharyoun* I
Din dasam pahuchyoun parlok I *keena pratham putrakau sok* II 77 II

35. Banarsidas, *Ardhakathanak*, verses 170–172, p. 237
Vidya padhi vidya mein ramae I *Solah sae sataavne samae* II
Taji kul-kaan lokki laaj I *Bhayon banarasi aasikhbaaj* II 170

Karae aasikhi dhari man dheer I *daradband jyon sekh faqir* II
ektak dekhi dhyaan so dharae I *pita aapnekau dhan harae* II 171
Chorae chuuni manik mani I *aanae paan mithai ghani* II
Bhejae peskasi hit paas I *aapu garib kahaave daas* II 172

36. Banarsidas, *Ardhakathanak*, verse 180, p. 237
Kaei padhna kaei aasikhi, magan duhoo rasmaahi I
Khaan-paanki sudh nahi, rojgaar kicchu naahi II 180 II
37. Ibid.
38. Nyayavijay, *Ajjhattatattaaloa*(Jamnagar: Shwetambar Murtipujak Shri Jain Sangha, 1938); Umasvati/Umasvami, *Tattvartha-sutra* (That Which Is), trans. Nathmal Tatia (Delhi: Motilal Banarsidass, 2007), 180.
39. Ibid., Chapter 7, sutra no. 1, p. 169.
40. Ibid., Chapter 7, sutra no. 7, p. 171. *Striragakathashravana-tatmanoranga-nirikshna-purvaratanusmaranavryeshtarasa-svasarirasmaskaratyagah pancha*
41. Tilaksagar, *Sri Rajsagar Suri Nirvana Raas*, Gujarati, 1723 VS, MS. no. 13771 (Koba: Sri Kailash Sagar Suri Gyan Mandir, Sri Mahavir Jain Aradhana Kendra, Koba, Gujarat); Mohanlal Dalichand Desai, *Sheth Shri Shantidas Tatha Mahamuniona Raas Jain Aitihasik Raasmala*, Part 1, no. 24 (Mumbai: Srimad Budhisagarji Granthmala, 1912), 3–5; Muni Darshanvijay et al. (Triputi Maharaj), *Jain Parampara no Itihaas*, vol. 3 (Ahmedabad: Shri Charitra Smarak Granthmala, 1964), 750–756.
42. Shri Vallabh Upadhyaya, *Vijayadevmahatamaya*, ed., Muni Jinvijay, (Ahmedabad: Jain Sahitya Samshodhak Granthmala, no. 9, 1928), 86–87.
43. Vijay et al. (Triputi Maharaj), *Jain Parampara no Itihaas*, vol. 3, pp. 733–734.
44. Tilaksagar, *Sri Rajsagar Suri Nirvana Raas*, MS.
45. Upadhyaya, *Vijaydevmahatmaya*, canto 19, verse 197, p. 126.
46. Vijay et al. (Triputi Maharaj), *Jain Parampara no Itihaas*, vol. 3, pp. 730, 756–757.
47. Tilaksagar, *Sri Rajsagar Suri Nirvana Raas*, MS.
48. Banarsidas, *Ardhakathanak*, verses 119–126, p. 233. Shahzadpur was part of *Sarkar* Kara, *Suba* Allahabad; Irfan Habib, *An Atlas of the Mughal Empire: Political and Economic Maps with Detailed Notes, Bibliography and Index* (New Delhi: Oxford University Press, 1986), 29.
49. Banarsidas, *Ardhakathanak*, verses 394–395, p. 253.
Chyaree maas lee keeno dhandh I *nahi bikaee kapraa pag bandh* II
Benidas khobra gout I *Taakaun 'das narrotam' pout* II 364 II
So banarsikau hitu, aur badliya 'than' I
Raat divas krida karhi, teenou mitra samaan II 365 II
50. Banarsidas, *Ardhakathanak*, verses 476–485, pp. 259–260.
51. Banarasidas, *Banarsi-Naamala* (1614), ed., Jugalkishore Mukhtar, (Saharanpur: Vir Sewa Mandir, 1941), 50.
Mitra Narottam thaan, Param vichakshan dharmanidhi I
Vasu vachan parwaan, kiyo nibandh vichari mani II 170 II
Sorahsae sattari samae, asu maas sit paksh I
Vijaydasam sasivaar teh, shravan nakhat partaksh II 171 II
Din din tej pratap jay, sada akhandit aan I

Paatsah thir noordi, Jahangir sultan II 172 II
Kusumraaji nana varan, sundar param rasaal I
Komal-gungarbhit rachi, naammaal jaimaal II 174 II
Jae nar raakhe kanth nij, hoy sumati parkaas I
Bhanu suguru parsaad teh, parmanand-vilaas II 175 II

52. Banarsidas, *Ardhakathanak*, verses 550–551, pp. 265–266.
Bahut bhanti banarasi, kiyo panthmein sog I
Samujhaavae mane nahi, ghire aaee bahu log II 550 II
Lobh mool sab paap kau, dukh kau mool saneh I
Mool ajeeran byadhikon, maran mool yeh deh II 551 II

53. Banarsidas, *Ardhakathanak*, verse 603, p. 270.
Nagan honhin charou jane, firhin kothri mahi I
Kahahin bhaye muniraj hum, kachhu parigriha nahi II

54. Banarsidas, *Ardhakathanak*, verse 654, p. 274.
Thore laabh harakh bahu gharae I *alap haani bahu chinta karae* II
Mukh awadhya bhaashat na lajaae I *seekhae bhandkala man laae* II 654 II

55. Banarsidas, *Ardhakathanak*, verses 654–655, p. 274.
Thore laabh harakh bahu gharae I *alap haani bahu chinta karae* II
Mukh awadhya bhaashat na lajaae I *seekhae bhandkala man laae* II 654 II
Bhakhae akathkatha birtant I *thanae nritya pae ekant* II
Andekhee ansuni banae I *kukatha kahae sabhamahi aaee* II 655 II

REFERENCES

Acharya Samantbhadra. *Ratnakarandak Shravakachara: The Jewel-Casket of Householders Conduct*. Translated by Vijay K. Jain. Dehradun: Vikas Printers. 2016.

Banarsidas. *Ardhakathanak: Half a Tale*. Translated by Mukund Lath. Jaipur: Rajasthan Prakrit Bharati Sansthan. 1981.

———. *Banarsi-Namamala*. Edited by Jugalkishore Mukhtar. Saharanpur: Vir Sewa Mandir. 1941.

———. *Natak Samaysaar*. Commentary by Buddhilal Shravak. Bombay: Jain Granth Ratnakar. 1929.

Bernier, Francois. *Travels in the Mogul Empire, 1656–1668*. Translated by Irving Brock, edited by Vincent A. Smith. Delhi: Low Price Publications. 2005.

Brunjin, Thomas de and Allison Busch. 'Introduction'. In *Culture and Circulation: Literature in Motion in Early Modern India*, edited by Thomas de Bruijn and Allison Busch, 1–20. Brill: Leiden-Boston. 2014.

Cort, John E. 'Making It Vernacular in Agra: The Practice of Translation by Seventeenth-Century Jains'. In *Tellings and Texts: Music, Literature and Performance in North India*, edited by Francesca Orsini and Katherine Butler Schofield, 61–105. Cambridge: Open Book Publishers. 2015.

Desai, Mohanlal Dalichand. *Sheth Shri Shantidas Tatha Mahamunio na Raas Jain Aitihasik Raasmala, Srimad Budhisagarji Granthmala*, Part 1 (24). Mumbai. 1912.

Goody, Jack. *The Development of the Family and Marriage in Europe*. Cambridge: Cambridge University Press. 1983.

Habib, Irfan. *An Atlas of the Mughal Empire: Political and Economic Maps with Detailed Notes, Bibliography and Index*. New Delhi: Oxford University Press. 1986.

Hasan, Farhat. 'Presenting the Self: Norms and Emotions in *Ardhakathanak*'. In *Biography as History: Indian Perspectives*, edited by Vijaya Ramaswamy and Yogesh Sharma, 105–122. New Delhi: Orient Blackswan. 2009.

Lal, Ruby. *Domesticity and Power in the Early Mughal World*. New York: Cambridge University Press. 2005.

Meghavijay. 'Yuktiprabodha'. In Mukund Lath. *Ardhakathanak: Half a Tale*. Jaipur: Rajasthan Prakrit Bharati Sansthan. 1981.

Mukhia, Harban. *The World of Mughals and Works on Mughal Household*. Massachusetts: Blackwell. 2004.

Muni Darshanvijay et al. (Triputi Maharaj). *Jain Parampara no Itihaas*, vol. 3. Ahmedabad: Shri Charitra Smarak Granthmala. 1964.

Nyayavijay. *Ajjhattatattaaloa*. Jamnagar: Shwetambar Murtipujak Shri Jain Sangha. 1938.

Orsini, Francesca and Katherine Butler Schofield. 'Introduction'. In *Tellings and Texts: Music, Literature and Performance in North India*, edited by Francesca Orsini and Katherine Butler Schofield, 1–30. Cambridge: Open Book Publishers. 2015.

Tavernier, Jean-Baptiste. *Travels in India*. Edited by Valentine Ball, vol. I. Delhi: Low Price Publications. 2000.

Tilaksagar. *Sri Rajsagar Suri Nirvana Raas*. VS. In Gujarati. Manuscript no. 13771. Koba: Sri Kailash Sagar Suri Gyan Mandir, Sri Mahavir Jain Aradhana Kendra: Koba 1723.

Umasvati/Umasvami. *Tattvartha-sutra* (That Which Is). Translated by Nathmal Tatia. Delhi: Motilal Banarsidass. 2007.

Upadhyaya, Shri Vallabh. *Vijayadevmahatamaya*. Edited by Muni Jinvijay. No. 9. Ahmedabad: Jain Sahitya Samshodhak Granthmala. 1928.

Vanina, Eugenia. 'The *Ardhakathanak* by Banarsi Das: A Socio-cultural Study'. *Journal of the Royal Asiatic Society of Great Britain & Ireland* 5, no. 2 (1995): 211–224.

6

'*AASHIQ KO TOW ALLAH NA DIKHLAAI BHUDHAPA*': NAZIR AKBARABADI AND THE CELEBRATION OF THE LITTLE PLEASURES OF LIFE IN URDU POETRY

*Raziuddin Aquil**

Gar shaal odhaai tow usi shaal mein khush hain
Puray hain wahi mard jo har haal mein khush hain
—Nazir Akbarabadi (quoted in Shahbaz 7)

Shaikh Wali Muhammad, better known by his pen-name Nazir Akbarabadi (1735–1830), is one of the most popular and respected classical Urdu poets. He was a fascinating character who was born and grew up in Delhi but flourished in the Agra–Mathura region. He rose above narrow religious and sectarian boundaries to compose a large number of works in different genres of Urdu poetry. His over 900-page *Kulliyaat* or *Collected Works*, published among others by Lucknow's classic Nawal Kishore Press, offers significant insight into the celebration of the little pleasures of life—fairs, festivals, a fresh burst of energy with the season changing for the better, natural bounties such

* I would like to thank Seema Bawa for encouraging me to write this chapter and patiently waiting for me to complete it for inclusion in this significant collection of essays on the history of discourses on pleasure. I am grateful to Charu Gupta, Jack Hawley, Anshu Malhotra and Shalini Shah for reading an early version of the chapter and providing critical comments and suggestions for improvement. I also take this opportunity to thank my usual interlocutors for all matters relating to the fascinating history of classical Urdu literature: Wasia Irfana, Sarwar Karim and Mazhar Mahdi. The usual disclaimers apply. I alone am responsible for any shortcomings at this stage of my research in this interesting area of literary and cultural history—reading literature to understand the many dimensions of entertainment and pleasure, historically.

as juicy summer fruits, some love as well as a chance or opportunity to interact with women in a regressive society, in wedding parties, along with other possibilities of fun. Nazir wrote at registers ranging from a popular or subaltern level to the high poetry of love of the fine *ghazal* variety.

The poet wrote extensively on Indian culture and traditions in the late 18th and early 19th centuries. Though the precocious Nazir was born and brought up in Delhi and much valued as the only surviving child, his family shifted base to Agra (Akbarabad, and hence the name 'Akbarabadi'), where his maternal grandfather Nawab Sultan Khan was once the fort's administrator. Thus, though coming from a politically resourceful background, Nazir steered clear of both the royal court and elite circles of poets to carve out a niche for himself as a prominent and popular Urdu poet. The poet vernacularised himself, deviating from traditional notions of elitist sophistication identified as *adab* and *shrafat*, mingling with people in the marketplace and fairs and writing on themes in local idioms catering to their interest—themes and writings that fit in our conventional understanding of syncretism and synthesis in India's cultural traditions and history. Besides large numbers of *nazm*s and poetry in other genres that made Nazir popular, over 600 *ghazal*s attributed to him and his performance and occasional participation in *mushaira*s of poets also meant he was well known to the fraternity of Urdu poets of his time (for Nazir's biography, see Abdul Ghafur Shahbaz's pioneering work, *Zindagani Benazir*, and, as for everything relating to the history of Urdu literature, Jamil Jalibi).

The vibrant cultural capital of the period of 18th and early 19th century Mughal decline—higher education, literary practices and performing arts—needs to be taken seriously. The entanglement of religious contestations and political churning also complicated the scenario, unleashing new questions of identity, whether sectarian, ethnic and, seemingly, even communal. Previous generations of historians confused weakening Mughal power and authority with all-round social, moral and economic degradation. The old-fashioned historians not only needed new sources, but also a new framework to look at historical processes in all their vitality than merely passing moral judgements, which is against the protocols of a historian's craft and method.

Take the case of the treatment of Urdu literature: at its height, it is imaginatively romantic, sensual and even pornographic, which prudish and perhaps homophobic modern historians are not equipped to handle. Not mentioning here what is called 'perversion': a Mughal prince accused by the famous satirist, Mir Muhammad Ja'far Zatalli (executed in 1713), of having intercourse with a goat, besides exploring other alternative possibilities of fun. Historians have tended to ignore the significance of reading the huge body of 18th-century Urdu literature on its own terms. A refreshing new approach to sources would further strengthen the arguments for cultural efflorescence in the 18th century. Literary sources actually reveal a vibrant cultural life even on the question of the decline of patronage to artists in Mughal Delhi, detailed in a text such as *Muraqqa-i Dehli* of Dargah Quli Khan, a Persian-origin visitor from the Deccan. Notwithstanding his political failures, the contemporary Mughal emperor Muhammad Shah (1719–1748), a cultural aficionado nicknamed as 'Rangila', certainly deserves a better treatment by historians than what has hitherto been the case. Besides, early in the 18th century, the enthusiastic reception of Wali Dakani's widely acclaimed *Diwan* in Delhi is also a momentous chapter in the history of Urdu literature.

Thus, the literary hyperbole of the poets who left Delhi for greener pastures should not be taken so literally, as Mir Taqi Mir (1722–1810) desperately tried to convince those who heard him in Lucknow that he belonged to the world-renowned magnificent city of Delhi that had just been ruined:

Dilli jo ek shahr tha aalam mein intekhab
Ham rahne wale hain usi ujde dayar ke

With as many as six collections of Urdu poetry to his credit, Mir Taqi Mir is widely regarded as the finest exponent of Urdu *ghazal*. Mir also wrote a collection of verses and three prose compositions in Persian, including *Zikr-i Mir*, a rare and remarkable autobiographical narrative, which has recently been published with an English translation by C.M. Naim, as part of the very impressive Murty Classical Library of India series. In this work, the poet offers glimpses into his family background and veritable struggles for survival, both in his native Akbarabad (Agra) and after having relocated to Delhi. Interestingly, Nazir's was a reverse trajectory: family shifting from Delhi for survival in Agra. These movements were forced by the politically volatile situation in northern India for much of the 18th century, with phases of relative peace in certain locations when political patronage to poets and intellectuals was possible. The situation compelled Mir to subsequently fall for the temptations of Lucknow, where he remained unhappy, with an attitude bordering on cynicism and even madness. Like other iconoclastic Urdu poets, Mir defied all norms, both in his private and professional life. His non-conformist compositions minced no words:

Qashqa khaincha dayr mein baitha
Kabka tarak Islam kiya

Mir's lamentation of the decline in the razzmatazz of the city of Delhi, fantastically mourned in the genre of poetry called *shahr-i ashob*, is in line with several examples of the frustrations and restlessness expressed by the poets in sufficient lack of patronage. Happily, for those with a *zauq* or carefully cultivated taste for the poetry of pathos, melancholy and loss, *shahr-i ashob* compositions are one of the best forms of poetry, touching the heart and evoking pain and sorrow. This is different from the lampooning and condemnation in *mazaah* or satire. Jafar Zatalli's condemnation of the grand Mughal capital city of Shahjahanabad as a veritable '*Chaupatabad*'—a despicable habitation—is a case in point. However, as a matter of fact, even though regional centres vied with Delhi, sometimes aggressively, in court cultures and patronage, old Delhi continued to flourish. We shall return below to the significance of the writings of other poets from the 18th and early 19th centuries for a political and cultural context leading to a better understanding of Nazir's work.

Further, recent research shows that even at the height of Mughal power, the vernacular literary scene was not as impoverished as it was made out to be by older historians. Expressed in local languages, regional aspirations were not only being powerfully articulated but were also making their presence felt at the Mughal court. By the early 17th century, the Braj variant of Hindi came to occupy an influential position, both for its sensuous poetry of love and as a language of scheming court-politics. Not surprisingly, despite all his pretensions of Persian sophistication, even the most powerful of the Mughal emperors, Akbar, would vent his occasional frustration by mouthing expletives in Hindi. Those obsessed with Persian in medieval India must read Allison Busch's fine work on classical Hindi literature of the Mughal period.

Certainly, by the mid-18th century, questions began to be raised on why the Mughal dynasty should continue to be in power if it was no longer able to produce strong and competent rulers. Some dynamic Mughal officials were touted as more capable ruler-material, but for them to come to power meant a revolution, which did not happen on an all-India scale even when regions got transformed for better or worse. A drastic change awaited in the form of a truly British colonial intervention in the 19th century. In his *Black Hole of Empire*, Partha Chatterjee offers one of the finest analyses of late-18th-century struggles and further political developments. Surely, not everything was lost in the 18th century. This was the period before Urdu was reduced to being the language of Muslims in the ghetto. Happily, Urdu poetry continues to be an important vehicle through which sublime emotions of love and longing could be expressed in the best possible form.

There have been times and moments in history when men of letters have marked their excellence through extraordinary ways of doing things, such as a Muslim poet composing fascinating Urdu poetry celebrating the Hindu festivals of Dussehra, Diwali, Basant and Holi in a language that captured the best of festive emotions. Nazir Akbarabadi's celebration of life is best reflected, among other compositions, in his poems on festivals, especially Hindu festive occasions such as the auspicious Diwali and the hooliganistic Holi. These poems also reveal the poet's narrativisation of Hindu beliefs and traditions associated with mythological figures on a scale meant to highlight as a matter of celebration the excellence of their character and the widespread devotion around them. Poems such as the one on the birth of Lord Krishna (*Janam Kanahaiyaji*), the celebration of events related to his brother (*Baldevji ka Mela*) and on devotion for the mother-goddess Durga (*Durgaji ke Darshan*), also offer fascinating details from popular Hindu legends.

The poems on Diwali reveal not only markets buzzing in preparation, with earthen lamps illuminated everywhere, but also some people going broke as a result of the widespread practice of gambling on the occasion. For the pious and the innocent, the poet would announce that the lamps were lit in all houses and sweetshops attracted customers (*Kulliyaat* 441–443):

Har ek makan mein jala phir diya Diwali ka
Har ek taraf ko ujala hua Diwali ka
Mithaiyon ki dukanen laga ke halwai
Pukarte hain ke lala Diwali hai aayi

On the other hand, the sinner is hell-bent on losing not only his house, but also his wife in Diwali-eve gambling, with almost all of her jewellery gone. The poet writes that the woman is abused as a loose character and threatened:

Woh uske jhonte pakad kar kahe hay marunga
Tera jo gahna hai sab taar taar utarunga
Haweli apni tow ek dao par mayen harunga
Yeh sab tow hara hun khandi tujhe bhi harunga

The poet also reminds the devout that though Dussehra is celebrated with much gaiety, Diwali is a much more auspicious festival (*Kulliyaat* 444):

Hai Dussehre mein bhi yun go farhat-o zinat nazir
Par Diwali bhi ajab pakizah-tar tehwaar hai

The endless possibility of fraughtful amusement is especially narrated by Nazir Akbarabadi in several compositions on Holi, when the participants are physically charged for amorous advances, taking advantage of the refrain later pronounced in Hindi, *bura na mano Holi hai*! Here is a polite sample of musical instruments used to announce the arrival of Holi-playing groups and friends and of lovers gleefully showering each other with colourful gestures (*Kulliyaat* 430–431):

Mridange baajen taal baje kuchh khanak khanak kuchh dhanak dhanak
Jab khubaan aaye rang bhare phir kya kya Holi jhamak uthi
Kuchh husn ki jhamken naaz bharen kuchh shokhi naaz adaaon ki
Sab chaahne wale gird khade nazara karte hansi khushi
Mahbub bhigoyen aashiq ko aur aashiq hanskar unko bhi

Some compositions of Nazir are truly meant to fit straight into classical Hindustani music, capturing the pleasant mood of the festive season and the veritable thrill in the air (*Kulliyaat* 437):

Jab phagun rang jhamakte hon tab dekh bahaaren Holi ki
Aur daf ke shor khadkate hon tab dekh bahaaren Holi ki

Though Nazir Akbarabadi and his patrons, on whose request he would compose extempore poetry, seemed particularly interested in the endless possibilities of fun during Holi, on which several poems were written by him and recorded in his *Kulliyaat*, the poet's work on festivals such as 'Id is equally interesting. After sketching a quite realistic picture of *Shabe Baraat* as a special night devoted to prayers in the traditional Muslim calendar, marked by both pietistic veneration for the dead and Diwali-like fireworks and lighting all around, Nazir records the celebration of 'Id, beginning with early morning bathing, wearing brand new clothes, going to 'Idgah for congregational prayers, meeting people and offering hugs and savouring special delicacies and sweetmeats such as mouthwatering *sewaiyaan*. Nazir writes on 'Id and practice of offering hugs, saying 'Id Mubarak and pleasures accrued from the festive emotions (*Kulliyaat* 418–420):

Aisi na Shabe Baraat na Baqrid ki khushi
Jaisi har ek dil mein hai iss 'Id ki khushi

Pichhle pahar se uthke nahane ki dhoom hai
Shir-o-shakar sewaiyaan pakane ki dhoom hai
Pir-o-jawan ko ne'maten khane ki dhoom hai
Ladkon ko 'Idgah ke jane ki dhoom hai

Mahbub dilbaron se hai jin ki lagi lagan
Unke gale se aan laga hai jo gulbadan
Sau sau tarah ke chaah se mil mil ke tan se tan
Kahte hain tum ko 'Id Mubarak ho jaane man

In another poem on 'Id, the poet expresses the deep disappointment of the lover who is unable to meet the beloved even on this festive occasion, leaving with feelings of pain (*dard*) over unfulfilled desires, *hasraten* (*Kulliyaat* 420–421):

Kyunkar lagen na meray dil mein hasraton ke tir
Din 'Id ke bhi mujh se hua woh kinara gir
Iss dard ko woh samjhe jo ho 'ishq ka asir
Jis 'Id mein ke yaar se milna na ho Nazir

Kya kya gharz saha sitame intezaar aah!

Another poem, *'Idgah Akbarabad*, typically sums up the mass celebrations in the overflowing 'Idgah premises, with the crowd lining up in adjacent gardens and vacant places and roads choked-a-block, *Kya kya mazay hain 'Id ke aaj 'Idgah mein* (*Kulliyaat* 421–423):

Aate hain ghar se apne jo ban-ban ke kuj kulah
Chhaati se lipte jate hain hans hans ke khwah-makhwah

Hathi wa ghode bayl o rath wa oont ki qataar
Ghul shor baale bhole khilaune ki hai pukaar

Kamren sabhon ne milne ki khaatir hain kasliyaan
Milte hain yun ke chhaati ki kadke hain pasliyaan!

Much of this celebration of festivities was possible also because Nazir Akbarabadi grew up in Delhi at a time of cultural efflorescence actively promoted by the later Mughal emperors, especially Muhammad Shah Rangila, the colourful, even as political power and authority were being continuously shaken by invaders from within and outside. Within the circle of eminent Urdu poets, Nazir's life and career overlapped with two stalwarts—Mir Taqi Mir and Mirza Asadullah Khan Ghalib (1797–1869)—with fruitful interactions across generations. Young Nazir received rare appreciation from an otherwise arrogant and veteran Mir Taqi Mir, and as a senior and popular poet Nazir heard the rising fame of Mirza Ghalib.

Some 2,000 Urdu couplets, *ash'ar,* of Mirza Ghalib, even if often not literally understood, warm up the inner cord of even a heartless crook. Look at this fine articulation of heartache:

Dil mera soz-i nehan se be-muhaba jal gaya
Aatish-i khamosh ki maanind goya jal gaya
Dil mein zauq-i wasl wa yaad-i yaar tak baqi nahin
Aag iss ghar mein lagi aisi ke jo tha jal gaya

Invoking the language of love in times of wretched political flux, general emotional loss and utter frustrations, Ghalib warns of the impending emotional disaster:

Ashiqi sabr-talab aur tamanna betaab
Dil ka kya rang karun khune jigar hote tak
Ham ne mana ke taghaaful na karoge lekin
Khak ho jayenge ham tum ko khabar hote tak

A voluminous collection of Ghalib's Persian letters, with an Urdu translation and bio-notes of addressees, has been collected and translated by Partav Rohilla. As it happens, the first letter may be noticed for doing *maska* or flattering a well-wisher in Bengal for a fresh supply of mangoes from Hugli before the season ends. Ghalib claims that Calcuttans (*ahle kalkatta*) have a consensus on this: yes, exactly, mango from Hugli, just as flowers from the garden (*aare anba az hugli wa gul az gulshan*)! Which Bengali *bhadralok* patron would not have been flattered to ensure a quick supply of a carton of ripe mangoes for Ghalib to plunder?

Another book on Ghalib, the widely acclaimed text by Gopi Chand Narang, one of the most respected scholars of Urdu literature and *Ghalib shanasi*—knowing or understanding Ghalib—is now available in an English translation. Celebration of the eminent poet's magnificent work in his iconoclastic style is obvious, as the poet himself announced:

A'ina kiyon na dun ke tamasha kahen jise
Aisa kahaan se laaun ke tum sa kahen jise

The poet has also warned any naysayers in his inimitable style, claiming to be a friend of God at night and ruthless infidel in daylight:

Dekhiyo Ghalib se gar uljha koyi
Hai wali poshida aur kafir khula

Urdu poetry defies regressive social norms, celebrates failures and invokes natural justice, often in the name of Mirza Ghalib, who arguably epitomises the best this literary tradition has to offer. Many others excelled in this art form for over three centuries and will continue to flourish, even though the last Mughal poet, Ghalib, pleaded simplicity and austerity which could be cross-checked on his death:

Chand taswir-i butaan chand hasinon ke khutoot
Ba'ad marne ke mere ghar se ye saamaan nikla

Together, these poets and their numerous contemporaries excelled in their own distinct ways at their literary practice, which was central to their lives. Nazir is often not counted in the history of classical Urdu literature because of the way he catered to popular taste in his compositions. His celebration of Hindu religious practices, traditions, myths and legends needs serious consideration, especially in times when the Hindi/Urdu and Hindu/Muslim divide and conflict serve as fodder for those who thrive on religious communalism.

Returning to his own time and compositions, Nazir Akbarabadi wrote stuff few could dare, yet these received wide public circulation and appreciation in 18th and early 19th-century Delhi, Agra and Mathura. Prudish later generations also read his work, mostly in private, and scholars of Urdu literature maintained studied ambiguity, though several compositions of Nazir were published in poetic collections of different kinds. The conservative and traditional milieu of the Urdu reading public may have been embarrassed by the kind of work Nazir produced. However, this ambiguity has an older history, which may be briefly referred to here. Hierarchical, prudish and patriarchal societies seek to discriminate against, marginalise and suppress what they perceive as abnormal through a violent process of othering. In doing so, they resort to finding a religious justification for actions for which there may be absolutely no legal grounds, as in the archaic law criminalising homosexuality. Homosexuality is considered abnormal in conservative circles because homophobic society deems it such, and families and societies use religion to justify their norms and thus control things—lives and bodies are minoritised and criminalised. Indeed, literature and history offer a window into the long struggle involving sex for pleasure and sex for reproduction. The iconoclastic Urdu literature offers some of the finest articulation and celebration of a variety of ways in which sexual pleasure was possible, whether hidden or in public, and despite attempts to suppress what is termed as perversion. The poet Ja'far Zatalli's sexy *Kulliyaat* (discussed in Aquil, Chapter 6) may be mentioned in this context. The fine work on *Rekhti* by Carla Petevich and Ruth Vanita on men masquerading as women and sharing things the latter were not expected to in polite and hypocritical society is also relevant. One of the foremost authorities of historical Urdu literature, C.M. Naim's interesting early work on transvestite and *Rekhti* poems in Urdu, is equally significant.

An interesting example of *Rekhti*, the feminine form of early Urdu poetry *Rekhta*, narrativising matters of love, often multi-sexual, and a whole lot of other concerns, may be mentioned here. The poet Nisar Husain Khan Shaida (born circa 1868) spoke in gendered terms, giving voice to a woman's concerns and struggles with in-laws for dominance in the domestic space:

Sasuraal mein jo paadun to maike mein ho khabar
Ik ishtihaar nand hai ik ishtihaar saas!

Indeed, words are deployed as weapons in classical Urdu poetry at its zenith. Not for nothing did Sa'dat Yar Khan Rangin (born 1755), one of the noted exponents of *Rekhti* and a younger contemporary of Nazir, preferred to call his work female *Angekhta* (aroused) as a response to male *Rekhta*, one literal meaning of which is the fallen one. Mostly written by men having *masti* (fun) in a feminine voice, the above *Rekhti* couplet by Nisar Husain Khan Shaida is quoted by C.M. Naim in his fine collection of essays, *Urdu Texts and Contexts* (especially see the chapters on homosexual or pederastic love and *Rekhti*, transvestic words). Reading these and the following might disorient or reorient and reconstruct those who take themselves for granted. These cultural narratives are not only significant for their entertainment value for fantastic articulation on love and sex but also for understanding the value of words as important weapons in the poetry of protest. It required a lot of courage to write the way the poets did. Zatalli's daring composition, *Gandu-nama* (*An Account of a Catamite*), on Mughal emperor Aurangzeb's son and successor, Bahadur Shah (ruled 1707–1712), provokes as much as it tantalises:

Badshahi hai bahadur shah ki
Ban-banakar gand marawwa kheliye

Zatalli's satire on Aurangzeb's youngest son Kam Bakhsh was equally imaginative, accusing him of screwing a goat which he especially maintained for that purpose (*ghusera ghuseri ke mi-kard shah, manohar pari khufiya mi-kard aah*)! However, Zatalli was eventually killed following the orders of the emperor Farrukh Siyar (ruled 1713–1719) for calling him, as a matter of fact, a leather-belt executioner, *tasme-*

kush—one who throttles to death anyone who dares to criticise him. So, Mughal authority was not yet entirely lost, but surely this kind of literature was impossible under Akbar (ruled 1556–1605) and Jahangir (ruled 1605–1627), and even under Shah Jahan (ruled 1628–1658) and Aurangzeb (ruled 1658–1707). Times were changing, and some dared to raise questions on the legitimacy of those in power and authority.

Continuing in the tradition of iconoclastic Urdu literature, Nazir wrote a poem which in times of political flux and moral policing might sound like sexual harassment or the sexist remarks of an old wretch who seeks to get close to the woman about to become the mother-in-law of his child, and, thus, a *samdhan*. Sample this composition on *Samdhan* (*Kulliyaat* 912–913):

Karun kis munh se aye yaaron bayan mayen shaan samdhan ki
Lagi hai ab tow meray dil ko piyari aan samdhan ki

Chaman mein husn ke hon uske rukh aur zulf par qurban
Agar dekhen zara surat gul-o rehaan samdhan ki

Kamar nazuk, matakti chaal, aankhen shokh, tan goru
Nazar chanchal, ada achhpal, ye hai pahchaan samdhan ki

Sunahri taash ka lahnga, ruphali got ki angiya
Chamakta husn joban ka jhamakti aan samdhan ki

Malai sa shikam, seena musaffa, khushnuma saaqen
Safa zaanu ka a'ina, mulaayam raan samdhan ki

Kahun kuchh aur bhi aage jo samdhan hukm farma den
Sifat manzur hai hamko toh ab har aan samdhan ki

Bara ehsaan manen ham tumhara aaj samdhi ji
Muyassar ho agar suhbat hamen ek aan samdhan ki

Hamen ek dow ghari ke waaste dulha dila dow tum
Jo kuchh lahnge ke andar cheez hai panhan samdhan ki

Nazir ab aafarin hai yaar teri taba` ko har dam
Kahi ta`rif toone khwub aalishan samdhan ki

This is clearly a wicked poem—Nazir could not have been naughtier. Yet, a head-to-toe description of the perfection of the female body is an established trope in Nazir's poetry, as in classical Indian aesthetics on bodily features and practices. In the above poem, he begins describing the beauty of the woman with her face (*rukh*) and hair (*zulf*) pitted against the flowers in the garden. The clean chest, slim waist, creamy belly, tender thighs of the well-groomed woman is a scintillating presence, completed by the naughty eyes, playful gaze and dalliance in movement, with a pair of lovely legs and the body as a whole sensuously fair. Indians are a racist people, especially when celebrating the female body, which should be fair and lovely, to the extent that when the woman sits her knees are so clean they shine like a mirror, with a mannerism that is puffed with pride further enhanced by their elegance.

Nazir develops these attributes further in the poem on his beloved, preciously named Moti (Pearl). The composition, *Moti,* is truly flattering (*Kulliyaat* 913–914):

Parizadon mein hai naam khuda jis shaan par moti
Koyi aisa nahin moti, magar moti, magar moti

Jhamak jaawe nigahon mein jawahir khana-i qudrat
Jo khaakar paan aur malkar missi hans de agar moti

Rag-i gul uss kamar ke saamne bharti phire pani
Lachak mein aur nazakat mein jo rakhti hai kamar moti

Udhar har ek makaan par motiyon ke dher ho jawen
Ada se naaz se hanskar qadam rakhe jidhar moti

Sada sunkar har ek chashm se moti tapakte hain
Faqat baithe he gaane mein yeh rakhti hai asar moti

Ajab naqsha ajab saj dhaj ajab ankhen ajab nazren
Bade taale`, badi qismat jo dekhe ek nazar moti

Sharf panne ko panne par, sharf heere ko heere par
Sharf sharfan ko la`lon par, rahi hai jis ke ghar moti

Har ek dandaan moti, husn moti, naam bhi moti
Sarapa chashm moti, tas pe pahne sar basar moti

Jo khubaan benazir iss daur mein hain nazuk-o rangin
Sharf rakhti hai yaaro, ab tow sab ke husn par moti

Nazir has once again emphasised on the fineness of the woman's body (waist has *lachak*, suppleness, and *nazakat*, elegance), wonderful features enhanced by a captivating gaze, and pearl-like (*moti*) teeth. The poet has also highlighted the emotions generated by her laughter and the overwhelming quality of her voice, which may cause pearl- or *moti*-like tears. Both the features of the body and emotions are doubly enhanced by her embellishments and make up—using *paan* (betel) and *missi* (a herbal concoction with a sexual connotation applied by women on their teeth during wedding ceremonies) as well as finely designed dress and accoutrement. All these would give shape to a particular *ada* and *naaz* (grace and pride) and a perfect profile, *naqsha*. Nazir provokes and challenges other exceptionally good-looking, slim and colourful women by claiming that his Moti is superior to all other pretty women of the time.

Nazir's real life beloved (*ma`shuqa*), Moti, may have been mighty pleased by the exaggerated praise heaped on her, and there is nothing sexist about it. Celebration of the beauty of the youthfulness in life (*joban*) is an important theme in Nazir's poetry. A well-groomed and chiseled body with an awe-inspiring style, mannerism or *ada* can be a deadly combination for connoisseurs of love, producing a variety of complicated emotions that have all been summed up by Nazir in his long poem, *Lutf i Shabaab, Pleasures of Youth* (*Kulliyaat* 485–488):

Kya ayesh ki rakhti hai sab aahang jawani
Karti hai baharon ke tay'in dang jawani
Har aan pilaati hai maye aur bang jawani
Karti hai kahin sulah, kahin jang jawani

Iss dhab ke mazay rakhti hai aur dhang jawani
Aashiq ko dikhati hai ajab rang jawani

Allah ne jawani ka woh aalam hai banaaya
Jauhar kahin aashiq kahin ruswa, kahin shaida
Phande mein kahin ji hai kahin dil hai tadapta
Marte hain sisakte hain, bilakte hain ahaha!

Iss dhab ke mazay rakhti hai aur dhang jawani
Aashiq ko dikhati hai ajab rang jawani

Na maye ka na ma`jun ke mangwaane ka kuchh gham
Na dil ke lagaane ka na gul khaane ka kuchh gham
Gaali ka na aankhon ke lara aane ka kuchh gham
Hansne ka na chhaati se lipat jaane ka kuchh gham

Iss dhab ke mazay rakhti hai aur dhang jawani
Aashiq ko dikhati hai ajab rang jawani

Ladti hai kahin aankh kahin dast kahin sayn
Jhuta hai kahin piyar, kisi se hai lagi nayn
Wa'dah kahin iqraar kahin sayn kahin nayn
Na ji ko kahin faraaghat hai na aankhon ke tay'in chayn

Iss dhab ke mazay rakhti hai aur dhang jawani
Aashiq ko dikhati hai ajab rang jawani

Ulfat hai kahin mehr-o muhabbat hai kahin chah
Karta hai koyi chah koyi dekh raha rah
Saaqi hai suraahi hai, parizaad hain hamrah
Kya ayesh hain kya ayesh hain kya ayesh hain wallah

Iss dhab ke mazay rakhti hai aur dhang jawani
Aashiq ko dikhati hai ajab rang jawani

Chehre pe jawani ka jo aakar hai chadha nur
Rah jaati hain pariyan bhi gharz uske tay'in ghur
Chhaati se lipat-ti hai koyi husn ki maghrur
Godi mein padi lote hai chanchal si koyi hur

Iss dhab ke mazay rakhti hai aur dhang jawani
Aashiq ko dikhati hai ajab rang jawani

Agar raat kisi paas rahe ayesh mein ghalataan
Aur waan se kisi aur ke milne ka ho adhiyan
Ghabra ke uthe jab tow gire paaon pe har aan
Kahti hai hamein chhod ke jaate ho kidhar jaan

Iss dhab ke mazay rakhti hai aur dhang jawani
Aashiq ko dikhati hai ajab rang jawani

Raste mein nikalte hain tow hoti hain yeh chaahen
Woh shokh ke hon band jinhen dekh ke raahen
Khanse hain koyi hanske koyi bharti hain aanhen
Parti hain har ek ja se nigaahon pe nigaahen

Iss dhab ke mazay rakhti hai aur dhang jawani
Aashiq ko dikhaati hai ajab rang jawani

Tante hain agar ayenth ke chalte hain ajab chaal
Jo paaon kahin raah, kahin saif kahin dhaal
Khaynche hain kahin baal, kahin tod liya gaal
Chadh baithe kahin haath kahin munh ko diya daal

Iss dhab ke mazay rakhti hai aur dhang jawani
Aashiq ko dikhati hai ajab rang jawani

Jaate hain tawa'if mein tow waan hoti hai yeh chaao
Kahti hai koyi 'inke liye paan bana laao'
Koyi kahti hai yaan baitho koyi kahti hai yaan aao
Naache hai koyi shokh batati hai koyi bhaao

Iss dhab ke mazay rakhti hai aur dhang jawani
Aashiq ko dikhati hai ajab rang jawani

Hans hans ke koyi husn ki chhal bal hai dikhaati
Missi koyi surma koyi kaajal hai dikhaati
Chitwan ki lagaawat koyi chanchal hai dikhaati
Kurti koyi angiya koyi aanchal hai dikhaati

Iss dhab ke mazay rakhti hai aur dhang jawani
Aashiq ko dikhati hai ajab rang jawani

Kahti hai koyi raat meray paas na aaye
Kahti hai koyi ham ko bhi khaatir mein na laaye
Kahti hai koyi kisne tumhen paan khilaaye
Kahti hai koyi ghar ko jaaye hamein khaaye

Iss dhab ke mazay rakhti hai aur dhang jawani
Aashiq ko dikhati hai ajab rang jawani

Gar dil ko kisi shokh puri ki huyi tak chaah
Aur naznin karne lagi uss waqt woh akaraah
Jon baaz ke chidiya ko kahin daab le nagaah
Machwa de lipat kar wahin ... se oyi aah

Iss dhab ke mazay rakhti hai aur dhang jawani
Aashiq ko dikhati hai ajab rang jawani

Aaya jo koyi husn ka boota ya koyi jhaad
Ja shokh se jhat lipte yeh panjon ke tay'in jhaad
Angiya ke tay'in cheer ke kurti ko liya phaad
Ekhlaas kahin piyaar kahin maar kahin dhaad

Iss dhab ke mazay rakhti hai aur dhang jawani
Aashiq ko dikhati hai ajab rang jawani

Kya tujh se Nazir ab mayen jawani ki kahun baat
Iss pun mein guzarti hai ajab ayesh se auqaat
Mahbub parizaad chale aate hain din raat
Sairen hain bahaaren hain tawazo` hai madaraat

Iss dhab ke mazay rakhti hai aur dhang jawani
Aashiq ko dikhati hai ajab rang jawani

This long poem clearly sums up the strength of youth and the celebrations of life attached to it, associated pleasures (*Iss dhab ke mazay rakhti hai aur dhang jawani*) expose youthful lovers to all kinds of fantastic possibilities (*Aashiq ko dikhati hai ajab rang jawani*). Some of the references are sexually explicit (*Angiya ke tay'in cheer ke kurti ko liya phaad*), and some encounters are euphemistically explained as attractions of love (*Kurti koyi angiya koyi aanchal hai dikhaati*).

The poetic expressions of a sense of loss in the poem on old-age helplessness are no less fantastic. Nazir laments in his poem on old-age, *Alam-i Piri*: *sab cheez ko hota hai bura haai budhapa / Aashiq ko tow allah na dikhlaai budhapa*. The poet compares the change in attitude towards the old man, faced with utter neglect, with the earlier youthful time, when one was much in demand (*Kulliyaat* 488–489):

Aage thhe jahan gulbadan aur yusuf-i saani
Dete thhe hamen payar se chhallon ki nishani
Mar jaayen tow ab munh mein na dale koyi pani
Kis dukh mein hamen chhod gayi haai jawani

Interestingly, some lovelorn old men do not give up easily, so Nazir offers a thoroughly imaginative dialogue between the powers of youth and the value of life-long experience. The old man challenges and provokes, saying that the youth is nothing before us: *ab bhi hamare aage, yaaro, jawan kya hai?* The poet elaborates on behalf of the old man's claims of exploits (*Kulliyaat* 498):

Karte hain hum jo, yaaro, ab dhum or dhadke
Dekhe jawan tow uske chhut jayen dum mein chhakke

The imaginative challenge continues in this interesting formulation of the contrast between the young and the old in risking being caught as they attempt to meet their respective beloved—while the youth can escape jumping from the wall, the old man might hop across the rooftops, *woh gar diwal kuden hum kotha phaand jawen* (*Kulliyaat* 498):

Ham aur jawan milkar gar dil ke tay'in lagaawen
Aur apne apne gul se milne ki dil mein laawen
Jaakar unhon ke ghar par jab zor aazmawen
Woh gar diwal kuden hum kotha phaand jawen

The old man also claims it did not matter if he did not have access to a vagina for sex. There are other ways of doing it, so long as the body is in fine fettle: *qaayam hai jism, go ke nahin kus ghanimat ast*. In *Budhape ka Ishq*, the poet explains that the desire for love and sex continues in old age (*Kulliyaat* 499):

Karte hain iss budhape mein khubaan ki ham tow chaah
Ahmaq hain khubru, jo woh hanste hain ham pe aah!
Aur woh jo kuchh sha`ur se rakhte hain dastgaah
So woh tow ham ko dekh yeh kahte hain 'wah wah'!

Nazir also reminiscences on good times spent in childhood, *kya din thhe yaaro woh bhi thhe jabke bhole bhale* (*Kulliyaat* 483):

Mote hon ya ke duble, goray hon ya ke kale
Kya aysh loot-te hain ma`sum bhole bhale!

In another poem on childhood, Nazir highlights the fun of being a breastfeeding child: *kya sair dekhte hain yeh tifl shir khoray*! The poet explains, sounding somewhat like a pervert (*Kulliyaat* 484):

Kya waqt tha woh ham thhe jab doodh ke chatoray
Har aan aanchalon ke ma`mur thhe katoray

Gul ki tarah se har dum seene pe phoolte thhe
Pipi ke doodh maan ka khush hoke phoolte thhe

Lest it all sound pornographic, Nazir Akbarabadi's oeuvre is vast. We began with Holi-Diwali festive blasts and extravaganza of Muslim festivals such as 'Id to move into the intricacies of bodily and other features and their celebrations in the poet's work. This was part of the established tradition in popular Urdu literature to speak about matters of love and sex at a variety of registers, explicit, in double-entendre or in a more sophisticated language of love and longing. Yet what Nazir has done is phenomenal.

Unlike Hindi *Riti* poetry, which was largely meant for a courtly audience, Nazir embraces a much more eclectic audience, and his language is also more accessible. The vernacularisation and democratisation of language itself, particularly in expressing the erotic, which was again earlier meant largely for the elite, is equally significant (I owe parts of the foregoing discussion to Charu Gupta, feminist historian and leading expert on obscenities in political literature in modern Hindi).

Generally, historians work separately on body and sexuality or body and spirituality. Boundaries are especially marked in contexts where sexuality is taboo and spirituality recommended. In an important new work on two important Urdu literary figures contemporaneous with Nazir but located in the Deccan, Scott Kugle has explicitly combined these two aspects for an interesting blend of gender, sexuality and spirituality. Some people will be embarrassed while others happily embrace it. Working on the lives and works of Shah Siraj (1715–1763) of Aurangabad and Mah Laqa Bai Chanda (1768–1820/1824) of Hyderabad, identified as Sun (Siraj) and Moon (Mah) respectively, Kugle has offered a fascinating discussion of the Urdu literary and cultural milieu of 18th-century Deccan, including the early decades of the 19th century. Outgrowing homosexual love in youth, Siraj styled himself as a Sunni Sufi-like poet. Mah Laqa (literally: moon-cheeked) rose above the filth around the life of a courtesan and composed an elegant Urdu *diwan* (a collection comprising at least one *ghazal* rhyming in each of the thirty-two letters of Urdu alphabet) of her own, once again anchoring herself in Sufi spirituality and revealing a disarming devotion (as a known Syed and Shi'i Muslim) for Prophet Muhammad's cousin and son-in-law, Imam 'Ali ibn abi Talib. Specialising in *ghazal* compositions, both the poets fused spiritual quest with erotic imagery for tantalising results. Their Urdu *diwans* should be a veritable treat for the connoisseur. As an accomplished scholar of bodily practices in Sufism and Deccani Urdu literature, Kugle has first treated the two poets (Sun and Moon) separately as two orbits of the cultural planet. The author has eventually brought them together in a literary conjunction, when the sun meets the moon.

Kugle has provided English translations of a number of verses, the original Urdu of which is a veritable treat for its sheer linguistic charm. A couple of interesting lines quoted by the author may be mentioned here. Siraj Aurangabadi points out the following:

Sharab-i shauq pi kar dow jahan ka jis ne gham bhula
Khayal-i kham-i aflatun-o fikr-i jaam-i jam bhula

Mah Laqa Bai Chanda sings, using the commonly deployed metaphor in Urdu-Persian poetry of intoxicating wine:

Bahut makhmur hun saaqi sharab-i arghawani de
Na rakh tishna mujhe saaghar bi-raah-i meharbani de

Mah Laqa also complains about the emotional pangs and feelings of frustration that lovers have to usually endure, especially the tantrums of the beloved:

Har roz jo yun sitam ijaad karoge
Dil aashiqon ke saikron barbaad karoge

Hyderabad must have been a truly cosmopolitan city, with a vibrant cultural and intellectual environment, in the 18th and 19th centuries, for another female poet with a well-known Urdu *diwan* to her credit, Lutfun Nisa 'Imtiyaz', was a contemporary of Mah Laqa Bai Chanda. Historians are now increasingly reading the vast corpus of Urdu poetry to discover a whole cultural world that was previously outside their narrow frame. However, they are still not equipped to make sense of the powerful poetic imagery and refined expression of overwhelming emotions. Savour these lines by Siraj Aurangabadi (quoted by Kugle):

A'ina-ru ke shauq mein hairaan hua hun mayen
Zulfon kon uski dekh pareshan hua hun mayen

Thus, Urdu poetry cannot be dismissed as vulgar expressions catering to the low-class taste of people in a decadent society. The poets could be highly imaginative, indeed, philosophical, with an understanding of both the material and spiritual worlds that could inspire awe in the eyes of contemporaries. They also offered powerful critique of and dissent against the flawed normativities of their time. The poet also celebrated the best of the bounties of nature, wrote tributes for their patrons, expressed devotion for popular religious figures, and more often than not poured out love for their motherland, city or country.

Besides matters of bazaars, festivities and fun, Nazir's devotional poetry dedicated to the extraordinary powers of religious gurus is equally powerful. The fine example of the celebration of Guru Nanak's career may be mentioned here. Nazir's composition is given below, and a fuller discussion is offered elsewhere (Aquil 2017, Chapter 7):

Hain kahte nanak shah jinhen woh puray hain aagah guru
Woh kaamil rahbar jag mein hain yun raushan jaise maah guru
Maqsud, muraad ummid sabhi bar laate hain dil khwaah guru
Nit lutfo karam se karte hain ham logon ka nirbaah guru

Iss bakhshish ke iss azmat ke hain baba nanak shah guru
Sab sis newa ardaas karo aur har dam bolo wah guru

Har aan dilon wich yaan apne jo dhyan guru ka laate hain
Aur sevak ho kar unke he har surat beech kahaate hain
Gar apni lutf-o inayat se sukh chayn unhen dikhlaate hain
Khush rakhte hain har haal unhen sab tan ka kaaj banaate hain

Iss bakhshish ke iss azmat ke hain baba nanak shah guru
Sab sis newa ardaas karo aur har dam bolo wah guru

Jo aap guru ne bakhshish se uss khubi ka irshaad kiya
Har baat woh hai uss khubi ki taàsir ne jis par saad kiya
Yaan jis jis ne un baaton ko hai dhyan laga kar yaad kiya
Har aan guru ne dil unka khushwaqt kiya aur shaad kiya

Iss bakhshish ke iss azmat ke hain baba nanak shah guru
Sab sis newa ardaas karo aur har dam bolo wah guru

Din raat jinhon ne yaan dil wich hai yaad guru se kaam liya
Sab mun ke maqsad bhar paaye khush waqti ka hangaam liya
Dukh dard mein apne dhyan laga jis waqt guru ka naam liya
Pal beech guru ne aan unhen khush haal kiya aur thaam liya

Iss bakhshish ke iss azmat ke hain baba nanak shah guru
Sab sis newa ardaas karo aur har dam bolo wah guru

Yaan jo jo dil ki khwahish ki kuchh baat guru se kahte hain
Woh apni lutfo shafqat se nit haath unhon ke gahte hain
Altaaf se unke khush ho kar sab khubi se yeh kahte hain
Dukh dur unhon ke hote hain so sukh se jag mein rahte hain

Iss bakhshish ke iss azmat ke hain baba nanak shah guru
Sab sis newa ardaas karo aur har dam bolo wah guru

Jo har dam unse dhyan laga ummid karam ki karte hain
Woh un par lutf-o inayat se har aan tawajjoh karte hain
Asbab khushi aur khubi ke ghar beech unhon ke bharte hain
Anand inayat karte hain sab mun ki chinta harte hain

Iss bakhshish ke iss azmat ke hain baba nanak shah guru
Sab sis newa ardaas karo aur har dam bolo wah guru

Jo lutf-o inayat unmein hain kab wasaf kisi se unka ho
Woh lutf-o karam jo karte hain har chaar taraf hain zaahir woh
Altaaf jinhon par hain unke sau khubi haasil hai unko
Har aan Nazir ab yaan tum bhi baba nanak shah kaho

Iss bakhshish ke iss azmat ke hain baba nanak shah guru
Sab sis newa ardaas karo aur har dam bolo wah guru

A better tribute to Baba Nanak Shah may not be possible. This was in conformity with the usual celebration of the Guru's life and teaching in the Muslim tradition, which is generally ignored by both followers of the Khalsa-mediated Sikhism and later historians. Nazir also wrote a fine *nazm* on Chishti Sufi Shaikh Farid-ud-Din Ganj-i-Shakar (Baba Farid), who is an equally important figure in the shared traditions of the cultural history of Punjab.

In conclusion, scholars are increasingly realising that literature and history are inextricably linked to each other. Earlier, literary scholars had generally no or little sense of history, and poorly trained academic historians thought literature was all about the fictitious imagination of writers, devoid of any sense of reality. Historians are now beginning to realise that government data, which they so valued for the writing of history, could be fudged, as it happens, to cover up failures of governance (as some learned theorists put it: government data tells us only what it wants to tell us). By contrast, all literatures are products of their time. Literature and society construct each other. Historians can study literature to understand its context which is what the parameters of research recommend—understand the past in all its varied dimensions, including literary cultures and intellectual traditions, to better understand a society. Scholars of medieval Indian history have traditionally emphasised the primacy of Indian-Persian sources for the writing of history, but few scholars have actually seriously studied Persian literary works. Thus, very little is available in terms of edited texts and translations. Happily, new historians have opened up in recent decades a whole new archive of material in several languages and across genres (see, for example, Sunil Sharma's recent book on Persian literature under the Mughals; the Urdu and Hindi scene have been dealt with in Naim and Busch; many examples of research in the literary traditions of other Indian vernaculars can also be given; for some discussion on history in the vernacular, see Aquil and Chatterjee [2008]).

In this chapter, our focus has been on highlighting the value of the intersection between literature, history and society, especially in matters of pleasure. For this purpose, we discussed samples of Nazir

Akbarabadi's exceptional work, which can be contextualised and understood with reference to the larger Urdu field—the classical Urdu literature of the 18th and first half of the 19th centuries. Some efforts were made here through examples of a literary tradition shared with equally important figures such as Ja'far Zatalli, Mir Taqi Mir and Mirza Ghalib, among others. It is a scintillating chapter in India's chequered cultural history, which needs more research into its many wonderful dimensions, including momentary celebrations of life and dealing with the lasting pain of death. Nazir himself concludes in his philosophical observations on life in this popular line (Shahbaz 8):

Sab thaath para rah jayega, jab laad chalega banjara!

REFERENCES

Aquil, Raziuddin. *The Muslim Question: Understanding Islam and Indian History*. New Delhi: Penguin. 2017.

Aquil, Raziuddin and Partha Chatterjee, eds. *History in the Vernacular*. Ranikhet: Permanent Black. 2008.

Busch, Allison. *Poetry of Kings: The Classical Hindi Literature of Mughal India*. New York: Oxford University Press. 2011.

Chatterjee, Partha. *The Black Hole of Empire: History of a Global Practice of Power*. Ranikhet: Permanent Black. 2012.

Ghalib, Mirza. *Diwan-i Ghalib*. New Delhi: Ghalib Academy. 1997.

———. *Kulliyaat-i Maktubat-i Farsi-i Ghalib*. Edited and translated by Partav Rohilla. New Delhi: Ghalib Institute. 2010.

Gupta, Charu, ed. *Gendering Colonial India*. New Delhi: Orient Blackswan. 2012.

Jalibi, Jamil. *Tarikh-i Adab-i Urdu*, multi-volume. Delhi: Educational Publishing House. 1977.

Khan, Dargah Quli. *Muraqqa-i Dehli*, Persian text with Urdu translation. Edited and translated by Khaliq Anjum. New Delhi: Anjuman Taraqqi Urdu (Hind). 1993.

Kugle, Scott. *When Sun Meets Moon: Gender, Eros and Ecstasy in Urdu Poetry*. Hyderabad: Orient Blackswan. 2016.

Kulliyaat-i-Nazir Akbarabadi. Edited by Maulana Abdul Bari Aasi and Maulwi Ashraf Ali Lukhnawi. Lucknow: (Raja) Ram Kumar Press Book Depot, Waris Nawal Kishore Press Book Depot. 1951.

Mir, Mir Taqi. *Remembrances* [autobiographical narrative], Persian text with English translation. Edited and translated by C.M. Naim. Murty Classical Library of India. Cambridge, MA: Harvard University Press. 2019.

Mukhia, Harbans. 'The Celebration of Failure as Dissent in Urdu Ghazal', *Modern Asian Studies* 33, no. 1 (1999): 861–881.

Naim, C.M. *Urdu Texts and Contexts: The Selected Essays of CM Naim*. New Delhi: Permanent Black. 2004.

Narang, Gopi Chand. *Ghalib: Innovative Meanings and the Ingenious Mind*. Translated from the Urdu by Surinder Deol. New Delhi: Oxford University Press. 2017.

Petievich, Carla. *When Men Speak as Women: Vocal Masquerade in Indo-Muslim Poetry*. New Delhi: Oxford University Press. 2007.

Shahbaz, Syed Muhammad Abdul Ghafur. *Zindagani Benazir*. Edited by Syed Muhammad Hasnain. New Delhi: Taraqqi Urdu Bureau. 1981.

Sharma, Sunil. *Mughal Arcadia: Persian Literature in an Indian Court*. Cambridge, MA: Harvard University Press. 2017.

Vanita, Ruth. *Gender, Sex and the City: Urdu Rekhti Poetry, 1780–1870*. New Delhi: Orient Blackswan. 2012.

Zatalli, Mir Muhammad Ja'far. *Zatal-nama (Kulliyaat-i Ja'far Zatalli)*. Edited by Rashid Hasan Khan. New Delhi: Anjuman Taraqqi Urdu (Hind). 2003.

7

PAINTING PLEASURE: THE GENEALOGY AND DICHOTOMIES OF GENDER-BASED IDENTITIES*

Preeti Sharma

INTRODUCTION

Transformations in the scripting of history and the métier of the historian from the last century have opened newer areas of historical exploration, providing insights into human pasts through uncharted trajectories. Scholars such as Foucault, while distinguishing the process of domination and power relationships within Western society, carried history deeper into the realms of the story of social control. With Derrida, Saussure and Barthes and the theory of historicism, history took a linguistic turn through discourse and deconstruction. Subsequently, the historian's focus, in a way, shifted away from the recovery and interpretation of hard evidence to theories of representation, to symbolism and collective memory for comprehending culture. Analysing the role of the hitherto marginalised groups, including women, also emerged as a potential area for historical investigations. The gap between assumptions and assertions was never so clear, and the link between ideology and a conceptualisation of the field nowhere so integrated as in the gender issue or the social relations between the sexes.[1]

The second half of the 19th century in particular was dominated by the Victorian ideology of separate spaces, postulating that women were destined to inhabit the private space that was identified with them and their life-giving and life-sustaining activities—the exclusive world of family, domesticity, delicacy and intimacy, separate from and untouched by the male-oriented public world. The scientific history and

* This chapter is a refined version of a talk delivered at the Rajasthan State Archives, Bikaner (2015) and a paper published in Proceedings, Rajasthan History Congress (2009).

the new social sciences substantiated theoretical assumptions of the dichotomous private and public worlds.

This dichotomy of private/public worlds was furthered by the postulate of nature/culture as reflecting the fundamental difference between women and men. Women, as mothers with birth-giving capacities, were celebrated as the beings close to nature while men, lacking the natural creative function, were prone to assert their creativity externally. Hence, while women were confined to the home, men created and controlled the contours of culture and imbibed the same through process of socialisation in the communities. Highlighting role of culture in defining women and gendering society, Simone de Beauvoir pronounced that women are made, not born and their cultural construction had rendered them weak and essentially outsiders in a society largely organised for the benefit of men.[2] Beauvoir cited thinkers from the ancient Greeks to Freud with salient tenets of the Genesis, Saint Paul and Karl Marx in support of her thesis.[3] Subsequently, gender as a coordinating concept brought together a variety of subjects relevant not just for an interpretation of history but also for the disciplines of sociology, psychology, anthropology, legal studies and literature. From the 1980s onwards, gender studies emerged as one of the tools for deconstruction and the decoding of literary and historical texts to reconstruct the past and explore areas where women's influence was assumed to be at its least.[4]

Such explorations provided congenial ground to nurture the history of women. The need to refocus the vision and review history from a perspective involving women was emphasised. Were women actors, initiating things, or just disinterested respondents? Were they involved or merely drawn into the unfolding of events? Did they act spontaneously and genuinely, or did they simply use strategies associated with subordinate positions: manipulating, pleasing, and just enduring? Henceforth, the scholarly inclination was to re-read the evidence available for any other purpose or alternative sources and 'discover' what has been 'left' out. Joan Gadol Kelly's query 'Did women have a Renaissance?' questioned the 'recorded past' and highlighted the need to reconsider events to bring forth women-specific experiences. She rightly held that the existing projections and interpretations were one-sided and all the advances of Renaissance Italy, its proto-capitalist economy, its states and humanistic culture, all worked to mould the noblewoman into an aesthetic object: decorous, chaste and doubly dependent on her husband as well as her prince.[5] She concluded, 'But I knew now that the entire picture I had held of the Renaissance was partial, distorted, limited, and deeply flawed',[6] and underlined the need to revisit the past afresh with all possible sources.

Art studies, from this perspective, provide a valuable insight into social history. Art is an influential, potential and vital shaper of culture. Exploring the representations of men and women in art is instrumental to examining ways of representing gender. Therefore, issues of gender and art need to be examined in the historical contexts of age, class and race. As also held by Lauretis, gender is both a sociocultural construct and a semiotic apparatus that produces meaning. If gender representations are social positions carrying differential meanings, then for someone to be represented and to represent oneself as male or as female implies the supposition of the whole of those meaning effects.[7]

If we view the traditional Indian cultural and knowledge systems and their projections in this context, it is apparent that apart from their intense philosophical purport, they also convey meaningful insights into prevailing social structures. In fact, the Indian cultural ethos was imbued with a vibrant discourse of pleasure, overtly and covertly expressed through visual and literary manifestations. With the emergence of monarchical states and subsequent normative socialisations, the royal court as well as the household evolved into sites of physical and mental enjoyment, including pleasurable thoughts and practices. The concept of pleasure symbolised a tangible and intangible matrix that provided spaces for leisure and recreations in the people's lived existences, while remaining within the prevailing social structures.

In fact, a reading of the genealogy of the discourse formation[8] on feminine social spaces in Indic cultures presents us with an interesting epistemic hierarchy between the women's private and the public realms. Such an epistemic hierarchy portrays itself into a contesting imagery, wherein women's private and public roles get categorised into a dichotomy. The dichotomous inferences may be gleaned through women's ubiquitous representational presence in arts, aesthetics and literature as refined pleasure-oriented engagements nurtured in their private world. Contrary to this, their structurally mediated social identity denies them any public space and projects them as passive conformists to the norms of patriarchy and masculinity and as operating therein. This renders a competing discourse on the social space of women in Indic cultures inevitable. It not only draws our attention to the epistemological indeterminacy that the sub-discipline of the history of women in India exhibits, but also directs our consideration to the contesting conception of the phenomenon of women's pleasure.

The chapter attempts to map this very epistemological indeterminacy. Knowledge formation in the context of women and their varied manifestations are ostensibly a problematic due to the lack of a seemingly convincing connotation. Issues such as double marginality or dual colonialism of biological womanhood and a socially submissive class, as also the women's question, have remained pertinent, particularly since colonial times. They render difficult the determination of any consistent implications. The women's question occupied a central position in the early and mid-19th century social reform-related debates over issues such as *sati*, widow remarriage, *kulin* polygamy, age of consent, etc., in the Bengal Presidency, the symbol of the Indian Renaissance. Towards the end of the century however, the discourse changed entirely—such issues were taken out of focus and replaced with the politics of nationalism, as has been discussed by Partha Chatterjee.[9] Women were still deemed vulnerable, but the nationalism debate appropriated the nature of their vulnerability in terms of a nature and culture discourse and advocated protecting them in their private space or the exclusive environs of their homes in order to sustain Indian culture.

This brings us to private space and its projecting contending concepts—a confinement, secluded place, internalising self, secure surroundings both autonomous and sacrosanct. Kaviraj has analysed how the modern genre of the autobiography revealed 'the historical invention of a private sphere, of a private life for individuals, a conceptual space in which they are sovereign, subject to some rules of sociability'.[10] However, regarding women, the notion of private space generally involves confining or relegating them to the world of domesticity and a denial of any accessibility to the public space in the façade of social structuration. Thus, the indeterminacy regarding the interpretation of women's issues and their social positioning percolates and persists.

The academic and implied purport of terms such as 'power/empowered/powerless' also implies inconsistencies when used for the women of privileged/elite classes and unprivileged/folk sections, respectively. While the former socially represent power circles, their actual status is powerlessness due to taboos and injunctions under the guise of cultural traditions. The women of the seemingly powerless 'subalternity'-ridden sections also confront double marginality: congenital, assigned to their biological status and social, as a by-product of their disadvantageous social position. However, when regarded comparatively, women of the mainstream social, political and economically privileged structures and enjoying the legacy of a superior and distinct social status are bound by fetters of patriarchy, which entrench them deep in the normative cultural folds, constantly shaping/reshaping their lives. Women of these sections apparently did not contest the patriarchal injunctions as demonstrated by expressions of the prevailing cultures. An examination of their core values presents a reified submission to the overarching normative constructions. In contrast, the unprivileged women, voicing their opinion and enjoying unrestricted access/movements though public/private spaces, appear more empowered. Thus, the gendered perspective of the epistemological treatment of history revolves around the two conceptions that have largely determined its nature: 'a reified subjugation to domination' and a 'radical resistance by the subjugated to the structures of dominance'.[11] The academic and actual expositions obviously remain at variance, creating sites of dual hermeneutics as far as aspects of womanhood are concerned.

Women, from the early societies, were lodged in the safe havens of homes, contributing to the sustenance of the family pedigree, continuity of race and cultural observances. Ours has been a society where conventionally the various roles of the woman as an ideal wife have been clearly delineated by sage Vyasa in the *Garuda Purāṇa*:

> *Karyeshu mantri, patni syat sakhi syat karyeshu cha*
> *sneheshu bharya mata syat vesya cha sayane shubha.*[12]

The above lines express the expectations from a wife, how she ought to perform her multiple roles: as a judicious advisor to the husband before he commences any work, as an ally in unison assisting the husband with work, as a mother in affection and selflessness for the husband and as a *vesya* in her skill in bed. The characterisation was nevertheless obligatory in the name of creating image of an ideal wife, as she *ought to* act accordingly.

A similar ideology conveyed by a 13th-century Telugu poet in *Neethi Sara* attests to the fact that parameters remained identical across time, communities and space as far as defining womanhood was concerned:

> *Karyeshu dasi, karaneshu manthri, bhojeshu mata,*
> *shayaneshu Rambha, roopeshu Lakshmi,*
> *kshamayeshu Dharitri, shat dharmayukta, kuladharma pathni.*

This translates to describing the good wife as one with the following six virtues: who works like a servant, advises like a minister, feeds like a mother, pleases in bed like Rambha, is beautiful like Lakshmi, has patience like Dhara (Earth).[13]

Ironically, the text has not elaborated on what was satisfying, fulfilling or enjoyable for the woman as an individual, implying that the phenomenon of pleasure was not uniformly applicable to all and smacks of incongruity. Located in this context, the chapter endeavours to explore how the notion of women's pleasure itself tends to confront a kind of dual hermeneutics. Confined to the 'private' space of domesticity, under the overarching institutions of patriarchy and *purdah*, their status usually divulged subservience and isolation, deprived of any pleasure or gratification. However, in artistic manifestations abounding in the public social space, the feminine motif is arguably amongst one of the most popular for lending embellishment or pleasure to the onlookers. Also, women as the creators and bearers of human progeny have contributed to cultural affluence since antiquity as practitioners of finer arts. However, such cultural practices as performing arts was largely pursued by the class of public/professional women to provide pleasure to the affluent sections, leaving women from dignified sections generally out of their ambit. In a way, the pleasure pursuits by women for self-gratification in the public domain were deemed unbecoming while their role in regaling the social classes was acceptable, suggesting contesting perspectives of the hermeneutics of pleasure. Further, how women within the confined private spaces themselves sought and experienced pleasure also necessitates an academic exploration.

The chapter seeks to comprehend this dual hermeneutics by specifically examining how the Rajput queens, customarily projected as inert conformists, mediated by the structures of patriarchy in the public—the male-oriented *mardana* domain—were able to experience pleasure in the private space within the *zenana* through art patronage and images of pleasurable activities represented therein. While the themes of the paintings of pleasure are generally woven around the king's persona, the chapter seeks to investigate whether they may be interpreted as a 'visual' expression of the pleasure in the lived reality of women's lives.

Towards this end, the chapter takes up the virtual, implicit presence of women, actually absent, in the normative public domain of the Rajput courts, from the closed and 'private' quarters of the *zenana* as an indicator ascertaining the place/space of women in history. It will be significant to envisage how women, through the influence and power exerted by the patronage of art, could seek not only fulfilment of pleasure pursuits but also seek and devise ways of interactions with the public space even when confined behind the veil or *purdah* and located in the secluded apartments of the *zenana*. Limited access to external environs did not result in a lack of information. Maharani Gayatri Devi of Jaipur reminisced how apart from their naïve theatricals, the *zenana* women followed outside activities keenly and would promptly rejoice at every achievement of their king. When Maharaja Man Singh II's team won the All-India Polo Championship, his *zenana* women embroidered their skirts and shawls with polo stick designs. Similarly, when he gained his flying license, the *zenana* ladies who, Gayatri Devi believed, had never and were unlikely to ever sit in an aircraft, loyally decorated their clothes with aeroplane motifs.[14]

In the light of this public/private dichotomy, usually put forth as a synonym of women's submissiveness, the chapter focalises the artistic patronage by the Rajput royals to deconstruct the ontological indeterminacy confronted in understanding the contesting conceptions of the phenomenon of women's pleasure. Citing records from the erstwhile Jaipur state *Suratkhana*, i.e., department of painting,[15] and instances of Rajput style painting representations, the chapter endeavours to project the art connoisseur queens largely as women of refined artistic tastes, specifically in light of the nature of the art they patronised—from portraits of their loved ones and relatives to profusely romantic depictions, mostly based on the literary conventions of the genre of *Ragamala* and *Barahmasa*. It is significant to postulate through art-centric inferences how the supposedly submissive and isolated inmates of the *zenana* observing *purdah* could indulge in gratifying pleasurable activities, in the surroundings of their 'private' world while vindicating norms of the 'public' world. It is of paramount importance to gauge the extent to which these women were actors, taking initiatives rather than being passive recipients. Were they actively involved or inadvertently drawn into shaping events? Generally, seclusion or isolation is equated with a lack of knowledge, passivity and restriction of space. However, the *zenana/zenani dyodi* in the erstwhile Jaipur state was an institution, politically and culturally vibrant, as discussed in the forthcoming sections.

THE PAINTING ATELIER: SURATKHANA

Following Akbar's conciliatory and syncretic strategies, several of the Rajput rulers were variously inducted into the Mughal administration, nobility and imperial family. They subsequently became Mughal-acculturated in several ways, absorbing and emulating their court culture and the artistic enterprises that they patronised in their native principalities (Figures 7.1 and 7.2). Patronage to painting, as a courtly art, led to the creation of fine artworks supported for secular and connoisseurly purposes. The Rajput kings also became the protagonists/subjects in these paintings, especially during the second quarter of 18th century, when the Mughal artist migrants to Rajput courts produced a plethora of paintings that replicated the Mughal exemplars in function and form. Such images included royal portraits, kings in court, royal processions or hunts, festival celebrations, musical soirees, love making, etc.

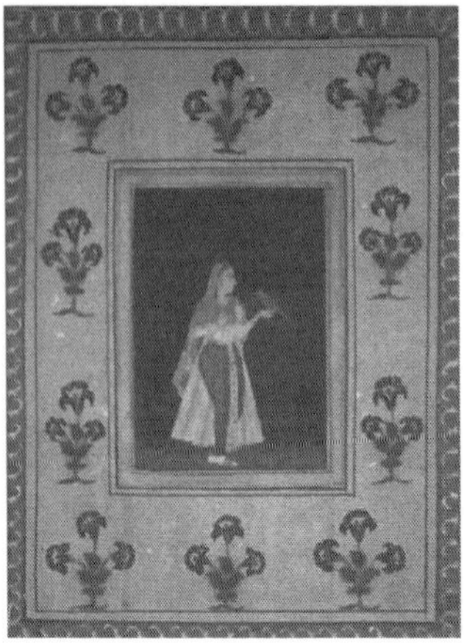

Figure 7.1: Lady with a Parrot, Late Mughal, ca 1800, Government Central Museum, Albert Hall, Jaipur

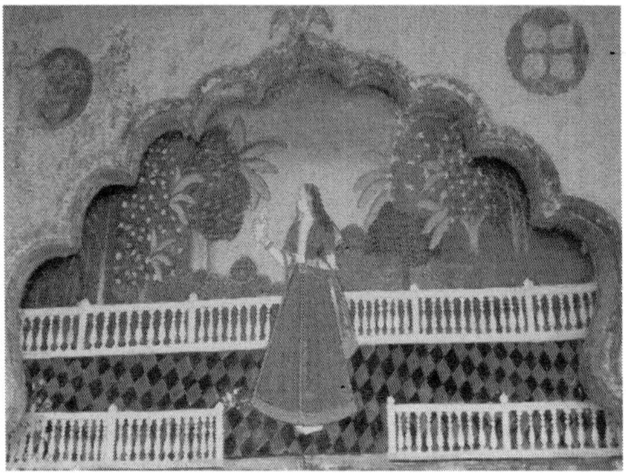

Figure 7.2: *Nayika* with a Parrot, Fresco, Sukh Mahal, Bundi

Maharaja Sawai Jai Singh, while conceptualising his capital city of Jaipur, made provisions for workshops on the Mughal model in the vicinity of his palace that would cater to all requirements of the royalty. Popular as *karkhana*, the 36 workshops that came up produced miscellaneous commodities for the royal court and household establishments, ranging from daily use to specific occasions such as royal processions, acts of piety, the royals' recreational pursuits and so on. The *karkhanas* included *Kapaddwara*, *Pothikhana*, *Suratkhana*, *Khyalkhana*, *Silahkhana*, *Farashkhana*, *Palkikhana*, *Bagghikhana*, *Rathakhana*, *Atishkhana* and *Rasoda*.[16]

The *Suratkhana* or the painting atelier was initially part of the *Pothikhana*,[17] i.e., the royal library, and was instrumental in nurturing painters, *suratgar*, artisans and scholars, besides preserving the literary heritage of Jaipur kings. Maharaja Sawai Jai Singh had brought two Mughal painters, Fazil Muhammad and Sadeq Muhammad, from the Delhi *durbar*. They worked in the *Suratkhana*, which was substantially reorganised in 1725 CE under the Maharaja's supervision.[18] The painters, traditionally called *chatera*, had mostly migrated from the Mughal court to Jaipur, where they eventually evolved splendid styles of painting under their royal patrons.

The *Suratkhana*'s most illustrious phase was under Maharaja Sawai Pratap Singh (1773–1803 CE). It prospered till the late 19th century, when the onset of photography during Maharaja Ram Singh's times (1835–1880 CE) relegated the *Suratkhana* to a mere repository of old pictures. Sahibram, Chhaju, Baksa, Harnarayan, Govind and Gopal were some renowned painters who worked under Pratap Singh. The Maharaja himself was a skilled artist and did several paintings of Radha Krishna, *Raslila*, *Nayika*, *Ragamala*, *Barahmasa*, etc. Embossed gold work, incised pearl, diamond, rubies, gold lining and huge paintings with *syah kalam* began under him. *Mussavir* (painter) Ramchandra was patronised by Maharaja Sawai Ram Singh, who commissioned paintings on the epics and *Bhagvata* stories.

Although miniatures were done profusely, the Jaipur school paintings were particularly characterised by their larger-than-life dimensions. Though active from the 18th century, the Jaipur School came to prominence only in the 20th century. Six paintings were sent by the Jaipur Regency Council for display in the first All India Art Exhibition held in London (1928).[19] Two of these were *barahmasa* paintings and were 6 × 3 feet in size.[20] The portraits of Maharaja Jai Singh and Pratap Singh were also exhibited and stood out for their life-size proportions and realistic projections of forms (Figures 7.3 and 7.4). Embossed jewellery, lively lines and immaculate facial expressions rendered distinct charm and class to the two portraits. This was the first-ever display of Jaipur School paintings on a public platform and resulted in projecting it as a world-class art style. Another huge painting entitled *Bahadurvijay Raso*, based on the identically titled epic by Chunnilal Bhatt, was painted by 11 artists of Pratap Singh's *chitrakarabaisi* group.[21] It measured $8 \times 2^{1/2}$ feet.[22] Amongst the masterpieces of this period preserved in the *Suratkhana*, *Radhakrishna Maharas* and *Govardhan Krishna* paintings made during Pratap Singh's reign constituted a class of their own. He also had thousands of paintings arranged thematically as albums—*muraqqa*. Besides these magnum opuses, the *Suratkhana* holdings included collections from various places, works commissioned by the royals and artworks gifted by the painters to their patrons.

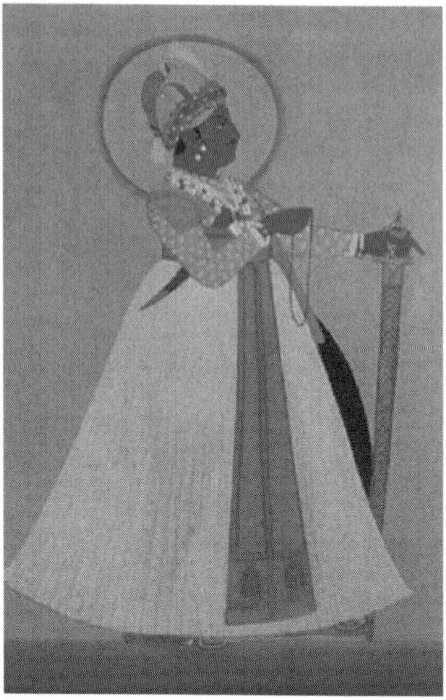

Figure 7.3: Maharaja Sawai Jai Singh, Government Museum, Hawamahal, Jaipur

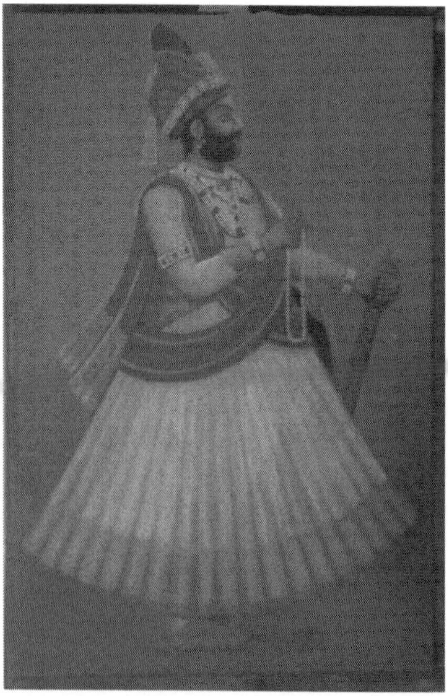

Figure 7.4: Maharaja Sawai Pratap Singh, Government Museum, Hawamahal, Jaipur

THE ZENANI DYODI/ZENANA

The royal women's quarters were known variously—*zenana*, *zenani dyodi*, *raniwas*, *rawala* or *antahpur*. It was generally an autonomous unit, with a series of self-contained apartments appended with ample resources for their maintenance. The *dyodi* was the part of the royal palace inhabited by the royal women such as the dowager queen or *Maji*, the Maharaja's wives or Rani and sub-wives, *paswan*, *khawas*, *paddayat*, and their retinue of ladies-in-waiting, broadly comprising *badaran*, *dhai*, *sahelya*, *davdia*, *gayania*, etc.[23]

The Jaipur queens were generally named after their natal houses, such as Rathoreji, Jadumji, Jhaliji, Tanwarji, etc., while the *paswan* were given names by the *dyodi* with the suffix '*raiji*', such as Basanti*raiji*, Bharat*raiji* and Heera*raiji*. The queens were generally proficient in the fine arts as well as martial arts, weaponry, horse riding and were capable of defending their fort in crisis, enthuse the husband to uphold the family's honour, participate in crucial war- and peace-related consultations, engage in philanthropic acts and assume regency if required.

Instances of the involvement of Jaipur queens in active state politics are profuse, indicating their political clout. Bhattiyani Rani acted as sovereign when Man Singh undertook campaigns for the Mughals and even sent him money until he acquired a position at the imperial court.[24] The ranis were consulted over political situations. For instance, Maharaja Madho Singh I shared state matters, including Maratha threats, with his rani in a letter dated VS 1821.[25] *Zenana* regencies were also effective in Jaipur state, thrice under Rani Chundawat (1768), *Maji* Bhattiyani (1818–1833) and *Maji* Chandrawat (1869). Such examples are available from various states[26] of Rajputana and extol the administrative competence as also independent functioning of the queens. As dowager queens, the *Majis* were revered and consulted by the kings. Thus, politically, as a classic stance of dual hermeneutics, although women were not seemingly powerful in a typical Rajput setup, they could exert substantial influence and power if need be. At times, they even managed the administration of their maintenance grants—*hathkharach jagirs*.[27]

Organised on the lines of the royal court, life in the *zenani dyodi* resonated culturally with revelry through periodic gatherings—*mehfils* of dance, music, plays and celebration of festivals. The *zenana* inmates did get occasional opportunities to witness the gaiety of the royal *mardana* courts. For instance, celebratory *mehfil-majlis* were regularly organised in Hawamahal during the reign of Pratap Singh and Jagat Singh, as hinted by Pratap Singh himself in his *rekhte*—couplets.[28] It is surmised that the royal women frequented Hawamahal from their apartments and joined such pleasure-inducing gatherings through the tunnel, made by Pratap Singh, from the Chandramahal *zenani dyodi* premises to Hawamahal. Though they did not have access to the open courts due to the customary *purdah*, such screened mechanisms might have oriented them into the pleasure worlds/pursuits of the menfolk. The merriment and festivities were probably replicated in the *zenana* quarters too, for the larger community of their inmates, as indicated by the categories of entertainers and performers as *davdia, gayania*, maintained in the *zenana* establishment itself. Can we read an appropriation of the male-centric mannerisms in such replications? Thus, an epistemological indeterminacy about pleasure may be seen wherein women provided pleasure—as subjects of paintings or performers—in public, male-centric gatherings. Simultaneously, the privileged women themselves derived pleasure and perpetuated it too through similar events organised in their precincts.

In the prevailing royal circles, professional dancers and singers also thrived as royal attendants and served the royalty as *paturs* and *bhagtans*. In Jaipur state, particularly in 1600–1800 CE, their numbers increased exponentially and a separate department, the *Paturkhana*, was set up to manage related matters. Trained at the behest of the state, they performed *muzara* on occasions as the king's anniversary, festivals, etc.[29] and were duly rewarded for the performances.[30]

Pratap Singh's favourite *bhagtans* included Didarbaksh, *patur* Rangrai, Kasturirai, Gatitarang Rai and Raspraveen. Some of them bore his offspring too.[31] Jagat Singh (1803–1818) was enamoured with Raskapur. Maharaja Madho Singh's (1880–1917) *zenani dyodi* was at the peak of its opulence. Hundreds of its inmates of varied categories attended upon the queens and *paddayat*—*Khalsabai* (state supported establishment), *Hazuribai* (personal attendant to *Maji*, queens and *paswan*), *Makkhibai* (for whisking away the bees), *Takiyabai* (for placing pillows), *Ghagharahali* or *Gararawali*, designated after their attire, etc.

The royals encouraged the cultivation and nurturing of the finer arts in the *zenana*. Ram Singh II deputed several courtesans, *tawaifs*, to train his *bandis*. *Mirza Raja* Jai Singh delegated Kulpati Mishra and Prannath Shrotriya to tutor the *zenana* inmates in performing arts.[32] Several copies of manuscripts prepared by them have been preserved in the *Pothikhana*. Experts from the *Gunijankhana* were often assigned to initiate the *zenana* women in singing, dancing, drama, etc. Maharani Gayatri Devi recalled how the *zenana* inmates entertained her, while Maharaja Man Singh II fought in the Second World War. They would stage plays dressed as soldiers, recreating the Maharaja's victories in his battles against the Germans in the Middle

East.[33] Copies of several drama scripts have also been recovered from the *zenani dyodi*.

ZENANI DYODI: PROFILING PLEASURE

The symbiotic relationship between women and pleasure remains constant from early times and was duly represented through arts and literature. The association of the sensuous female body with fertility, abundance, growth and auspiciousness constituted the core of the plastic arts, while the projections of women indulging in pleasure activities have been visualised in different phases of Indian art—the bacchanalian frenzied *Vasantsena*, the Mathura school female sculptures, the Khajuraho temple sculptures, to cite a few. Texts such as Vatsyayana's *Kāmasūtra* provide literary insights into the sexual aspect of pleasure.

Freed from mundane concerns, the women in the Rajput *zenana* were obviously more drawn towards refined aesthetic and pleasure pursuits, consequently exhibiting cultural exuberance. As in polity, the impact of the Mughal court must have been cultural as well, as evident from several painted representations in the Kishangarh, Bundi, Bikaner and Jaipur art styles. For example, the painter Sitaram's work *Radha and Krishna Entertained with Fireworks*, painted in Kishangarh style,[34] was a replication of the palatial ambience of the terrace scene from Hashim's Mughal style painting, *Ladies of the Imperial Harem Celebrating the Night of Shab-i-Barat*.[35] The former projects the idealised royal as Radha, Krishna and attendant females with fireworks and illumination settings and exhibits the possible appropriation of imperial Mughal traditions by the regional schools of art. As to the popularity of idealised forms in Rajput art, the rulers expounded a mythical lineage to validate their claims to sovereignty. Many of them, as *chandravanshi* and *suryavanshi*, traced their dynastic lineage from Krishna and Rāma. Bardic literature—*khyats* and *prashastis*—was instrumental to some extent in propagating such notions.

Art was another device to stake claims for an elevated social hierarchy. Idealised forms emerged as characteristic features of various regional schools of painting, lending them distinct identities. The rulers' identity as possessors of military might was substituted by their connoisseurship of arts and themes of the paintings wherein battle scenes or the line of forts were disfavoured. They commissioned paintings in which a halo around the king's head emphasised his sacrosanct status and likeness to God, a retinue of attendants, images of performing arts (Figures 7.5 and 7.6), gardens, palace, festival celebrations, seemingly represented a refined cultural ambience instead of military prowess.

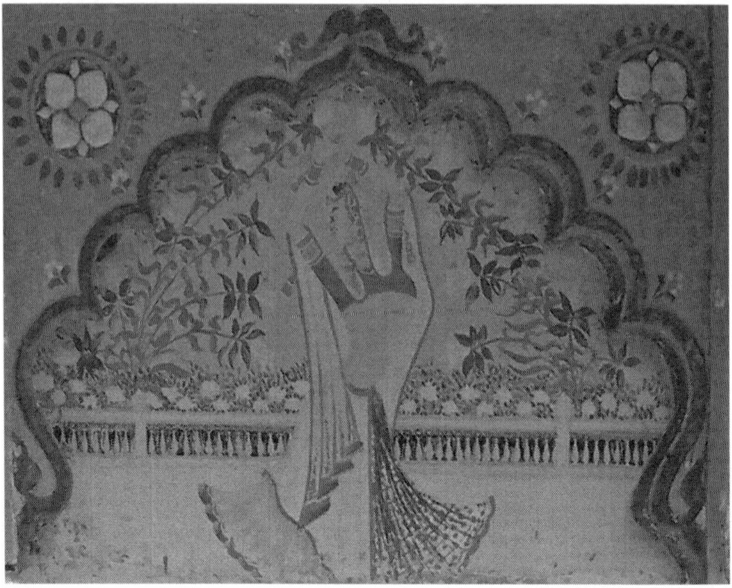

Figure 7.5: Dancing *Nayika*, Fresco, Sukh Mahal, Bundi

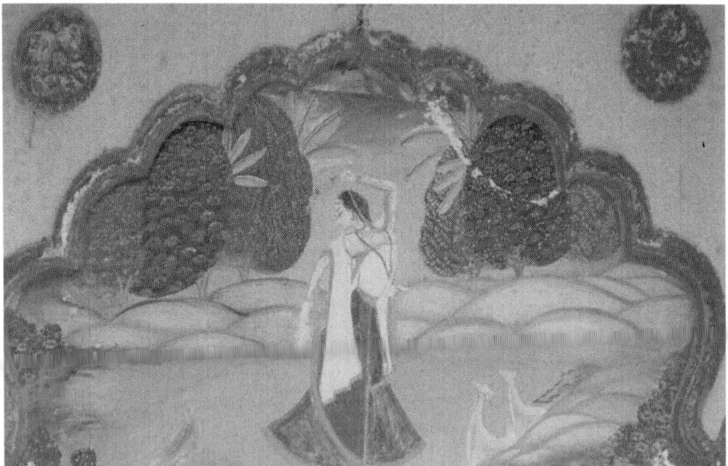

Figure 7.6: Dancing *Nayika*, Fresco, Sukh Mahal, Bundi

As befitting adjuncts, the *Ragamala* paintings convey moods of musical compositions besides devotional significance. *Barahmasa*-themed paintings were also done profusely as idealised imagery components.

A prolific use of the Krishna theme remained intrinsic to Rajput painting styles, especially Jaipur and Kishangarh. The association of the patron with Krishna and the *nayika* as Radha, the divine consort of Krishna, transcended courtly environs to the realm of the divinities. A classic case is that of Raja Sawant Singh of Kishangarh and his beloved *paswan* Bani Thani (Figure 7.7), who not only worshipped but even identified themselves as Krishna and Radha.

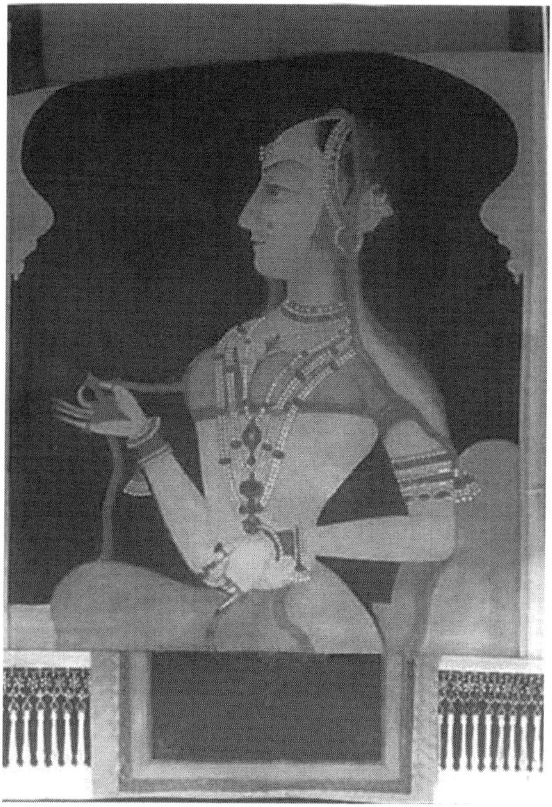

Figure 7.7: Bani Thani, Kishangarh Style, Government Central Museum, Albert Hall, Jaipur

The adoption of conventions developed to frame the visual presence of the Mughal Emperors in terms of their court etiquettes as well as painted representations is equally significant. The elaborate behavioural norms and associated architectural settings have been highlighted by Necipoğlu (1993)[36] and Singh (2013).[37] The daily practice of *jharokha darsana* to showcase the Emperor's imperial persona to his subjects from the palace balcony had been institutionalised into an ostentatious ritual of the personality cult. In the heydays of the Empire, no regional rulers could transgress upon and recreate the visual codes thus determined. However, with the waning of imperial might and the migration of Mughal artists to regional courts, the appropriation of such idioms was comparatively normative. Several instances are extant wherein the Mughal settings have been transformed to a Rajput ambience to recreate the imagery. These can also be taken up as attempts at subverting the hierarchy within which the Rajput kings were hitherto subordinated. As suggested by Singh, the appropriation of imperial imagery to a Hindu god would have had similar resonances to its appropriation to a Rajput king, for god and king were in senses more than one interchangeable in these realms.[38]

As the Kachhwaha dynasty of Amer-Jaipur had close relations with the Mughals from the times of Akbar, the acculturative influence of the imperial culture percolating into their *zenana* and impacting its inmates is very probable. Extolled for their physical beauty and valued as mothers and nurturers, royal women were generally sheltered from the public eye. The social organisation, family structures, social traditions, festivals, religious rituals, etc., acted as catalysts for the overall process of socialisation (Figures 7.8–7.10). The representations too primarily exhibit activities instrumental in socialisation by highlighting the behavioural norms acceptable in the prevailing milieu (Figure 7.11).

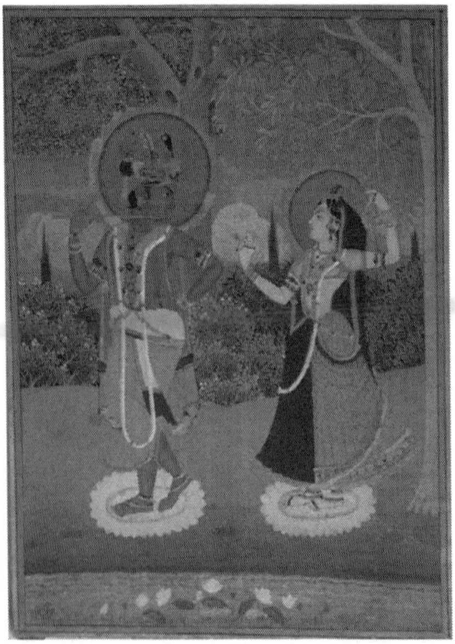

Figure 7.8: Radha Krishna, ca 1775, Alwar Style, Government Museum, Hawamahal, Jaipur

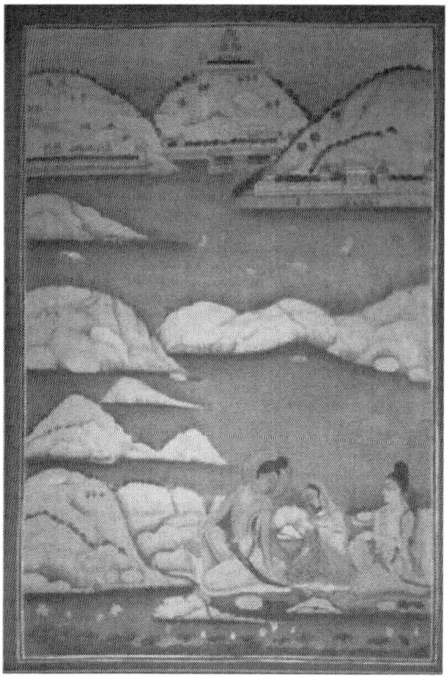

Figure 7.9: Ram, Lakshman and Sita Beside a Lake—Palace and Fort in the Background, 19th Century, Kishangarh, Government Central Museum, Albert Hall, Jaipur

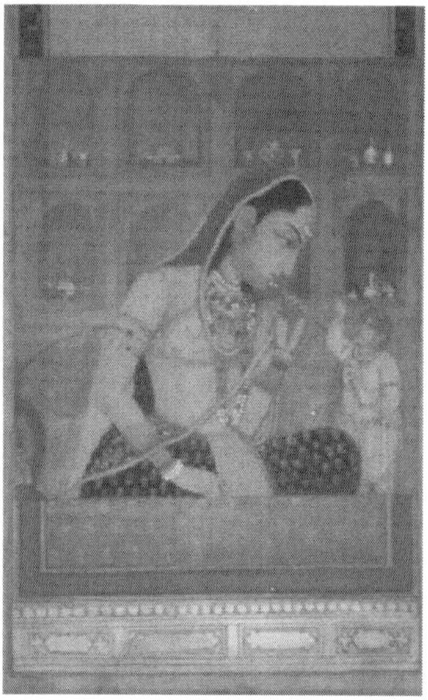

Figure 7.10: A Lady with a Child, Government Central Museum, Albert Hall, Jaipur

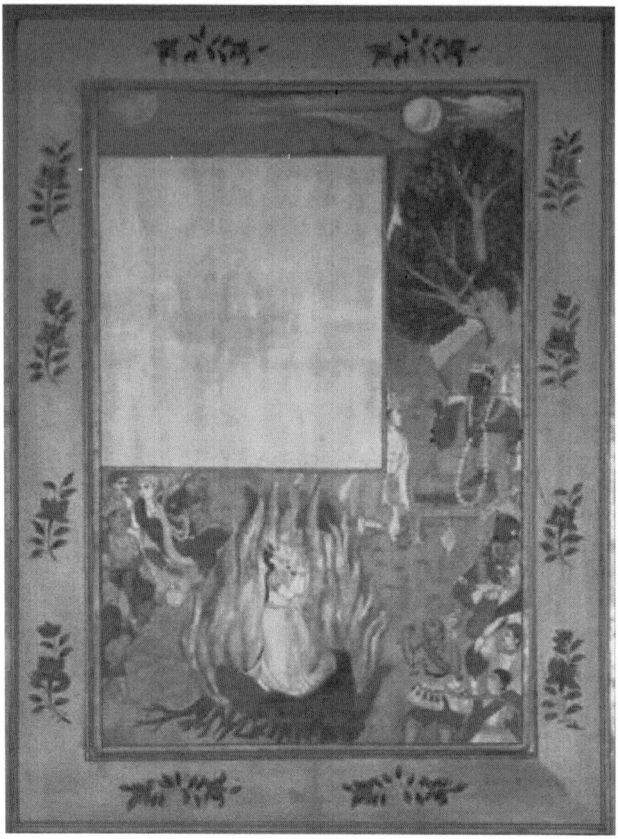

Figure 7.11: Ram Compels Sita to Go through a Fire Ordeal—Reproduction from Razmnamah, 19th Century, Government Central Museum, Albert Hall, Jaipur

Royal women were inclined towards reading and learning and nurtured literary pursuits. Ram Singh I's mother Anand Kunwar Chauhan was mentioned in one verse of *Bihari Satsai* for her scholastic competence. His two wives and princesses of Rewa brought manuscripts and books to their husband's home. A painting in the royal collection in Jaipur City Palace shows a princess artistically reading book on a bookstand. Bundi style collections include the painting of a girl with a wooden slate, pen and inkpot. The collection in the Oriental Research Institute, Udaipur, comprises a painting of a teacher with female and male disciples, suggesting that education was provided to girls and was at times common for both genders.[39] Several religious texts were either intended readings for or were written by royal ladies, including Puranic texts and texts about religious fasts.[40] The inmates of Pratap Singh's *zenana* authored several books, mostly *bhajan* compilations. They also had an inclination for love stories.[41] *Paswans* also nurtured literary inclinations. A famous instance is of Kishangarh Maharaja Sawant Singh Nagaridas's *paswan* Bani Thani Rasik Bihari, who was a devout Krishna follower and composed several Radha-Krishna verses—*pada*. The royal consorts also wrote letters, generally to the kings, at times focusing on political, religious and social issues indicative of their literacy levels.

A celebration of seasonal festivals such as Teej, Gangaur, Holi and Dussehra remained an important constituent in the pleasure profiling of *zenana* women. *Gangaur* was especially coveted as known through royal documents and *bahis*. In Jodhpur, dancers, *patur* and *bhagtan*, were especially summoned to perform in front of the *Gangaur* procession till Gulab Sagar Taal (Figure 7.12).[42] In the Kota *zenana*, women of *kunjadi*, *lakhera* and *bhadbhuja* castes performed and were sent off respectfully after the celebration was over.[43]

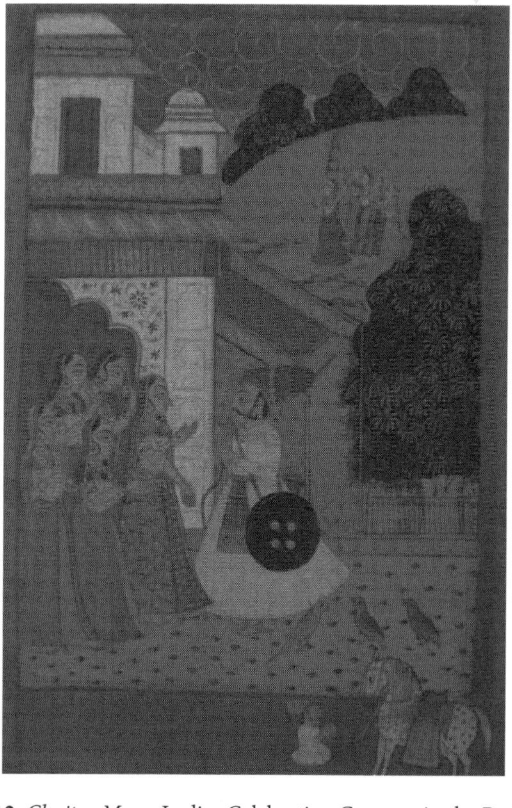

Figure 7.12: *Chaitra Masa*, Ladies Celebrating Gangaur in the Background, *Barahmasa* Series, Jodhpur Style, Government Central Museum, Albert Hall, Jaipur

Parvati tritiya or Teej celebrations have been mentioned by Colonel Tod.[44] Goddess Saraswati was invoked through *Vasantpanchami* celebrations, while popularity of Holi is represented in various paintings of Krishna playing colours with *gopis* (Figure 7.13). Evidences of Holi songs, dances, royal processions through city streets, etc., are abundant. In Jodhpur, the male royal party was followed by the *zenana sawari* to play colours outside the palace. In 1772 CE, it was played in the Balasamand Garden.[45] In Jaipur, *Zenana Mazlis* preserved in the *Suratkhana* projects *zenana dyodi* environs during Madho Singh I (Figure 7.14).

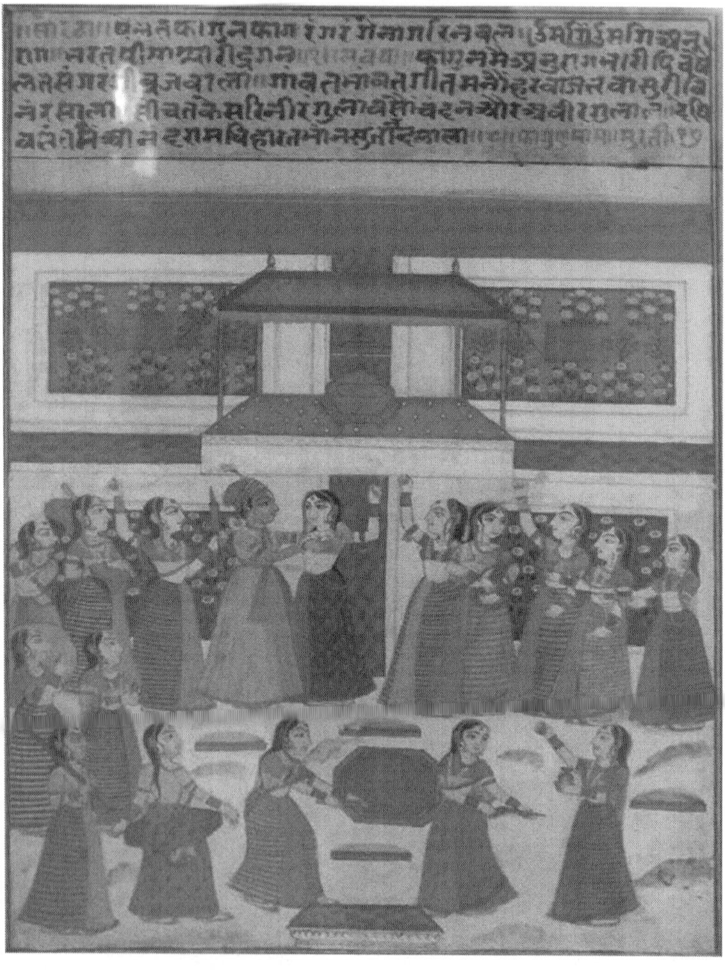

Figure 7.13: *Nayak* Playing Holi with *Nayika*, *Phalgun Masa*, *Barahmasa* Series, Alwar Style, 19th Century, Government Museum, Alwar

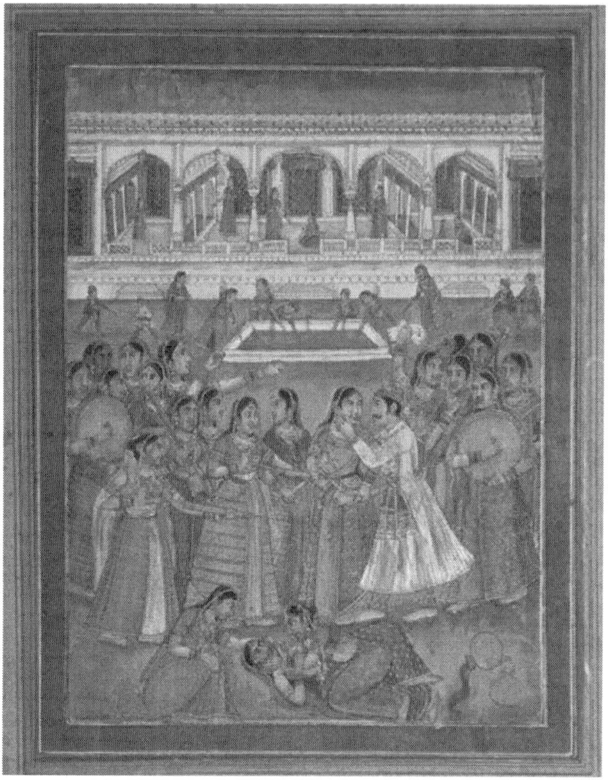

Figure 7.14: Maharaja Sawai Madho Singh Playing Holi with Ladies, Government Museum, Hawamahal, Jaipur

Pleasure activities within the *zenana dyodi* included the popular sport of kite flying.[46] In *Rajasthani Raniwas*, Rahul Sankrityayan has vividly represented kite-flying competitions—*kankhwa dangal*—at times between the *maharaja* and his queens, wherein even silver threads were used if the cotton threads were not strong enough to hold the kite against the currents of wind.[47] He also described the revelries of dance and musical gatherings or *mehfils* by the queens' *patars* in the royal courts and *dholnis* at the feudal *thakurs*' places.[48] Dance forms such as *ghoomar*, *garba*, *toysa* and *gharwa* were favourite pastimes within the royal households.

Chess was played either with female attendants or with the king.[49] Several paintings suggest hide and seek as a popular sport in the *zenana*, symbolised by Krishna playing with his friends or *gopis*.[50] Royal women at times accompanied the king on hunting outings.[51] They derived pleasure from ecclesiastical inclinations such as patronising temples, donations and pilgrimages to holy cities. The Jodhpur Maharaja Vijai Singh's *paswan* Gulabrai travelled 800 kilometres to Haridwar (1773 CE). Six years later, she visited holy centres in Kota and Jaipur. Evidence reveals the building of temple shrines by Jaipur royals as *Maji* Chundavat,[52] *Maji* Sri Ranawatji,[53] the elder *Maji* Bhatiyaniji,[54] and *badaran* Imratraiji,[55] to cite few. Painted illustrations (Figure 7.15) make it evident that women were familiar with yoga, and references of some *yoginis* taking up residence in forest shrines are also available.[56] A 17th century painting in Jaipur City Palace art gallery represents a *yogini*.[57] Paintings of women saints preaching to a gathering are also on display in the same gallery.[58]

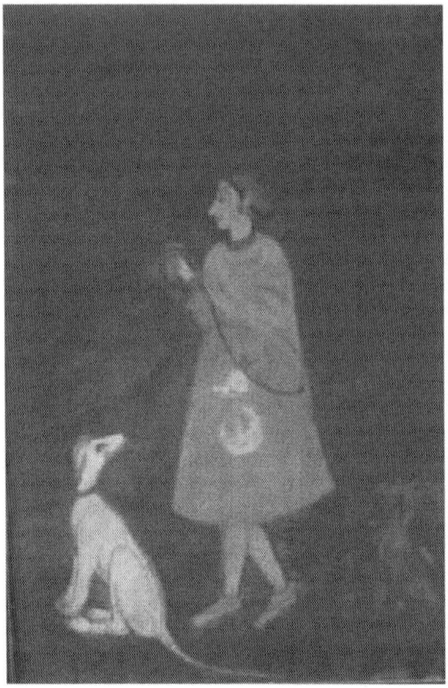

Figure 7.15: *Yogini* with Dogs, Jaipur Style, Government Central Museum, Albert Hall, Jaipur

As connoisseurs of art, the Jaipur queens seemingly enjoyed the privilege and pleasure of patronising various fine arts. The *Suratkhana* and *Pothikhana* records furnish abundant instances of art patrons who were wealthy and politically influential queens. Amongst the *Pothikhana* collections, several paintings affixed with Maharaja Sawai Jai Singh's *zenani dyodi nadir* or in-charge, *khoja*—eunuch—Panna Miyan's seal documents his royal consorts, 27 at the time, as art connoisseurs and patrons, contributing to art in the *dyodi* precincts. Patronage to portraitures remained a popular tradition throughout the 18th and early 19th centuries, as discussed in the later sections. Portraits with stylised characteristics might have been a probable influence of the Rajput association with imperial courts, as discussed above. The development of portraiture signified a trend of political gifts to ensure loyalty and allegiance, though other dynamics involved could not be overlooked. The probable motives have been discussed under the dynamics of art patronage. The queens patronised male portraits in various ways, whether commissioning, making or collecting the paintings. They often purchased portraits from the *Suratkhana*, as evident from its records, particularly entries of the later half of the 18th century and early decades of 19th century. For instance, Maharani Jadam bought ten portraits in 1778 from the *Suratkhana*, including those of her son Prithvi Singh, husband Pratap Singh, father-in-law Madho Singh and her brothers.[59] In 1783, she bought portraits of Pratap Singh and his seven *thakurs*.[60] Sometimes the ranis commissioned portraiture work by availing the services of renowned artists. For instance, Rani Chandrawat bought a portrait of her husband Maharaja Sawai Pratap Singh by the painter Ramji (1780 CE),[61] Rani Chundawat's mother acquired four paintings of Maharaja Sawai Madho Singh worshipping at Nathdwara by *chatera* Sahib Ram in 1765 CE,[62] Rathore Rani received the portraits of her husband Pratap Singh and his ancestors[63] painted by *chatera* Govind Ram (1801 CE).[64] Occasionally the ranis gifted portraits to their husband and kinsmen. For example, Maharaja Jagat Singh's Vikawat Rani gifted 27 paintings to the royal court in 1804–1806, which included two portraits of Jagat Singh and his four nobles.[65] Around the same time, *Maji* Jadam gifted 100 paintings to the royal court, 39 officially recorded.[66] At times, the portraits of Mughal emperors were also commissioned and collected. Rani Chundawat purchased a 40-page *muraqqa* of *padshah*(s)[67] amongst 29 paintings from the *Suratkhana* (1773 CE).[68]

On occasions, the royal consorts were rewarded with portraits by the Maharaja as *inam*. Rani Chundawat was the recipient of two portraits of Maharaja Madho Singh (1763 CE),[69] while Rathore Rani was gifted six portraits by her husband Maharaja Pratap Singh depicting the Kachhawaha lineage from himself to Maharaja Sawai Jai Singh. Interestingly, the queens refrained from commissioning self-portraits, whether proclaiming their authority or suggesting their names. For instance, *Maji* Chundawat patronised portraits of her husband and sons, but despite exerting sovereign authority as the Regent Queen, she confined herself to collecting or gifting of the males' portraits.

Among other themes pursued by the artistically inclined queens, *Maji* Chandrawatji embellished her apartment, *rawala*, with *Kavipriya Barahmasa* and *Ragamala Rasikpriya* themed frescoes. Rani Chundawat had bought an illustrated 49-page version of Keshavdas's *Rasikpriya* (1778 CE). In the same year, Maharani Jadam also bought an album or *muraqqa* of 36 *Ragamala*-themed paintings.[70] *Barahmasa* paintings were amongst the coveted possessions of *Maji* Jadam, *Maji* Khichani and *Maji* Rathore.

Ragamala paintings represent a genre of painted, illustrative miniature manuscripts, based on musical *ragas* or melodies, popular in Indian royal courts from the 16th century CE onwards.[71] The term *raga*, meaning 'that which pleases',[72] in itself connotes their relation to pleasure. *Ragamala* paintings are best known to evoke emotions of passionate love of the lovers and epitomise synthesised creations of Indian traditions of poetry, classical music and miniature painting (Figure 7.16). Each of the six *ragas*—Bhairav, Dipak, Sri, Malkaus, Megha and Hindola—represented a specific emotion or *rasa*—*śṛṅgāra*, *veer*, *karuna*, *hasya*, *raudra*, *adhbutha*—and related to a specific deity, particular time of the day or *prahar* and corresponding season or *ritu*. Subsequently, *raga* families also came up with 36 *raginis*, *ragaputras* and *ragaputris* as their consorts, sons and daughters, respectively. Keshavadas' *Rasikpriya* is amongst the most renowned adaptation for *ragamala* illustrations, in particular the courtship, squabbles and reunions of the divine couple, Radha and Krishna.

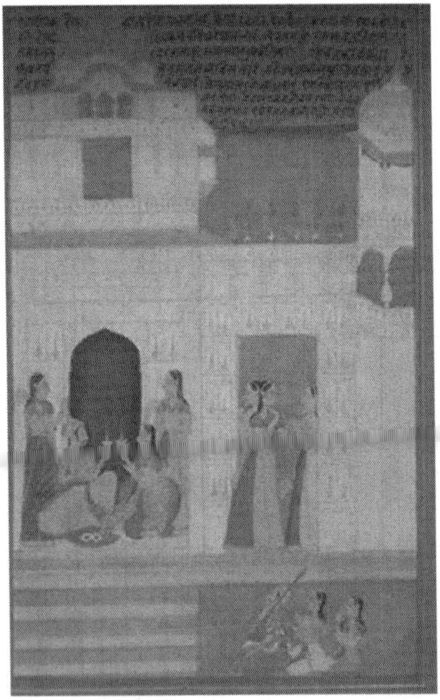

Figure 7.16: *Raga* Dipak is Associated with Light. In This Painting, He is Depicted Seated in His Palace with All *Raginis*, Holding a Lamp in His Hand, while Music is Being Performed. *Ragamala* Series, Government Central Museum, Albert Hall, Jaipur

Corresponding with the seasonal cycle of the 12 months of the year—*Chaitra*, *Vaishakha*, *Jyestha*, *Asadha*, *Sravana*, *Bhadon*, *Ashvin*, *Karttika*, *Margasirsa*, *Pausa*, *Magha* and *Phalguna*—*Barahmasa* is a genre of poetry celebrating changes in nature, its influence on humans, animals, social customs, etc. This genre mainly conveys the pangs of separation, lovers' longings and ecstasy in probable union. The *nayika* or *virahni* pines for the return of her beloved throughout the year, her agony aggravated with changes in monthly cycles (Figure 7.17). During the 17th and18th centuries CE, the *Barahmasa* remained a recurrent theme for miniature paintings, evoking season-specific emotions (Figure 7.18). For instance, summer was represented by the sun in the sky; blooming trees, humming bees, cuckoo and joyous people characterised spring; rains were conveyed through dark, laden clouds and lightning in the sky; autumn had the imagery of fruit-laden trees and ripened corn in the fields, swans and lotuses in ponds, and so on. Patronage to artistic renditions of such romantic literature-based illustrations of passionate dalliance exemplifies the natural inclinations and passion pursuits of the ranis. Most of the paintings thematically projected women of pleasure and reproduction, activities that women in the *zenana* actually indulged in—sensorial pleasures, wine,[73] swings, garden outings, boating, partying and relishing music, celebrating Teej and Gangaur, enjoying *tamasha*, visiting *faqirs*, etc.

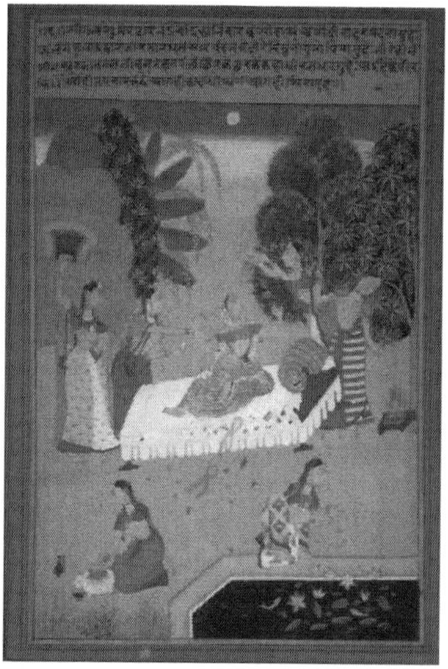

Figure 7.17: *Nayika's* Inconsolable Sorrow of Separation Being Eased by the Application of Sandalwood Paste, Sprays and the Waving of a Fan. Government Central Museum, Albert Hall, Jaipur

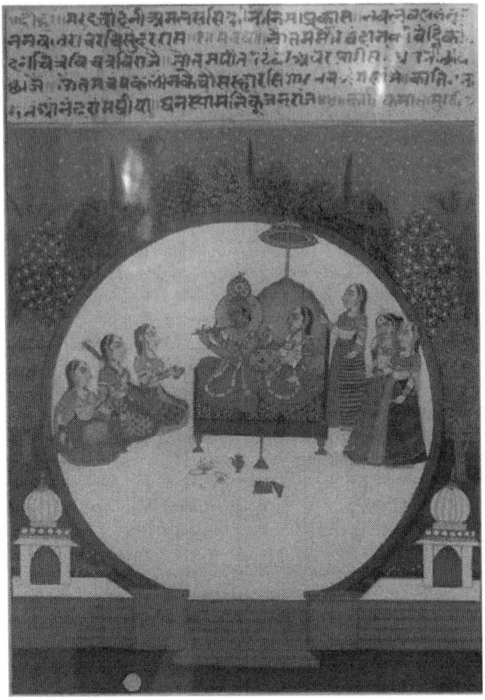

Figure 7.18: Radha Krishna, *Karttika Masa*, *Barahmasa* Series, Government Museum, Alwar

The personal assets of the *zenana* ladies were, after their death, taken up by the state/household and deposited separately in respective *karkhanas* under the holding label *amli*, *amla* or *amwali*, entitled after their specific establishment.[74] The term *amla* usually symbolised the extended or enlarged family/establishment and was constituted by members of certain castes only, forming part of the queen's entourage. Paintings commissioned by the queens, *pardayats*, *paswans* and *badarans* were passed on to the *Suratkhana*, books/manuscripts to the *Pothikhana*, jewellery and clothes to the *Kapaddwara*, and so on. The immobile assets were transferred to the state—for example, Rambagh Palace on Tonk Road, after the death of Kesar *badaran*, was taken up as the state guest house.[75]

Though the female patrons kept their individual self out of the frame, they loved to paint their beloved.[76] The paintings also exemplified the romantic self-pride of the feminine *nayika* in beautifying herself for the lover (Figures 7.19 and 7.20). In a way, by promoting the paintings of the popular stylised *nayika* Radha, patrons such as *Maji* Chundawat endorsed their own omission from the visual sources and followed the

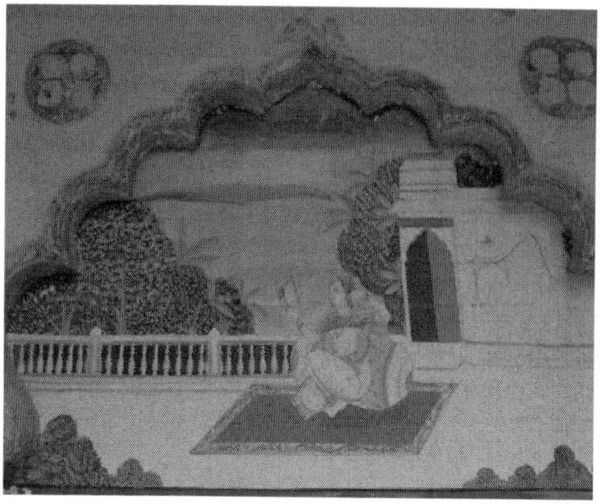

Figure 7.19: *Nayika* Anointing and Admiring Herself, Fresco, Sukh Mahal, Bundi

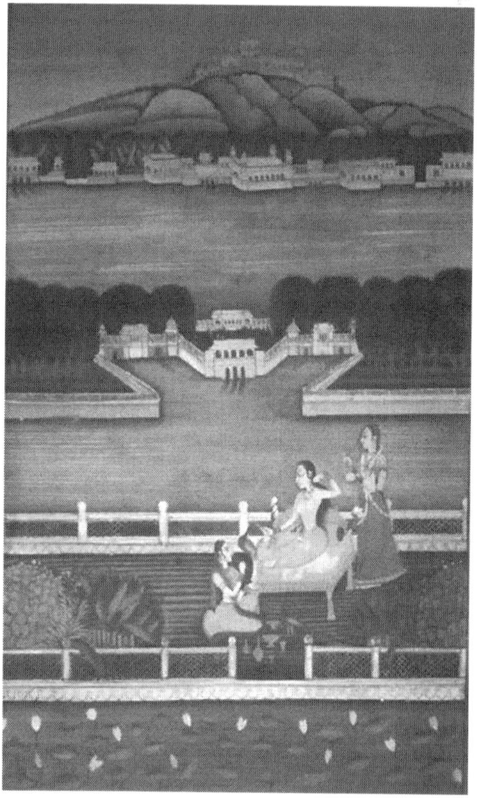

Figure 7.20: *Nayika* Beautifying Herself—Bani Thani, Kishangarh, 19th Century. Government Central Museum, Albert Hall, Jaipur

cultural norms of *purdah*. Consequently, their patronised art comprised assimilated images of the patrons' male relatives besides illustrated textual types of the romantic—*śṛṅgāra* paintings' idealistic stylised women as lovers.

Several queens collected generic paintings of attractive females, sans any textual or poetic affiliations. For instance, *Maji* Jadam possessed paintings titled women as *maherya* and mates as *sahelya*, denoting *zenana* categories. Rani Chundawat's collection also included two albums of pictures of women in romanticised ambiences. In 1773, she obtained around two dozen paintings from the *Suratkhana* representing different kinds of women, individually or in groups, without a name.[77] Therefore, as far as feminine projection in paintings commissioned/collected by *zenana* women was concerned, it is evident that they were replicating the hetero-normative conventions of representation and disfavoured self-portraiture. This inference is apparent through the male portraits they patronised, wherein the artists accurately captured the external likeness as well as the personality of the king. The feminine-oriented paintings primarily represented idealised types, determined mostly by literary and poetic metaphors, and the generic forms despite their ubiquitous presence exposed the fact that women's identity was not postulated on similar grounds as the men's.

THE DYNAMICS OF ART PATRONAGE

Such comprehensive patronage to the art of painted forms makes it imperative to discuss why the ranis patronised or collected male portraits and stylised female forms without any identity, thereby promoting the visual history of male power. Molly Aitken has also discussed at length how the elite Rajput women, as patrons and collectors, promoted male visibility and their own effacement in paintings.[78] What was the use and effect of the predominantly individualistic male and stereotyped female representations on the women who patronised them? At first glance, the probable incentives could have been personal, emotional or political. The ruler's portraits might have resulted out of reverence to his sovereignty, wherein patronising his representations may be likened to expressions of devotion echoing a personal relationship with the painted form as a devotee or *bhakt*'s bond with the personal god. In several such representations, the flanking, serving or gazing females reinforce the sanctity of the central figure. The configuration of such paintings reveals the conventional method used in Rajput images of gods and kings, wherein by putting the attendants to either side of the figure in a framed space, the middle of the picture was emphasised as the centre of attention and importance. This may particularly be true about personal motives of patronising the rulers' portraits.

Under the emotional aspect of the patronage, the ranis possessing portraits of their husband, sons and father-in-law as well as those of their kinsmen might have been due to their sentimental concerns and expressions of fondness for close relatives. Politically, under the prevailing dynamics of polygamous domestic establishments and court politics, impressing the Maharaja and captivating his attentions must have been crucial as a cause of rivalry amongst his various wives. Patronising relevant artistic representations might have served as a strategic manoeuvre for a wife to gain ascendancy in power circles for herself and her folks while taking power away from the other wives of the king. This might have served to minimise the element of subjection/ seclusion and expand their influence over events in the public space, outside the private world of the *zenana*. Or maybe it was an implicit attempt by the royal patrons, living but refusing to align with the patriarchal norms of submissive femininity by moving away from the prevailing status of solitude in the *zenana* through their pro-active ploys.

Alternatively, it may be assumed that through the romantic paintings patronised, the patrons were at times venting out their suppressed passionate longings, a probable offshoot of polygamous households/establishments. Further, it can be surmised that the viewing of an aesthetic piece of art is naturally pleasurable experience for its onlooker. Keats has immortalised the sentiment in his line 'A thing of beauty is a joy forever' from *Endymion* (I.1).[79] In the same sense, patronage to an artistic representation might have also evoked a sense of creative pleasure in its creator. Therefore, patronising representations or collecting painted versions would surely have delighted their *zenana* patrons. That the patrons derived pleasure from their sponsored art is suggested by an exquisitely executed painting of Jodhpur Maharaja Abhay Singh (1724–1749 CE) watching a dance performance,[80] produced by erstwhile Mughal painter Dalchand. It was a reproduction of a painting of Emperor Muhammad Shah at a musical gathering.[81] Comparing both the paintings, Abhay Singh must have derived pleasure and joy as a patron in seeing his own representation executed grander than the majestic Mughal emperor's magnificence.

The patronage may, at the level of the sublime, be analysed from the perspective of Indian aesthetics of *rasa* evocation and its experience—*rasanubhuti*. While Western aesthetics differentiates between the subject and object or observer and observed, the Indian aesthetics of seeing or gazing perceive seeing as *darshan*, through gazing, knowing and touching, establishing an affinity between the subject and object and thereby awakening *rasa* within the spectator or onlooker. On a larger scale and as suggested by Abhinavagupta, the collective pleasure that is experienced in *rasa* is activated through the permanent emotion latent in a person's subconscious or *sthayibhava*. It is, therefore, not unlikely that the patron ranis, through a recreation of the imagery of Krishna's dalliances with the *gopis*, dance with Radha, or music-making with the flute, visualised or experienced pleasure or *rasanubhuti* by visualising the divine to experience the worldly.

One more perspective may be considered to understand the dynamics of patronage. Socially, patronage to art might have provided the ranis with a *modus operandi* to minimise the inhibitions associated with normatively constructed gender identities in a traditional society. They could perhaps assume mainstream vibes and connect even while relegated to the *zenana* and rendered invisible in the public domain by the exclusionary practices of *purdah* and non-intervention with *mardana* spaces. In fact, the royal consorts could gaze at the world outside through their screened *jharokhas*, windows, and curtained balconies. Their access to Hawamahal *mehfils* through a secret tunnel has already been mentioned. Architecturally, the perforated windows in the *zenana* premises enabled its inmates to observe the hustle and bustle of the world outside. The royal women use to watch the street scenes below from the Hawamahal's pierced windows.[82] Painted representations also produce images of women looking from their balconies (Figure 7.21). So, it may be held that the practice of women looking at men, whether in their painted portrait forms or in person through screened outlets, was integral to the Rajput *zenana* culture.

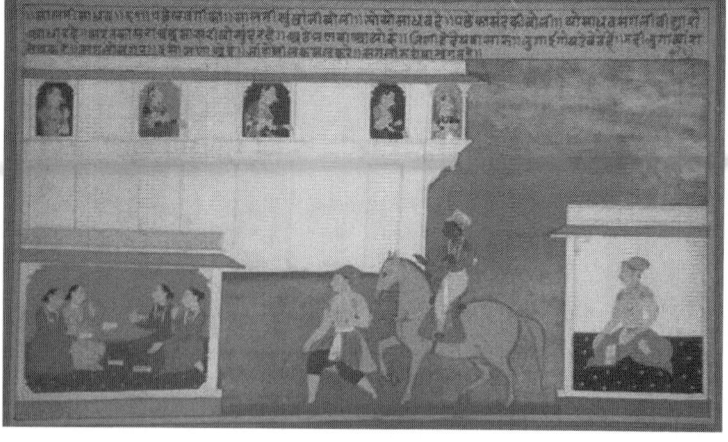

Figure 7.21: As Madhava Comes Riding in, All the Ladies Appear at Their Windows to Gaze at His Beauty. Government Central Museum, Albert Hall, Jaipur

In this sense, the ones in the public space seems to provide the pleasure of onlooking to the ones in the private space—reversing the purport of power and powerless, pleased and pleasing, public and private spaces—and makes the entire gendered discourse contesting and intriguing.

CONCLUSION

An artistic perusal of the patronage possibilities availed by each sex at a given time indicates that women were not just another group in history, and it is imperative to develop some affinity towards the differing experiences of women and men under historical enquiry. The consequent gain would be a multiplicity of gendered perspectives to enrich our appreciation of the past beyond certitudes of objectivity and scientific history. Thus, historians doing history must seek all types of alternative sources, ask new questions and seek newer interpretations from that vantage point. The concept of pleasure is one such potent area for historical investigations, symbolising a tangible and intangible matrix that provided spaces for leisure/recreations, within prevailing social structures. Herein gender representations appear as social positions carrying differential meanings, overtly and covertly expressed through visual and literary manifestations and highlighting the dynamics of space connotations, especially for women.

As mentioned earlier, the genealogy of the discourse formation on feminine social spaces in Indic cultures presents an interesting epistemic hierarchy between the women's private and public realms, creating contesting imagery wherein women's private and public roles get categorised into a dichotomy. The dichotomous inferences may be gleaned through women's ubiquitous representational presence in arts, aesthetics and literature as refined pleasure-oriented engagements nurtured in their private world. Contrary to this, their structurally mediated social identity denies them any public space and projects them as passive conformists to the norms of patriarchy and masculinity and as operating within these bounds.

The chapter has attempted to map this very epistemological indeterminacy through such concepts as public/private space and power/empowered/powerless and highlighted their inconsistencies, implying different meanings for the genders as well as women of different sections. Thus, the academic and actual expositions remain at a variance, creating sites of dual hermeneutics as far as aspects of womanhood are concerned. The chapter further endeavours to explore how the notion of women's pleasure, confined to the private space of domesticity, confronted a kind of dual hermeneutics. Pleasure pursuits by women for self-gratification in the public domain were deemed unbecoming, while their role in regaling the social classes was acceptable. The chapter examined the landscape of art patronage by Rajput queens within the *zenana* to deconstruct the ontological indeterminacy confronted in understanding the contesting conceptions of the phenomenon of women's pleasure. It probed the extent to which the royal women were actors, taking initiatives rather than being passive recipients, actively involved or inadvertently drawn into shaping events. This is even more relevant when seclusion or isolation are usually equated with a lack of knowledge, passivity and restriction of space.

Pleasure seeking in the *zenana* may be profiled variously—the inmates nurtured literary inclinations, philanthropic acts, sports; the *dyodi* resonated with revelry through *mehfils* of dance, music, plays and the celebration of festivals. Patronage to artistic renditions of the romantic *ragamala*, *barahmasa* genre and literature-based illustrations, Radha and Krishna's passionate dalliance, love stories, etc. exemplifies the natural inclinations and passion pursuits of the patron ranis.

As apparent instances of powerlessness, the projections reinforced a politics of male visibility and female invisibility by effacing the women's identity, documenting visual male-oriented genealogical histories while denying the same to women. This stands equally true that being bearers of tradition and shapers of the progeny, women themselves partnered in the process of creating gender-related identities through such representations.

In terms of wielding power, as cited earlier, women could exert substantial political influence if need be. Aitken has compared Rani Chundawat's presence for the art historian to 'a pair of eyes' which were not 'powerless eyes' as the queens had influence enough to act on what they saw.[83] The power of patronage through portraits was most likely utilised to entice the king as well. Further, can we read an appropriation of the male-centric mannerisms in replications of *zenana mehfils*? Can patronage to romantic paintings be related to venting out their suppressed passionate longings, a probable offshoot of polygamous households? Or did it create a *modus operandi* for them to minimise the inhibitions associated with normatively constructed gender identities in a traditional society, assuming mainstream vibes/connect while relegated to the *zenana* and rendered *invisible* in the *public* domain by the exclusionary practices of *purdah* and non-intervention with the *mardana* space?

It will not be irrelevant to point out here that the practice of women looking at men, whether in their painted portrait forms or in person through screened outlets, was integral to the Rajput *zenana* culture. In this sense, portraits of the ones in the public space (menfolk) may be seen providing pleasure of looking to the ones in the private space (*zenana* ladies), reversing the purport of power and powerless, pleased and pleasing, public and private spaces and making the entire gendered discourse contesting and intriguing and loaded with hermeneutical inconsistencies. The *zenana*, indeed, presents a picture of intertwining networks of power and pleasure.

To this extent, the Rajput royal consorts' patronage initiatives are conducive to making an 'art history of pleasure' valid, viable and visible. Scholastic explorations into that domain facilitate interpretations of how such representational patronage provided women patrons a freedom not found in the male-oriented public space and how the private and public spaces could be bridged and pleasure could be sought and availed. Such an approach would also contribute towards transforming the normative imagery of the *zenana* from isolated, stagnant sites to effervescent places pulsating with cultural dynamism.

It is through moving beyond dichotomous thinking that we may understand not only how gender encodes or symbolises matters considered critical to culture and society but also how they were embraced by the women. It is only when we comprehend how gender functions as a system of social relations that we will be doing history that holds multiple lived realities.

This chapter is a refined version of a talk delivered at the Rajasthan State Archives, Bikaner (2015) and a paper published in Proceedings, Rajasthan History Congress (2009). The illustrations are from Government Central Museum, Albert Hall, Government Museum, Hawamahal, Jaipur and Government Museum, Alwar, duly acknowledged wherever used. The ones from Bundi are self-clicked.

NOTES

1. Joan Wallach Scott, 'Gender: A Useful Category of Historical Analysis', *American Historical Review*, 91, no. 5 (1986): 1053–1075; Joan Kelly-Gadol, 'The Social Relation of the Sexes: Methodological Implications of Women's History', *Signs: Journal of Women in Culture and Society* 1, no. 4 (1976): 809–824.
2. Simone de Beauvoir, *The Second Sex* (London: H.M. Parshley, 1954 [1949]).
3. Olwen Hufton, 'Women, Gender and the Fin De Siècle', in *Companion to Historiography*, ed. by Michael Bentley (London and New York: Routledge, 1997), 910.
4. Miri Rubin, 'A Decade of Studying Medieval Women, 1987–1997', *History Workshop Journal*, 46 (1998): 213–39, 230.
5. Renate Bridenthal and Claudia Koonz (ed.). *Becoming Visible: Women in European History* (Boston: Houghton Mifflin, 1977), 161.
6. Joan Kelly-Gadol, 'The Social Relation of the Sexes: Methodological Implications of Women's History', *Signs: Journal of Women in Culture and Society* 1, no. 4 (1976): xiii.

7. Teresa de Lauretis, *Technologies of Gender* (Bloomington and Indianapolis: Indiana University Press, 1987), 5.
8. Discourse, for Foucault, refers to the 'general domain of all statements, sometimes an individualisable group of statements, and sometimes as a regulated practice that accounts for a number of statements'. Michel Foucault, *Archaeology of Knowledge*, trans. A.M. Sheridan Smith (London: Routledge, 1972), 80; further, according to him, the empirical reality of the world does not dawn upon us through any pre-discursive providence. But the world is subject to our understanding, through our own act of violent imposition of meanings on the object to be known. Michel Foucault, 'The Order of Discourse', in *Untying the Text: A Post-Structuralist Reader*, ed. by Robert Young (London: Routledge, Kegan and Paul, 1981), 67.
9. Partha Chatterjee, 'Colonialism, Nationalism, and Colonialized Women: The Contest in India'. *American Ethnologist* 16, no. 4 (1989): 622–633; also Partha Chatterjee, 'The Nationalist Resolution of the Women's Question', in *Empire and Nation* (New York: Columbia University Press, 2015), 116–135.
10. In his essay 'The Invention of Private Life: A Reading of Sibnath Sastri', Kaviraj suggested that the modern literary form of the autobiography imagines the self as an autonomous private space, informed and influenced, to some extent, by the rules of the public. Sudipta Kaviraj, *The Invention of Private Life: Literature and Ideas* (New York: Columbia University Press, 2015), 334.
11. Preeti Sharma, 'Hearing the Hidden Voices of Feminine Sexuality: Folkloric Challenges to Patriarchic Traditions in Rajasthan'. *The International Journal of Interdisciplinary Cultural Studies* 7 no. 2 (2013): 37–47.
12. *Srikrishnadvaipayanvyaspraneetam Garuda Puranam*, The Vidyabhawan Prachyavidya Granthamala 3, ed. by Pt. Shri Ramtej Pandey (Varanasi: Chowkhamba Vidyabhawan, n.d.), *purvakhand, Aacharkhand*: 64/6.
13. Kalyanaraman Srinivasa, 'Noble Virtues of a Women'. Available at https://www.speakingtree.in/blog/noble-virtues-of-a-women (accessed 12 May 2020).
14. Gayatri Devi of Jaipur and Santha Rama Rau, *A Princess Remembers: The Memoirs of the Maharani of Jaipur* (New Delhi: Vikas Publishing House Pvt. Ltd., 1982), 160.
15. *Jaipur Suratkhana Jamakharch and Rozanama* Records (*1763 to 1806*) available in Rajasthan State Archives, Bikaner.
16. Gopal Narayan Bahura, *Literary Heritage of the Rulers of Amber and Jaipur: With an Index to the Register of Manuscripts in the Pothikhana of Jaipur (1. Khasmohor Collection)* (Jaipur: Maharaja Sawai Man Singh II Museum, 1976).
17. The *Pothikhana* as an institution was established even before Jaipur city came into existence, while the Kachhawaha dynasty was still based in Amer. As the royal library, it preserved valuable collections of the rulers. Maharaja Sawai Jai Singh included it amongst his 36 *karkhanas* and made it more utilitarian. As a *karkhana*, it was presumed to be functional and evolve consistently rather than serve as a mere repository of books and manuscripts. During the entire span of the state, it patronised poets,

scribes and *katib* or translators who enriched the collections with copies of manuscripts and original works.

18. Asok Kumar Das, 'Amber-Jaipur Painting', in *Cultural Heritage of Jaipur*, ed. by Jai Narayan Asopa (Jodhpur: Rajasthan History Congress, 1979), 126.
19. It was held to select Indian artists for adorning the British Government's upcoming building project of India House in London. The Exhibition was circulated to various European cities from 1928 to1932 and contributed to showcasing Indian art to an international audience on a grand scale.
20. The paintings are comparable with banner paintings of Tibet and kakimino paintings of Japan in technique. In the *asadha* (the summer season) painting a female stands under a mango tree, clad in a Rajput and Mughal synthesised dress with an onlooking deer. In the *pausha* (winter) painting, the deer is replaced by a crane, the mango tree with a *champak* flower-laden tree, and she holds a *maina* in one hand. Nandkishore Pareek, *Jaipur Jo Tha – I, Raj-Darbar aur Raniwas* (Jaipur: Rajasthan Patrika Pvt Ltd., 1984), 59.
21. Pratap Singh was fond of patronising experts in their respective areas of arts and designated them *baisi* as they generally numbered 22. *Chitrakarabaisi, gandharvabaisi, vaidyabaisi, panditbaisi* were some such patronised groups.
22. Nandkishore Pareek, *Jaipur Jo Tha – I, Raj-Darbar aur Raniwas* (Jaipur: Rajasthan Patrika Pvt Ltd., 1984), 57.
23. The *Paswan*, as confidant to the king/queen, enjoyed various rights, including possession of land grants; *khawas*—closest attendant; *paddayat*—female put under the *purdah* by the king smitten by her beauty; *badaran*—manager of the *zenana dyodi*, generally a senior, experienced attendant; *dhai*—nurse, *saheliya*—friends; *davdia* and *gayania*—singers and attendants.
24. Rani Laxmi Kumari Chundawat, 'Rajasthan ki Rajniti Mein Nari', *Maru Bharati* 27, 7–13 (1969): 9.
25. Varsha Joshi, *Polygamy & Purdah: Women and Society among Rajputs* (Jaipur: Rawat Publications, 1995), 98.
26. Rani Gangabai after Maharaja Rai Singh and Sisodani Rani after Maharaja Anoop Singh, respectively in Bikaner; Hadi Rani in Jodhpur after Maharaja Jaswant Singh, Dowager Queen in Mewar after Maharana Arisingh in Mewar, to cite few instances.
27. Ibid., 86.
28. Pratap Singh was a man with highly commendable scholastic tastes. He wrote poetry in BrajBhasa and *dhundhari* under the name of Brajnidhi. The cited couplet is part of his *Brajnidhi Granthawali*, 368–369 referred by Pareek, 129.
29. *Toji Jamakharach Paturkhana Hazuri*, Jaipur, VS 1804/1747 AD (Bikaner: Rajasthan State Archives).
30. *Dastur Komwar, Rajlok Patar, Sawan Sud* 3, VS 1774/ 29 July, 1717, Pt. 25, 933 (Bikaner: Rajasthan State Archives).
31. *Brajnidhi Granthavali* (Kashi: Nagari Pracharini Sabha, 1933), 45–46.
32. Nandkishore Pareek, *Jaipur Jo Tha – I, Raj-Darbar aur Raniwas* (Jaipur: Rajasthan Patrika Pvt Ltd., 1984), 94.

33. Gayatri Devi of Jaipur and Santha Rama Rau, *A Princess Remembers: The Memoirs of the Maharani of Jaipur* (New Delhi: Vikas Publishing House Pvt. Ltd., 1982), 157–160.
34. Kavita Singh, 'A Knowing Look: Appropriation and Subversion of the Mughal Idiom in Rajput Paintings of the Eighteenth Century', in *Synergies in Visual Culture/Bildkulturenim Dialog: Festschrift für Gerhard Wolf*, ed. by Manuela di Giorgi, Annette Hoffman and Nicola Suthor (Munich: Wilhelm Fink, 2013), 172, Figure 13.4.
35. Ibid., 171, Figure 13.3.
36. Gülru Necipoğlu, 'Framing the Gaze in Ottoman, Safavid, and Mughal Palaces', *Ars Orientalis*, 23 (1993): 303–342. Available at https://www.jstor.org/stable/4629455.
37. Kavita Singh, 'A Knowing Look: Appropriation and Subversion of the Mughal Idiom in Rajput Paintings of the Eighteenth Century', in *Synergies in Visual Culture/Bildkulturen im Dialog: Festschrift für Gerhard Wolf*, ed. by Manuela di Giorgi, Annette Hoffman and Nicola Suthor (Munich: Wilhelm Fink, 2013), 168–175.
38. Ibid., 173.
39. Shashi Arora, *Rajasthan Mein Nari ki Stithi (1600–1800 AD)* (Bikaner: Tarun Prakashan, 1981), 93.
40. Instances of *zenana* ladies in Mewar: Rani Bhatiyani wrote *Ramacharit Sampuni Samapt*, *Kunwari* Pushpa wrote *Dhruva Charit*; *Ramacharit* was written for Gulabrai, *paswan* of Vijai Singh of Jodhpur. Amongst fast oriented texts:*Chauthmatari Vaat* and *Nasiketri Vaat* were written for Mewar's Rani Bhatiyani and *Kunwari* Jaitkunwar while *Grhalila Haridas* was written by *Kunwari* Pushpa. Ibid., 94.
41. Gopi Nath Sharma, *Social Life in Medieval Rajasthan (1500–1800 AD): With Special Reference to the Impact of Mughal Influence* (Agra: Lakshmi Narain Agrawala, 1968), 121.
42. *Jodhpur Hakikat Bahi*, VS 1835-40/1778-83 AD, No. 3 (Bikaner: Rajasthan State Archives), 319.
43. Shashi Arora, *Rajasthan Mein Nari ki Stithi (1600–1800 AD)* (Bikaner: Tarun Prakashan, 1981), 102.
44. Lieut. Col. James Tod, *Annals & Antiquities of Rajasthan or the Central and Western Rajput States of India*, ed. by William Crooke (London: Oxford University Press, 2018 [1920]), 134.
45. *Jodhpur Hakikat Bahi*, VS 1820–1830/1763–1773 AD, No. 1 (Bikaner: Rajasthan State Archives), 65–66.
46. *Dhola Maruri Baat*, 63; Exhibit Painting, *Women with charkhi*, VS 1830/1773 AD, Bikaner Art Gallery.
47. Rahul Sankrityayan, *Rajasthani Raniwas* (Allahabad: Kitab Mahal, 1984), 43.
48. Ibid.
49. *Dastur Komwar*, VS 1857/1800 AD, No. 25, 81, 138 (Bikaner: Rajasthan State Archives).
50. *Khajanchi Collection*, *Women playing hide and seek*, referred by Shashi Arora, 111.

51. Gopi Nath Sharma, *Social Life in Medieval Rajasthan (1500–1800 AD): With Special Reference to the Impact of Mughal Influence* (Agra: Lakshmi Narain Agrawala, 1968), 137.
52. *Dastur Komwar*, VS 1818/1761 AD, No. 8, 69 (Bikaner: Rajasthan State Archives).
53. *Dastur Komwar*, Jaipur, VS 1819/1762 AD, No. 24, 943 (Bikaner: Rajasthan State Archives).
54. *Dastur Komwar*, Jaipur, VS 1804/1747 AD, No. 8, 1 (Bikaner: Rajasthan State Archives).
55. *Dastur Komwar*, Jaipur, VS 1822/1765 AD, No. 25, 893, (Bikaner: Rajasthan State Archives).
56. Shashi Arora, *Rajasthan Mein Nari ki Stithi (1600–1800 AD)*. (Bikaner: Tarun Prakashan, 1981), 98.
57. *Yogini*, VS 1750/1663 AD, No. AG 1202.
58. *Female Sanyasi*, VS 1675-1700/1618-43 AD, No. AG 1203; VS 1700-20/1643-63, No. AG 1206.
59. *kati, sudi* 3, *samvat* 1835, *Jamakharach* Records: 175 and *Rozanama*.
60. *asoj, sudi* 5, *samvat* 1840, *Jamakharach* Records: 270.
61. *Maghavadi* 11 *samvat* 1837, *Jamakharach* Records: 270 and *Rozanama*.
62. *Bhadrapadasudi* 1 *samvat* 1822, *Jamakharach* Records: 113.
63. Maharaja Sawai Jai Singh, Maharaja SawaiIsvari Singh, Maharaja Sawai Madho Singh and Maharaja Prithvi Singh.
64. *Kativadi* 11 *samvat* 1858, *Jamakharach* Records: 383 and *Rozanama*.
65. Jiva Raja Paliwal, Thakur Syo Das, his son Syambhu Das—*vaisakhavadi* 1 *samvat* 1861–1863, *Jamakharach* Records: 136.
66. Of these twelve were portraits of Maharaja Sawai Madho Singh, Maharaja Sawai Jai Singh, and Raja Gopal Das of Karauli, her natal state—*sravanasudi* 5 *samvat* 1861–1863, *Jamakharach* Records: 137.
67. *Chaitravadi* 10 *samvat* 1830, *Jamakharach* Records: 157.
68. *Pausasudi* 1 *samvat* 1830, *Jamakharach* Records: 154.
69. *Margasirsavadi* 1 *samvat* 1820, *Jamakharach* Records: 102.
70. *Kartikasudi* 15 *samvat* 1835, *Jamakharach* Records: 176.
71. Sahibdin's *Ragamala* series painted under Maharana Jagat Singh of Mewar is amongst the earliest (1628 CE) Rajput instances of the genre. Bundi painters excelled in *Krishnalila* and *Rasikpriya* illustrations.
72. S. Mukund, *Sangeetha Laalithya Lahari* (*The Waves of Elegance in Music*) (Bangalore: WQ Judge Press, 1989), 16.
73. *Ladies enjoying wine*, Painting Exhibit, Eastern Gallery, City Palace Museum Art Gallery.
74. This was akin to the *khalsa* practice of the state taking over assets, which would no longer be deemed as personal belongings of the person concerned.
75. Nandkishore Pareek, *Jaipur Jo Tha – I, Raj-Darbar aur Raniwas* (Jaipur: Rajasthan Patrika Pvt Ltd., 1984), 119.
76. Gopi Nath Sharma, *Social Life in Medieval Rajasthan (1500–1800 AD): With Special Reference to the Impact of Mughal Influence* (Agra: Lakshmi Narain Agrawala, 1968), 121–122.
77. *Pausasudi* 1 *samvat* 1830, *Jamakharach* Records: 154.

78. Molly Aitken, 'Pardah and Portrayal: Rajput Women as Subjects, Patrons, and Collectors', in *Artibus Asiae*, 62 no. 2 (2002): 247–280.
79. John Keats, 'A Thing of Beauty is a Joy Forever', *Endymion, Book I*. Available at https://literarydevices.net/a-thing-of-beauty-is-a-joy-forever/ (accessed 12 July 2020).
80. Kavita Singh, 2013, Dalchand, *Maharaja Abhai Singh Watching a Dance Performance*. Jodhpur, c. 1725. Collection: Mehrangarh Museum, 170, Figure 13.2.
81. Ibid., *Emperor Muhammad Shah at a Concert*. Delhi, middle of the 18th century. Kasturbhai Lalbhai Collection. L.D. Institute, 169, Figure 13.1.
82. Varsha Joshi, *Polygamy & Purdah: Women and Society among Rajputs* (Jaipur: Rawat Publications, 1995), 175.
83. Molly Aitken, 'Pardah and Portrayal: Rajput Women as Subjects, Patrons, and Collectors', in *Artibus Asiae* 62, no. 2 (2002): 265.

REFERENCES

Aitken, Molly. 'Pardah and Portrayal: Rajput Women as Subjects, Patrons, and Collectors'. *Artibus Asiae* 62, no. 2 (2002): 247–280.

Arora, Shashi. *Rajasthan Mein Nari ki Stithi (1600–1800 AD)*. Bikaner: Tarun Prakashan. 1981.

Bahura, Gopal Narayan. *Literary Heritage of the Rulers of Amber and Jaipur: With an Index to the Register of Manuscripts in the Pothikhana of Jaipur (1. Khasmohor Collection)*. Jaipur: Maharaja Sawai Man Singh II Museum. 1976.

Beauvoir, Simone de. *The Second Sex*. London: H.M. Parshley. 1954 [1949].

Brajnidhi Granthavali. Kashi: Nagari Pracharini Sabha. 1933.

Bridenthal, Renate and Claudia Koonz, eds. *Becoming Visible: Women in European History*. Boston: Houghton Mifflin. 1977.

Chatterjee, Partha. 'Colonialism, Nationalism, and Colonialised Women: The Contest in India'. *American Ethnologist* 16, no. 4 (1989): 622–633.

———. 'The Nationalist Resolution of the Women's Question'. In *Empire and Nation*, edited by Partha Chatterjee, 116–135. New York, NY: Columbia University Press. 2015.

Chundawat, Rani Laxmi Kumari. 'Rajasthan ki Rajniti Mein Nari'. *Maru Bharati* 27 (1969): 7–13.

Das, Asok Kumar. 'Amber-Jaipur Painting'. In *Cultural Heritage of Jaipur*, edited by Jai Narayan Asopa, 121–132. Jodhpur: Rajasthan History Congress. 1979.

Devi of Jaipur, Gayatri and Santha Rama Rau. *A Princess Remembers: The Memoirs of the Maharani of Jaipur*. New Delhi: Vikas Publishing House Pvt. Ltd. 1982.

Foucault, Michel. 'The Order of Discourse'. In *Untying the Text: A Post-Structuralist Reader*, edited by Robert Young, 48–79. London: Routledge, Kegan and Paul. 1981.

———. *Archaeology of Knowledge*. Translated by A.M. Sheridan Smith. London: Routledge. 1972.

Hufton, Olwen. 'Women, Gender and the Fin De Siècle'. In *Companion to Historiography*, edited by Michael Bentley, 907–917. London and New York: Routledge. 1997.

Joshi, Varsha. *Polygamy & Purdah: Women and Society Among Rajputs*. Jaipur: Rawat Publications. 1995.

Kaviraj, Sudipta. *The Invention of Private Life: Literature and Ideas*. New York: Columbia University Press. 2015.

Keats, John. 'A Thing of Beauty is a Joy Forever'. *Endymion*, Book I. Available at https://literarydevices.net/a-thing-of-beauty-is-a-joy-forever/ (accessed on 12 July 2020).

Kelly-Gadol, Joan. 'The Social Relation of the Sexes: Methodological Implications of Women's History'. *Signs: Journal of Women in Culture and Society* 1, no. 4 (1976): 809–824.

Lauretis, Teresa de. *Technologies of Gender*. Bloomington and Indianapolis: Indiana University Press. 1987.

Mukund, S. *Sangeetha Laalithya Lahari* (*The Waves of Elegance in Music*). Bangalore: WQ Judge Press. 1989.

Necipoğlu, Gülru. 'Framing the Gaze in Ottoman, Safavid, and Mughal Palaces'. *Ars Orientalis* 23 (1993): 303–342.

Pareek, Nandkishore. *Jaipur Jo Tha – I, Raj-Darbar aur Raniwas*. Jaipur: Rajasthan Patrika Pvt. Ltd. 1984.

Rubin, Miri. 'A Decade of Studying Medieval Women, 1987–1997'. *History Workshop Journal* 46 (1998): 213–239.

Sankrityayan, Rahul. *Rajasthani Raniwas*. Allahabad: Kitab Mahal. 1984.

Scott, Joan Wallach. 'Gender: A Useful Category of Historical Analysis'. *American Historical Review* 91, no. 5 (1986): 1053–1075.

Sharma, Gopi Nath. *Social Life in Medieval Rajasthan (1500–1800 AD): With Special Reference to the Impact of Mughal Influence*. Agra: Lakshmi Narain Agrawala. 1968.

Sharma, Preeti. 'Hearing the Hidden Voices of Feminine Sexuality: Folkloric Challenges to Patriarchic Traditions in Rajasthan'. *The International Journal of Interdisciplinary Cultural Studies* 7, no. 2 (2013): 37–47.

Singh, Kavita. 'A Knowing Look: Appropriation and Subversion of the Mughal Idiom in Rajput Paintings of the Eighteenth Century'. In *Synergies in Visual Culture/ Bildkulturenim Dialog: Festschrift für Gerhard Wolf*, edited by Manuela di Giorgi, Annette Hoffman and Nicola Suthor, 168–175. Munich: Wilhelm Fink. 2013.

Srikrishnadvaipayanvyaspraneetam Garuda Puranam. The Vidyabhawan Prachyavidya Granthamala 3, edited by Pt. Shri Ramtej Pandey. Varanasi: Chowkhamba Vidyabhawan. n.d.

Srinivasa, Kalyanaraman. 'Noble Virtues of a Women'. Available at https://www.speakingtree.in/blog/noble-virtues-of-a-women (accessed on 12 May 2020).

Suratkhana Jamakharch, Dastur Komwar and *Rozanama* Records of Jaipur; *Hakikat Bahis* of Jodhpur (select year as cited in notes), Rajasthan State Archives, Bikaner.

Tod, Lieut. Col. James. *Annals & Antiquities of Rajasthan or the Central and Western Rajput States of India*. Edited by William Crooke. London: Oxford University Press. 2018 [1920].

8

CELEBRATING ADVERSITIES IN THE 17TH AND EARLY 18TH CENTURY NORTH INDIA: THE CASE OF MIR JA'FAR ZATALLI*

Saifuddin Ahmad

In the 18th century, the Mughal rule witnessed radical changes in politics and governance. Rapid succession of kings one after the other subsequently brought about changes in the administration, perpetrating indifference and apathy towards the future of the state. Institutions rapidly lost their verve and efficacy. The age of conquest and expansion ended, with that of corrupt politics and internal strife setting in. Older ideals on which the foundations of the society rested had become hollow and stagnant, and they had slowly started to fade out of society's conscience. The futility of these values in real life led to contradictions in an individual's percept and practice. However, despite the predicament and weakening of political authority, 18th century was culturally, intellectually and spiritually more vibrant than the one preceding it.[1]

In such a milieu of political turmoil that created social instability, adulation of wit and reason came to the forefront of literature in the form of poetry and satires, which, through keen observation and agility of thought, exposed the shallowness and moral corruption of the society. This paper is an attempt to investigate the historical trajectory of the life of a poet from North India-Mir Muhammad Ja'far Zatalli (d. 1713 CE). Ja'far was a master of invective satires, known for his ribald humour and acerbic criticism of society and its morals. His verses reveal him as a brave and determined yet socially committed personality of the decaying times of the late 17th and 18th century. He infuses his verses with proverbs, maxims and astute words expressed manifestly. Ja'far's satire aims at pointing out the shortcomings of the social order through ridiculing accepted standards of thought, exposing the failings of North Indian society and chastising the hypocrisy of the time.

* Financial support for this research, under short-term Faculty Research Programme, 2020–2021 of University of Delhi is gratefully acknowledged.

The chapter endeavours to analyse the contribution of Ja'far Zatalli in the evolutionary stage of the Urdu language and the benefaction and support he received as a poet. What was the rationale behind Ja'far's use of invective idioms in his poetry, and how was it received among his peers, people and patrons? Based on the analysis of his poetry, it is argued that Ja'far's profound annoyance towards the prevailing circumstances of the times offended and provoked him to ridicule the high and mighty through his writings. His subsequent penury and the adversities of life he faced did not prevent the poet from being blunt and heedless, which finally culminated in his death.

MIR JA'FAR ZATALLI: THE FIRST URDU PROSE WRITER OF NORTH INDIA

Ja'far was the first major Urdu literary figure and the first Urdu prose writer, satirist and humourist of North India. His talent was extraordinary and shows in the matchless range and variety of words he uses in his verses. He had complete mastery of and an innate dexterity with words and the formulation of ideas and invectiveness. Despite his alleged nonsensicality and obscenity, he cannot be ignored. His contribution to the evolution of Urdu in its formative phase is significant. Mir Muhammad Ja'far was a phenomenon in many ways, being himself the creator and concluder of his tradition. His verses modify the prime assumption of the *ghazal* as the starting point of Urdu verse in North India that ensued with the arrival of Wali Deccani's *diwan* (collection of *ghazals*) to Delhi. Urdu verse in Delhi had already begun with Ja'far. Wali's *diwan* reached Delhi seven years after the death of Ja'far. Urdu verse in northern India started with Ja'far's poetry of social criticism and not with the poetry of love. His poetry enjoys the status of a historical and cultural document and is an early step in the development of linguistics in North India.[2]

Contrary to the noteworthy contributions of Ja'far, historians and literary critics remain indifferent to him. His compositions have generally been discarded on the pretext of allegedly being ludicrous, obscene, improper and of petite significance. He suffers the neglect and even derision of modern critics with the exception of only a handful few who have studied him from historical, cultural and linguistic perspective.[3] Mahmud Sherani is the first modern author of Urdu who went against the established convention to highlight the significance of the poetic compositions of Ja'far in his book, *Punjab Mein Urdu*.[4] Sherani writes that preceding biographers in the 18th century have counted him (Ja'far) among the Urdu poets but modern writers have overlooked him.

Muhammad Husain Azad attempted to distance himself by 'casting aspersion on the integrity and untrustworthiness of a non-sense'.[5] However, in the history of Urdu literature, Ja'far cannot be circumvented, for his role in the evolution of the Urdu language is noteworthy.

Ja'far was a unique poet whose compositions help us not only to appreciate the actual state of affairs and dynamics governing his era but also understand the societal, cultural, political and moral matrices. Ja'far was forthright in his comments, blunt and unmindful of the consequences. Thus, he was fêted by many and was found to be annoying and at times dangerous by others. He had the integrity and guts to speak his mind, and stood resolutely for the freedom of expression and wrote fearlessly with utmost honesty, righteousness, specificity, severity and sharpness of temperament that was his characteristic style. Ja'far is the only poet in whose compositions we find a true representation of his times. He was witness to the whole reign of Aurangzeb—his ascendancy, death and the subsequent decline of the Mughal Empire and the gradual erosion of the dominant Mughal culture. Candour was Ja'far's principal feature, and in upholding this integrity in expressions, he didn't spare anyone, not even himself. This frankness of expression and integrity is manifested uniformly in his entire corpus of poetry and prose. In one of the poems, he expresses the strangeness of the times he lives in, where earnestness has become futile and silly talks have become popular.

Mara ajab za taqāza i waqt mī āyad
Ke harzah gōi aziz wa muzaffar wa mansūr.[6]
(I am appalled at the importunity of times
Absurd talk is magnificent, popular and successful.)

Background and Origin

Almost nothing is known of Ja'far's life, except that he came from an elite (*ashrāf*) family of Narnaul, a small town in present-day Haryana, not very far from Delhi. He possessed an amiable temperament.[7] He was an unusual personality of the time and wrote in stinging language.[8] The basic theme of his poetry was mostly obscenity and to this effect he was called 'Zatalli' and his poetry got popular among the masses.[9] Ja'far's poetry is not devoid of meaning and carries with it his observations of the social situation of the time and human behaviour in general. According to *Tazkira-i Shorish*, Ja'far was an inhabitant of Shahjahanabad. He upheld his unmatched ingenuity and became the expert of his time at this art. One of his satires annoyed Emperor Farrukh Siyar, who then dispatched Ja'far to heaven.[10]

These are the only accounts found in the anthologies through which we get to know that he belonged to a respectable family of Narnaul and had been living in Delhi for a long time. He was erudite and possessed a poetic bent of mind. Ja'far was matchless, his compositions were universally popular, and he had the potential to become poet laureate. His style was distinctively unique and demonstrated his brilliance and expertise in both prose and poetry. Ja'far's was probably born in 1658 CE. A leading critic and literary historian, Jameel Jalibi, has expressed his opinion that 'he was Mirza and not Mir' on the basis of a satire composed for his wife titled *Kin Khudai i Mirza Ja'far. However*, this has been contradicted by Mir Qudratullah Qasim in *Majmu'a-i Naghz* and Mir Hasan in *Tazkira-i Shu'ra-i Urdu*, who refer to him as Mir Ja'far Zatalli.[11] Besides, on a number of occasions, Ja'far refers to himself as Mir Ja'far.[12] Qudratullah Qasim, quoting Ja'far, writes that '... he used to say that irrespective of how much efforts is put in, I cannot attain the position of Sādi Shīrazi, Firdausi and Tusi, and therefore I utter non-sense, so that I become popular'.[13]

Jafar! Shukr kun ke dar ālam
Ja ba ja nām-e tū zatalli shud
Shohrat-i mard behtar az har qism
Har ke gumnām zīst lalli shud.[14]
(O! Ja'far thank God that in the entire world
You are famous by the name of Idle-talker
Fame of man whether it is by any means is better,
Than the one, who is obscure and is of no value.)

Following is another couplet from his poem *Dar Ahwal-i Isteghna* (*On Conditions of Content*), where he identifies himself as Zatalli:

Gharīb wa Ājiz wa miskīn Zatalli am Ja'far
Hazār Shukr na zar wa na zahra dāram man.[15]
(O! Ja'far I am feeble, poor and unhappy idle talker
A thousand thanks to the Almighty that I don't have hypocrisy and courage.)

Ja'far even named his diwan *Zatalnama*, and writes:

Zatal nama kardam adīm-ul badal
Ke har misra-i ōost zarab-ul mash'l.[16]
(I have composed *Zatalnama* which has no alternative
Of which every word is an exemplar.)

According to Mahmud Sherani, the enthronement of Aurangzeb and birth of Ja'far took place in the same year; however, he has not provided any source to support this claim.[17] It is generally accepted that Ja'far was put to death on the orders of Emperor Farrukh Siyar in 1713 CE for allegedly criticising him for eliminating his rivals and creating a reign of terror. The all-powerful minister Asad Khan and his son Zulfiqar Khan, Sad'ullah Khan (Deputy Minister), Hidayat Kesh (the news-writer), Sidi Qasim (the police perfect of Delhi) and Shah Qudratullah of Allahabad (a learned Sufi) were all strangulated to death by the innovative use of a leather belt. The tongue of Sabha Chand, the right-hand man of Zulfiqar Khan, was cut and his house and properties were seized.[18] Shorish, in his *tazkira*, has pointed out that Zatalli met with the same fate of being strangulated to death, when after the execution of Zulfiqar Khan, he composed a *sikka* 'that the emperor was outraged and the poet was dispatched to the heaven'.[19]

Sikkah zad bar gandum wa moth wa matar
Badshah-i tasmah kush Farrukh-Siyar[20]
(Struck coin on wheat, lentil and peas,
Farrukh Siyar, the butcher king, who kills by leather strap.)

The year of the death of Zatalli is also corroborated by an entry in another diary which Jameel Jalibi has quoted in his work *Tarikh-i Adab-i Urdu*:

Chhute sab ba-wafa jeevan ke sāthi
Lagi tan man mein ab wetagh ki aag
Haveli 'chhod', yun bola Zatalli
'Andheri gor mein latkan lage paag.[21]
(Left are all the faithful friends of life
My body and mind is aflame with the fire of sacrifice?
Leaving the mansion thus spoke Zatalli
The legs were dangling in the dark grave.)

The wordsmiths have worked out the arithmetical correspondence from the fourth line—*andheri gor mein latkan lage paag*—of the above *qita'* as 1189 AH and taking out the numbers (64) derived from the word '*haveli*' from the third line, they derived the date of execution of Zatalli to be 1125 AH/ 1713 CE. The exact age of Ja'far at the time of his death is not known, though Ja'far himself refers to his age as 60 in a *qita'*.[22]

Ja'far! ba lahu wa luab-i jahan umr bākhath
Yak dam ba-fikr-i towshah-i aqba nah sakhtah

Dar umr-i shasht sāl tu khud kardah-i do zan
Hast ein mashal qadīm keh: yak gaz do fākhtah.
(O Ja'far! You have spent your time in the worldly affairs
Not giving a moment of thought about the things of the life hereafter
At the age of sixty, you have two wives
And there is an old proverb: one arrow and two marks.)

We get to know from this that Ja'far was of 60 years when he composed the above verse. In all probability, he was born in the reign of Mughal Emperor Shah Jahan and was executed in 1713 CE during the reign of Farrukh Siyar (1713–1719 CE).

Ja'far has largely been ignored despite his linguistic agility and candid reflection on the rampant corruption, hypocrisies and inabilities of the political class of the time by the modern day scholars with few exceptions (as pointed out earlier). Ja'far's role needs a fair and impartial assessment to understand his valuable contribution to the evolution of the Urdu language and also acknowledge him as a keen observer and critic of the deteriorating sociopolitical conditions and moral duplicity of Mughal India. Although the contemporary and later generation *tazkira* writers do not consider him as a poet on the pretext of alleged absurdity, only a small number of compositions from among a wide range of his poetry are guilty of this.[23] Ja'far's writing was in many ways innovative in terms of his natural agility with words and formation of ideas. On the other hand, his writing was contemptuous and scathing with the capability to shock, affront, despise and ridicule others.

Character and Temperament

There are three moral conducts available to an individual in trying times or in acting against something that is perceived as unjust—one is to follow the trend, second is to consider it bad and withdraw like the Sufis and the third is to fight against it and establish justice or truth. Ja'far opted to criticise the hypocrisies prevalent in society through his satire.[24] His poetry acrimoniously articulates the depravity of the elite class and ruthlessly lampoons and reviles them with utmost severity and sharpness.

Ja'far's deep knowledge and complete command over languages such as Persian, Hindi as well as Rekhta manifested itself in poetic and prose compositions that were compiled into a collection (*kulliyāt*) in the last quarter of the 17th century, possibly sometime around the 39th regnal year of Aurangzeb (c. 1697 CE). However, the earliest known manuscript of Ja'far's works dates to 1791–1792 CE.[25]

Zatalli had an ingenious temperament, acerbic tongue and quick-witted and domineering attitude. He was an expert in language and expression to the extent that he invented innumerable new words and styles for communication according to his wish. Brindavan Das Khushgo, one of the contemporaries and friends of the great Persian poet Mirza Abdul Qadir Bedil (1644–1720 CE) writes, 'One night Ja'far Zatalli, who was a satirist and pornographer of his age, brought a *masnavi* (couplet) composed by him in praise of Bedil. He had recited the first line (hemistich):

> *Cheh Faizi cheh Urfi ba pesh-e tu phus,*
> (What is 'Urfi, and what Faizi is before you? A stifled fart.)

Bedil stopped and thanked Ja'far by saying, "We don't have the right to listen to such tales that are said in favour of our teachers (*ustads*)". He took out two gold coins (*asharfis*) from the pocket and gave them to Ja'far and kept quiet thereafter'. Khushgo, along with the other people present at the gathering (*majlis*), requested Bedil's permission for the recital of the second line (*misra*), so as to know the rhyming of the word '*phus*', but it was turned down.[26]

Another incident quoted by the 18th-century poet Mir Hasan in his biographical anthology (*tazkira*) is as follows: one day Ja'far visited Mirza Bedil, who was engaged in composing a verse and did not attend to him. A bit irritated, Ja'far asked, '*Sahib Qibla*, which hemstitch have you composed?' Bedil responded by reciting a line of the couplet (*she'r*), stymied and uninspired in putting up the second line in order to complete the verse, and looked at Ja'far: [27]

> *Lalah bar sīnah dāgh chun dārad,*
> (Why does the poppy flower have a scar on its breast?)

Ja'far retorted, 'What's the hitch in it?' and completed the verse spontaneously:

> *Chubake sabz zeyr kun dārad.*
> (It has a green stick wedged in its arse.)

The exuberance, spontaneity and versatility of Ja'far is also attested to by an incident narrated by Laxmi Narayan Shafiq, who writes[28] that Ja'far composed a double entendre verse (*Ihām*) for a person named Muhammad Ashraf:

> *Muhammad Ashraf-i paighambaran ast,*
> (Muhammad is supreme amongst the prophets)

When Ashraf did not respond positively, Ja'far disgustingly composed an extempore second line to complete the verse:

Na ein Ashraf ke mardud-i zaman ast.
(Not this Ashraf, who is rascal of the time.)

Ja'far once composed a eulogy and sent it to one Qamr-un Nisa Begum, the daughter of Nawab Khan-i Jahan Bahadur, who, pleased at the tribute, ordered for rupees 30 as a reward to him. However, Fateh Khan, the *diwan*, made a payment of only five. When Ja'far got to know of this, he lampooned him through a satire (*hajv*), while praising Fakhr-un Nisa.[29]

Jo maine madah Begum ki banai
Likhi aur jaye kar main padh sunai
Zahe dharmatama ka shukr beti
Sakhi data bahadur ki hai beti
Ja asmat Maryam wa Bilqis-i sani
Khuda ke na'on ki ashiq diwani
Dilaye tees lekin paanch nikle
Ilahi Fateh Khan ki kanch nikle.
(When I composed eulogy of the Begum, and read it out to her
She [the daughter] is the gratitude of great saint
She is the daughter of a brave and generous bestower,
She is at par with Marry and Bilqis in holiness
She is madly in love with God
She sent thirty, however only five came
O! God, Fateh Khan's money turns out to be useless.)

Ja'far's Patrons

Ja'far was in employment with a number of Mughal princes, and at one point he was in the service of Muhammad A'zam, the third son of Aurangzeb. According to Mir, when Ja'far was presented before the prince, he impromptu composed and recited an eulogy (*Saja'*) verse in his praise:[30]

Nagin-i Sulaiman ke tabindah būd
Hamin ism-i Āzam baru aan kandah būd.
(Engraved on the sparkling stone of the ring of Solomon
Was this exceptionally great name, Azam.)

The above-quoted verse, according to Islamic tradition, refers to the most powerful name of God (*isme a'zam*/the supreme name), which the Prophet Solomon possessed. The prince was very happy and rewarded him. Ja'far thereafter joined in the army of Prince Kam Bakhsh, the fifth (youngest) son of Aurangzeb in Delhi and went with him to Deccan. However, he did not like the war and the adversity of a soldier's life and hence complained to the prince in this regard. When nothing came out of it, Ja'far wrote an awfully nasty and obscene satire on Kam Bakhsh, accusing him of alleged bestiality with a goat. The prince, who had developed a liking and high regard for Ja'far and had bestowed on him many material comforts, had no option but to sack him from service, though he spared his life for the vulgar indiscretion. Ja'far was exiled from Dakan:[31]

> *Zahe Shah-i wala ghuhar Kam Bakhsh*
> *Keh ghachchi buz kard pichchi wa pakhsh.*[32]
> (Kudos! Gem of the prince, Kam Bakhsh
> The slight cavity of the goat is ripped apart into a wide hole.)

The damage and downturn of his fortune and the consequent penury and hardships on the way to Delhi made the poet realise the stupidity of his action and even regret it.[33] He reminisces his old days of comfort and ease and the savouring of delicious delicacies in the employment of the prince. He vividly depicts the state of affairs after his dismissal from the service of Kam Bakhsh in a poem *Hasb-i haal-i khud guftah*, which is considered to be one of his finest poems.[34]

> *Az hajv-i āan Sultan-i khud kar di pareshān jān-i khud*
> *Dar māndah-i be bāl-o par ke Ja'far ab kaisi bani!*
> (You ridiculed and lampooned your King, and made your life pathetic
> Plunged behind, shorn of arm and quill, say now, Ja'far, how does it feel like!)

Pen Doused in Acrimonious Gall: Ja'far's Invective Tongue

Ja'far has been deliberately marginalised on account of being allegedly non-sensical and obscene. Some scholars have attempted to analyse his work from a historical and linguistic perspective. It might be true that one section of Ja'far's compositions is based on obscenity; however, it is quite strange that most of the scholars of the past and present have inferred it to be all that he had in his repository. No one attempted to actually look into the spirit of this vulgarity or bother to verify if it is only cheekiness or if it has any other aspect hidden in it? Possibly one theme in the poetry was profound acrimony, and in a situation of helplessness, it is quite natural to turn aggressive and revile. For a man whose weapon is his pen, what else can he do but to use it when he feels extremely appalled and aggrieved? Ja'far used strong words to highlight the intensity of oppression, hypocrisies and the ills that had crept in the society, accentuating with time. A society where the inhabitants had become insensitive, dumb and deaf, seriousness of thought had become extinct; satire and vulgarity were the best mediums of expression of one's agony and derision. Ja'far was only holding up a mirror to the society. The degeneration of the nobility, rampant corruption, duplicity and immorality of the elites was severely criticised by the poet. This contention is not merely a demonstration of his taste of language or an expression of depravity on part of Ja'far. If the contemporary literature of the time is explored, one would find its widespread existence at places. Upon reading the sections of Dargah Quli Khan's *Muraqqa-i-Dehli*, which is a contemporary account of the 18th-century Delhi just prior to and after the invasion of Nadir Shah (1739 CE), that chronicle the tastes and furtive desires of the nobles of Delhi for beautiful young boys,[35] one would easily comprehend Ja'far's use of vulgar language. It was difficult for an honest and fearless person like Ja'far to control his tongue in the era of indecency and baseness. The poet even explains the rationale behind his stinging satires and obscenity:[36]

Na in hājv az rāh-i hars wā hawāst
Dil azād rā hajv kardan rawāst.
(I don't write satire for any purpose of greed or desire
For it is permissible for free heart individual to compose satire.)

Indubitably, a section of Ja'far's composition employs obscene language. Some personal satire also forms part of it. However, only a fraction of his prose and poetry taken together contain such language, while the remaining majority work is not obscene or vulgar.[37] One of Ja'far's compositions worth consideration are those where he deals with the belief in God and renunciation of the world. From the point of view of efficacy too, this section of verses has a special significance. On analysing these compositions, it becomes obvious that the poet was alive to the situations prevailing around him in the society. The poignant hopelessness in society brought in the idea of contentment and renunciation of the world to his mind. Poems such as *Qinatnama* (A Report on Contentment), *Dar bayan-i Tawakkul* (On the Declaration of Trust in God) and *Dar ahwal-i Istaghna* (On Conditions of Content) fall under this category. One notices the changed accent and thoughts of Ja'far in these compositions as compared to the earlier ones. He also wrote a striking eulogy for the Prophet Muhammad (*Na't wa Manqabat*):[38]

Muhammad pār utaran hār sab ka
Muhammad sarwar wa sālar sab ka.
(Muhammad is the saviour of all
Muhammad is the leader of all created beings.)

Mir Ja'far did not choose the *ghazal* as his preferred mode of expression. He had a unique temperament laced with ruthlessness, a sharp tongue and honesty and courage to speak his mind. He is the only poet of the era whose compositions truly represent the times. Forthrightness is the greatest virtue of Ja'far's compositions, prose and poetry alike. In this quest of conveying the truth, Ja'far is unsparing towards others and even towards himself.

In an era when nonsense was appreciated, Ja'far echoes a deep sense of sadness and disappointment at the deteriorating social conditions of the society. The *ghazal* would not have been the appropriate medium to awaken the society from its deep slumber. To bring about this evolutionary process, it was imperative to use language that had noise value and the ability to enduringly impact the person/s and institutions concerned. In his efforts to revive the long-dead feelings and to bring back affirmative incantations from pessimism, this was perhaps the only course of action, and Ja'far accomplished the same through his writings.

The contours of a new language taking shape are quite perceptible in Ja'far's writings. Additionally, there is a feeling of restrained Persian tenor. The literary practises of Ja'far encompass a mélange of Persian and Urdu language usages, which gives an impression of the waning of the dominant Persian culture that is drawing support from the regional language and culture. In the age of Ja'far, the Urdu language had in it the living traditions of Persian and the foundation and soul of the vernacular languages. There is a perceptible influence of vernacular language in Ja'far's style of exposition and choice and chronology of words in poetry. Amir Khusrau assimilated the local dialect with the foreign language in his compositions, which were dominated by Persian styles. In Afzal Jhanjhanwi's *Bikat Kahani* (written at the end of 16th century), wherever Persian is used, there is a spontaneity in expressions and where Urdu is employed in the lines (*misra*), one immediately feels the incongruity.[39] There is also a perceptible influence of the Hindavi language in Ja'far's Persian poetry. However, firmness and dynamism in his vernacular language can easily be felt in his compositions, and one can actually discern the waning of Persian and the rise of a new language, i.e., Urdu.

Tarbuza wa kharbuza narsad gar tera ba-dasht
Yak sabz phānk khira-i bālam ghanimat ast.[40]
(If you do not get watermelon or musk-melon
Then even a slice of green cucumber is a blessing.)

Zahe Shāh-i Shāhān ke rōz-i waghā
Na hillad na jumbad na tullad jaza.[41]

In this hemstitch, one could see the Persian language and tradition adopting a new form influenced with the Hindavi style. The first part of the *misra* is conventional. However, in the second part, where in the Persian style *hillad* (to move) from *hilna* and *tullad* (get out of the way) from *tulna* are created, from these two new words the verse becomes pleasurable and effective. From the blending of Persian and Hindavi disposition, these two words (*hillad, tullad*) are pointing to a third culture in the making, i.e., Urdu.[42]

Literature attempts to imitate reality and hold a mirror up to it, with a view to make the society realise its mistakes and make amendments. Ja'far's writings have extraordinary implications from this perspective. His poetic composition can be divided into four parts. The first section is based on the poetry where youthful vigour and old age, feeling of annihilation, admonition and moral values are part of the discourse. His poetic compositions such as *Rab-i Yasir* (*Tutinama*), the ephemeral mode (*be-sabati dahr*), *Kallarnama/dar bayan-i zayifi* (description of old age),[43] *Budhapanama/dar sifat-i piri ghufta* (discourse on the traits of spirituality)[44] are part of this classification. Drawing from these compositions, it is evident that Ja'far had a deep anxiety of his fading youth and the annihilation of everything worldly. Only good deeds would be carried forward to the next world, and so one should prepare for the life hereafter.[45]

In the poem *Rab-i-Yasir*, addressing a parrot, Ja'far says, it is futile to love the imprisoned bodies (i.e., worldly desires) where neither you nor the cage would live on eternally. His poetic composition displays subterranean sensitivity and philosophy and the sense of annihilation keeps cropping up persistently. Efficacy with idioms is one of the characteristics that manifest consistently in all forms and styles of Ja'far's poetry, making his poetry striking in its entirety. The same theme of the transience of life is yet again reaffirmed in *Dar bayan-i zayifi* (description of old age). The structure of the building in the poem is dilapidated; the bricks have become old and worn out, enfeebling the foundation. In situations like this, Ja'far asks himself what should be done.

Kallar laga dīwar ko ke Ja'far ab kya kijiye
Khatrah hua āsār ko ke ab kyā kijiye
Ye rāt ab tārīk hai aur bāt bhi bārik hai
Chalna kathin bīmār ko, ke Ja'far ab kya kijiye.[46]
(Walls have become brackish, Ja'far what should be done now?
Danger to the foundation of the building, what should be done now?
The night is dark now and the road is narrow
Hard is the journey for the sick, Ja'far what should be done now?)

In the second part of the poetry, Ja'far uses obscene and plain words together in the same sentence; the crucial significance of this section for a historian is the exposition of the honesty and truth for which the poet is acknowledged. Ja'far is unflinchingly candid in expressing his mind or shedding light on the state of affairs of the era he lived in. The society was passing through a difficult time with the overall familial relations generally weakened, immodesty among women, and widespread prostitution and avidity to gain fame. Prostitutes, catamites and eunuchs dominated the society. Truthfulness was rare and deception and lies had become one of the cultural traits. *Dar Ekhteläf-i Zamānā and Daurnāmā Goyad* effectively depicts Ja'far's exasperation and disenchantment with the times. He connects the larger picture of everyday lives of the common people along with the coercion of a repressive establishment.

Gaya ikhlās ālam se, ajab ye daur āya hai
Dare sab khalq zālim se, ajab ye daur āya hai
Na yāron mein rahi yāri, na bhāiyon mein wafādāri
Mohabat uth gayi sari, ajab ye daur āya hai
Na bole rāsti koi, umar sab jhooth mein khoi
Utāri sharm ki loi, ajab ye daur āya hai.[47]
(Sincerity has vanished from the world, these are strange times
People are fearful of the tyrant, these are strange times
Camaraderie is missing among friends, and constancy between brothers
All the love is lost, these are strange times
No one speaks truth; all the life is lost in falsehood
Removed the vestiges of modesty, these are strange times.)

In poems his *Dastūr-ul-Amal* and *Nasihatnāmā mawāfiq zamāna mi gōyad*, Ja'far contrasts good and bad practices, which vividly portray the actual state of affairs within the confines of the home and the outside world of this era. Women wrangled with their husbands and wanted a life of ease and sumptuousness; the son-in-law had become acquisitive and demanded dowry. Entire society encountered a number of malaises, smugness and lack of knowledge. Ja'far had the self-realisation that his criticism was not going down well with the people with vested interests, and he even reprimands himself to keep his tongue in check.

Ja'far! Zabān rā band kun, bā-rāsti paiwand kun
Dil khastah rā-khursand kun, in shewah az har kar beh.[48]
(O Ja'far! shut up your tongue and enjoin the habit of speaking truth
Make people happy, who are upset with you and it is better to leave your ways.)

Ja'far was an eyewitness of the reign of Aurangzeb and hence his writings are an important contemporary historical source. He had profound approbation for Aurangzeb and composed at least three poems and one elegy (*marsiya*) on his death in different styles. *Dar tā'rīf-i Aurangzeb* (In praise of Aurangzeb)[49] deals with the victory of Deccan. Here, Ja'far praises the emperor for his valour and determination that made his adversaries tremble in fear and no one could withstand him since he stood like a mountain in the battlefield.[50] The second poem describes the struggle for the throne among the sons of Aurangzeb after his death. The third poem is an elegy (*marsiya*) to the emperor where his character, valour and piety have been extolled. Ja'far, in the early days during Aurangzeb's rule, despite feeling angry and disapproving of the conduct of ruler, did appreciate his charismatic power, effective leadership and administrative qualities. After Aurangzeb's death, there was no redeeming factor for Ja'far and the elegy (*Marsiya-i Aurangzeb Alamgir*) is a reflection of it:

Kahān ab pāyen aisā Shahanshāh
Mukam̃al Akmal wa Kāmil dil āgāh
Rakt ke aansū jag rota hai
Na meethi nīnd koi sota hai.[51]
(Where shall we find so perfect a king?
Complete, accomplished, ideal, knowing hearts,
The world is weeping tears of blood
And gentle sleep to no one begets.)

Ja'far expresses his genuine feelings in the poems that all the sons of Aurangzeb were out rightly incompetent. They were the ones responsible for the mismanagement and ruining of the Deccan campaign of Aurangzeb. Prince Muhammad Muazzam, the eldest son of Aurangzeb successfully ascended the throne with the title of Bahadur Shah I. Ja'far labels him as a confused king, echoing the feeling of the common masses.

Takhsin kalān tar chah parkhand kard
Hamah kā-rō-bā-r-i pedar bhānd kard.[52]
(The one [Muazzam] who most excessively and increasingly ruined
And destroyed the business of his father.)

Rahe rāt din gānd ke zikr mein
Ba lahu wa la'b chut ki fikr mein.[53]
(Round the clock was [Azam] engrossed in remembrance/fascination of anus,
And in the solicitude of drenched vagina.)

These compositions are especially significant from the historical viewpoint as they have profound genuineness and are reflective of the diverse thoughts prevailing in the era. Here, even obscene language does not remain obscene but become a means of expression.

The third part of Ja'far's poetry is based on satire (*hajv*), which is an admixture of awe-inspiring ridicule. The people on his radar were tyrant rulers, spoilt princes, cruel officials, dishonest ministers, coward soldiers, corrupt revenue officials (*diwans*) and police officials (*kotwals*). All of them have been exposed of their cruelty and coercion and their hypocrisy is ridiculed through satire and lampooning. He uses strong words to highlight the intensity of the oppression and fearlessly expresses and shames the concerned person by the use of invectives and terms that are not only derisive but obsessively wicked and instantly get popular among the masses.[54] Ja'far expresses his profound anger, disgust and candour against the prevailing state of affairs. The sentiment of distress, pain and affliction in his satire is reflective of the mutilated and dejected soul of the age. He deliberately uses expressions laced with acute severity meant to afflict shock and injure. He uses the Urdu and Persian languages, at times together creating a unique charm in the composition. His poetry strengthens the Urdu language by reinvigorating energy and fixing a purpose for the poetry.

In an age when morality, love and kindness had become meaningless with no regard for civility and good deeds, and deceit and plunder, sexual perversion, immodesty and debauchery had become the standards of conduct, Ja'far rose as the living voice of a truthful self and drew the attention of the masses through a touch of fierceness, tussle and movement of poetry. In the cacophony and melee, Ja'far is screaming to make people listen to the actual realities of the society. In such circumstances, expecting refined and elegant traditional language would be a futile proposition.

Invective poetry such as *Gand-marrawa-nama, Hajv Khan-i Jahan, Hajv Mirza Zulfiqar Beg Kotwal Shahr Dehli, Hajv Fateh Khan, Hajv Shakir Khan Faujdar, Hajv Sabha Chand, Hajv Ismat-un Nisa Begum* and *Hajv Khuda Yar Beg,* Ja'far belittled and ridiculed Mughal princes, nobles, officials and elite women known for their insatiable sexual promiscuity. He wrote *Gand-marrawa-nama,* a nasty satire on Bahadur Shah I.

Pān kha kar gand marawwa kheliye
Bagh jakar gand marawwa kheliye
Bādshāhi hai Bahādur Shah ki
Ban banakar, gandmarawwa kheliye.[55]
(While chewing paan have the fun of anal sex
While in the garden have the fun of anal sex

It's the kingdom of Bahadur Shah
Get ready for the fun of anal sex.)

Ja'far wrote savage and obscene satire against women of the high class such as Ismat-un-Nisa Begum, a maternal granddaughter of Ma'mur Khan (a nobleman at Aurangzeb's court) as also the wives of Sabha Chand (the *diwan*). They have been portrayed as sexually promiscuous women, whore and cheats with other derisive appellations.[56] One could in fact spot that Ja'far's feat of linguistic dynamism is at its best. He is equally vituperative and derisive of Sabha Chand (a confidant of Zulfiqar Khan, noble of Aurangzeb's court). Sabha Chand was known for his corruption and Zatalli has attacked him for the lack of honesty and warns him to follow his advice (*nasihat*) and be God fearing:

Sabha Chand Ji! Tum bade dhīyīng ho
Ke garh pankh aur bail ke sīng ho
Nazar mat karo sāat aur pāanch par
Mabda pade bojh ab kanch par
Hamari nasihat rakho gosh beech
Japo Ram mala, raho hosh beech
Manam Ja'far āndar zatal naam daar
Chughal ki uchhal gand phadun pachaar.[57]
(Sabha Chan Ji! You are utterly stupid
You are a bird with large wings and horn of the bull
Don't eye anymore about fives and sevens
Lest the inner lining of your tummy come under pressure;
Let my advice be stuck in your ears,
Take the name of Ram and keep to your senses.
I am Ja'far, infamous for nonsense,
I am capable of jumping and ripping apart the back-biter's arse.)

The fourth part of Ja'far's poetry is the one where satire is embedded in humour. He mocks and laughs at his hardship and also makes others laugh at him. *Joban Nama, Hasb-i haal-i khud guftah,* and others are part of this genre of poetry. It describes the hardships Ja'far had to endure because of his own silly action in antagonising his masters/ patrons. He was critical of others and even did not spare himself for the mistakes committed and was prone to self-afflicted sufferings.

Tanha shudi andar safarke Ja'far ab kaisi bani
Uftadi andar bāhar-o bar ke Ja'far ab kaisi bani!
Az hajv-i āan Sultan-i khud kar di pareshān jān-i khud
Dar māndah-i be bāl-wa par ke Ja'far ab kaisi bani!
Faludah wa firni che shud pan bhatta wa shirni che shud

Āan bistar-o bālin kidhar ke Ja'far ab kaisi bani!
Dil ko thī¯kane lao ab, kar sabr mat pachtao ab
Hargiz magu ba¯re dagar, ke Ja'far ab kaisi bani![58]
(Travelling alone, say now, Ja'far, how does it feel like!
You've been cast away in land and sea, say now, Ja'far, how does it feel like!
You ridiculed and lampooned your King, and made your life pathetic
Plunged behind, shorn of arm and quill, say now, Ja'far, how does it feel like!
Where are now the *faluda*, and *firni* [milk rice-pudding], *pan bhatta* [rice cooked in water] and sweets?
Where's the squashy bedding, and the pillow? Say now, Ja'far, how does it feel like!
Fix and reconcile your heart now, be patient and don't feel sorry
Never say again, Say now, Ja'far, how does it feel like!)

Ja'far was matchless in his expertise and command over the language and use of idioms and proverbs in spontaneous ways that made his compositions lively. It is worth pointing out his style of creating sound from the usage of words that makes evident his viewpoint and feelings. One can comprehend the context through the phonetics of the words without actually understanding the meaning of each word. The phonetics, through the selection of words and idioms, creates an atmosphere leading to a profound impact of the satire and lampoon. The sociopolitical scene after the death of Aurangzeb, the ensuing political instability and internecine war among his sons for the throne that shook the empire are expressed by the following sound in the elegy composed on the death of Aurangzeb (*Marsiya-i Aurangzeb Alamgir*):

Sada-i tūp wa bandūq ast har sū
Basar-asbāb wa sandūq ast har sū,
Jhatā jhat wa patā pat ast har sū
[illegible] kat walatā latast har sū,
Bah har ja mār mār wa dhār dhār har ast
Ucchal chāl wa tabar khanjar katār ast
Az ān sū A'zam wa az in sū Mu'azzam
Jhara jhar wa dhara dhar har do bāham
Be-binam ta Khuda az kīst rāzi
Ba-khawand khutbah bar nāme ke qazi.[59]
(Because of cannon's noise and guns
Men carrying goods and guns on their heads
And fleeing here and there on every side
Beds on their heads and children in their arms

Cutting and smiting on all sides
On all sides death and violence,
Turmoil, axes, daggers, poniyards
That side Azam, this side Muazzam
Fighting, struggling, both I find
But let us see whom God approves as king,
For whom the faithful offer Friday prayers.)

Ja'far used language very intelligently and with the utmost sensitively in order to make his communication more effective. His juxtaposition of Hindavi words/phrases/proverbs with Arabic and Persian and vice versa seems effortless and natural. He creates new names for people as per the situation. His *Kulliyat* is full of names such as Mirza Ghach Ghach Beg, Mirza Gandfodwa, Loot Khasot Khan Ruhela, Qazi Rishwat Talib Khan, Tang Zafar Khan, La'nat Quli Khan, Nafs Parwar Khan, Gobar Chand Wakil and Shah Nikhatoo, among others. While analysing the significance of these names, it becomes apparent that this invention (of names) induces meaning and thought and portrays the persona fittingly.

His *kulliyat*, though a short one, has in it a cache of peculiar words, which are obsolete in modern terms and encompass a large horde of Urdu words.[60] He is no less than Nazir Akbarabadi in eloquence and no one can deny his quick-wittedness and sharp intellect. Few lines from the poem, *Dar Ahwāl Isteghna Wa Be Parwa'ī Khud* ('On Conditions of Content')[61] are quoted below, which gives the reader an ample idea of the multitude of words (*zakhirā-i-alfāz*) used by Ja'far.

Na doop[62] *wa Barchī wa guptī na tarkash wa na kamān*
Na bānk[63] *wa dashnah*[64] *na khanjar sunhara dāram man*
Na pākhar ast wa na chalqad na baktar wa na salah
Na dotahi wan a jāma' akharah dāram man
Na dar na deorhi wa dar bān na asam wa rasm-i jahān
Na dol wa mashaq wa pakhāl[65] *wa tatharah darām man*
Na chulah wa na kadahi na hāndi wa doi
Na jhajjar[66] *wa na ghadonchī*[67] *na bajharh darām man.*

The atypical linguistic novelty of Ja'far helped accelerate this process through the insertion of Persian words and expressions into Urdu couplets and newly coined Urdu words and phrases in Persian couplets. Sometimes, Ja'far wrote a couplet in Persian followed by the one in Urdu, and in other instances a line of the couplet in Persian and the other in Urdu, at times even Urdu and Persian expressions in the same line, displaying his mastery over the languages as well as embodying literary and cultural appropriation.[68]

CONCLUSION

Mir Ja'far established the tradition of the satirical verse (*hajv*) in Urdu, which ultimately led to the evolution of a new mode of expression that became known as *shahr Ashob* in later times. There are distinct imprints and influence of Ja'far on the themes and expressions in the poetry of the later generation of poets such as the great satirist of the 18th-century Mirza Rafi Sauda, Mir Taqi Mir, Shakir Naji and Sadullah Khan Rangin. Shah Hatim (1699–1783 CE), the first poet of Delhi to garner a big fan following, wrote satire on the physicians of the times by imitating Ja'far.[69]

Ja'far's personality is uniformly articulated in his poetry and prose. Since Persian was the official language of the time, all petitions, epistles and court chronicles were written in this language. Ja'far has used these models for writing satirical prose in Persian language. Nevertheless, the basic words, phrases and adages are more or less in Urdu. In Ja'far's prose, one gets a feeling of cultural and linguistic demur and perplexity between Persian and Urdu and the amalgamation of other languages such as Arabic and Turkish resulting in a linguistic hotchpotch (*lesanikhicchdi*).[70]

Both of Ja'far's prose and poetry are fine examples of Urdu writing, though the language got this name only later. His dexterity in the language was outstandingly brilliant and could not be dismissed despite his alleged incongruous style. His contribution to the linguistic evolution of Urdu is significant. Ja'far's poetry enjoys the status of a historical and cultural document and is an early step in the linguistics experiments in Urdu in North India.[71] It is believed that there was no poetry or prose in Hindavi/Hindi in Delhi before Ja'far. He chose the *rekhta* style over Hindi/Hindavi, and his compositions are an excellent manifestation of early Urdu writing that serves as a link between the older and a more refined variant of the Urdu language that developed in the 18th century in North India. He is one of the most excellent poets of Urdu, whose compositions unwaveringly represent the social issues and difficulties of his era. From the point of view of both the language and expression, Ja'far's writings need serious attention. The history of the evolution of the Urdu language and culture in North India cannot be written without analysing Ja'far's composition. Urdu had not yet acquired the sophistication of a developed language, and Ja'far was quite aware of it, the dynamics of which he aptly summarises in his own words:

Agar che sabhi kuda wa karkart ast
Ba-hindi wa rindi zuban lat pat ast
Wa lekin kisi ne bhali yeh kahi

Jise piyu chahe, suhagan wahi
Baya Ja'far in ja sukhan kun tamām
Ke ma qall wa dall ast khair ul kalam.[72]
(Even though what I have said is rubbish
This Hindi language is smeared with free thinking tongue-lashing
But as someone has rightly said
One whom husband loves most, is the lucky wife
Come Ja'far and end your discourse here
Because that speech is best which is short and abounding.)

NOTES

1. Recent researches have questioned and argued for a reconsideration on the very idea of Mughal decline in the 18th century, see Christopher A. Bayly, *Rulers, Townsmen, and Bazaars: North Indian Society in the Age of British Expansion, 1770–1870* (New York: Cambridge University Press, 1983); Muzaffar Alam, *The Crisis of Empire in Mughal North India: Awadh and Punjab, 1707–1748* (New Delhi: Oxford University Press, 1986); Muzaffar Alam and Sanjay Subrahmanyam, eds., *The Mughal State, 1526–1750* (Delhi: Oxford University Press, 1998); P.J. Marshall, ed., *The Eighteenth Century in Indian History: Evolution or Revolution?* (New Delhi: Oxford University Press, 2003); David Washbrook, 'Progress and Problem: South Asian Economic and Social History c. 1720–1860', *Modern Asian Studies* 22, no. I (1988): 57–96; also see Tabir Kalam, *Religious Tradition and Culture in Eighteenth Century North India* (Delhi: Primus Books, 2013).
2. Rasheed Hasan Khan, ed., *Zatalnama: Kulliyat-i-Ja'far Zatalli* (Delhi: Anjuman Taraqqi Urdu Hind, 2003), 19; Jameel Jalibi, *Tarikh-i Adab-i Urdu, Atharvin Sadi* (Delhi: Educational Publishing House, 2000), Vol. 2, Part I, 98.
3. Hamid Hasan Qadiri, *Dastan-i-Tarikh-i Urdu* (Agra: Azizi Press, 1957), 27–28, has summed up Zatalli in almost a single page, describing him as a minor clownish figure; Muhammad Sadiq, *A History of Urdu Literature* (New Delhi: Oxford University Press, 1984), does not mention him at all; Annemarie Schimmel, *Classical Urdu Literature from the beginning to Iqbal* (Wiesbaden: Otto Harrassowitz, 1975), 157–158, accords little importance to Zatalli as a social satirist; Ali Jawad Zaidi, *A History of Urdu Literature* (Delhi: Sahitya Academy, 1993), 69, discusses him in brief, devoid of any appreciative value of the linguistic significance of Zatalli. There are a few exceptions to this 'overriding trend', Jameel Jalibi, *Tarikh-i Adab-i Urdu*, 90–118, gives adequate space to discuss his importance and accords a respectable position to him as the one with whom starts the tradition of Urdu writing in North India even before Wali. Shamsur Rahman Faruqi, *Early Urdu Literary Culture* (New Delhi: Oxford University Press, 2001), 121–124, is affirmative of Zatalli's role in the evolution of the Urdu language. For appreciating Ja'far Zatalli through the historical perspective, see

Raziuddin Aquil, *In the Name of Allah: Understanding Islam and Indian History* (New Delhi: Penguin India, 2009), Chapter 6.

4. Mahmud Sherani, *Punjab Mein Urdu* (Delhi: National Council for Promotion of Urdu Language, 2005), 195–202.
5. Muhammad Husain Azad, *Āb- i Hayāt* (Lucknow: Uttar Pradesh Urdu Academy, 1998), 22.
6. Jalibi, *Tarikh-i Adab-i Urdu*, 97.
7. Hakim Abul Qasim Mir Qudratullah, *Majmu'a-i Naghz*, ed. Mahmud Sherani (Delhi: National Council for Promotion of Urdu Language, 2002), 167; Mir Taqi Mir, *Nikat-us Shu'ra*, ed. Maulvi Abdul Haq (Aurangabad: Anjuman Taraqqi Urdu, 1935), 30–31. *Tazkiras* such as Mir Hasan's, *Tazkira-i Shu'ra-i Urdu*, ed. Maulana Muhammad Habibur Rahman Khan Sherwani (Delhi: Anjuman Taraqqi Urdu Hind, 1940), 39–40; Qaim Chandpuri, *Makhzan-i Nikat*, ed. Maulvi Abdul Haq (Aurangabad: Anjuman Taraqqi Urdu, n.d.), 13; Mir Ghulam Husain Azimabadi, 'Shorish', *Tazkira-i Shorish*, ed. Kalimuddin Ahmad, *Do Tazkire* (Patna: Ma'asir, n.d.), 161–63, and others only mentions that Ja'far was famous as Ja'far Zatalli. Lakshmi Narayan Shafiq, *Chamanistan-i Shu'ara'* (Aurangabad: Anjuman Taraqqi Urdu, 1928), 47, 49, writes that he was blunt (outspoken) and haughty. His compositions were lucid, representing day-to-day affairs of life and famous among masses that needed no introduction. Emperor Muhammad Azam stated that if Ja'far did not compose nonsensical poetry, he would have been *malik-us shu'ara'* (poet laureate).
8. *Ba Ja'far Zatalli mashūr ast. Nadirah zamān wa ajōba-i daurān-i khud būd. Zabān gazidah dāsht*, see Maulana Muhammad Habibur Rahman Khan Sherwani, ed., *Muqaddima-i Nikatus Shu'ra* (Badaun: Nizami Press, 1922), 31.
9. Qaim Chandpuri, *Makhzan-i Nikat*, 13.
10. *Tazkira-i Shorish*, 161–163.
11. Jalibi, *Tarikh-i Adab-i Urdu*, 91; Mir Qudratullah, *Majmu'a-i Naghz*, 167; Mir Hasan, *Tazkira-i Shu'ra-i Urdu* 39.
12. Rasheed Hasan Khan, *Zatalnama*, 13.
13. *'Mi guft ke har chand sa'i khwahīm kard, Sādi-i Shīrazi wa Firdausī, Tusī na khwāhim shud. Zatal mi gōyam ta mumtaz-i ālam bāsham'*, see *Majmu'a-i Naghz*, 167. See 'Shorish', *Tazkira-i Shorish*, 161–63 for a different version of Ja'far taking up the title of Zatalli. It is reported that Ja'far once recited a Persian couplet to his contemporaries:
    Mara agar chah deedan-i durr-i yatim nist
    Nazar suwye dana-i shabnam ghanimat ast.
    The poets present, unanimously adjudged the *sheir* as nonsense (*zatal*) out of envy (*az rashk-i bālā tafāq*). To this Ja'far replied, if it's nonsense then, I will say nonsense only and recited this couplet:
    Gar nechah pechdār mayas̄ar na āiydat
    Nā chār humar huqq-i sag dum ghanimat ast.
14. Rasheed Hasan Khan, *Zatalnama*, 14, 252 (*lalli* is used here in the sense of 'impotent').
15. Ibid., 211.
16. Ibid., 266.

17. Ibid., 248; also see Mahmud Sherani, *Punjab Mein Urdu*, 183; Jalibi, *Tarikh-i Adab-i Urdu*, 92, where in the fourth line instead of *khāyah*, the word *kānd* has been use. I have relied on *Zatalnama*.
18. Wolseley Haig, *The Cambridge History of India: The Mughal Period*, Vol. IV, ed. Sir Richard Burn (Delhi: S. Chand & Co., 1971), 330–332.
19. See *Tazkira-i Shorish*, ed. Kalimuddin Ahmad, *Do Tazkire*, 163, for this information, '*azyin khabar mizaj badshah barham gasht. Ishān rā ba-jannat farastād*'; Shahnawaz Khan, *Ma'asir ul Umara*, Vol. II, Eng. tr. Henry Bevridge and Baini Prashad (Calcutta: Asiatic Society, 1952), 1042–1043, for the details of the execution of Zulfiqar Khan and Jahandar Shah on the same day (16th Muharram 1125 AH/11 February 1713). Zulfiqar Khan was murdered by putting a strap (*tasma*) around his neck; see William Irvine, *The Later Mughals*, ed. Jadunath Sarkar (Delhi: Low Price Publications, 1995), Vol. I, 240, 248–253; also see Jalibi, *Tarikh-i Adab-i Urdu*, 94; Rasheed Hasan Khan, *Zatalnama*, 14–15; Aquil, *In the Name of Allah*, 140.
20. Rasheed Hasan Khan, *Zatalnama*, 15; *Tazkira-i Shorish*, 163; Ale Ahmad Suroor, ed., *Aligarh Tarikh-i Adab Urdu*, Vol. I (1200 AD–1700 AD), 501.
21. Jalibi, *Tarikh-i Adab-i Urdu*, 94.
22. Rasheed Hasan Khan, *Zatalnama*, 16, 246; Jalibi, *Tarikh-i Adab-i Urdu*, 94; Aquil, *In the Name of Allah*, 140.
23. Saiyid Mohiuddin Qadri Zor, 'Ja'far Zatalli', in *Ja'far Zatalli ki Ehtejaji Shayeri*, ed. Ali Javed (Delhi: Writer's Guild India, 2000), 14.
24. Jalibi, *Tarikh-i Adab-i Urdu*, 90.
25. Aquil, *In the Name of Allah*, 136; see also Shamsur Rahman Faruqi, 'Burning Rage, Icy Scorn: The Poetry of Ja'far Zatalli', lecture under the auspices of the Hindi–Urdu Flagship, University of Texas at Austin, 24 September 2008, 1–10.
26. For details, see Bindraban Das Khusgho, *Safina-i- Khushgo*, ed. Syed Shah Muhammad Ataur Rahman Ata Kakovi (Patna: Silsila-i Intesharat Idarah-i Tahqiqat Arabi wa Farsi, 1959), 113. Also see Mir Taqi Mir, *Nikat-us shu'ra*, 30–31; Qaim Chandpuri, *Makhzan-i Nikat*, 13; *Tazkira-i Shorish*, 163; Mahmud Sherani, *Punjab Mein Urdu*, 187, for the story in brief with slight variations.
27. Mir Hasan, *Tazkira-i Shu'ra- i-Urdu*, 40.
28. See Lakshmi Narayan Shafique, *Chamnistan-i Shu'ra*, 69; also see Rasheed Hasan Khan, *Zatalnama*, 262. It is reported that whenever Ja'far went to see someone, he had two papers ready with him; one contained a couplet of eulogy (*madāh*) and the other a satire (*hajv*) for the person concerned. If Ja'far was treated well and given something as a reward, then the eulogy would be read. Otherwise, he would popularize the satire (*wa khidmat mi namudand wa mi nawisand ke chun ba-khānah-i kase mi āmad do kāghaz hamrah dasht. Bar-yak parcha hajv sahib-i khānah wa bar digar-i madāh ō. Agar mila rā mi deyad madāh mi khwānd digar na parcha kāghaz hajv rā bal shohrat mi dād*), see *Tazkira-i Shorish*, 163; also Naim Ahmad, 'Mir Ja'far Zatalli: Ek Mut'ala', in *Ja'far Zatalli ki Ehtejaji Shayri*, ed. Ali Javed, 57.
29. Rasheed Hasan Khan, *Zatalnama*, 166–167.

30. Mir Taqi Mir, *Nikat-us shu'ra*, 30; Mir Hasan, *Tazkira-i Shu'ra-i Urdu*, 40; *Tazkira-i Shorish*, 163; Rasheed Hasan Khan, *Zatalnama*, 262.
31. Rasheed Hasan Khan, *Zatalnama*, 140.
32. The prince has allegedly been accused of bestiality with a goat, see Rasheed Hasan Khan, *Zatalnama*, 144; Gyan Chand Jain and Sayyida Ja'far, *Tarikh-i Adab Urdu* (Delhi: NCPUL, 2011), Vol. V, 59–60; Aquil, *In the Name of Allah*, 137.
33. Rasheed Hasan Khan, *Zatalnama*, 140.
34. Ibid., 147–148; Suroor, *Aligarh Tarikh-i Adab Urdu*, Vol. I, 500–501; Jain and Ja'far, *Tarikh-i Adab Urdu*, Vol. V, 60.
35. Dargah Quli Khan, *Muraqqa-i Dehli*, ed. Khaliq Anjum (Delhi: Anjuman Taraqqi Urdu Hind,1993), 11–38, 123–124.
36. Rasheed Hasan Khan, *Zatalnama*, 173.
37. Ibid., 22–23.
38. Ibid., 121–122.
39. Jalibi, *Tarikh-i Adab-i Urdu*, 100.
40. Rasheed Hasan Khan, *Zatalnama*, 18.
41. Ibid., 27.
42. Jain and Ja'far, *Tarikh-i Adab Urdu*, Vol. V, 66–67.
43. The title of the poem has differing names in different manuscripts. The Bombay MS has *Kallarnama/Dar bayan-i zayifi wa piri*; the London MS1 has *Kallarnama/Dar bayan-i zayifi*; the Berlin MS has *Kallarnama goyad;* the Alavi MS has *Dar sifat-i pirigoyad* and the Naim MS has *Kallarnama*, see Rasheed Hasan Khan, *Zatalnama*, 224.
44. The Bombay MS has the title *Masnavi Mir Ja'far*; the London MS1 does not have a title; the London MS2 has the title of *Budhapanama*; the Berlin MS has *Dar bayan-i umar goyad*; the Naim MS has *Dar sifat-i piri* and the Muhammadi MS has *Dar sifat-i piri ghufta*, see Rasheed Hasan Khan, *Zatalnama*, 220.
45. Ibid., 213–225.
46. Rasheed Hasan Khan, *Zatalnama*, 224–225.
47. Jalibi, *Tarikh-i Adab-i Urdu*, 103.
48. Rasheed Hasan Khan, *Zatalnama*, poem titled *Dastūr-ul Amal*, 193.
49. The title of the poem differs in different manuscripts: the London MS1 has the title *Zafarnama-i Badshah Alamgir Ghazi*; the Alavi MS has *Zafarnama-i Aurangzeb Shah Alamgir Ghazi Nurullah Marqadah;* the Kolkata MS has *Dar Bayan-i Pīrsāli*, see Rasheed Hasan Khan, *Zatalnama*, 125–136.
50. *Zahe dhak-i Aurang Shah-i bali/dar aqlim-i dakhan padi khalbali; Mahasur* (extraordinarily brave), *jodha, bali be badal/Chu al-burz* (a big mountain in the northern Iran) *qaiyam, chu parbat atal*, see Rasheed Hasan Khan, *Zatalnama*, 125–136; Aquil, *In the Name of Allah*, 148.
51. Rasheed Hasan Khan, *Zatalnama*, 137–139; Suroor, *Aligarh Tarikh-i Adab Urdu*, Vol. I, 499.
52. ibid., 133.
53. ibid., 135.
54. Jalibi, *Tarikh-i Adab-i Urdu*, 105–106.
55. Rasheed Hasan Khan, *Zatalnama*, 149–151.

56. *Har do zan hāye Sabha Chand che makkārā* (cheat) *wa badkarā* (immoral) *wa aiyyārā* (cunning), *dhagabāz wa latak sāz wa tannāz chapel chanchal wa achpal, matak chāl wa janjāl wa chhināl* (whore) *and wa khawāne spārā*, see Rasheed Hasan Khan, *Zatalnama*, 90–91.
57. Ibid., 164–165.
58. Ibid., 147–148.
59. Ibid., 138–139; Suroor, *Aligarh Tarikh-i Adab Urdu*, Vol. I, 499.
60. Mahmud Sherani, *Punjab Mein Urdu*, 183–187.
61. Rasheed Hasan Khan, *Zatalnama*, 209–211.
62. *Dhoop* is a type of sword.
63. *Bānk* mean curved stick, which is curved at the tip.
64. *Dashnah* means a kind of dagger.
65. *Pakhāl* is large bag made of animal skin, which is used in the transportation of water on the backs of oxen or ponies.
66. *Jhajjar* is big earthen pitcher.
67. *Ghadonchī* is wooden stand on which a pitcher is kept.
68. Jalibi, *Tarikh-i Adab-i Urdu*, 100–101; Aquil, *In the Name of Allah*, Chapter 6.
69. Ibid., 115.
70. Ibid., 109.
71. Jalibi, *Tarikh-i Adab-i Urdu*, 98.
72. Rasheed Hasan Khan, *Zatalnama*, 266.

REFERENCES

Alam, Muzaffar and Sanjay Subrahmanyam, eds. *The Mughal State, 1526–1750*. New Delhi: Oxford University Press. 1998.

Alam, Muzaffar. *The Crisis of Empire in Mughal North India: Awadh and the Punjab, 1707–1748*. New Delhi: Oxford University Press. 1986.

Aquil, Raziuddin. *In the Name of Allah: Understanding Islam and Indian History*. New Delhi: Penguin India. 2009.

Azad, Muhammad Husain. *Āb- i Hayāt*. Lucknow: Uttar Pradesh Urdu Academy. 1998.

Bayly, Christopher A. *Rulers, Townsmen, and Bazaars: North Indian Society in the Age of British Expansion, 1770–1870*. New York: Cambridge University Press. 1983.

Chandpuri, Qaim. *Makhzan-i Nikat*. Edited by Maulvi Abdul Haq. Aurangabad: Anjuman Taraqqi Urdu. n.d.

Faruqi, Shamsur Rahman. 'Burning Rage, Icy Scorn: The Poetry of Ja'far Zatalli', lecture under the auspices of the Hindi–Urdu Flagship. Austin: University of Texas, 24 September 2008, 1–10.

———. *Early Urdu Literary Culture*. New Delhi: Oxford University Press. 2001.

Haig, Wolseley. *The Cambridge History of India: The Mughal Period*. Edited by Sir Richard Burn, Vol. IV. Delhi: S. Chand & Co. 1971.

Hasan, Mir. *Tazkira-i Shu'ra-i Urdu*. Edited by Maulana Muhammad Habibur Rahman Khan Sherwani. Delhi: Anjuman Taraqqi Urdu Hind. 1940.

Irvine, William. *The Later Mughals*. Edited by Jadunath Sarkar, Vol. I. Delhi: Low Price Publications. 1995.

Jain, Gyan Chand and Sayyida Ja'far. *Tarikh-i Adab Urdu*. Delhi: National Council for Promotion of Urdu Language. 2011.

Jalibi, Jameel. *Tarikh-i Adab-i Urdu, Atharvin Sadi. Vol. 2, Part I*. Delhi: Educational Publishing House. 2000.

Kalam, Tabir. *Religious Tradition and Culture in Eighteenth Century North India*. Delhi: Primus Books. 2013.

Khan, Dargah Quli. *Muraqqa-i Dehli*. Edited by Khaliq Anjum. Delhi: Anjuman Taraqqi Urdu Hind, 1993.

Khan, Rasheed Hasan, ed. *Zatalnama: Kulliyat-i-Ja'far Zatalli*. Delhi: Anjuman Taraqqi Urdu Hind. 2003.

Khan, Shahnawaz. *Ma'asir ul Umara*. Translated by Henry Bevridge and Baini Prashad, Vol. II. Calcutta: Asiatic Society. 1952.

Khusgho, Bindraban Das. *Safina-i- Khushgo*. Edited by Syed Shah Muhammad Ataur Rahman Ata Kakovi. Patna: Silsila-i Intesharat Idarah-i Tahqiqat Arabi wa Farsi. 1959.

Marshall, P.J., ed. *The Eighteenth Century in Indian History: Evolution or Revolution?* New Delhi: Oxford University Press. 2003.

Mir, Mir Taqi. *Nikat-us Shu'ra*. Edited by Maulvi Abdul Haq. Aurangabad: Anjuman Taraqqi Urdu. 1935.

Qadiri, Hamid Hasan. *Dastan-i-Tarikh-i Urdu*. Agra: Azizi Press, 1957.

Qudratullah, Hakim Abul Qasim. *Majmu'a-i Naghz*. Edited by Mahmud Sherani. Delhi: National Council for Promotion of Urdu Language. 2002.

Sadiq, Muhammad. *A History of Urdu Literature*. New Delhi: Oxford University Press. 1984.

Schimmel, Annemarie. *Classical Urdu Literature from the Beginning to Iqbal*. Wiesbaden: Otto Harrassowitz. 1975.

Shafiq, Lakshmi Narayan. *Chamanistan-i Shu'ara'*. Aurangabad: Anjuman Taraqqi Urdu. 1928.

Sherani, Mahmud. *Punjab Mein Urdu*. Delhi: National Council for Promotion of Urdu Language. 2005.

'Shorish', Mir Ghulam Husain Azimabadi, *Tazkira-i Shorish*, Edited by Kalimuddin Ahmad, *Do Tazkire*. Patna: Ma'asir. n.d.

Washbrook, David. 'Progress and Problem: South Asian Economic and Social History c. 1720 1860', *Modern Asian Studies* 22, no. I (1988): 57–96.

Zaidi, Ali Jawad. *A History of Urdu Literature*. Delhi: Sahitya Academy. 1993.

Zor, Saiyid Mohiuddin Qadri. 'Ja'far Zatalli'. In *Ja'far Zatalli ki Ehtejaji Shayeri*, edited by Ali Javed. Delhi: Writer's Guild India. 2000.

9

PLEASURES OF FASHION AND SORROWS OF PRODUCTION: THE HANDLOOM INDUSTRY IN UNITED PROVINCES, INDIA, 1860s–1940s

Santosh Kumar Rai

Scholars often see *pleasure* as an escape from reality or distraction from real world issues. Thus, we also tend to neglect the forms of pleasure people enjoy, what they do for such expressions and, in turn, how they produce the world around us. In search of preconceived ideas of what is politically, economically or socially significant in the history of textiles, we often ignore its relationship with fashion trends, i.e., the dresses people enjoyed and took pleasure in wearing, the choices they appreciated and the types of fabric they were moving towards. Traditionally, fashion studies have focused either on material diachronic or synchronic moments of cultural production. One of the first modern scholars to recognise the economic implications of fashion was Joan Thirsk, who accused economic historians of ignoring evidence by relegating fashion to a secondary explanation in accounting for the development of the clothing industries. She also pointed out the power of the 'tyranny of fashion' on all social classes.[1] Recently, scholars in the field have begun to question the role of authenticity, ethics, identity and sustainability in the practice of making, marketing and consuming clothes. It has been accepted that political and economic conditions, knowledge and skills intermingle with the cultures of production and consumption and they fertilise each other within a typical set of characteristics. Now, it is premised that the relationship between how a designed product is produced and how it is distributed and consumed is central to any definition of fashion.

While exploring such issues, one needs to underline the fact that colonial modernity revolutionised every dimension of Indian life including fashion, which scholars cannot comprehend without bringing material culture into the domain of cultural history. Fashions showed the innovative attitude of colonial society and economy; markets, styles, trends and philosophies towards clothing were a direct result of the ongoing changes in attitude. Thus, the fields of fashion and luxury, otherwise seen as intertwined, were also in flux. Consumers had realised the value of their purchasing power and, like producers, could not easily shift to new sites of action. Similarly, reduced profits for traditional luxury conglomerates, changed the creative processes that determined product creation. This chapter seeks to explore fashion trends, examining the way they shape cultural attitudes towards textile production and influence national politics in colonial and global contexts. To further the argument, how the shaping of dress and dress practices resulted in experiences of sorrow for the producers, the handloom weavers in this case, has been discussed.

INTRODUCTION

The politics of dress in colonial, post-colonial and globalised contexts and the circulation of items of clothing across time and space have just been seen as concerns of the colonial economy. Until the recent past, South Asian researchers have tended to overlook the realm of ordinary life through the interface of material culture of production and pleasure. For instance, critics have dismissed modern clothing introduced under European influence and appropriated by millions of Indians as merely an expression of the colonial policies, market and nationalist response. The existing historiography on textile and fashion largely functions with three overarching arguments: (1) the economic historians have analysed the whole process within the globalisation and modernisation paradigm, which for them created; (2) the conditions for a creative reorganisation of the institutional structures; (3) additionally, the political adaptation of the handloom industry is another approach to study this subject.

In the first instance, Tirthankar Roy emphasises on an economic transformation where commercialisation and market forces are the main players leading to the analytical eclipsing of cultural experiences of workers and consumers and the ways in which they crucially transformed economic processes. This explanation goes back to the second point regarding the modernisation of the industry.[2]

In contrast, the third school has interpreted the popularity of handloom as a sign of intensified nationalism. Emma Tarlo examines the sartorial style in India from the late 19th century to the present, showing how trends in clothing are linked to caste, level of education, urbanisation and a larger cultural debate about the very nature of Indian identity.

Clothes have been used to assert power, challenge authority and instigate social change throughout Indian society. During the struggle for independence, members of the Indian elite incorporated elements of Western style into their clothes, while Gandhi's adoption of the loin cloth symbolised the rejection of European power and the stark contrast between Indian poverty and British wealth. Similar tensions are played out today, with urban Indians adopting 'ethnic' dress as rural populations seek to follow the culture of urban dressing in fashions.[3] Similarly, in her study of craft production in colonial India, Abigail McGowan explores 'how knowledge was created about craft during British rule and how this knowledge helped shape development efforts at that time'.[4] While McGowan's work acknowledges that craft was a central theme of the colonial and nationalist discourse, it fails to recognise the life-world of cloth outside the domains of colonial and national appropriations of art and craft. Lisa Trivedi takes a broader approach, as she discusses the transformation of Khadi into a national symbol in modern India.[5]

In another interpretation, clothes became the symbol of power relations in terms of links between discourse and power via the agency of the rituals surrounding clothes. Moreover, the interaction between the traditional society of South Asia and the colonial approaches has been explained in terms of rituals and European anxieties surrounding cloth. As Thomas Metcalf has argued, the British understood India largely in terms of the differences among Indians themselves. Clothing played a crucial role in this process. The British came to view the subcontinent as a place of multiple communities defined by various languages, religious practices and, significantly, dressing styles.[6]

C.A. Bayly has argued that after 1905, the import of British-made cloth into India and the ensuing destruction of the Indian handicraft industry became the key theme of Indian nationalism. In the hands first of Bengali leaders such as Bipin Chandra Pal, Benoy Kumar Sarkar and Radhakamal Mukherjee and later of Mahatma Gandhi and his followers, the need to support *swadeshi* (home) industries and boycott foreign goods was woven through with notions of neighbourliness, patriotism, purity and sacrifice, all of which provided unifying ideologies more powerful than any single call for political representation or independence. The destruction of indigenous weaving and influx of foreign cloth became visible, material symbols for nationalists, comparable to those represented in other societies by literary or legendary motifs: 'loss of country' in Indochina and China, the coming of the Just King in Indonesia or the notion of the ending of Babylonian Exile in Caribbean and African societies. The decline of 'nativity' of production was, in a way, the denial of indigenous pleasure as well. That cloth could be such a powerful symbol of the community and of right conduct was due to the important role that cloth and clothes played in Indian society, and not merely in fixing and symbolising social and political statuses but also in transmitting holiness, purity and pollution through their colour, hygiene and uses.[7] Bernard S. Cohn has also examined how the English cloth and 'modernisation' altered the norms and standards of clothing and how new classes, as well as behavioural codes, upset the ceremonial and status function of the cloth.[8]

However, such emphasis on colonial experience as well as sacred nuances and skill of the handloom industry discouraged an understanding of the craft's true social and economic premise, diluting the 'historical narrative' in the analysis of modern craft. Should we resist conceptions of tradition as inherently vague and mystifying? Or does tradition still have an important role to play, as an anchor and binding agent of a society? How should we understand the phenomenon of knowledge transmission while remembering that the once guild-based apprenticeships began to decline drastically in the late 19th century? One should also pose the question of how far European fashion also initiated a process of homogenisation within Indian society. As far as the material culture of pleasure is concerned, one requires to ask to what extent innovations in products, technology and marketing strategies for textiles and clothing during the colonial regime in India responded to the social emulation and rapid change characteristic of fashion. How did different types of consumers and behaviours stimulate or suppress the manufacture and trade in textiles, clothing and dress accessories? Did particular price points or changing distributions of income allow consumers to make more choices about the dresses that propelled their individual aspirations? What role did cross-cultural contact play in the intensification of fashion in terms of the range of products available, new processes in the production of clothes and marketing strategies? How can historians draw on methodologies and a new set of arguments for understanding the relationship between fashion and cloth production?

Such interpretations regarding clothes and their material production do not take their implications in terms of the meaning of pleasure and its corollary production of textiles *outside* the construct of fashion—beyond the grasp of the protagonists or the consumers themselves. Scholars believe that meaning lies in buried symbols or ideological undercurrents rather than in the synchronic movement of dress wear, pleasure or enjoyment itself. If we locate fashion in modern times in terms of modern culture, two important insights have to be highlighted with reference to 18th century France. In pre-modern times, fashion was a non-inclusive right among the nobles of the court. However, with the amalgamation of new philosophies, ideas and inventions, the style of dressing became a mirror for the dynamic changes taking place within the society. Fashions displayed the innovative attitudes of the time. Markets, styles, trends and philosophies towards clothing were a direct result of the changes taking place.[9] Here, the decline of the handloom industry requires to be connected to the idea of fashion and its evolution, as the objects of fashion are intimately connected with corporeal, cultural, social and gender-based experiences as well as the economies of fashioning and re-fashioning across places and times. Items of clothing reflect the priorities of local and international economies, political agendas and also national identities, in addition to collective and personal inclinations. Objects of fashion are highly charged cultural instruments, animated by cross-cultural and transnational flows that actively influence the social world and cultural history. Political and economic conditions, knowledge and skills intermingle with cultures of production and consumption and they fertilise each other within a typical set of characteristics. Raising the issue of concretely organising work also means being directly interested in the concrete functioning of the fashion market and demand networks.

The colonial economy was redefining the textile sector in such a way that an 'adolescent' market whose customers belonged to all classes was no longer catering within the confines of a habitus but wishing to play with individual identity, assert a personal 'right' or live a unique fashion experience. Together, producers, purveyors and consumers were struggling to build a new meaningful space for new fashion and luxury objects to express social and personal meaning and create value beyond the pecuniary. There is a need to document local histories of handloom production that escape the pleasures of fashion, reveal its novelty and suggest the stirring possibility that the social history of nationalism is incomplete and impermanent without the social histories of production and pleasure. This chapter considers three perspectives on the handloom industry: (a) the changing clothing habits and fashion, (b) the contextualisation of new trends and documentation of the handloom industry's continued resilience and (c) the weaver's own perception of day-to-day problems of livelihood and survival vis-à vis the realm of the pleasure of production and earning. The basic question to answer is how did the modern trends of fashion generated under the colonial regime negotiate with the existing structure of handloom production? How did handloom localities fit into fashion territories inside the colonial space? As an industrialised nation, Britain was expanding her markets and producing more goods; fabrics and materials in the Indian colony were becoming more diverse and less expensive. Both the production and consumption of clothes were not just matters of choice; the colonial economy and nationalist politics of the *Swadeshi* movement too were playing an overly significant role.

The response of the traditional handloom industry to the new situation through simultaneous introduction and display of many new styles at the cost of older ones, the selections available to and made by the innovative consumer with reference to their purchasing power and the desire to wear 'modern' costumes provided both an impediment as well as an impetus to the handloom production and fashion.

CHANGING CONSUMER PREFERENCE

The deciding factors in the choice of cloth were its cheapness or suitability to the clothing habits, as in the late 19th century, indigenous-made finer cloths were preferred either because the English cloth of same kind was more expensive or because it was not adapted to suit the local conditions. The division of higher and lower classes was also a deciding factor in the fate of handloom industry, as it was reported that the persons 'with whom it is an object of necessity to dress with a certain degree of gloss' were mostly using English cloth or local cloth made from English yarn, while those for whom appearance was a secondary consideration and cloth was meant for covering the body were mostly using local cloth made from native thread. Here, the inherent qualities of the local cloths, i.e., 'more durable, thicker, warmer and better suited to the wants of the people',[10] and also its affordability gave it a upper hand over English cloth, since it was more suitable for the labour class and for household ladies. At the same time, due to its fineness, sheen and lightness, English cloth was also popular as 'holiday attire'[11] even amongst the lower classes.

The strategy of the handloom industry of adopting coarser cloth also did not become successful, as the English mills had successfully imitated and had actually put into market the coarse cloths preferred by the poor peasantry and working men, 'with whom the object is to obtain cloths, which will stand, rough wear and tear'.[12] Here, opting for the mill-made cloth had a double-edged effect. On the one hand, the 'gloss' of 'new cloth' gave a sense of pleasure, while on the other hand, its durability was doubtful. Similarly, the members of the urban middle class, such as lawyers, surgeons and schoolmasters, preferred the 'coat and trousers of the Englishmen', which was certainly an indicator of their social mobility in the era of 'colonial modernity'. To some extent, the native art industry was attracting European patronage. 'The English lady uses the embroidered shawls of the Jat women as hangings or curtains; she invests her surplus cash in Lucknow silver work or Delhi embroideries; she orders carved tables from Saharanpur, native chintzes from Bulandshahr, brass trays and bowls from Benares'.[13] Now, native patterns were being modified to suit the 'vile taste of the globe trotters'[14] and occupational groups were constantly, by a process of fusion, giving birth to fresh combinations.

Perhaps the most spectacular of changes in fashion was the discontinuation of the use of turbans, whether *pagri*, *pheta* or *safa*. Earlier, all over India, about 70 per cent of the men, both Hindus and Muslims, would wear some kind of turban, and some of these were many yards long. By the late 1930s, only a small proportion of people were wearing such headgear (to cover the head) even in the rural areas, and caps of all kinds, including Gandhi caps and *Fez* caps, had taken their place. Those who still continued to wear turbans changed over to cheap, mill-made, mostly imported muslins, and the demand for the hand-woven turban cloth nearly disappeared.

Even more revolutionary was the change in the dressing style of children, both boys and girls. Earlier, boys used to wear little dhotis or pyjamas, but by the late 1930s, a growing number of boys, especially in towns, had started wearing khaki shorts and knitted vests. Similarly, little girls, unlike their mothers who wore saris or *khans* (bodice cloth) in their childhood, opted for frocks. So by this time the weaving industry was having only an insignificant share in the new dressing choices of children that greatly affected this industry.[15]

The Report of the Indian Industrial Commission of 1919 stated that the tenacity of the handloom industry was attributable in part to

> the great number of types of cloth of which slow moving Indian custom decrees the use, to the fact that the demand for many of these is on a small scale, while the types themselves are so special as to render it difficult for this power loom to produce them at profit.[16]

Artisans managed to sustain themselves by making cloth for niche markets and catering to specialised demand. Every centre tended to focus on making one or two products for regional markets marked by the demands of specific caste groups and gender-specific tastes. The demand for cloth within these niches, however, was very unsteady. Purchases generally went up during the harvest and marriage seasons, when the peasant class had some cash to spare and special reasons to buy cloth. But at other times of the year, when there was low demand, the looms had to greatly reduce output, and production would even come to a complete halt.

The awareness of the changing consumer tastes was a vital factor for the survival of the weaver. In 1900, the Azamgarh handloom industry was in a very deplorable condition, but it was still important. The fabrics of Azamgarh district were mixed silk or *tasar* with cotton in deference to the prohibition of pure silk fabrics for Muslim men. The cotton weaving industry had no doubt suffered in the race against cheap Manchester fabrics, but when it came to silk fabrics, especially of the mixed kind, there was a peculiar adaptation to local conditions and prejudices, which enabled the industry to hold its own. A great proportion of the products of the Azamgarh looms was no doubt cotton fabrics, but the mixture of silk and cotton or *tasar* and cotton was so common in the district that it was difficult to estimate the worth of silk or *tasar* separately.[17]

By mid-1920s, a change in the tastes of the people was quite visible. Earlier, fine fabrics such as jamdani were much in demand, but people were now moving towards European garments. Thus, at places such as Tanda in Faizabad district, where earlier jamdani used to be a very high paying industry, weavers had almost abandoned manufacturing jamdani and other fine fabrics of use by wealthy people. Now, the demand for coarser fabrics such as that of *lungis* was greater and more consistent, and weavers thus preferred them. The weavers of the United Provinces were now catering on a much larger scale to the needs of the middle and the poorer classes. Though the clothes in demand by these classes could be made from readily available Indian yarn, there was an increasing trend to use Japanese yarn owing to its relative cheapness. Demands were being made to increase the import duty by another 13 per cent to ensure an appreciable rise in the price of imported yarn so that weavers could give up the imported yarn in favour of the indigenous yarn. Although Indian mills in Kanpur and other manufacturing centres were supplying most of the yarn counts, they could not compete with the imported yarn in terms of the price.[18] Here, the consumer base was expanding vertically from top to bottom in terms of the class structure, but this shift cannot be analysed merely in terms of change in the fashion, as this shift was also influenced by the purchasing power of the consumer. This increase in the social base of European dresses, at least in the case of the middle and lower classes, could be interpreted through the politics of yarn tariff, which pre-fixed the affordability of the imported yarn and subsequent decrease in the cost of European dresses being manufactured by this yarn. By the late 1920s, it was reported that the *gota* (lace) industry of Lucknow, the cap-making industry of Meerut and the embroidered caps of Lucknow all were suffering because of the peoples' changing tastes. *Lehangas* were going out of fashion, and their replacement *saris* would have very little *gota* work. Similar was the state of *zardozi* and *kamdani* patterns of Lucknow. The change in fashion and a certain standardisation led to a continued fall in demand of the above-mentioned objects. This process ultimately reduced the wages, particularly in the sectors where the wages earned by the workers were already very meagre. The wage fixation was a gendered process; for example, the *gota* weavers or the embroiderers of Lucknow were women who could not take care of their interest 'on account of *purdah*'.[19]

Over half a century, there were distinct changes in the patterns of the apparel preferred by the consumers, which vitally affected the handloom weavers. Some of these changes favoured the handloom industry, while others were distinctly detrimental to it. The consumption pattern went through a major change from 1914 to 1941.

Table 9.1: Changes in the Proportion of People Wearing Different Garments in the United Provinces, 1914–1941 as per the RFFC, 1942[20]

	Urban Areas (%)		**Rural Areas (%)**	
	1914	**1941**	**1914**	**1941**
Men				
Dhoti or *lungi*	94	85	99	99
Kurta or *shirt*	99	99	40	70
Achkhan or coat	10	40	(a)	(a)
Turban	5	(a)	70	10
Cap	60	85	5	35
Women				
Lehenga and *dupatta*	95	5	100	40
Sari and dhoti	5	95	(a)	60
Petticoat	(a)	70	(a)	(a)
Choli	50	(a)	70	5
Jumper	(a)	75	(a)	(a)
Children: Boys				
Shorts	(a)	50	50	50
Trousers	50	5	(a)	(a)
Children: Girls				
Frocks	11	40	(a)	(a)

The changes in apparel, at least in some fabrics, appear quite drastic if one studies the data in Table 9.1. The most striking change occurred in women's clothes. The proportion of women wearing *lehengas* fell from 95 per cent to 5 per cent in the urban areas and from 100 per cent to 40 per cent in the rural areas, whilst the proportion of people using saris increased from 5 per cent to 95 per cent in the urban areas and from nil to 60 per cent in the rural areas. The proportion of women using the old-fashioned *cholis* dropped from 50 per cent to nil in the urban areas and from 70 per cent to 5 per cent in the rural areas, while the proportion using petticoats and jumpers in the towns increased from practically nil to 70 per cent and 75 per cent respectively. For men, the change in the preference of headgear was most striking in terms of numbers. In the towns, 5 per cent of the men wore turbans in 1914 but hardly anyone wore them in 1941. In the rural areas, the proportion of turban users fell from 70 per cent to 10 per cent. At the same time, the proportion of cap wearers increased from 60 per cent to 85 per cent in the towns and from 5 per cent to 35 per cent in the rural areas.

Of these changes, the most significant was the massive increase in the preference for saris and the stark decline in turban wearing amongst men. The popularity of saris helped the handloom industry to an extent because mills could not produce cloth with borders on it. A decline in turban wearing, on the other hand, meant that the niche market for it dissolved, necessitating the adaptation of the handloom weaving industry to newer fabrics. Thus how the decline in the popularity of turbans necessitated a wholesale shift to sari production in both Mau and Mubarakpur. As seen earlier, by then, the cotton cloth handloom production had adjusted and reduced in comparison to mill-made cotton cloth. Yet, the handloom sector's shifting focus towards silk production in certain segments was a new development in the eastern region of the United Provinces.

SURVIVING THE PRECARIOUS CHANGES

In the above-mentioned circumstances, the traditional producers, i.e., the local weaving communities, particularly the *Julahas,* started to lose their exclusive character. This was more so because the demand for indigenous goods was left only for two kinds of products. First, the quite significant demand was for the 'roughest production for the use of the very poor classes'. But the problem for the *Purabiya* weavers was that these kinds of cloth required more raw material, which was not produced locally and was very expensive. Second, there was a demand for the 'articles of great artistic and intrinsic worth',[21] which only very rich classes could afford. The rise of some new crafts such as *chikankari* embroidery, which was popularised mainly from the 1860s onwards and was in demand in big cities, also helped this trend. This was mainly domestic work pursued by women.[22] However, only highly specialised weavers could satisfy such a demand, so a vast range of weavers who could produce only medium quality cloth had no future, as it was this class of weavers which was the most hit by the influx of English goods.

Due to its specialised nature, the silk industry had a greater chance of survival as compared to cotton. In Azamgarh district, there was a peculiar adaptation to local conditions and prejudices in silk fabrics, especially in the mixed kind manufactured in this district, which enabled the industry to hold its own or, at least, to decline at a slower pace than it would otherwise have done.[23] Among the main silk varieties of the district, *gatta* or *ghalta* (mixed silk and cotton) was favoured for women's dresses, and even the Europeans admired it. Another pure silk fabric called *sangi* was very much appreciated by Muslims for their *payjamas*. The annual production of *ghalta* and *sangi* in Azamgarh was estimated at three lakh fifty thousand rupees. Here, the weavers were settled in villages, so the city-based emerging firms in the textile industry had few chances to engage them, and traditional *grihastas*, *dalals* and *kothiwals* continued to exploit these weavers. In 1882, there were only 315 weavers working with 65 firms as compared to 2,168 weavers working 'independently'.[24] The word 'independence' was used for want of a better word, but how independent they really were is the question. Now, there was competition between different firms as the elites in cities and *talukdars* were highly interested in expensive and well-decorated silk cloth, a fancy which could not be found in English goods.[25]

The weaver was not in a position to draw advantage out of selling his product as a manufacturer, as he neither had the sources to purchase raw material nor to sustain his family. So, for the survival of his household, the weaver had to forego rights over his labour by entering into a contract with the *mahajans* and firms which would give him an advance and intercept much of his profits. In Banaras, 408 firms were active in the trade of *kamkhab* (brocade), *saris* and *dupattas*. They had engaged 2,115 weavers, and only 636 weavers were independently active in the manufacture of these varieties.[26] It seems that the '*bani*'[27] *pratha* evolved at this time. The emergence of modern firms was attributed to highly specialised and very expensive cloth. It was noticed that the 'misery of the craftsmen of this country appears to increase with the value of the wares they produce'.[28] Weavers were employed with such firms with hopeless indebtedness, and here again a situation similar to the one with the previous commercial residency of the British East India Company engagement was emerging. So the weavers who produced brocade worth rupees two hundred were not getting more than two annas per day.[29] In contrast, the master weavers (*grihasta*) were very well off. Three of them were land holders and also owned indigo factories[30] in Banaras. Thus, the producers experienced changes in fashion and demand as per their class status. The mediators, such as the *grihasta*, were prospering, while the subaltern weavers were losing their manoeuvring power.

The Fact Finding Committee for the Handloom and Mills of 1942 found that, contrary to the general perception about the census reports and other authoritative publications, the great majority of weavers in India were full-time workers. The proportion of full-time weavers was 75 per cent in the United Provinces, and they formed a considerable part of the population in Banaras, Barabanki, Mirzapur and Maunath Bhanjan.[31] The strategies adapted by these full-time workers saw significant changes in the nature and work of the handloom. Specialised centres at local levels were now emerging—such as Banaras and Maunath Bhanjan in the United Provinces—which specialised in silk and cotton fabric. In these centres, auxiliary trades required for the sale of the silk fabric also congregated. Indeed, the lines of specialisation changed owing to recent shifts in demand. Due to changes like the decline of hand-spinning, growing dependence on mill yarns and settlement in urban areas, the handloom weavers increasingly came into the grip of the middlemen. Yarn had to be purchased, and as the average weaver had no cash for such purchases, he had to either purchase on credit or engage with the yarn merchant or with the financier on a contract or wage basis. The weaver was also forced to give up independent business as the growing fluctuations in the price of yarn and cloth made weaving a risky business. Only the weavers with some financial backing—which most of them actually lacked—could undertake such risks. Further, the weavers selling in distant markets had to wait for a long time before their investment on yarn could be realised. But impecunious weavers could not wait; they had to sell their labour in advance and for them dependence on financiers was almost a Hobson's choice. Most of the weavers needed not only the money for the yarn but also an advance for their maintenance during the time of production. Thus, mortgage of future labour was a familiar feature in the exchange. Normally, a weaver had to depend on advances, and because he needed those advances so badly, he had to sell his labour cheap. In most middlemen's systems, 'the working weaver is so inexorably tied to the financier that he is not able to sell his labour in a free market, nor sell his products at the highest available price'.[32] The proletarianisation of weavers of coarse cloth continued, but they survived by reducing their prices and immiserating themselves and their families. Weaving continued to be a source of livelihood for many, but it was no longer a link to the world economy as it had been earlier.

There were thus overwhelming odds which the handloom weaving industry had to face over the first 50 years of the 20th century. Yet, evidently, certain events were shaping the livelihood of the weavers. According to the census statistics, the number of persons in the United Provinces that were supported by hand-weaving is given in Table 9.2.

Table 9.2: Number of Persons in the United Provinces Supported by Hand-Weaving[33]

Year	People Supported by Hand-Weaving
1901	947,873
1911	853,133
1921	731,813

Census statistics suffer from a number of flaws. Yet, the decline in the number of weavers indicates that the condition of the weaving industry remained precarious. According to the census of 1911, the total population of weaving castes (Muslim and Hindu) in the province, excluding the native states, was 961,672, of whom only 53 per cent were actually engaged in their traditional occupation. These figures did not include the nomadic Gadarias, who spun and wove wool, nor the non-weavers by caste, who were in the occupation of weaving. The total population depending on textiles connected with handloom, including the actual workers and their dependents, was 895,447. The following was reported in the census report:

> Welfare of such a large number of people is manifestly a fit object of the Government's concern. They are all, as a class, deeply attached to their industry, but their economic and social condition leaves much to be desired.... They are almost illiterate and wholly unorganized and are habitually improvident. They need outside impetus and assistance and these can only be provided on the Government's initiative and with its help.[34]

This stereotype continued to dominate the colonial views on weavers of the region:

> The weavers are one of the most ignorant, conservative and improvident communities of India. They are poor and are generally so heavily indebted that it is difficult to wean them out of the clutches of the petty money-lender. It is perhaps our weavers who have suffered most from the commercial intercourse that has sprung up between East and the West and their present degraded condition is the result of their sufferings.[35]

Each rise in the price of cotton and yarn drove a large number of these workmen to agriculture and other trades.[36] Factors such as the purchasing power of consumers and inflation also determined the demand for cloth. It was reported from Gorakhpur in 1908 that, 'Owing to scarcity and high prices having rendered it difficult, and in some cases impossible for them, [the weavers] to find a market for their manufactured goods'.[37] The weaving industry certainly declined in the early years of the 20th century, first as a result of the plague, from 'which the weaver class appears to have suffered greatly', and second, as a result of the rise in the price of yarn combined with unfavourable agricultural seasons.[38]

> In times of scarcity the weavers who are the most numerous of the artisan classes, are the first to be thrown out of work; the demand for the articles produced by them decreases as the intensity of famine increases. They became dependent on state relief and the subject of affording relief to them has occupied the special attention of all the three Indian Famine Commissions.[39]

> In the majority of cases the weaver at present lives a hand to mouth existence; his method of working, the appliances used by him, and the amount he has to pay to the moneylender to obtain money to purchase his materials, cut down his earnings to such a narrow limit that they are barely sufficient to supply his daily wants.[40]

Yet, even in this precarious survival pattern, there were times when the handloom weaving in the region did revive. One such time was in the immediate aftermath of the First World War. At this time, the prices of imported and mill cloth advanced to a rate that had been unheard of for many years, and the indigenous industry benefited through this rise. The revival of the handloom industry was in no small measure due to the stimulus that was given to it by the establishment of weaving schools and the introduction of fly shuttle looms. Handloom factories had sprung up in the vicinity of all weaving schools and even at a distance from them. By 1922, as many as 3,400 fly shuttle looms were working at Tanda, 3,000 at Mau, 800 at Ghosi, 200 at Mubarakpur, 300 at Etawah, 500 at Moradabad and many more at other places. The total number of fly shuttle looms, which worked in 31 districts in 1923, was 19,000 and, although the hand-weaving industry lost ground, many weavers found employment in Indian mills.[41] There was a marked increase in the number of new weaving sheds started in the villages for the weaving of dhotis and coarse cloth. A number of cotton weavers in many districts of the United Provinces were engaged in manufacturing *doosuti* and other cloth suitable for making bedsheets. The decline in imports during the war gave the industry quite a decisive incentive, but in the post-war period it was very necessary to devise means by which the industry could continue to progress. The regular supply of cotton yarn and other requisite accessories at market rates and the formation of cooperative societies were some ways out.[42]

However, the deep sorrow of economic dislocation was a continuous phenomenon to be seen in the actual condition of the weavers in the region. William Hoey, in his survey on the trades of northern India in 1880, noted the following:

> ... the spinning of cotton has dwindled to almost nothing for it has been found cheaper to import European twist and yarn for weaving purposes than to spin the cotton produced locally. The Jolahas of Lucknow are fast leaving the city of Lucknow and seeking a livelihood in service.[43]

He stated that some years ago, a most extensive business in handloom weaving existed in Lucknow but that English goods were gradually pushing country fabrics out of the market. The work of an average weaver family was described in the Dufferin Report in 1888 thus:

> One more instance may be taken this time of a weaving family consisting of husband, wife and young son. Both man and wife worked at trade. The wife made the thread ready for weaving; the husband wove and cleaned the cloth. The thread was usually supplied by other people and he received wages for preparing and weaving it, sometimes in cash but more frequently in grain.[44]

For a similar feedback to the Dufferin Enquiry, the collector of Ghazipur described the fate of one such weaver family. The family was that of Raza, a 70-year-old *Julaha* and his family comprising his wife, two married sons, their three wives and his three grandsons. One of his sons had left for Calcutta three months earlier in search of work and since his departure had not been heard of. Raza had no land and was entirely dependent on the proceeds he got from the weaving business. However, he and his wife were too old to weave and the second son could not weave more than five yards of cloth daily. There was nothing to supplement this income beyond the little work the women used to get during the harvest season.[45] The report further noted:

> In the rural areas there is one class of artisans which as it seemed to me in the course of my enquiry probably more nearly approached than any other the position in which the sufficiency of daily food becomes a question of uncertainty. These are the weavers and in a less degree the cotton carders, whether Hindus or Mohammadans. In the villages the weaver seldom uses his own cotton, his employer supplies the cotton and he is paid at the rate of an anna for five yards, this quantity representing a day's work.[46]

For a large number of such weavers, the search for an alternative occupation was gradually becoming mandatory for survival. This remains a continuous phenomenon. After the riots of 1927 at Bahadurganj Qasba and the nearby villages in Ghazipur, the tehsildar gave an estimate of the annual income of the inhabitants of the village of Ranbirpur. There were five *Julahas* by caste in the village whose names and annual income are given in Table 9.3.

Table 9.3: Sample Annual Income of *Julahas* from Ghazipur District, 1927[47]

Name of the *Julaha*	**Occupation**	**Estimated Income (in ₹)**
Suleiman s/o Mangroo	Cultivator in other villages	200
Husain s/o Mangroo	Caste profession (weaving)	80
Shakur s/o Thalu	Caste profession (weaving)	80
Jabbar s/o Thalu	Service (in Calcutta)	144
Bakash s/o Jhingur	Caste profession (weaving)	20 (income very poor as per official estimate)

This data clearly shows that the earnings of the people involved in the weaving of traditional items were very low compared to the earnings of those who moved to other professions. Under the above-mentioned circumstances, artisans and crafts persons in the *mofussil* regions, locally experienced and responded to the larger process changes occurring in the global fashion. From the late 19th century onwards, the social context for the emergence of silk production as the main segment of the cloth industry was getting decided by the fashion trends in this region. This major shift adapted some of the fashion trends as a strategy of survival for the weaving sector in this region, leading to the rise of new occupational hierarchies and reducing the majority of weavers to positions of dependence up to the level of a loom-less weaver. The heavy investment required in procuring raw materials and designs strengthened merchant control. A vast majority of the artisans, whose skill made the cloth vibrant and presentable to the wider market, could, however, not acquire independence and move beyond their occupational niche.

By the mid-1930s, it was realised that the livelihoods of the handloom weavers would be adversely affected by the indiscriminate expansion of mill cloth. Mill cloth being cheaper, glossier and lighter, was much in demand. Consequently, though the functioning of spinning mills was not disturbed, the growth of the mill sector was regulated. Certain concessions came to be given to the handloom industry, while excise duty was levied on mill cloth. By 1940, the outbreak of the Second

World War created serious difficulties for most cottage industries, particularly the cotton sector. Shortage in the supply of yarns, dyes and chemicals created difficulties for handloom weavers. By then, there was an increase in the demand for *khadi* and imitation *khadi*. Some new designs were introduced, but at the same time, due to competition from mill-made yarn and costly cotton, the price of *khadi* also rose, adversely impacting the sale of finished goods. The silk weaving industry, despite an increase in the prices of silk yarn, dyes and chemicals, could maintain its demand. Here also, old and traditional designs were being replaced by new and more attractive floral shapes and multi-colour shades, which appealed to the modern taste.[48] During the course of the Second World War, some industries began to languish and stagnate while some others found themselves forging ahead beyond expectations. The demand for handloom products was augmented because of the unusual concentration of mills producing for war purposes. Thus, the handloom industry remained a major supplier of cloth. However, the rise in the prices of Indian and foreign yarn brought about a reduction in the average profits of the weaver. The handloom sector thus received a setback, as the prices of the finished products did not rise in proportion to the rise in the price of the raw material.[49]

To conclude, instead of studying fashion and pleasure as individual constructs in isolation, the study of the domain of fashion together with pleasure leads us to certain interlinked processes of pleasure as well as sorrow moving around the human factors associated with the textile industry that critics can only explain in relation to larger political, social or economic forces. The pleasures derived from fashion and creativity of production are not two autonomous domains. Rather, a common thread of material culture binds them together. The participation of multiple actors is required for something to be defined as fashion. Hence, fashion and the pleasure drawn out of it are both socially constructed processes, as a social context constantly shapes the taste, imagination and acceptability as well as the consumer base in this human segment. The diversity of fashion depends not solely on the binary of pleasure and sorrow; rather, as the experience of the handloom weavers in colonial India shows, in between these two factors, the global material circumstances set the tone for a cultural transformation and forms of survival of producers. Here, the commercialisation of the production network constantly negotiates with the relevance of consumer culture. However, the evolution of textiles and designs lies in their own location and content of production. Hence, beneath the gloss of fashion lies a traditional community enterprise negotiating with technology, materials, distribution, finances and, of course, human factors getting shaped by as well as shaping the pleasure of wearing clothes.

NOTES

1. Joan Thirsk, 'The Fantastical Folly of Fashion: The English Stocking Knitting Industry (1500–1700)', in *Textile History and Economic History: Essays in Honour of Miss Julia de Lacy Mann*, eds. N.B. Harte and K.G. Ponting (Manchester: *Manchester* University Press, 1973), 50.
2. Tirthankar Roy, *Artisans and Industrialisation: Indian Weaving in the 20th Century* (New Delhi: Oxford University Press, 1993): 25–30; Tirthankar Roy, *Traditional Industry in the Economy of Colonial India* (Cambridge: Cambridge University Press, 1999); Tirthankar Roy, 'Acceptance of Innovations in Early 20th-century Indian Weaving', *The Economic History Review* 55, no. 3 (2002): 507–532.
3. Emma Tarlo, *Clothing Matters: Dress and Identity in India* (Chicago: University of *Chicago* Press, 1996).
4. Abigail McGowan, *Crafting the Nation in Colonial India* (New York: Palgrave Macmillan, 2009), 4.
5. Lisa N. Trivedi, *Clothing Gandhi's Nation: Homespun and Modern India* (Bloomington: Indiana University Press, 2007).
6. Thomas Metcalf, *Ideologies of the Raj* (Cambridge: Cambridge University Press, 1995).
7. C.A. Bayly, 'The Origins of Swadeshi (Home Industry): Cloth and Indian Society, 1700–1930', in *The Social Life of Things: Commodities in Cultural Perspective*, ed. A. Appadurai (Cambridge: Cambridge University Press, 1986), 285–322.
8. Bernard S. Cohn, 'Cloth, Clothes and Colonialism: India in the 19th Century', in *Cloth and Human Experience*, eds. A. Weiner and J. Schneider (Washington: Smithsonian Books, 1989), 106–162.
9. Jennifer M. Jones, 'Repackaging Rousseau: Femininity and Fashion in Old Regime France', *French Historical Studies* 18, no. 4 (Fall 1994): 943; Edward Maeder, *An Elegant Art: Fashion and Fantasy in the 18th Century* (New York: Abrams, 1983), 15; Peter McNeil and Giorgio Riello, 'The Art and Science of Walking: Gender, Space, and the Fashionable Body in the Long 18th Century', *Fashion Theory* 9, no. 2 (2005): 182; Joan De Jean, *The Essence of Style: How the French Invented High Fashion, Fine Food, Chic Cafes, Style, Sophistication, and Glamour* (New York: Free Press, 2005), 39; Madeleine Delpierre, *Dress in France in the 18th Century*, trans. Caroline Beamish (New Haven: Yale University Press, 1997), 1; Aileen Ribeiro, *The Art of Dress: Fashion in England and France, 1750 to 1820* (New Haven: Yale University Press, 1995), 35.
10. 'Information Regarding the Slackness of Demand for European Cotton Goods', Art. 4, *Selection from the Records of Government, North Western Provinces, part XL* (Allahabad: Government Press, 1864), 118.
11. J.R. Reid, *Reports on the Settlement Operation in the District of Azamgarh: As Also in Parganas Sikandarpur and Bhadaon* (Allahabad: Government Press, 1881), 170.
12. W. Irvine, *Report on the Revising of Records and Settlement Operations in the Ghazipur District, 1880–85* (Allahabad: Government Press, 1886), 127.

13. William Crooke, *The North Western Provinces of India: Their History, Ethnology and Administration* (London: Methuen and Co., 1897), 209–210.
14. Ibid.
15. P.J. Thomas, *Report of the Fact-Finding Committee (Handloom and Mills)* (Delhi: Ministry of Commerce, 1942), 17.
16. Vaman Govind Kale, *Introduction to the Study of Indian Economics* (Poona: Aryabhushan Press, 1922), 274.
17. A. Yusuf Ali, *A Monograph on Silk Fabrics Produced in the North-Western Provinces and Oudh* (Allahabad: Government Press, 1900), 103.
18. *Report of the Indian Tariff Board (Cotton Textile Industry Enquiry)*, vol. III (Calcutta: Government of India Central Publication Branch, 1927), 124.
19. Pandit Champaram Mishra, Replies to the Questionnaire, Report of the United Provinces Provincial Banking Enquiry Committee, 1929–30, vol. III, Evidence (Allahabad Government Press, 1930), 364–365.
20. *RFFC*, 162–163.
21. *Report on the Railway-Borne Traffic of the North-Western Provinces and Oudh, during the year ending March 31, 1882* (Allahabad: Government Press, 1883), 30.
22. William Hoey, *A Monograph on Trade and Manufactures in Northern India* (Lucknow: American Methodist Mission Press, 1880), 28.
23. A. Yusuf Ali, *A Monograph on Silk Fabrics Produced in the North-Western Province and Oudh* (Allahabad: Government Press, 1900), 103.
24. *Report on the Railway-Borne Traffic ... year ending March 31, 1882*, 38.
25. *Report on the Railway-Borne Traffic of the North-Western Provinces and Oudh, during the year ending March 31, 1884* (Allahabad: Government Press, 1884), Appendix A, ii.
26. *Report on the Railway-Borne Traffic ... year ending March 31, 1882. Kamkhab* was sold at ₹125 per yard, and a *sari* or *dupatta* were priced at ₹ 35 per yard. So these types of cloth had an exclusive consumer class.
27. Abdul Bismillah, 'Jhini Jhini Bini Chadariya', personal interview with Qazi Zafar Masood and Imtiyaz Ahmad Julaha, Mubarakpur, 31 January 1998; *Bani* was the system in which the weavers' wages were fixed for a particular cloth and they had to weave cloth from raw material provided by the *grihasta* on their own looms.
28. *Report on the Railway-Borne Traffic of the North-Western Provinces and Oudh during the Year ending 31st March, 1883* (Allahabad: Government Press, 1883), 35.
29. *Report on the Railway-Borne Traffic ... year ending March 31, 1882*, 38.
30. *Report on the Railway-Borne Traffic ... year ending March 31, 1883*, 37.
31. *RFFC*, 63, 66.
32. *East India (Census): General Report of the Census of India, 1901* (London: His Majesty's Stationery Office, 1904), 546; *RFFC*, pp. 68–70.
33. *Report of the R. Burn Committee on Provincial Industries*, Industries Department file 287/1924, 234, Uttar Pradesh State Archive (henceforth UPSA).

34. *Report of the Weaving Schools Committee*, Industries Department file 407/1920, Box 226, UPSA.
35. S.B. Misra, 'What Steps Should be Taken to Further the Development of Co-operation among Weavers?', *Proceedings of Ninth Conference of Registrars of Co-operative Societies in India*, held at Bombay on 12–15 January 1926 (Calcutta: Government of India Central Publication Branch, 1926).
36. Lala Baij Nath, 'On Some of the Leading Industries of Upper India,' *Report of the First Indian Industrial Conference held at Benares on Saturday, December 30, 1905* (Allahabad: The Indian Press, 1906), 311.
37. J.M. Holms, *Rules for Relief of Distressed Weavers*, No. 358/5 of 1908, Dept. XIII, File 40/1905–9, Gorakhpur Commissioner's Record Room.
38. D.L. Drake Brockman, *Azamgarh: A Gazetteer, being Vol. XXXIII of the District Gazetteers of the United Provinces of Agra and Oudh* (Allahabad: Government Press, 1911), 61.
39. Ibid.
40. Rai Sri Ram Bahadur, 'Industrial Conference', *Full Text of the Papers Read at and Submitted to the Industrial Conference, Nainital*, August 1907, 44.
41. *Report of the R. Burn Committee on Provincial Industries*, Industries Department file 287/1924, UPSA.
42. *Annual Reports of the Director of Industries for 1918–19*, Industries Department, file 533/1919, Box 218, UPSA.
43. William Hoey, *A Monograph on Trade and Manufacture of Northern India* (Lucknow: American Methodist Mission Press, 1880), 28.
44. Letter from J.J.D. Latohche, Chief Secretary, NWP&O to Secretary to the GOI, Revenue and Agriculture Department, Proceedings of the Government of NWP&O, for the month of March 1893, Revenue (Scarcity) Department, file 16/1888, Box 1, UPSA.
45. Letter from E. Rose, Collector Ghazipur to J.J.F. Lumsden, Commissioner, Banaras Division, no. 2420/VII 49, Dated 10 April 1888, 'Economic condition of the agricultural and labouring classes in India', Revenue (Scarcity) Department, file 16/1888, Box 1, paragraph 17, UPSA.
46. Ibid.
47. Letter from J.H. Darwin, Deputy Secretary to Government, to the Commissioner, Banaras Division, Nainital, 1 June 1928, Bahadurganj (Ghazipur) Riots, February 1927, Department XX, file 9/1927–28, Azamgarh Collectorate Record Room.
48. *Administrative Report of the Department of Industries and Commerce, United Provinces, for the year ending March 31, 1940* (Allahabad: Government Press, 1941), 13.
49. *Administration Report of the Department of Industries and Commerce, United Provinces, for the year ending March 31, 1941* (Allahabad: Government Press, 1941), 14–15.

REFERENCES

Administrative Report of the Department of Industries and Commerce, United Provinces, for the year ending March 31, 1940. Allahabad: Government Press. 1941.

Administrative Report of the Department of Industries and Commerce, United Provinces, for the year ending March 31, 1941. Allahabad: Government Press. 1941.

Ali, A. Yusuf. *A Monograph on Silk Fabrics Produced in the North-Western Provinces and Oudh*. Allahabad: Government Press. 1900.

Annual Reports of the Director of Industries for 1918–19. Industries Department, file 533/Box 218. Uttar Pradesh State Archive, Lucknow. 1919.

Bahadur, Rai Sri Ram. 'Industrial Conference'. *Full Text of the Papers Read at and Submitted to the Industrial Conference*, Nainital. August 1907.

Bayly, C.A. 'The Origins of Swadeshi (Home Industry): Cloth and Indian society, 1700–1930'. In *The Social Life of Things: Commodities in Cultural Perspective*, edited by A. Appadurai, 285–322. Cambridge: Cambridge University Press, 1986.

Bismillah, Abdul. *Jhini Jhini Bini Chadariya*. New Delhi: Rajkamal Prakashan. 1998.

Brockman, D.L. Drake. *Azamgarh: A Gazetteer, being Vol. XXXIII of the District Gazetteers of the United Provinces of Agra and Oudh*. Allahabad: Government Press. 1911.

Cohn, Bernard S. 'Cloth, Clothes and Colonialism: India in the 19th Century'. In *Cloth and Human Experience*, edited by Weiner A. and J. Schneider, 106–162. Washington: Smithsonian Books. 1989.

Crooke, William. *The North Western Provinces of India: Their History, Ethnology and Administration*. London: Methuen and Co. 1897.

De Jean, Joan. *The Essence of Style: How the French Invented High Fashion, Fine Food, Chic Cafes, Style, Sophistication, and Glamour*. New York: Free Press. 2005.

Delpierre, Madeleine. *Dress in France in the 18th Century*. Translated by Caroline Beamish. New Haven: Yale University Press. 1997.

East India (Census): General Report of the Census of India, 1901. London: His Majesty's Stationery Office. 1904.

Hoey, William. *A Monograph on Trade and Manufacture of Northern India*. Lucknow: American Methodist Mission Press. 1880.

Holms, J.M. *Rules for Relief of Distressed Weavers*, No. 358/5 of 1908, Dept. XIII, File 40/1905–9. Gorakhpur Commissioner's Record Room. 1908.

'Information Regarding the Slackness of Demand for European Cotton Goods'. In Art. 4, *Selection from the Records of Government, North Western Provinces, part XL*. Allahabad: Government Press. 1864.

Irvine, W. *Report on the Revising of Records and Settlement Operations in the Ghazipur District, 1880–85*. Allahabad: Government Press. 1886.

Kale, Vaman Govind. *Introduction to the Study of Indian Economics*. Poona: Aryabhushan Press. 1922.

M. Jones, Jennifer. 'Repackaging Rousseau: Femininity and Fashion in Old Regime France'. *French Historical Studies* 18, no. 4 (1994): 939–967.

Maeder, Edward. *An Elegant Art: Fashion and Fantasy in the 18th Century*. New York: Abrams. 1983.

McGowan, Abigail. *Clothing Matters: Dress and Identity in India*. Chicago: University of *Chicago* Press. 2009.

McNeil, Peter and Giorgio Riello. 'The Art and Science of Walking: Gender, Space, and the Fashionable Body in the Long 18th Century'. *Fashion Theory* 9, no. 2 (2005): 175–204.

Metcalf, Thomas. *Ideologies of the Raj*. Cambridge: Cambridge University Press. 1995.

Mishra, Champaram. Replies to the Questionnaire, *Report of the United Provinces Provincial Banking Enquiry Committee, 1929–30*. Vol. III. Evidence. Allahabad: Government Press. 1930.

Misra, S.B. 'What Steps Should be Taken to Further the Development of Co-operation among Weavers?'. In *Proceedings of Ninth Conference of Registrars of Co-operative Societies in India,* held at Bombay. Calcutta: Government of India Central Publication Branch. 1926.

Nath, Lala Baij. 'On Some of the Leading Industries of Upper India'. In *Report of the First Indian Industrial Conference held at Benares on Saturday, December 30, 1905*. Allahabad: The Indian Press. 1906.

Reid, J.R. *Reports on the Settlement Operation in the District of Azamgarh: As Also in Parganas Sikandarpur and Bhadaon*. Allahabad: Government Press. 1881.

Report of the Indian Tariff Board (Cotton Textile Industry Enquiry), Vol. III. Calcutta: Government of India Central Publication Branch. 1927.

Report of the R. Burn Committee on Provincial Industries. Industries Department file 287. Lucknow: Uttar Pradesh State Archive. 1924.

Report of the Weaving Schools Committee. Industries Department file 407, Box 226. Lucknow: Uttar Pradesh State Archive. 1920.

Report on the Railway-Borne Traffic of the North-Western Provinces and Oudh, during the year ending March 31, 1882. Allahabad: Government Press. 1883.

Report on the Railway-Borne Traffic of the North-Western Provinces and Oudh, during the year ending March 31, 1883. Allahabad: Government Press. 1883.

Report on the Railway-Borne Traffic of the North-Western Provinces and Oudh, during the year ending March 31, 1884. Allahabad: Government Press. 1884.

Ribeiro, Aileen. *The Art of Dress: Fashion in England and France, 1750 to 1820*. New Haven: Yale University Press. 1995.

Roy, Tirthankar. 'Introduction'. In *Artisans and Industrialisation: Indian Weaving in the 20th Century*, 25–30. New Delhi: Oxford University Press. 1993.

——. *Traditional Industry in the Economy of Colonial India*. Cambridge: Cambridge University Press. 1999.

Roy, Tirthankar. 'Acceptance of Innovations in Early 20th-Century Indian Weaving'. *The Economic History Review* 55, no. 3 (2002): 507–532.

Tarlo, Emma. *Clothing Matters: Dress and Identity in India*. Chicago: University of *Chicago* Press. 1996.

Thirsk, Joan. 'The Fantastical Folly of Fashion: The English Stocking Knitting Industry (1500–1700)'. In *Textile History and Economic History: Essays in Honour of Miss Julia de Lacy Mann*, edited by N.B. Harte and K.G. Ponting, 50–73. Manchester: *Manchester* University Press. 1973.

Thomas, P.J. *Report of the Fact-Finding Committee (Handloom and Mills)*. Delhi: Ministry of Commerce. 1942.

Trivedi, Lisa N. *Clothing Gandhi's Nation: Homespun and Modern India*. Bloomington: Indiana University Press. 2007.

10

DEVOTION AND PLEASURE: VANTAGES OF REBELLION

Kota Neelima

yat karosi yad asnasi
yaj juhosi dadasi yat
yat tapasyasi kaunteya
tat kurusva madarpanam

(Whatever you do, whatever you eat, whatever you offer,
whatever you give,
the *tapsya* you do, Kaunteya; think of everything as an offering to Me.)
—*Bhagavad Gita IX.27*

INTRODUCTION

All religions and spirituality are based on the belief that god can be found. It is immaterial that this is contrary to evidence, which shows that god is consistently inaccessible, elusively omnipresent and most probably a concept too vast to be comprehended by the human mind. Instead of being discouraged by its stunning failure to find god, the same human mind continues to constantly search for ways to reach god and achieve some level of conversational informality with god without the mediation of middlemen from the priestly classes.

This is because, to a human being blessed with faith, god is not just a higher purpose or an enduring mystery. God is the visionary and the architect of the entire world as well as of every single life in it. There are three main reasons why such a human being would want to find and reach god. First, there is a long-pending and desperate need to get in touch with the One who 'runs the show' and find some answers to the nagging questions of life and death. Second, understanding god would provide much-needed clarity on the original purpose of the world and the role an individual plays in the grand plan. Third, finding god is essential to the investigation of the 'what', like for instance, what do we accomplish on earth, chasing seemingly pointless objectives while floating through an ominously empty universe? Fourth, only god can answer the 'why' of everything: of *dharma*, *artha*, *kāma*, *moksha* and everything in between.

These and other factors inform the pursuit of god, an activity for minds that are exercised by difficult questions and complicated answers. Or no answers at all. The answers become even more elusive because human beings seem to require both the Unmanifest and the Manifest god. Essentially, the human mind seeks a higher consciousness, a greater 'mind' that possesses all the keys and every secret map of destiny. The individual is naturally inclined towards 'a higher spirit, a guide, a friend, a support' (Radhakrishnan 2006a, 75), who can be petitioned for help, who moves in mysterious ways and who never refuses any version of attachment, devotion, worship or prayer. One can be sure that even if there is conclusive, wide-spread and irrefutable proof that god can never be found or accessed, it will not lead to the end of religion. Like the transitions of the Vedic gods, new gods would be personified from nature, and the show will go on. Also, it helps that there is belief in heaven or a higher plane. Even if god cannot be found on earth and in a lifetime, there is another world where this quest can continue and reach its destination.

This also introduces the moral dimension and provides insights into the conceptualisation of societies and their organisation. The key word is *dharma*, around which the narratives of right and wrong, good and evil, just and unjust are woven. But *dharma* also extends to rituals, religious ceremonies, customs, and laws of justice, rules of power and even rites of penance (Hacker 2009, 479). Such *dharma* has been instrumental in structuralising human communities because it promises the ideal life or a life that god would approve of. In other words, people organise themselves in a better way and for better results in the belief that they are being watched in their public and private life by a divine witness.

The divine panopticon over mortal life guides individuals and communities to define themselves and judge as well as decide their future. It is under the god's benevolent yet critical eye that the human life is led, and there is fear of consequences for those who stray from the defined path. For those who follow the path, on the other hand, there is peace, order, fulfilment of wishes and contentment that they serve god through their own morality and goodness. For all this to happen, however, there is a prerequisite—devotion. The concepts surrounding *dharma* can find resonance only if people are devoted to god and feel the divine presence within as a constant companion who cannot be betrayed at any moment in life. Devotion, therefore, is critical for establishing communities, societies and nations. However, a major contradiction lies at the heart of devotion itself.

Devotion, paradoxically, is an act of revolt against the systematic existence that the civilisational project must promote. Unlike religion, devotion falls outside the perimeters of aspiration and achievement. This includes post-regimented desire for freedom, which arises from within the structure and is a revolt against the framework. Devotion is also more than freedom; it is happiness. It is not only beyond all structures but also refuses to recognise them. The objective of finding god leads to a consistent defiance of all norms and a regular pleasure in doing so.

Such pleasure of devotion, protected internally in the privacy of thought, manifests itself externally through the ways of religion. This chapter interrogates devotion and pleasure and examines whether the externalisation of symbolic religion and spirituality provides context for the internal devotional space, or if it is the other way around. The hypothesis is that devotion is an internal subversive counteraction fulfilled through external reference points of pleasure and that all god-making is inherently a connection with the self's inherent desire for choice, freedom and *ānanda* or bliss. The defiance of devotion is the spatial transference and objectification of the abstract and the pleasure obtained from the subversive pursuit of the Inaccessible through very accessible, simple activities (Figure 10.1).

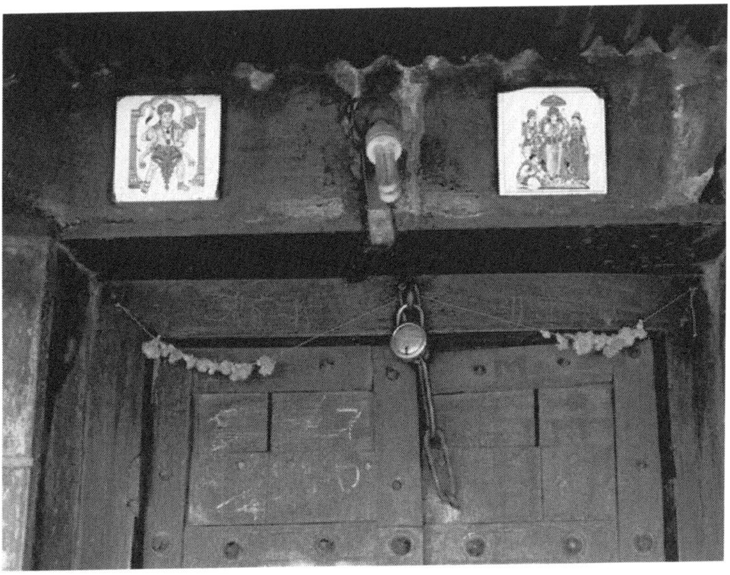

Figure 10.1: The Watching God: Moral Stories of *Rāmāyaṇa* are the Guiding Force in the Form of Images Over the Front Door of a Village Home in Patoda *Taluka* of Marathwada in Maharashtra, India (Photo by the Author, 2019)

DEFIANCE OF DEVOTION

Devotion is a voluntary state of oneness with god that is attained through internal and external measures, which create and recreate this state at various degrees of intensity and achievement. The three ways of finding salvation in the *Bhagavad Gita* are *jnana yoga* or knowledge, *karma yoga* or action and *bhakti yoga* or devotion. Of these, *bhakti yoga* is the most preferred path because it transcends the rules of society and religion. Finding salvation through the *bhakti marga* or way of devotion also signifies a defiance towards the established rites of passage to reach god. It is inherent in this path that a devotee walks alone and abides by nothing but god. Like all things spiritual, devotion defies normative and doctrinal explanations but appears to rely on the circumstance of rituals. At the same time, like all things ritual, devotion defies interpretative and deductive evidence but seems to depend on the *atman* or the soul of the devotee. The defiance of devotion to paradigmatic descriptions is most evident in the paradox of the personal or the 'interior' god and the 'public' god.

The interior god defies imposed forms and is continuous with the infinite, formless Absolute. The veneration of such an Absolute requires non-locational and non-referential faith, with no rules, no restrictions and no penalties. The personalisation of god symbolises that which the devotee very well knows cannot be symbolised. When places of worship are defined, the One who is everywhere and nowhere is made to belong 'somewhere'. But such location of the Absolute in time and space is an act of the highest and the purest objectification that the human mind is capable of. Yet, the same mind is not always satisfied by this attempt of religion and knows that the Absolute is not bound by the walls of a sanctum. It knows that that which is bound cannot be the Absolute. As Radhakrishnan (2006a, 97) says, 'If God is perfect, religion is impossible; if God is imperfect, religion is ineffective'. So, if the Manifest is necessary for all faith and religion, then it is also necessary that devotion be free of all religion. Devotion hacks its way through the forest of ceremonial religion and normative spirituality to arrive at its own inner temple and inner sanctum.

But the forest is thickest close to the destination. Both spiritual and ritualistic religion appear to guard the entry points into their fold. There are rules to do worship or *puja*, to do *dhyanam* or meditate and even for *darshan* or to see god. Devotion defies all regulation through its depth of intent, most vividly evident in the imagining of the interior god. This internal veneration is a protest against agencies that regularly appropriate and externalise the divine. But such regimentation is also a human creation, and it is also the reason why the rebellion of devotion is inevitable. The interior god is the result of the exclusion from regulatory religious and spiritual practices; it is disobedience of the same heart which envisages universal love and consciousness. The space outside the strict constructs of religion and spirituality is populated by devotees who engage with god not out of the fear of right or wrong, or the hope of heaven or fear of hell, but merely for the pleasure of the constant companionship of god. God is personalised through a continuous sharing of the life and times of the devotee. The interior god knows the troubles, triumphs and aspirations of ordinary people without them articulating these, and in return, people ensure that their life lives up to the expectations of their god. Internalisation of god makes devotion a highly individualistic and immersive experience. However, as no two devotees are the same, no two interior gods can be similar; and this, ironically, feeds the cautionary urge against chaos and the need for regulated spaces of religion and spirituality to converge millions of individual experiences into the pursuit of one single public god.

The public god is the focus of all devotion and a reflection of the infinite divine interiorities carried to the temples in the hearts of the devotees. The targeted devotion in a place of worship socialises an interior god and treats all devotion as equal. This is achieved by outsourcing the pleasure of devotion to neutral and qualified mediators, and rightly so. But the distance at which the devotee is from actually conducting the rituals at a temple deepens their bond with their interior god. As a result, the interior god becomes the primary god with whom the devotee spends an entire lifetime. This defiance of devotion is at the heart of the revolutionary question that Arjuna asks in the *Bhagavad Gita* (XII.1): who is wiser between the two—those who *paryupasate* or properly worship the god or those who meditate upon the *avyaktam* or the Unmanifest? Lord Krishna answers that all devotees are dear to Him but praises those who take the difficult path to know the Unmanifest (*Bhagavad Gita* XII.2–5).

Devotion is also the individual assertion of one's access to the Inaccessible divine. In the outer world, the vast area outside places of worship is strewn with the evidence of the 'Inaccessible' god. In the internal world, the heart of the devotee is filled with faith in the Accessible god. The inner world exists in defiance of the outer and exerts influence over the outer world to become more like the inner.

Devotion mediates this transformation by accommodating the religio-spiritual quest through spatio-temporal pathways while finding alternative access to god. Despite such defiance, devotion remains an integral part of structured faith because access to god is at the heart of all conceptualisations of religion and spirituality. And as intuitively as the mind comprehends the difficulty of this construct, it knows that religion and spirituality are not about making god accessible; they are about making god 'less' inaccessible. This marks an enduring failure that continuously inspires devotion to search deeper, farther and also closer. However, as the failure is shared, it levels the playing field for all human beings, whether a devout thief or a devout sanyasi, creating scope for conscious humanism and a sense of common destiny. And also a sense of common defiance, because devotion not only equalises failure to find god without but also equalises the finding of the god 'within'.

Then why does devotion endure, through centuries of progress and modernisation? Is it because the human mind must chase that which is inaccessible in the hope of finding a larger, greater purpose and plan? The *jnana* or knowledge and the intuition that god cannot be accessed in the worldly manner adds to the allure of god. The mind is fatigued with the achievable, the immediate and the temporary. The Inaccessible preserves its permanence, which is also dynamic and changes with the times. The knowing mind has endured the reality check of the Inaccessible god through devotion to the Accessible one. Devotion reassures the mind that there is no dichotomy between the two; the difference is merely in geography between the internal temple and the external one. Devotion covers the internal distance instantly to find itself proximal to the Unknown, who is willing to travel to the limits of imagination and play the role of a friend, a companion and a guide, besides being the omniscient Absolute. With every such act of devotion, the mind senses a movement closer to its objective and a merger of the sensations of god with those of the devotee.

Devotion is an act of immersion and a point of convergence where no difference exists between the sensory and the spiritual. The mind deconstructs all *karma*, and slows down *kaala*, to separate each movement in the pursuit of god for its own criticality. It is indulgence of the soul and individualisation of the abstraction called god. The inaccessibility is sign of the Immortal who does not vary depending on cause and effect. In this personalisation, there is the ownership of time and space in the mortal world, and the satisfaction of the self that carries around the source of its own happiness, independent of the outside world (Figure 10.2).

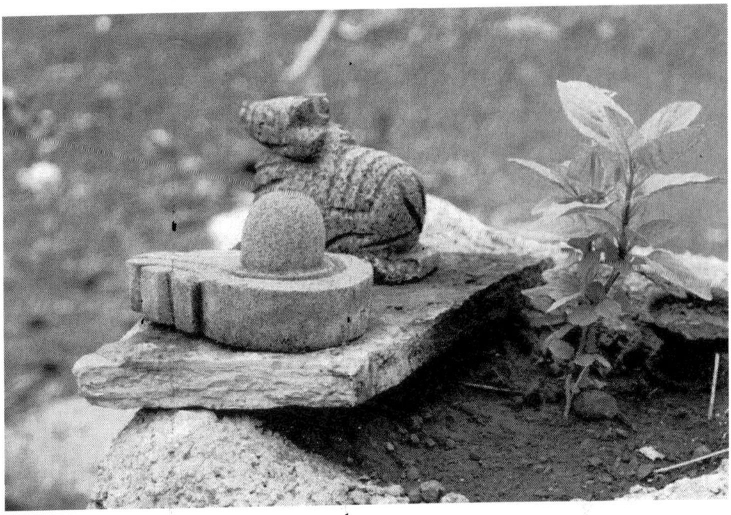

Figure 10.2: Personal Gods: Hand-Crafted Figurines of Lord Shiva and Nandi Next to a *Tulasi* Plant in a Rural Front Yard in Gevrai *Taluka* of Marathwada in Maharashtra, India (Photo by the Author, 2019)

Pleasure, therefore, is an important part of devotion, because the knowing mind constructs the methods in which personal happiness can be repeatedly recreated and maintained. The public god provides every opportunity to the devotee to conjure the signifiers for devotion to the interior god. Socialised devotion, even though it is endorsed by religion, intensifies the isolation of the devotee. It is also because the pursuit of the Inaccessible is a friendly chase in a beautiful garden and not a dusty race for a coveted trophy. The inner state provides the intimacy necessary to experience the pleasures of devotion, which the public participation may not facilitate. But for the devotee, there is an easy equality and interchangeability between the social state of devotion and the 'non-social' state of devotion, because the pursuit of god is seamless and unconditional.

The defiance of devotion is an everyday construct of normalised interiority. For example, the taxi driver who keeps a flower at god's idol in the car is reaching out to the Inaccessible to the same extent as the person who has climbed 4,000 steps to a place of worship on a mountain. The distressed person who prays to god in a hospital has as much ownership over the Inaccessible as the one who, expressing gratitude, dedicates a new house to god. The result of the pursuit in all cases is happiness, and this internalisation of devotion provides pleasure at every turn and in every moment.

THE ACCESSIBLE GOD

Altering with each consciousness, devotion also expands the meaning and purpose of the pursuit of god. Like all revolts, discontent is at the heart of devotion. The restlessness with the momentary propels the search for more enduring versions—of god and of the human being. Unlike *jnana*, which may be timeless but still has to be acquired, devotion is inherent, as *Shandilya Bhakti Sutra* (I.1.vii) says. Therefore, devotion is a social equaliser as well as a practical one. Irrespective of the class, caste or even actions of the individual, they can be devout.

Both *jnana* and *karma* serve *bhakti* to help reach the ultimate objective. *Jnana* and *karma* are evolutionary and dynamic and also dialectical and democratic, but even at their most directional, they appear self-referential to the discerning mind. Both fail to impress because they are temporary and fall short of the larger, deeper impact that a lifetime can make. As a solution to this, the Manifest god intersects action and knowledge with devotion to create a higher purpose in pursuit of a greater truth.

The rituals around Manifest god mark the various levels to be crossed for reaching the Unmanifest Absolute. The worship of the Manifest is functionally critical in the modern age because it is the most accessible for *archana* or worship (Tirumala 2016, 35–36). In essence all the forms, as *Bhagavad Gita* (IV.6) states, represent the same Unmanifest. The diversity allows devotion to be manifold and more adaptable to the external challenges of change. Whether devotion leads to the manifestations or it is the other way around could be debated in the context of *jnana* and *karma*. But the impact of the Manifest has been to establish flexible parameters of the internal space for devotion and the merging of the *karma* of worship with the *jnana* of context and the *bhakti* of the Unmanifest.

The unification of the Manifest and the Unmanifest at the level of devotion offers an important insight into the nature of the *atman*, or the human soul. As an objective of the devotion within, the *sakara* and the *nirakara* are non-contradictory. The form is only a distinction and not a distraction from the original, and the *atman* is aware of its unconflicted nature. Perhaps that is because the *atman* itself is made of everything (Olivelle 2009, 76). As *Brhadaranyaka Upanisad* (IV.4.v) says,

> *tejomayo'tejomayah kamamayo'kamamayah,*
> *krodhamayo 'krodhamayo dharmamayo' dharmamayah*
>
> *(made of light and of light-less, of desire and of desire-less, of anger and of anger-less, of dharma and of adharma)*

The Manifest is an impression of the Unmanifest, and it is equally dear and divine. The difference is in the perception of pleasure between the two. Devotion to the Manifest is the actualisation of an internal conversation on the pleasure of devotion to the Unmanifest. So then, what kind of pleasure is not real: the devotion to the public god or to the interior god? Both are real, but the Manifest has its advantages. The mind seeks something tangible to believe in, something that can be touched and felt, like the *tilak* on the forehead or a symbol to be worn. The human need for an external manifestation of the inner, private god is the reason for the inevitability of the *sakara saguna Brahmā*.

The objective of the devotion to the Manifest is access and, like all access, it is referential. Access through various means—rituals, people or places—creates reference points that can be accomplished. The access is a sensory experience that actualises feelings of pleasure as well as pain. When a pilgrimage is of particular difficulty, it holds a special place in the hearts of the devotees. The same is true also for rituals and practices that demand perseverance and exertion. The pleasure obtained from overcoming the ordinariness of pain neutralises the physical world for the devotee. Endurance, discipline, austerity and other such qualities associated with religious practices challenge the human nature and the sociocultural habits, to facilitate self-realisation.

The internal impact of these external reference points, however, varies from individual to individual. Tangibility makes god accessible to the degree to which the devotee assigns value to the external reference point. To this is added the significance of these points, such as the locational powers of a pilgrimage or the effects of ritual. Cultural and community mobilisation around festivals, places of worship and religious ceremonies assist in socialising devotion and making it part of individual identity. Participatory devotion endorses the public god as well as the personal god. Sharing the public god encourages the devotees to build sociocultural structures with the Manifest god at the centre. Life plays out in reference to this Manifest. The sensory experience of access, therefore, naturalises as the main path towards the Inaccessible. But there can be many such paths, and the question arises on the difference.

Difference in access is at the heart of the important verse that speaks of the vast and inclusive vantages of the *Bhagavad Gita*. The *Gita* (VII.21) says that the *bhakta* or the devotee may *architum* or worship god in any way that they *icchati* or desire and with *shraddha* or faith, and that god shall make that faith *achalam* or steady and support it. There is no lesser or greater god, there are no lesser or greater devotees and, therefore, there is no lesser or greater religion. This verse endorses diversity of manifestations as the result of the unending search of the devotee to find the right path to god. Therefore, it is also a warning of the possible discontent in the experience of religion. But, as Radhakrishnan (2009, 10) asks, 'If religion is experience, the question arises, what is it that is experienced? No two religious systems seem to agree in their answers to this question'. The question is profound; it is not just about imagining god but also about the 'experience' of god. This is an important step in understanding the source of the pleasure of devotion and the reason why all pathways to god eventually lead one inwards to the self.

Devotion towards the higher realities of god necessitates that devotion must examine the internal first. The self is the gateway to all devotion, and devotion necessitates a separation of the self from the Higher Self of god. The question that arises then is: what is the reason for the existence of devotion? What identifies the devotee with god in a way that any separation is possible only by the end of the self itself, or in death? These questions foray into the intense and highly addictive debate on whether god and the self are the same or different entities, and whether religion is right in trying to return the self to god. This question, like some of the greatest philosophical inquiries of human thought, has been variedly answered through the ages. Here are some of the answers: the self is either (i) part of god, (ii) not part of god, (iii) form of god, (iv) is god or (v) is just the self. If there are other possibilities, they are further proof of the spectacular journey of the question across over a few thousand years.

In the context of devotion, every one of these definitions of the self is important. This is for two reasons; one, the self's infinite *upadhi* or attributes create a variety of paths to god; and two, the self's essential purity makes it identify with the divine and seek god. Narada argues that the self is born and reborn into *samsara* not due to the lack of knowledge but due to a desire for devotion. The 'fire' of devotion destroys the *ahamkara* in the self, which is the cause of the separation of the self from god. Forgetting the self and identifying it with god leads to *mukti*, says Shandilya. *Mukti*, which may also be interpreted as freedom from the world, is the objective of *para bhakti* or the highest form of devotion. Besides this, there are 81 lesser states of devotion, as per the choice of objectives and activities (Sinha 1998a, xvi–xx). While in *para bhakti* the devotee only seeks *mukti*, in the lower forms of devotion, the devotee seeks the world. Consequently, focusing on *mukti* or release from the world provides greater peace to the self rather than the temporary fulfilment of worldly desires.

These and other accesses to god are varied and still evolving. Experientially, access can be of multiple kinds, and the following is a select list. The first access is physical, and is available in places of worship, which the devotee will reach through the rigours of travel and planning. The second is the sensory access, where the human senses recognise the similarities between the human form and the form of god. The third access is discipline that creates pathways to staying in the vicinity of god. The fourth kind is storytelling, to conversationalise the divine. The fifth access is portability, where the physical presence of god is reimagined in places outside the places of worship. The sixth access is the systemisation of god through regularisation in culture, society and power. The above-mentioned are but a glimpse of the mind's need for a nobler entity to live and die for (Figure 10.3).

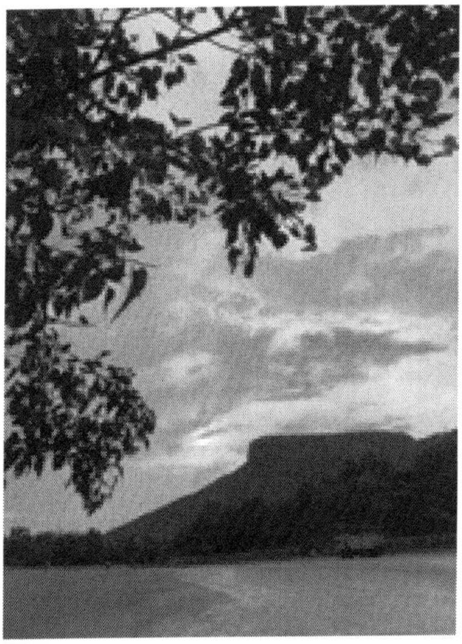

Figure 10.3: Access to the Unmanifest: A Speaking Sky at Alipiri (*Aadi Padi*), the First Step towards the Tirumala Temple, Andhra Pradesh, India (Photo by the Author, 2019)

Access normalises the divine, but only for the devout. Without devotion, the access to places of worship, performance of rituals and participation in a display of faith are devoid of context. The defiance of devotion ensures that there are no entry-point checks. Devotion constitutes a relationship with god, and anyone can enter into it unconditionally. And further, devotion is the sign of a free soul. The breaking free of the soul from the shackles of the material world is internal and invisible. As the detachment of the *atman* increases, there is a growing attachment with god. This bond is absolute and *anuraktih*, and this attachment is supreme (*Shandilya Bhakti Sutra* I.1.ii).

Devotion ensures that the idea of god is a tactile, tangible feeling that can be regenerated with faith and a little bit of practice. Unlike the inaccessible Absolute, who is *nischala* and *nirbheda*, the Accessible god undergoes modernisations with humanity and is constantly made contemporary. The changing god, whether through popular culture or through urbanised rituals, adds to the pleasure of accessibility. True, the moment the rules are fixed on how one's devotion must materialise, the devotion transforms into religion and spirituality. But the reinterpretations, often suspected of dilution, instead strengthen devotion towards the changing god. For example, for the Hindu festival of Ganesh Chaturthi, when the *Ganapati* idol is made with environment-friendly materials, the god has only become more beloved and more precious. Rebellion, therefore, is intrinsic to devotion, as it is to the self.

THE TANGIBILITY OF PLEASURE

The mere fact that a large section of humanity has been dedicated, through most of history, to being devoted to a higher power proves the human mind's love for the abstract. It also points to the successful conversion of devotion into physical applications that, even though only representative, have endured through time.

Religion is applied devotion. Desire and devotion are intertwined with causation, because the *atman* contains all desire and is also devoid of any desire (*Brhadaranyaka Upanisad* IV.4.v). Devotion without desire is highly problematic because the idea of seeking salvation is also a desire. Desire for worldly things is driven by the pleasure of acquiring the outside. Devotion is driven by the pleasure of acquisition of the inside. The highest devotion prefers the One beyond all the acquisitions of the world. But even the will to leave the world is a desire, and there is pleasure in finding ways of rejecting other, lower pleasures. Pleasure usually has moral value fixed to it and is always in danger of slipping down on the *karmic* scale. Like, for example, the distinction drawn between what is 'good' and what is 'pleasant' (*Kaṭha Upaniṣad* I.2.i).

This is not the case when it comes to devotion, as even the extreme isolation that a devotee feels away from god is pleasurable along with the pain of waiting for divine guidance or companionship. This is because devotion at source is *nishkama bhakti* or devotion that desires nothing and that which is *nirupadhi bhakti* or without attributes. Such devotion is also self-dependent through knowledge and action, and it is self-realised (Sinha 1998a, xviii–xxi). Nothing that emerges directly from the self and reflects the *atman* can be easily categorised or explained. The wide variety of perspectives on devotion reveal its dimensions, which seem to cover the scope of human thought, imagination as well as individual nature. Following is a sample of this ocean, in the form of a list of the kinds, phases, forms and types of devotion.

1. Kinds of devotion: Religious references provide a glimpse of the diverse kinds of devotion, all of which are variants of the pleasure the devotee derives from *bhakti*. Following is a brief list, based on the *Narada Bhakti Sutras* and *Shandilya Bhakti Sutras* of the textual references from the stories of god and devotion:

   (i) *Sammana* or honour: The devotee honours both friends and enemies alike because he/she finds divinity in everyone.
   (ii) *Bahumana* or reward: The devotee finds great joy in the service of god, whatever may be the activity.
   (iii) *Prīti* or fondness: The devotee loves any action or thought that is about god.
   (iv) *Viraha* or separation: The devotee is extremely sad to be separated from god.
   (v) *Itara-vicikitsa* or disinterest: The devotee does not care for anyone/anything but god.
   (vi) *Mahima-khyati* or glory: The devotee is ecstatic when glorifying god.
   (vii) *Tadartha prana sthana* or purpose: The devotee finds purpose to live only in god.
   (viii) *Tadiyata* or belonging: The devotee believes everything belongs to god.
   (ix) *Sarva-tad-bhava* or being: The devotee believes everything is god.
   (x) *A-pratikulya* or harmony: The devotee is never in opposition to god.

2. Phases of devotion: There is pleasure in discovering how every facet of devotion to god is a perfect match to the various aspects of the soul itself. It is a small wonder then that the long history of devotion is a map of the pathways that meander through life and society looking for god, and finally return to the *atman*. The following nine phases of devotion, based on the *Shandilya Bhakti Sutras* (Yati 1991, 137), are a roadmap:

   (i) *Shravanam* or listening to the glory of god
   (ii) *Kirtanam* or reciting the stories of god
   (iii) *Smaranam* or remembering god at all times
   (iv) *Padasevanam* or service at the feet of god
   (v) *Archanam* or worship of god
   (vi) *Vandanam* or veneration of god
   (vii) *Dasyam* or dedication to god

(viii) *Sakhyam* or friendship with god
(ix) *Atma nivedanam* or self-surrender to god

3. Forms of devotion: More specifically, there are ways in which the human mind might lose itself in devotion, so much so that there is no difference between the sensory and the spiritual experiences. The following list is based on *Narada Bhakti Sutras* (Sinha 1998a, xviii), on how this could transpire:

(i) *Leela* or the singing of and listening to god's names and stories
(ii) *Nistha* or a stable and constant worship
(iii) *Ruci* or great inclination towards devotion
(iv) *Asakti* or deep interest in devotion
(v) *Rupa asakti* or interest in the form of god
(vi) *Mahatmya asakti* or interest in the greatness of god
(vii) *Puja asakti* or interest in worship
(viii) *Dasaya asakti* or interest in service to god
(ix) *Sakhya asakti* or interest in friendship with god
(x) *Vatsalya asakti* or interest in god as a parent
(xi) *Kanta asakti* or interest in god as a consort
(xii) *Atma nivedana asakti* or interest in the soul's surrender to god
(xiii) *Tanmaya asakti* or losing oneself in devotion to god

4. Types of devotion: As the earlier sections demonstrate, devotion is all-encompassing and finds representation in a myriad, mesmerising ways in the world of the devotee. A lot of what religion is, depends heavily on how this world is translated by the devotee from the privacy of their mind to the public sphere. This makes devotion subjective to the devotee and, as discussed earlier, to the individualised contexts for the pursuit of god. Every devotee is different, but the *Gita* (VII 16) gives a unique view of the devotee seen from the divine perspective:

caturvidha bhajante mam
janah sukrtino arjuna
arto jijnasur artharthi
jnani ca bharatarsabha

There are *caturvidha* or four kinds of devotion to god: that which aims at relief from problems, that which desires wealth in return, that which seeks advantages and that which seeks knowledge. This broad categorisation covers mainly two sorts of devotion; that which seeks this world and that which does not. The latter is the most intriguing type, not just because of its search for the Unmanifest but also because it gives more pleasure to the devotee. There is no gap between the god and the devotee, no more distance to be traversed, when the devotion is *ekabhakti* or is single-mindedly focussed on the Absolute. This oneness dissolves all duality of the *atman* and the interior god—a reason why the *jnani* or the wise prefer this. God is very dear to such devotees and such devotees are very dear to god: '*Priyo hi jnanino tyartham, aham sa ca mama priyah*' (*Bhagavad Gita* VII 17).

5. Devotion and pleasure: Essentially, it matters neither who the devotee is nor why he or she is seeking god; only the intensity of their devotion matters. The subtle rebellion of thinking of god even when not at worship or in religious places provides the pleasure of togetherness with god. This pleasure is experienced through conventional and unconventional ways, none of which can be controlled or charted by any religion. There can be, after all, no framework for happiness.

   (i) The pleasure of effort: Devotion and the pursuit of god are far more pleasurable when the effort put into the act of worship is particularly substantial. A temple at the top of a hill, therefore, may require more input from the devotee, and is therefore dearer to the devotee. It tests her or his devotion by testing the physical or the mental strength to reach the temple. Therefore, an external and arduous journey is also symbolic of the internal journey. (Figure 10.4)

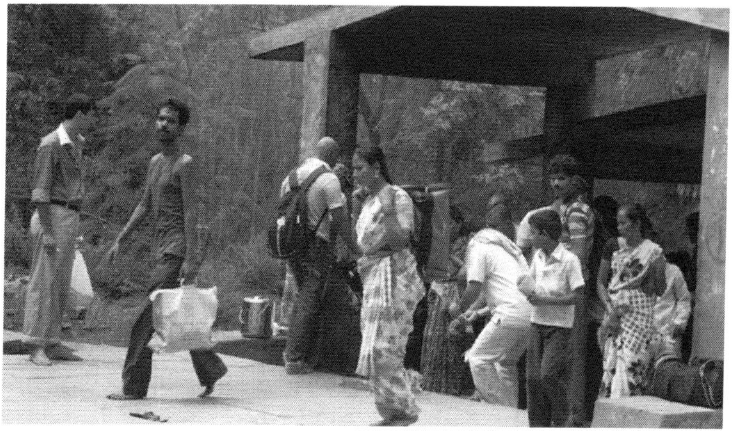

Figure 10.4: To the Temple Within: Devotees Climb the Sacred Venkatachala Mountain Barefoot, Heading towards Lord Sri Venkateshwara Temple in Tirumala, Andhra Pradesh, India (Photo by the Author, 2019)

The length of the way is also a period of contemplation. Hills and mountains assist in assigning a higher position to places of worship. But, as in the case of the Tirumala temple of Lord Sri Venkateshwara, these also reward the pilgrim with a meaningful journey. The distance of over 9 km uphill is covered daily by devotees who walk up the 3,500 steps. The Venkatachala mountain itself, where the temple is situated, is worshipped as god before the ascent. Every step that a devotee takes on that mountain is with gratitude and happiness that the journey towards god will be accomplished soon in the physical world (Neelima 2012, 207–210).

The places of worship of the Accessible god are surrounded by rituals of secondary access. These contextualise the glory of god and the reasons for worship. The devotee, however, may or may not consign her or his devotion to ritualistic justification or spiritual positioning but can merely participate in these activities and derive pleasure in their representative beauty and serenity. The offering of *naivedyam* or food is a crucial part of personification of god in the *archa* form. The rules of *naivedyam* at the Tirumala temple are guided by the rules of Agama Shastra, and after the offering, this food is distributed among the pilgrims as *prasadam*. Every day, hundreds of ingredients are carefully procured and mixed in perfect quantities to be cooked with great love and dedication for the offering in the sanctum. Then, the food is distributed with immense care and diligence to the millions of waiting devotees. Such an effort is considered a blessing, and such a service a pleasure and a matter of good fortune (Dikshitulu and Neelima 2016).

(ii) The pleasure of ritual: The Manifest god receives worship in the form of *puja* through sacred rituals following prescribed rules. There may be different kinds of rituals, but a simple *puja* consists of offerings of very basic nature, such as flowers, water, turmeric powder, *kumkum* and the like. The more complex *puja* requires several sequences of *upacara* or services accompanied by ritual *mantras* or recitations. Significantly, any ritual done in contemplation of god, without any training, knowledge of the *mantras* or *upacaras* or even many offerings is also considered *puja* (Buhnemann 1988, 29–30).

The ritual circumstance has its own significance in the different forms of worship. Each ritual reimagines a particular event or feeling that has been attributed to god. This allows an access point for immersion. Immersive experiences are facilitated through rituals, and devotion makes it possible for the boundary between the real and the imagined to be dissolved, even if only momentarily.

Personal conduct, strict timing, the quality of food and water, and the rigidity of the rules of the rituals are some factors of devotion. The constant demand on the devotee to improve her or his life is achieved in the service of god. This is a way to get in touch with the divinity within and discover tangible connections with god.

At the same time, it does not matter what one offers to god, as long as it is offered with love. The *Bhagavad Gita* (IX. 26) says,

pattram puspam phalam toyam
yo me bhaktya prayacchati
tad aham bhaktyupahrtam
asnami prayatatmanah

As the *Gita* says, everything that is offered with devotion, be it a leaf, a flower, a fruit or just water, is acceptable to god. The offering is immaterial; what matters is the devotion. In other words, devotion does not have to be in any form or framework, such affection is free to choose what it wants to be.

(iii) The pleasure of song: Devotion finds the highest expression in lyrics of love and dedication, seen in the diverse expanse of *bhakti* poetry in India. The highest form of devotion is singing, says *Shandilya Bhakti Sutra* (II. ii.56–57). Every imagining of god, from the plucking of flowers to the contemplation of the universe, is an act of pleasure. There is also an intense knowledge in the lyrics that praise the physical and the accessible actions, to say that even the simplest actions can open the eternal path to the divine. Thyagaraja personifies and de-personifies god through his timeless *kirtanas* in a magnificent movement between the two realms of thought, creating and erasing dualities. The spectacular transcendence in Thyagaraja *kirtanas* is due to the fearless rebellion against all rules of thought. In a way, it is like love, as he sings in the composition, *Marugela ra:*

Annee neevanuchu antaranga muna
Thinnaga veydaki thelisi kontinayya

(I learnt when I searched deep within that everything is You.)
The pleasure of the worship of god, and the slow and deliberate ceremonies move the heart of the devotee. Every word is a key to an interior door, as in the composition,

Gandhamu puyyaruga:
Tilakamu didargua kasturi tialakamu diddaruga;
Kalakala manu mukhakala gani sokkuchu;
Palukula amrutamu lolikaydu swamiki.

(Will you not apply the tilak of kasturi, on the forehead of the god who looks so good and speaks so sweetly?)

Pujalu sayyaruga, mansara pujalu sayyragu;
Jaajulu mari virivajajulu davanamu;
Raajitha thygaraja nuthiniki.

(Will you not worship with all your hearts,
with every fragrant flower and leaf, the One Thyagaraja venerates?)

The personalisation is a rebellion in the case of Meera against the socio-cultural impositions of her time. The stunning defiance in Meera *bhajans* is a testimony of the unequivocal merger with the interior god and her assertion to the exterior world that this is a viable choice. She gives up sensory sustenance of the outside world for the spiritually nourishing love of the god within. Meera's poetry contemporises disbelief and holds the world at a distance, studying it with the disdain of a rebel, as if from the window of a temple of her own. She sings in the following composition, *Ab to mera*:

Ab to mera Shyam naam dusra na koi

(There is only the name of god for me, and no other)

Ab toh baat phayl gaye, jaane sab koy;
Dasi Meera Lal Girdhar, honi ho soh hoy

(It is now well known; I serve only god, no matter what.)

Beyond the rituals and the ceremonial worship, the world of the devotee is filled with an anticipation of god because god is everything and every emotion. So there is pleasure in waiting for god, in longing for god and in thinking of life as a medium to reach god. Meera sings this in *Ghadii eka nahi:*

Panth nihaarun dagar buharoon ubhi marg joye;
Meera ke prabhu, kabre milogey, tum miliyo sukh hoy

(I wait at the path, preparing it;
Meera's god, when will You come for me, so I can rest in peace and happiness.)

VANTAGES OF REBELLION

Devotion is a comprehensive subversion of the visible, tangible world, in favour of the invisible and intangible god. It is often simplified as dedication to god, and often to the accessible forms of god, because these seem the shortest route to the Inaccessible. Devotion creates a world of possibilities of finding god, which can then be processed through religion, rituals and the inner world of spirituality. However, as this chapter endeavoured to establish, devotion is a much more complex and a much more irreverent version of religion than what religions would like the pious to believe. Hinduism serves as the classroom of learning about this aspect of devotion for two reasons: one, the Hindu path is both external as well as internal; it is ritualistic as well as spiritual, and so are its reference points, and two, the ideation of Hinduism is universal, inclusive of the rebel as well as the follower. It provides the basis for combined consciousness and thought, which seek to represent the quest of entire mankind since the beginning of time (Figure 10.5).

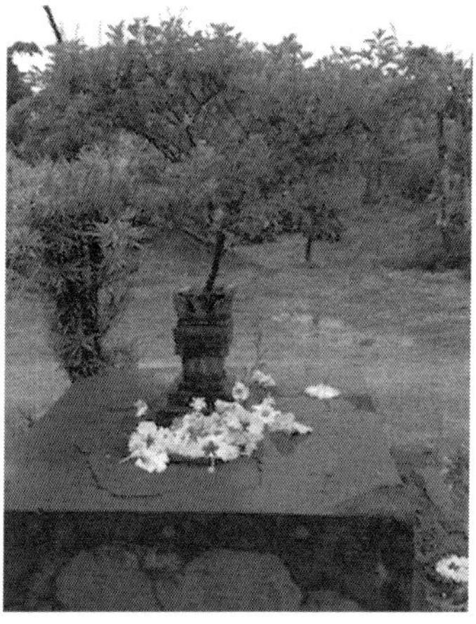

Figure 10.5: A Simple Worship: Flowers of the Garden Soon after the Morning *Puja* at a Village Home in Shimoga *Taluka*, Karnataka, India (Photo by the Author, 2020)

Devotion has two indefatigable vantages of rebellion: interiorisation and individualisation. Interiorisation is the curation of an internal space for the contemplation and worship of god, distinct from the rest of the community, group, household and the like. A sovereignty is established over this personal space, which is upheld by faith. Such a space maintains its own contours, which cannot be infringed upon by the activities taking place beyond its borders. It does not abide by the outside construct of religion, neither does it adhere to the established ways of finding god. While it charts new ways of reaching out into the world to look for god, it also makes deeper inroads into the soul to find the divine within. This allows a full expression and freedom to the self, which now identifies more with the devotee than the individual. Perception of such duality entrenches the separation of the public and private space and further demarcates the personal god from the public one. Thus, the interiority continuously creates its own cause and effect—except that not all external stimuli lead to an external reaction. Therefore, paradoxically, it is necessary for the internal rebellion that the self remain attached to the world so that it may become aloof from it.

Further, the superiority of the internal over the external is known only to the devotee. The proximity to god in the internal space is too abstractly constant to be compared to the elusive results of religious activities in the physical world. Also, the exterior derives any meaning only if it can resonate in this interior space of devotion. Religion is an attempt to socialise the private space of devotion so that a common devotional territory can be found populated with devotees seeking an external manifestation of the internal god. However, this throws light on the second vantage of the rebellion of devotion—individualisation.

Individualisation recovers god from the clutches of the logical world, which requires demonstrability and repetition of observable phenomenon before supporting it with sociopolitical systems and elevating it to fact. The devotee is assisted by various civilisational structures that construct and maintain an environment conducive for the smooth and productive functioning of the society. For example, individuals' rights and freedom allow people to thrive within a framework that has been tried and tested for desired results, such as peace, wealth, order and stability. All structures contain an inherent seed of revolt, even if they were built by choice and in pursuit of freedom. The first moment of a structure's existence coincides with the first thought of its ultimate end. The mind constantly searches for the space beyond the walls, whether real or imaginary, even though it obeys the rules that uphold such walls. No rule, however, can restrain the mind from mentally living in a vast space that has no lines and corners, no centres and peripheries, no insiders and outsiders. Interestingly, this inherent rebellion of the mind is despite the knowledge that the systems will not support such conduct. The preference given to the observable phenomenon has no impact on the wandering of the mind, whether into the depths of the universe or of the soul. In a way, all history is a record of the insecurities with this tendency of the human mind to be incurably free.

The subversion of the devotee is not unrequited. Individualisation of devotion is facilitated because god also individualises the devotee. As the *Gita* (IX. 34) says,

mam evai syasi yuktvai 'vam
atmanam matparayanah.

(*Seek me with your soul and I shall come to you.*)

The vantages of pleasure and devotion allow the reinterpretation of god for an individual and by an individual. God may be thought of and worshipped outside the limits set forth by the scripted rules and in a way that best suits the individual. Whatever may be the conduct outside, the devotee may within have a different and direct interaction with god. There are restraints in the external world, but in the internal world, there are no rules; god and the devotee are on the same plane. The rebellion of devotion makes all external obedience to religion possible and, at the same time, redundant. Without the rebel devotee on the inside, the obedient one on the outside does not exist. And the reverse is also true.

REFERENCES

Aurobindo, Sri. *On The Mahabharata*. Pondicherry: Sri Aurobindo Ashram Trust .1996.

Bhuteshananda, Swami. *Narada Bhakti Sutras*. Kolkata: Advaita Ashram. 2013.

Buhnemann, Gudrun. *Puja: A Study in Smarta Ritual*. Vienna: The De Nobile Research Library. 1988.

Dikshitulu, Acharya V.R. and Kota Neelima. *Tirumala: Sacred Foods of God*. New Delhi: Roli Books. 2016.

Gandhi, Mohandas K. *Songs from Prison*. Whitefish, MT: Literary Licensing. 2011.

Hacker, Paul. 'Dharma in Hinduism'. In *Dharma: Studies in Its Semantic, Cultural and Religious History*, edited by Patrick Olivelle, 475–492. Delhi: Motilal Banarsidass Publishers. 2009.

Neelima, Kota. *Tirupati: A Guide of Life*. New Delhi: Random House Publishers. 2012.

———. 'Tirupati: The God for a Modern Age'. In *Travelling In, Travelling Out: A Book of Unexpected Journeys*, edited by Namita Gokhale, 176–188. New Delhi: HarperCollins Publishers India. 2014.

Radhakrishnan, S. *Indian Philosophy, Vol. 1*. New Delhi: Oxford University Press. 2006a.

———. *The Bhagavadgita*. New Delhi: HarperCollins Publishers India. 2006b.

———. *The Principal Upanisads*. New Delhi: HarperCollins Publishers India. 2006c.

———. *The Hindu View of Life*. New Delhi: HarperCollins Publishers India. 2009.

Rao, Suryanaranana and Mallikarjuna Rao. *Thyagaraja Geetha*. Chennai: All India Vishnusahasranama Federation. 2008.

Rishi, Sri Shandilya. *Sri Shandilya Bhakti Sutras*. Translated by Tridandi Sri Bhakti Prajnan Yati. Madras: Sree Gaudiya Math. 1991.

Sarasvati, Madhusudana. *Bhagavad-Gita*. Translated by Swami Gambhirananda. Kolkata: Advaita Ashrama. 2017.

Sinha, Nandalal. *Bhaktisutras of Narada*. Delhi: Munshiram Manoharlal Publishers Pvt. Ltd. 1998a.

———. *Sandilyasutram*. Delhi: Munshiram Manoharlal Publishers Pvt. Ltd. 1998b.

The Brhadaranyaka Upanisad. Translated by Swami Madhavananda. Kolkata: Advaita Ashrama. 2008.

ABOUT THE EDITOR AND CONTRIBUTORS

EDITOR

Seema Bawa teaches at the Department of History, University of Delhi, and specialises in history of South Asian art and culture. She was the recipient of DAAD Fellowship to read at the University of Bonn. Books by her include *Gods, Men and Women: Gender and Sexuality in Early Indian Art* and *Religion* (2013) and *Art of the Chamba Valley, A.D. 700–1300* (1998). Her areas of research include Indian art, ancient Indian art and iconography, western Himalayan art and religion, and modern and contemporary Indian art on which she has published extensively in both scholarly journals and popular publications.

CONTRIBUTORS

Ashish Abrol is a career bureaucrat who has done research in English literature and political science. His papers have been published in national and international journals and books. He has an interest in Sanskrit philosophy and theatre.

Saifuddin Ahmad is Associate Professor at the Department of History, University of Delhi. He teaches medieval Indian history.

Raziuddin Aquil teaches at the Department of History, University of Delhi. His books include *The Muslim Question: Understanding Islam and Indian History* (2009) and *Lovers of God: Sufism and the Politics of Islam in Medieval India* (2017).

Parul Pandya Dhar teaches South and Southeast Asian art history at the Department of History, University of Delhi. She has authored *The Toraṇa in Indian and Southeast Asian Architecture* (2010), edited *Indian Art History: Changing Perspectives* (2011), and co-edited *Temple Architecture and Imagery of South and Southeast Asia* (2016), *Asian Encounters: Exploring Connected Histories* (2014) and *Cultural Interface of India with Asia: Religion, Art and Architecture* (2004).

Shalin Jain teaches medieval Indian history at the Department of History, University of Delhi. He has been a post-doctoral fellow at Claremont Lincoln University, California, USA, under UGC-Raman Fellowship Scheme for post-doctoral research in the United States in 2013–2014. He has published a monograph *Identity, Community and State: The Jains under The Mughals*. He has also published several research papers in *Studies in History*, *Indian Historical Review*, *Social Scientist* and other history journals.

Kota Neelima is an author and political scientist. She writes on poverty and spirituality. She studied at Jawaharlal Nehru University and the University of Delhi and was a senior research fellow at SAIS, Johns Hopkins University, Washington, DC. Her book *Tirupati: A Guide to Life* (2012) explores the *Skanda Mahapurana*and sets the Sri Venkateshwara Temple in the contemporary period. Her second book, *Tirumala: Sacred Foods of God* (2018, co-authored with the then temple chief priest, Sri Ramana Dikshitulu), examines the tradition of *naivedyam*, food offerings. Her other books include *Widows of Vidarbha* (2018), *Making of Shadows* (2018), *Riverstones* (2007), *Death of a Moneylender* (2009), *Shoes of the Dead* (2013) and *The Honest Season* (2016).

Janica Paul is a research assistant with a deep interest in social history.

Santosh Kumar Rai teaches modern Indian history at the Department of History, University of Delhi. He started his research–teaching career as a research associate. Between 2003 and 2014, he also served as Assistant Professor in history at S.G.T.B. Khalsa College, University of Delhi. He has published more than 25 research papers, 10 articles and numerous book reviews in various journals and conference proceedings. His book *Weaving Hierarchies: Handloom Weavers in Early Twentieth Century United Provinces* has recently been published.

Preeti Sharma is Professor of history at Banasthali Vidyapith, specialising in ancient Indian history, art studies and rock-cut temple architecture. Her current research interests include feminine representations in art and literature, philosophy of history, feminine sexuality and folkloric studies, among others. She has authored *Rock Cut Temples of South India: Architectural Dimensions* (2015) and *Cultural Heritage of Rajasthan* (2008). She is a former Erasmus Mundus IBIES Visiting Fellow to Leiden University, The Netherlands, and recipient of the Charles Wallace India Trust visiting grant to the UK. She is Chief Editor of the departmental magazine *Kushagraa*.

Jaya S. Tyagi is Professor at the Department of History, University of Delhi, and holds the position of Director, Women's Studies and Development Centre for Advanced Study, University of Delhi. Her books include *Contestation and Compliance: Retrieving Women's Agency from Puranic Traditions* (2014) and *Engendering the Early Indian Household, Brahmanical Precepts in the Gṛhyasūtras* (2008).

INDEX

V

W

Y

Z